C. Alves

D0072136

INTRODUCTION TO COMMERCIAL AND ENTREPRENEURIAL RECREATION

John C. Crossley and Lynn M. Jamieson

Sagamore Publishing

a division of
Management Learning Laboratories

Champaign, IL

Published by: Sagamore Publishing
a division of Management Learning Laboratories, Inc.
501 S. Sixth St., P.O. Box M, Station A
Champaign, Ill. 61820

Artwork: John Stuff

Design by: Anne McClellan

Printed by: Braun Brumfield, Ann Arbor, Mich.

Copyright 1988, by ©Sagamore Publishing. All rights reserved. No part of this book may be reproduced in any form, electronic or mechanical, including photocopy, recording, or any information storage and retrieval system, without permission in writing from the publisher.

Library of Congress Catalog Card Number: 88-60968
ISBN: 0-915611-16-3

Printed in the United States of America

Dedication

This text is dedicated to several individuals who were of profound influence when we first entered the field of recreation. They are: Dr. William J. Tait, former chairman, Department of Recreation and Lei-sure Services, Florida State University; Nick McMullin, Director of Recreation and Parks, Brevard County, Florida; Dr. Theodore Deppe, former chair-man, Department of Recreation and Park Administra-tion, Indiana University; and Dr. Mary Duncan, former chairman, Department of Recreation, San Diego State University. Each of these individuals provided superb leadership and encouraged creativity and innovation at an important stage of our careers.

PREFACE

The purpose of this text is to provide an introduction to the scope, characteristics, and management aspects of the commercial recreation industry. It is intended that the book offer a blend of conceptual and practical material to help achieve a basic understanding of this diverse industry. While some of the content is oriented toward large and established recreation providers, the text also has an entrepreneurial orientation which is particularly beneficial to the smaller businesses and organizations. Hopefully, many future recreation entrepreneurs will gain some useful ideas in these pages.

It is the absolute goal of this text to be different from all others in this field. Several strategies were employed in pursuit of this goal. First, it was decided to avoid coverage of content that is usually included in other courses: recreation philosophy, activity leadership, generic recreation programming, management theory, staff supervision, facility planning/design, legal liability, and accounting principles. Second, it was decided to give substantial coverage to several topics that have received little attention in other commercial recreation texts: entrepreneurial strategies, economic concepts applied to commercial recreation, steps of the feasibility study, operations management, and several specific types of commercial programs. Finally, it was decided to present the content in a way that parallels a logical course sequence. That is, from general to specific as explained below.

The first three chapters provide an introduction to the overall commercial recreation industry including history, definitions, economic impacts, profile of the entrepreneur, entrepreneurial strategies, economic concepts and problems, and general strategies to overcome barriers.

Chapters 4 through 7 present content about the initiation and management of a commercial recreation enterprise. The information is intended to have general application to the overall commercial recreation industry, even though there are some differences between the diverse sub-industries. Content includes feasibility studies, financing sources, financial management, operations management, and commercial recreation programming.

Chapters 8 through 10 narrow the focus to three categories of the industry: travel, hospitality, and local commercial recreation. Each chapter examines the status, operations, trends and opportunities in numerous specific types of commercial recreation.

A final chapter examines the future of the commercial recreation industry and suggests some strategies for students who seek careers in this area.

This text was developed for a variety of uses. The primary purpose is, of course, as a textbook for an introductory course in commercial recreation. The text could also function as an introduction to the recreation industry for majors in travel/tourism or hotel management.

iv

Whatever the academic use, a course instructor should try to supplement the text concepts with local examples.

Hopefully, the text may also be of value to practitioners in specific recreation industries who seek an illuminating overview of the entire commercial recreation industry. Similarly, investors and entrepreneurs may find useful content that will help them direct their resources more productively.

It should also be pointed out that the choice of gender nouns "he" or "she" throughout the text was made by random selection. As the commercial recreation industry matures, males and females seem to be less relegated to stereotypical roles either as staff or managers.

ACKNOWLEDGEMENTS

Acknowledgements are sincerely owed to numerous people who have made this text possible. The initiating and driving force behind this text has been Dr. Joseph Bannon, President of Management Learning Laboratories. His confidence in us and his encouragement are greatly appreciated. The efforts of MLL Production Coordinator Susan Williams and Marketing Coordinator Michelle Wagner were also critically important contributions. At the University of Utah, Leslie Headman was the word processor genius who worked as hard as any of us. Our academic institution supervisors Dr. Dale Cruse and Dr. Dwayne Head are thanked for giving us the entrepreneurial elbowroom to complete this project. Lynn Jamieson acknowledges the support and encouragement of her husband Stephen Wolter during the development of the text.

We would like to give special recognition to Dr. Larry Allen for reviewing the manuscript and offering numerous excellent suggestions. Dr. Taylor Ellis also provided worthwhile ideas for improvement.

Space does not allow thanking the dozens of people who gave interviews or provided references for this text. However, Mary Lou Wood, Executive Director of the Travel and Tourism Research Association must be recognized for her help with the travel industry chapter. Graduate student Dolph Conrads also helped provide content for several industry profiles.

Finally, we must recognize the pioneering work of Dr. Arlin Epperson, who wrote the first commercial recreation text. His foresight in the 1970s paved the way for all of use who write today about the commercial recreation industry.

TABLE OF CONTENTS

PART I

INTRODUCTION TO COMMERCIAL AND ENTREPRENEURIAL RECREATION

CHAPTER 1

WHAT IS COMMERCIAL RECREATION?

A BRIEF HISTORY OF COMMERCIAL RECREATION

Early Travel and Commercial Recreation

While family and community recreation activities in one form or another have existed since prehistoric times, the same cannot be said for tourism and commercial recreation. The invention of money by the Sumerians in Babylonia and their development of trade probably mark the beginning of the modern era of travel (McIntosh and Goeldner, 1984). Early travel, however, was primarily for war or business purposes. Few recreation seekers would put up with the discomforts and dangers of travel in those days.

Eventually, the Greeks and Romans improved roads and naval travel in order to control their empires. With these improvements, tourism became safer and more comfortable. This theme, of military technology literally paving the way for tourism, has been repeated throughout history.

As early as 334 B.C. Alexander the Great attracted 700,000 tourists in a single season to Turkey, where they were entertained by acrobats, animal acts, jugglers, magicians, and circus performances. The ancient Greeks traveled to the Olympic Games, to spas, to festivals, and to the pyramids in Egypt. Romans also traveled extensively, having 175 holidays for leisure and recreation. It was possible to cover up to 100 miles per day on the paved roads and even more by ship. Roman tourists were much like today's tourists, visiting the pyramids, shopping for souvenirs, and carving their names on the monuments (McIntosh and Goeldner, 1984).

Early tourists stayed in guest rooms that were part of private dwellings or in commercial inns. Housing, feeding, and entertaining the travelers became an important industry. About this time, seaside resorts and spas with medicinal waters became popular destinations.

Middle Ages and the Renaissance

With the decline of the great empires, tourism also declined. The wealthy class declined in number, roads deteriorated, and the countryside became overrun with bandits and thieves. Throughout history, tourists tend to cease their travel when economic conditions sour or when travel becomes unsafe.

In the Middle Ages, tourism related travel came to a virtual standstill. Similarly, the emphasis on religion and abstinence resulted in a dry spell for many of the recreational pursuits of the classical period. Nevertheless, some forms of commercially oriented recreation did exist. The nobility engaged in tournaments, gambling, feasting, and watching traveling entertainers. Peasants enjoyed fairs, pageants, racing, cock-fighting, and gambling (MacLean, Peterson, and Martin, 1985).

During the Renaissance, a revival of learning, cultural arts, and travel occurred. Fairs, exhibitions, operas, theater, and beer gardens were popular. "Travel for Education" was introduced, and was exemplified by the "Grand Tour." It became fashionable for young aristocrats, as well as members of the rising middle class, to travel and study throughout Europe, Egypt, and the Holy Lands. Sometimes these grand tours took up to three years and included indulgence in recreation and revelry.

Travel for health also became important during the Renaissance. At first, only the infirm went to the hot springs or spas to drink or bathe in mineral waters. Later, people began to go in order to dry out from alcoholism and other urban leisure vices. Next, entertainment, recreation activites, and gambling were added. Dozens of spas grew to become high quality resorts. Switzerland, for example, had over 100 spa/hotels (Lundberg, 1976).

It is important to note that there was no clear distinction between private/commercial and government sponsored recreation throughout history to this point. Many of the trips by nobility were actually financed by government funds. Similarly, feudal kingdoms sponsored some of the festivals, contests, and mass entertainment events provided for the working class and peasants. Church involvement in local and national governments further complicated the separation of church/state/private enterprise.

The First Travel Agent

In 1841, Englishman Thomas Cook chartered a train to carry 540 people to a temperance convention. Although Cook made no profit for himself on that trip, he saw the potential in arranging travel for others. By 1845, Thomas Cook had become the first full-time travel excursion organizer. A "Cooks Tour" was likely to turn up anywhere. Switzerland, the Nile, the Holy Lands, Mount Everest, India, Norway, and Yellowstone Park were a few of the destinations. Cook was dedicated to making his tours as interesting and convenient as possible. To allow access to cash while away from home, he invented "circular notes," which later became known as travelers checks (Lundberg, 1976).

Early Commercial Recreation in the United States

By the 1800s, the energy of America was still being spent primarily to build the new nation. Travel was not easy, but as stagecoach lines developed, taverns and inns were built along the routes. The inns provided food, drink, and sleeping accommodations. Soon enterprising innkeepers learned to see the value of recreation. Shooting matches, contests, and festivals were organized, and tidy profits were made from food, beverage, and lodging for those who came to participate (Epperson, 1986).

In urban areas, people began to arrange competition in tennis, boxing, cockfighting, drinking, and other activities. By the late 1800s dance halls, shooting galleries, bowling alleys, billiard parlors, beer gardens, and saloons flourished. Many cities had red light districts offering prostitution, gambling, and other vices. In such an environment, commercial recreation deservedly gained an unsavory reputation. In reponse, city councils passed restrictive ordinances including "Blue Laws," which closed recreation enterprises on Sundays. It was also in this environment that public parks and recreation became a major social movement.

Travel and commercial recreation were uplifted by improvements in transportation, specifically the railroad and later the automobile. Railroads carried urban residents to amusement parks on the outskirts of town and to major resorts across the country. In many cases, the amusement parks and resorts were built by the railroads to stimulate travel volume. For example, Sun Valley, Idaho, was built by Averell Harriman and the Union Pacific Railroad. Many resorts along the southeastern coast of the United States were similarly filled by tourists traveling by rail.

The automobile provided additional mobility and independence for Amercian tourists. Vacationing by auto became the great American middle class tradition. The auto also opened a whole range of local recreation opportunities. Urban and rural residents alike could drive to movie theaters, sports events, and many other commercial recreation attractions.

Postwar Commercial Recreation in the United States

A healthy economy and technological innovations continued to fuel growth in commercial recreation after World War II. The average work week decreased while discretionary income increased, thus providing opportunity and means to enjoy new forms of recreation.

Perhaps the greatest technological advances again involved travel. Construction of the U.S. interstate highway system greatly expanded the area accessible to American tourists, and airlines enabled even more distant destinations to be reached easily. Some resort areas such as Las Vegas, Central Florida, and Colorado experienced tremendous growth due to improved accessibility.

Other technological advances also had huge impacts on commercial recreation. Electronic innovations generated a huge home entertainment industry of television, stereo equipment, video recorders, and computers. Synthetic materials improved the performance and durability of ski equipment, golf clubs, skateboards, and sport balls of all types. Theme parks and water theme parks capitalized on a variety of innovations. Service innovations such as timesharing have also had significant impact. Undoubtedly, the future holds a continuing variety of new facilities, products, and services.

Common Themes Throughout History

Several themes have appeared throughout the preceding section about the history of commercial recreation. These themes include the following:

- Commercial recreation has existed when people have free time, discretionary income, transportation/accessibility, and the technology for recreation products or services.
- Many of the technological innovations for travel and for recreation products were first developed for military purposes.
- The fortunes of certain industries such as restaurants, lodging, and entertainment are closely linked to travel and tourism.
- When economic conditions sour, when travel is inconvenient or unsafe, or when services are inadequate, there are declines in many types of commercial recreation.

The significance of the above themes is related to the nature of history. Scholars always tell us that history tends to repeat itself.

DEFINITIONS

The previous section mentioned how the provision of recreation throughout history has been an undefined mix of governmental (public) and private efforts. Figure 1-1 illustrates a continuum depicting the traditional difference between public agency recreation and private/commercial recreation. It must be realized that few public park and recreation agencies exist in the pure/traditional form at the left of the continuum. Most have evolved a little or a lot toward the middle. The characteristics analyzed include philosophic orientation, service origin, financial base, originating authority, and service focus.

Philosophic Orientation—Public recreation is based on the value of recreation as a necessary service for society. Private sector recreation is provided to make a profit for a business.

Service Origin—Public recreation began as a social welfare movement, and public parks had roots in conservation ethics. Private recreation originated as a business response to people who desired to travel and/or purchase leisure experiences.

Financial Base—Taxes and grants have traditionally provided the bulk of public recreation finances. On the other hand, private recreation is funded by private capital and operated through fees revenue.

Originating Authority——City councils, county commissions, citizen boards, and other legislative bodies create public park and recreation departments. Individual initiative is the source of private recreation business.

Service Focus—Public recreation must be open to the collective interest of its community. On the other hand, private recreation can focus on any special market interest that it chooses.

Based upon this continuum, a definition of commercial recreation may be developed that differentiates it from public recreation. Definitions for commercialized public recreation, entrepreneurial recreation, and intrapreneurism are also included in this section.

Figure 1-1
Public-Private Recreation Continuum

Public Recreation————————————————Private Recreation

	Philosophic	Profit Making
Free, Necessary	Orientation	Business
Service for Society		

| Social Welfare Movement | Service | Consumer Desire for Travel |
| Conservation Ethics | Origin | Willingness to Pay |

| Taxes and Grants | Financial | Private Capital |
| | Base | Fees Revenue |

| Governmental Bodies | Originating | Individual Initiative |
| Citizen Boards | Authority | |

Nonrestrictive	Service	Can Focus on Any
Open to Collective	Focus	Special Market
Community Interest		Segments

Commercial Recreation

Authors of a popular recreation text define commercial recreation as "recreation for which the consumer pays and for which the supplier expects to make a profit" (MacLean, Peterson, and Martin, 1985, p. 220). While this definition covers the basic revenue orientation, it does not really differentiate between public and private provision of the service. This is a distinction that must be made, since private enterprise must overcome barriers that do not face governmentally sponsored recreation.

While some government agencies may charge a fee for recreation and claim that it is self-supporting, such fees seldom cover capital development and full overhead costs. These are major cost factors that private enterprises cannot escape. Government also has the advantage of using tax revenues to subsidize its revenue generating activities. Similarly, nonprofit organizations such as YMCAs often have United Way and other charitable donations as revenue sources. Another important difference is that public recreation agencies and nonprofit organizations do not have to pay property taxes and income taxes. Private enterprise, however, often pays substantial amounts of money for taxes.

To account for the differences between public and private orientations, the following definition for *commercial recreation* is offered:

The provision of recreation related products or services by private enterprise for a fee, with the long-term intent of being profitable.

In addition to the aforementioned public/private distinction, this definition offers two other key points. First, "recreation related" may be interpreted very broadly and includes any product or service that supports a leisure pursuit. Such an interpretation would mean that leisure related aspects of the travel industry and hospitality industry (including hotels and restaurants) are included within the broad framework of commercial recreation.

The second key point is that the "long-term intent" is to be profitable. This recognizes the fact that commercial recreation is not always profitable; it may fail. It may also take a company many years to become profitable because it may have to overcome very high start-up costs. Some companies may never be profitable on a day-to-day operational basis, but may yield large profits through the long-term appreciation of its land and facilities.

Commercialized Public Recreation

What can we call governmental and nonprofit recreation organizations that are operated in a commercial manner? *Commercialized Public Recreation* is the term suggested for this concept defined below.

The provision of selected recreation related products or services by a governmental or nonprofit organization in a commercial manner, such that much or all of the costs are covered by fees, charges, or other nontax revenues.

A key point of this definition is that the overall agency may operate under traditional funding sources, but that "selected" aspects may be operated in a commercial manner. An example of this would be a city parks and recreation department that funds its parks through tax revenues, but expects its recreation programs to be self-supporting through fees.

Entrepreneurial Recreation

It is a premise of this book that private, public, and nonprofit organizations can all operate in an entrepreneurial manner. The term entrepreneur is commonly used in reference to a person who starts his own small business. This definition, however, can exclude government and nonprofit organizations that initiate recreation services by utilizing entrepreneurial strategies. According to authorities on entrepreneurism (Drucker, 1985, and Van Voorhis, 1980), key strategies include searching of the environment for trends and changes that present opportunity.

The entrepreneur then locates, acquires, and manages resources (money, facilities, people, etc.) to exploit those opportunities. Therefore the following definition is offered for *entrepreneurial recreation*:

> The actions of a recreation related organization that searches for trends and changes in its environment then brings together and manages resources to exploit those changes as an opportunity.

Intrapreneurism

Some organizations may conduct commercial recreation (or commercialized public recreation) and not necessarily be entrepreneurial. This is because those organizations are not oriented toward exploiting change. They just continue to repeat proven and traditional concepts. It is more likely, however, that recreation organizations operate many of their facilities and programs in a traditional way, but are innovative and entrepreneurial in certain areas. The aspect within an organization that is innovative and entrepreneurial may be called "intrapreneurial." Pinchot (1985) defines the *intrapreneur* as:

> One who takes responsibility for creating innovation of any kind within an organization.

The topics of entrepreneurism and intrapreneurism will be covered in greater depth in Chapter 2. Throughout the remainder of this text, most of the concepts may be applied to some degree by public and nonprofit organizations as well as by private enterprise. Therefore, for simplicity, the term commercial recreation will be used interchangeably for both commercial recreation and commercialized public recreation as previously defined.

TYPES OF COMMERCIAL RECREATION

According to the definitions presented in the previous section, commercial recreation can include such diverse businesses as resort hotels, movie theaters, sporting goods stores, airlines, racquet sport clubs, dance studios, craft shops, restaurants, travel agencies, casinos, and campgrounds. Obviously there are commonalities and interrelationships between some of these enterprises. On the other hand, some have little or no relationship to the other types listed. This diversity makes it very difficult to grasp the breadth of the industry and understand its components. What is needed is some structure or logical classification system into which the many industries can be grouped. Such a system would allow a better organized study of commercial recreation because similar industries often have similar problems, trends, and management practices.

Bullaro and Edginton (1986) have suggested a classification system using the following types of commercial leisure service organizations: (a) travel and tourism, (b) entertainment services, (c) leisure services in the natural environment, (d) hospitality/food services, and (e) retail activities. Similarly, McIntosh and Goeldner (1984) have suggested the following basic parts of tourism: (a) transportation, (b) accommodations, (c) shopping, and (d) activities.

A New Classification System

Proposed here is a classification system that recognizes the overlapping nature of many of the categories suggested previously. This is essential if one is to gain a realistic grasp of a complex, diverse, and interrelated industry. Consider for example: Is a ski resort in the hotel, travel, entertainment, restaurant, retail, or recreation program business? It could be all of those and serve local residents as well as tourists.

The classification system proposed here has three main components: travel/transportation, hospitality, and local commercial recreation. Each of the components has its "purist" aspects and each has subindustries that overlap with the other component classifications (see Figure 1-2). The key to the classification system is that each major industry has certain common characteristics, but that some components of an industry overlap with another recreation industry.

The Travel/Transportation Industry has as its primary function the movement of people, and the provision of travel related services. The purist forms of this industry are the airlines, rental cars, bus lines, and railroads, which move tourists as well as business travelers. This industry overlaps with local commercial recreation when retail products and recreation activities are provided for tourists. Examples are heli-ski services, river guide trips, souvenir shops, and RV dealers. Travel/ transportation overlaps with hospitality when lodging, food, or certain amenities are provided for tourists. Examples are cruise ships, campgrounds, and historical attractions.

The Hospitality Industry has as its primary function the provision of accommodations, food and beverage, and related amenities. The purist forms of this industry are hotels and motels, restaurants, resort condominiums, taverns, motor home parks, campsites, and recreation communities. Hospitality can overlap with travel/transportation as previously mentioned. It also overlaps with local commercial recreation when recreation activities are provided at restaurants, camps, or other hospitality settings that predominantly serve local residents. Examples are leisure theme restaurants, local sports camps, and hunting day lodges.

The Local Commercial Recreation Industry has as its primary function the provision of retail products, entertainment, and recreation programs for people in their home communities. The purist forms of this industry include racquet clubs, dance studios, sporting goods stores, movie theaters, and small amusement parks. As previously mentioned, local commercial recreation can overlap with the travel/transportation and hospitality industries.

Facilitators of many types support the three main industries. Some facilitators, such as travel agencies, travel schools, and time share trade services, support the hospitality and travel/transportation industries. Other facilitators, such as equipment wholesalers, publishers of fitness

Figure 1-2
The Commercial Recreation Industry

LOCAL COMMERICAL RECREATION

Activities & Programs	Retail Products	Entertainment
Racquet Clubs	Sporting Goods	Theaters
Health Clubs	Outdoor Specialty	Concerts
Dance Studios	Hunting/Fishing	Sports Arenas
Golf Courses	Music	Fairs/Festivals
Skating Rinks	Arts & Crafts	Carnivals
Bowling Lanes	Hobby, Toys & Games	Amusement Parks
Party Services	Video	Water Parks
Promotional Events		Race Tracks

Primary and Secondary Facilitators

Equipment Manufacturers
Equipment Wholesalers & Reps.
Magazines, Books, Guides

TRAVEL/TRANSPORATION
(Move People + Services)

Airlines
Rental Cars
Bus Lines
Railroads

Heli-Ski
River Guides   Fishing Guides
RV Dealers   Boat Dealers
Expedition   Tourist Gift Shop
Companies

Major Entertainment Events
Resorts-many types   Summer Camps
Theme Parks   Sports Camps
Casinos   Hunting Lodges
                                      Residential Rec.
                                         Facilities
Travel Campgrounds   Leisure Theme
Cruise Ships   Restaurants
Tour Operators   Night Clubs
Meeting/Convention Services
Historical/Cultural Attrax

Primary and Secondary Facilitators
Travel Agencies
Travel Schools
Travel Info. Services
Time Share Exchange Services

HOSPITALITY
(Accommodations, Food & Beverage, Amenities)
Hotels & Motels
Restaurants
Recreation Communities
Resort Condominiums
Motor Home Parks & Campsites
Bars/Taverns

magazines and writers of "how to do it" crafts books support the local commercial recreation industry.

All of these industries overlap when accommodations, food, activities, retail shops, and entertainment are provided for tourists and local residents. This occurs in many types of resorts, at major entertainment events such as a Worlds Fair, and other large theme parks.

PARTICIPATION AND EXPENDITURES IN THE RECREATION INDUSTRY

Data regarding participation and expenditures in the recreation industry are important in order to assess the present and to make projections for the future. Such data is used in many ways, including:

- Feasibility studies for new or expanded facilities.
- Operational decisions involving demand estimates, pricing, marketing, employment of seasonal staff, etc.
- Projections by government for sales taxes, hotel occupancy taxes, etc.
- Policy decisions by governmental agencies.
- Lobbying efforts of industry/trade associations.

Unfortunately the data produced through measurement of the recreation industry are often inconsistent. The conflicting reports of the total expenditures for recreation and leisure in the United States for 1985, shown in Figure 1-3 are a good example of this problem.

Why is there such a discrepancy in these figures? Certainly the data collecting organizations have competent researchers. Nevertheless, there are problems in measuring recreation participation and expenditures. Different definitions are used for recreation, travel, and other categories, and those definitions can change over the years. Also, some agencies have a bias regarding the topics they survey and the methodology used. Finally, it is difficult to separate leisure related expenditures from business expenditures for topics such as hotels, restaurants, airlines, and gardening.

Even though there are problems in measurement, it is possible to gain a general idea of the participation and expenditure levels for major categories of recreation in the United States. The next two sections will present several studies of recreation participation and expenditures.

Figure 1-3
Total Expenditures for Recreation and Leisure

Source	Expenditure for 1985
Bullaro and Edginton (1986)	$300 Billion
U.S. News and World Report (1981)	$300 Billion projected
U.S. Travel Data Center (1986)	$269 Billion (travel only)
U.S. Department of Commerce (1986)	$216 Billion

Recreation and Leisure Participation

According to United Media Enterprises (1983), 72 percent of Amercians watch TV almost every day. In addition, almost every day, 70 percent read a newspaper, 46 percent listen to music, 35 percent exercise, 24 percent read a book, 23 percent pursue a hobby, and 22 percent work in the garden.

Figure 1-4 presents a further breakdown of the percentage of adults participating in recreation activities during 1985. Notice how the various surveys show general agreement for participation levels for most activities. It is important to note, however, that the surveys reflect a bias toward sports and outdoor recreation. Participation in crafts, music lessons, dancing, gambling, dining out, and many other popular activities are not mentioned in the four major surveys. This reflects the bias problem of recreation measurement mentioned in the previous section.

Figure 1-4
Recreation and Leisure Participation-- 1985

Participation Category	Percentage Adults Participating in Past Year			
	Market Opinion Research (1986)*	Gallup Org. Inc. (1986)	USA Today (1986)	Amer. Sports Data Inc.(1986)
Walking for Pleasure	84 (50)	-	-	17
Driving for Pleasure	77 (43)	-	-	-
Sightseeing	77 (34)	-	-	-
Picnicking	76 (28)	-	-	-
Swimming	76 (43)	41	41	-
Visiting Zoos, Fairs, Amusement Parks	72 (17)	-	-	-
Attending Outdoor Sports Events	60 (22)	-	-	-
Visiting Historic Sites	59 (14)	-	-	-
Fishing	51 (25)	32	34	-
Bicycling	46 (17)	31	33	-
Camping	45 (21)	-	21	-
Playing Softball/Baseball	43 (16)	20	22	12
Running/Jogging	42 (17)	23	23	14
Attending Outdoor Plays & Concerts	42 (11)	-	-	-
Studying Nature	35 (15)	-	-	-
Playing Tennis	30 (10)	12	13	12
Playing Basketball	27 (10)	14	15	18
Motor Boating	27 (15)	15	16	-
Hiking	27 (12)	-	18	-
Driving ORV's	24 (11)	-	-	-
Canoeing, Rafting, Kayaking	22 (5)	10	-	-
Golfing	22 (10)	12	13	9

Figure 1-4 (cont.)

Participation Category	Percentage Adults Participating in Past Year			
	Market Opinion Research (1986)*	Gallup Org. Inc. (1986)	USA Today (1986)	Amer. Sports Data Inc.(1986)
Playing Football	21 (6)	-	-	-
Hunting	21 (11)	13	14	-
Backpacking	17 (5)	-	-	11
Sledding	17 (4)	-	-	-
Horseback Riding	15 (3)	8	9	-
Sailing	15 (4)	5	5	-
Skiing	14 (5)	7	8	-
Ice Skating	12 (3)	5	-	-
Playing Soccer	10 (3)	-	-	-
Cross-country skiing	8 (3)	-	-	-
Bowling	-	23	25	-
Playing Volleyball	-	15	16	15
Playing Table Tennis	-	12	-	-
Rollerskating	-	9	-	-
Practicing Archery	-	3	-	-
Playing Handball	-	3	-	-

*First figure represents percentage of adults participating at least once a year. Figure in parentheses represents percentage of adults participating often or very often.

Recreation and Leisure Expenditures

As noted previously, data regarding expenditures for recreation and leisure vary significantly from source to source. Figure 1-5 presents expenditure levels for many of the major categories of commercial recreation. Notice how the figures for hotels and motels are extremely different. This probably reflects a major difference in definition and survey methodology.

It is interesting to note that the sum of the low figures for each industry totals almost $516 billion if legal gambling is included and $357 billion if gambling is not included. This figure exceeds the industry totals suggested previously. Of course there is some overlap, which accounts for some of the difference. For example $6.2 billion of the amusement park industry expenditures was for food and drink, some of which may have been included under "Eating and Drinking Places." Again, notice the absence of data regarding hobbies, crafts, music lessons, tour services, and other small but important industries.

Figure 1-5
Recreation and Leisure Expenditures 1985

Expenditure Category	Billions of Dollars Spent			
	U.S. Dept of Commerce (1986)	Standard and Poors (Urciuoli, 1986)	USA Travel Data Center (1986)	*Leisure Ind. Digest* (1986)
Eating & Drinking Places	142.1	153.5	131.6	--
Toys & Sports Supplies	20.6	26.2	--	--
Magazine & Newspaper	13.8	--	--	--
Hotels & Motels	11.1	--	42.2	--
Cable TV	8.6	--	--	--
Boats	6.0	--	--	--
Gardening Supplies	5.5	--	--	--
Live Theater/Entertainment	3.0	--	--	--
Spectator Sports	2.8	--	--	--
Motion Pictures	--	3.8	--	--
Photography	--	16.7	--	--
Recorded Music	--	4.4	--	--
Airlines	--	--	33.5	--
Entertainment & Recreation *	--	--	49.3	--
Amusement Parks	--	--	--	18.6
Legal Gambling	--	--	--	159.1
Cruise Industry	--	--	--	2.5
Consumer Electronics	--	--	--	25.0

*Includes many subcategories, some previously listed.

ECONOMIC, SOCIAL, AND ENVIRONMENTAL IMPACTS OF COMMERCIAL RECREATION

Depending upon how the recreation and leisure industry is defined, it accounts for between $181 billion and $516 billion expended in the United States in 1985. Even the low estimate makes recreation and leisure one of the country's largest industries. One component, travel and tourism, is the second largest employer in the country, and is one of the top three industries in at least 39 states (National Recreation and Parks Association, 1984).

Within this huge industry, most expenditures occur in the private sector. Epperson (1986) calculates that only about two percent of all leisure related spending occurs through local, state, or federal government agencies. However, the role of government in the economics of the industry is much greater than the two percent share would indicate. Consider that government lands are often leased to commercial enterprise as the sites for many types of resorts and tourist attractions. At the local level, many expenditures at retail sporting goods stores and arts and crafts shops are for equipment used in city park and recreation programs.

Commercial recreation has many positive impacts on a given community. These include:

- Employment opportunities.
- Stimulation of local economy through increased commerce.
- Attraction of outside capital (new businesses, new investors for existing businesses).
- Increased property values.
- Increased tax revenues—property, sales and hotel room taxes.
- Increased recreation opportunity for local residents.

Commercial recreation can also have negative impacts:

- Many types of commercial recreation have high failure rates and/or short life cycles, thus resulting in unemployment and decreased economic contribution to the local community.
- The local infrastructure (roads, sewers, utilities, etc.) can become overburdened, thus requiring capital improvements costing huge sums of money.
- Crime can increase since tourists can be easy prey and transient type employees may be more crime prone.
- Increased land values can backfire on young residents wishing to buy property for the first time.
- Natural resources can be overused to the point of ruining the attraction that is the center of the commercial recreation industry.
- Undesirable types of commercial recreation may appear, trying to capitalize on increased traffic to the prime commercial attraction.

Ultimately, each community must assess both the pros and cons of commercial recreation development. Zoning regulations, control and pricing of business permits and licenses, and other local government regulations can encourage or discourage a commercial recreation enterprise. An example of the impact of commercial recreation on a specific community is illustrated in the "Spotlight" section of Chapter 3.

THE ROLE OF GOVERNMENT IN COMMERCIAL RECREATION

As mentioned in the previous section, government is concerned with the success of commercial recreation because of its economic impacts on the community. In addition to assessing property taxes, sales taxes, and fees for licenses and permits, government at all levels is involved in the regulation of private enterprise. Government has a duty to protect the public interests and therefore establishes standards and regulations for practically every aspect of business operation. This topic of government regulation is addressed in greater depth in Chapter 4.

While taxes and regulations are necessary evils for commercial recreation, there are many positive relationships possible between government and private enterprise. Epperson (1977) and Kelly (1985) have suggested numerous relationships which could be grouped into three categories: complementary relationships, cooperative arrangements, and planning relationships.

Complementary Relationships

Government is not structured to meet all the recreation needs of all the people. Also, the resources of government are stretched too thin, and conditions are not getting better. Therefore, government should act to complement the efforts of private enterprise in order to provide the maximum recreation opportunity for its residents. Specific complementary actions by government can include:

- Provide, maintain, and/or regulate the infrastructure (roads, waterways, utilities, etc.), that supports commercial recreation.
- Promote tourism and commercial development.
- Provide public facilities where residents use recreation equipment that was purchased at retail outlets.
- Provide low cost introductory programs; advanced levels can be offered by commercial enterprise.
- Refer people to commercial recreation opportunities.

Cooperative Arrangements

There are many types of cooperative arrangements where government and private enterprise can interact directly to provide recreation facilities or programs. Examples (Crossley, 1986) include:

- Public programs conducted at commercial facilities.
- Commercially organized programs conducted at public facilities.
- Co-sponsorship of promotional events.
- Loans or sharing of equipment, supplies, or staff expertise.
- Leased concessions for food, beverage, or other amenities.
- Contracted management of entire facilities or entire programs.
- Cooperative facility development.
- Financial assistance such as low cost loans or property tax abatements.
- Lease of land for commercial development.

Planning Relationships

Long-range planning for recreation is best served when government and private enterprise work together. Unfortunately, this does not always happen. Nevertheless, the following guidelines indicate areas where mutual planning efforts can be beneficial.

- Commercial recreation representatives should be involved in public hearings concerning recreation and natural resources.
- Commercial recreation representatives should be active in the community, serving on advisory boards, planning commissions, etc.
- Comprehensive recreation plans should include commercial recreation in the planning process.

KEY TRENDS IN THE RECREATION AND LEISURE INDUSTRY

Government, private enterprise, society, and mother nature all interact constantly to create an everchanging environment for the commercial recreation enterprise. Events of the past set the stage for the future whether we choose to pay attention or not. Throughout this text several trends and themes will appear constantly. Chapter 11 focuses specifically on trends and opportunities for the future. Some of these trends are introduced here to alert the reader to them.

- International, national, regional, and local economic conditions will affect the ability of people to spend for recreation and leisure.
- Demographic changes underlie significant changes in the market for recreation and leisure.
- Energy availability will affect all forms of commercial recreation.
- Foreign policy, war, and terrorist activity will alter tourists', choice of destinations.
- New technology will continually improve travel and recreation products, and entire new concepts/products will emerge.

Obviously these are not earthshaking revelations. They are, however trends and themes that will arise constantly and affect the commercial recreation manager's efforts to develop a profitable enterprise. If a manager does not deal with these trends, dramatic problems and business failure can result.

THE COMMERCIAL RECREATION EXPERIENCE

Utlimately, the objective of a commercial recreation enterprise is to become profitable. Some commercial recreation managers, however, may limit their opportunity for profit by defining their business too narrowly. For example, a retail sporting goods store that sells only sports equipment and sports wearing apparel is not reaching its fullest potential. What commercial recreation managers should do is look at their company in light of the total recreation experience.

There are five major steps or components of the recreation experience: (1) anticipation, preparation, and planning; (2) travel to; (3) on-site participation and/or purchase; (4) travel from; and (5) recollection.

Continuing with the sporting goods example, the traditional manager would concentrate only on the third step, on-site sales of equipment and wearing apparel. On the other hand, the resourceful manager would see the potential to serve the consumer at each step of the recreation experience. Examples of this aggressive approach are given for each component.

The anticipation, preparation, and planning stage would find the manager selling products or services that would help the consumer prepare for a recreation experience. This could include:

Instructional classes to show people how to use the equipment and
perform the activity.
- "How to do it" books, records, and tapes to instruct and prepare the
participant.
- Guide books showing trails, accommodations, etc.
- Equipment repair services such as ski tuning and racquet restringing.

The travel to and travel from stages would suggest an opportunity
to sell travel packages to consumers with special interests. For example,
several Dallas, Texas, sporting goods stores contract with travel agencies
to operate travel desks at the store during peak periods. Many customers,
who come in to buy ski equipment at a Labor Day sale, sign up for group
ski trips to Colorado resorts. The sports stores earn a percentage of the
travel agents' commission.

Modern Resorts
combine all aspects of
the Commercial
Recreation Industry:
Travel and Tourism,
Hospitality, and
Recreation Activity.
(Photo: Courtesy of
MarineWorld)

On-site sales continue to be the mainstay of the store's revenue, but
are boosted by people coming in for the other products and services. For
example, people who come in to the store to register for a 10K race may
stay to shop around.
The recollection stage suggests opportunities for the store to sell
products or services that help the consumer relive the enjoyable experience. Ideas for the sporting goods store include:

- Cameras, film, photography accessories and film developing.
- Classes in outdoor or sports photography.
- Taxidermy or mounting services for trophy-size fish and game.
- Trophies, plaques, and medallions to honor competitive or humorous
aspects of the main experience.

All commercial recreation enterprises should analyze the potential
for products and services that target each of the five steps of the recreation
experience. Sometimes this extra effort can have a significant impact on
the overall profitability of the business. Prime examples of this occur-

rence in other commercial recreation industries include: (1) roving commercial photographers on cruise ships and at resorts; (2) souvenir shops at resorts; (3) instructional classes at crafts and fabric shops; (4) hotels, rental cars, and airline companies organized under one parent corporation.

SUMMARY

Commercial recreation is the provision of recreation products or services by private enterprise for a fee, with the long-term intent of being profitable. Public and nonprofit organizations can also provide recreation in a commercialized manner. Whether serving public, private, or nonprofit organizations, the entrepreneurial (and intrapreneurial) manager can exploit changes in the environment to create new recreational opportunities.

Throughout history, the provision of commercial recreation has paralleled the availability of free time, discretionary income, and transportation. Technological advancements such as railroads, autos, airplanes, plastics, and microchips have created huge industries. In the process, recreation has grown to become one of the nations largest industries. Estimates of annual expenditures range from $181 billion to $516 billion. Differences in definition and methodology make it very difficult to assess how big the industry actually is. It is certain however that recreation is one of the top three industries in almost every state.

The development of commercial recreation can have very positive impacts on a community, including attraction of outside capital, increase of the tax base, creation of new jobs, and the improvement of the local infrastructure. Negative impacts can also occur, including failure of businesses, overburdening of the infrastructure, and abuse of the environment. In order to protect the public interests, government regulates and taxes commercial recreation businesses. Government should also interact with commercial recreation by providing complementary services, by establishing cooperative ventures, and by including private sector representation in the planning process.

Most commercial recreation businesses tend to focus their efforts on only one aspect of the leisure experience. The aggressive manager will exploit revenue opportunities by providing products or services at many stages of the leisure experience, including preparation, travel, and recollection stages, as well as at the traditional on-site stage.

STUDY QUESTIONS

1. What common themes have affected the history of commercial recreation?
2. Differentiate between provision of recreation by the private and public sector.
3. Define commercial recreation and differentiate this from commercialized public recreation.
4. What are the major components of commercial recreation?

5. What are facilitators?
6. Why is it difficult to measure the recreation and leisure industry?
7. How may government assist commercial recreation ventures?
8. Describe five steps in the commercial recreation experience.

PROJECT IDEAS

1. Select a leisure pursuit and trace its historical development as a business.
2. In your community, find at least five examples of each major component of commercial recreation (as illustrated in the classification system in Figure 1-2).
3. Check with your local chamber of commerce and find out if the economic impact of commercial recreation (or tourism or any other component) has been determined.

SPOTLIGHT ON: Marineworld-Africa, USA

Marineworld-Africa, USA, is a good example of entrepreneurial ability and commercial success. It has flourished under the leadership of Michael Demetrios, who was the 1987 recipient of the California Travel Industry Association award for "Entrepreneur of the Year."

Demetrios' success began after his graduation with an MBA from Harvard. He worked with an advertising agency, became marketing director of the ICE Follies, managed the Ontario Motor Speedway, and was general manager of Sea World in Florida. Through the owner of Sea World, Resorts International, he became general manager of Marineworld-Africa, USA, in 1974.

Marineworld, located in Redwood City, California, was a theme park that emphasized aquatic animals and environmental education. Although the park was popular, it did not have an entertainment focus and was losing attendance to other theme parks. To better compete, Demetrios developed a concept of "educating through entertaining." He bought the park from Resorts International when he found several partners who would help finance the venture. After this financial stability was achieved, he set out to improve the park itself and

make his concept operational. The purchase of water flumes added entertainment value, and drew young people. Changes in hours, aggressive marketing techniques, and constantly changing programs helped to improve park attendance by 25 percent.

A big challenge occurred in 1980 when Demetrios' partners decided to sell the park in order to develop an office complex that could yield more profit. Demetrios created a nonprofit foundation, mortgaged everything he owned, and found a new site for Marineworld in Vallejo, California. Construction of the new park began in May, 1985. Once holding facilities for the animals were built, the entire park was moved in 21 days. Over 500 animals and 5 million pounds of equipment were transported, much of it in an Ark-like ship with Demetrios dressed as Noah.

The new Marineworld opened in June 1986 and has enjoyed great success. There are plans for future expansion. Demetrios has proven that dedication, creativity, and sound business management can result in a thriving commercial recreation enterprise (Demetrios, 1987).

REFERENCES

American Sports Data, Inc. in "New Rules of Exercise," *U.S. New, and World Report*, August 11, 1986, pp. 52-56.

Bullaro, J., and Edginton, C. *Commercial Leisure Services*. New York: Macmillan Publishing Company, 1986.

Crossley, J. *Public-Commercial Cooperation in Parks and Recreation*. Columbus, Ohio: Publishing Horizons Inc., 1986.

Demetrios, M. Personal Interview. August 1987, Vallejo, California.

Drucker, P. *Innovation and Entrepreneurship*. New York: Harper & Row Publishers, 1985.

Epperson, A. *Private and Commercial Recreation: A Text and Reference*. New York: John Wiley & Sons, Inc., 1977. Venture Publishing, Inc., 1986.

Gallup Organization, Inc. in "The Business of Leisure," *The Wall Street Journal*, April 21, 1986, Section 4, p. 130.

Kelly, J. *Recreation Business*. New York: John Wiley & Sons, 1985.

Leisure Industry Digest. Data from assorted bi-monthly issues, 1986.

Lundberg, D. *The Tourist Business* (3rd Edition). Boston: CBI Publishing Company, Inc., 1976.

MacLean, J., Peterson, J., and Martin, D. *Recreation and Leisure: The Changing Scene* (4th Edition). New York: John Wiley & Sons, 1985.

Market Opinion Research. *Participation in Outdoor Recreation Among American Adults and the Motives Which Drive Participation*. Washington, D.C.: The Presidents Commission on Americans Outdoors, May, 1986, p. 21.

McIntosh, R., and Goeldner, C. *Tourism: Principles, Practices, Philosophy* (4th Edition). New York: John Wiley & Sons, 1984.

National Recreation and Park Association. "Editors' Diary," *Dateline NRPA*, May, 1984, p. 2.

Princhot, G. *Intrapreneuring: Why You Don't Have to Leave the Corporation to Become an Entrepreneur*. New York: Harper & Row, 1985.

United Media Enterprises in "How People Spend Free Time." *Dallas Morning News*, September 5, 1983, p. C1.

Urciuoli, J. "Leisure Time Outlook." *Standard and Poor's Industry Survey*, February 6, 1986, p. L15.

USA Today. "The Way We Are." December 31, 1986, p. 4D.

U.S. News and World Report. "Our Endless Pursuit of Happiness." August 10, 1981, pp. 58-60.

Van Voorhis, K. *Entrepreneurship and Small Business Management*. Boston: Allyn and Bacon, Inc., 1980.

U.S. Travel Data Center. In "The Business of Leisure," *The Wall Street Journal*, April 21, 1986, Section 4, p. 130.

U.S. Department of Commerce. In "The Business of Leisure." *The Wall Street Journal*, April 21, 1986, Section 4, p. 130.

Chapter 2

THE ENTREPRENEUR AND
THE INTRAPRENEUR

In recent years the word "entrepreneur" has become a "buzzword" in popular literature as well as in business related literature. Even more recently, the word "intrapreneur" has begun to appear in our vocabulary. Although we use these terms frequently, do we really know who the entrepreneur and the intrapreneur are? Where do they get their ideas? How do they develop those ideas into a fledgling business? What strategies do they follow to manage the new enterprise to success? These and other issues are the focus of this chapter.

MISCONCEPTIONS ABOUT THE ENTREPRENEUR

Several times a year we see newspapers or television shows highlight an individual who has become a successful entrepreneur. The most newsworthy stories often tell about a high school or college dropout who turned a bright idea into a million dollar business. Variation A of this story is that the entrepreneur slaved 20 years to make a dream come true. The more glamorous variation B tells how the entrepreneur gambled everything his family owned on a long shot that came through.

In motion pictures we often see the entrepreneur portrayed as the sociable huckster who, with no sense of guilt, exploits friends or swindles strangers. This popular version shows the entrepreneur with an "easy come easy go" attitude. Another popular view is that the entrepreneur has such an instinct for the business that he never needs to be analytical. Finally, some people think that the entrepreneur is motivated primarily by money and will do anything to make a buck.

These views of the entrepreneur may be popular for newspapers, television, and motion pictures, but they do not square with facts. Research has shown the entrepreneur to be quite different from the popular misconceptions.

PROFILE OF THE ENTREPRENEUR

According to Drucker (1985, p. 28) the entrepreneur "always searches for change, responds to it, and exploits it as an opportunity." This implies that the entrepreneur constantly studies the environment, especially social change, market trends, technological advancements, and economic conditions. After careful study and analysis, the entrepreneur finds resources, brings them together, and manages them in such a way as to create something new and different. In this perspective, entrepreneurism is just the opposite of a risky "easy come-easy go" venture. Rather, entrepreneurship is a well thought out shift of resources from an area of low productivity to an area of higher productivity and yield. While there is still an element of risk, careful scrutiny of the market and careful planning of the business helps to reduce the risk. This section profiles the characteristics of these often misunderstood entrepreneurs.

Psychological Portrait

Many profiles of entrepreneurs are oriented toward inventors and manufacturers. Berger and Bronson (1981), however, studied successful hospitality entrepreneurs, who as a group, are probably more representative of the commercial recreation industry. Specific findings from their study found that entrepreneurs tended to:

- be the eldest among siblings of the same sex.
- have parents who were entrepreneurs and/or professionals.
- college graduates.
- motivated to create something unique on their own.
- dislike working for other people.
- liked to work with and serve people.
- rated themselves highest on the following characteristics: fighting spirit, ability to juggle tasks, leadership, motivation, willingness to take risks, creativity, and foresight.

On the basis of these and additional findings, Berger and Bronson concluded that successful hospitality entrepreneurs came from a family value system that emphasized an independent work life, leadership, and a strong educational background. The goals of accomplishment, self-respect, freedom, and family security are strong. In addition, the means (honesty, independence, competence, and ambition) to achieve those goals are present. There is also a strong understanding of human nature and a desire to serve others. Unfortunately, the pressure of maintaining a successful enterprise made it difficult to keep close, warm relationships with others.

Van Voorhis (1980), Mancuso (1974), Merwin (1981), Gregory (1986), and Hammond (1986), have suggested additional characteristics of entrepreneurs including:

- A high sense of morality because they work in a small circle of people they trust.
- Sensitivity to good ideas.
- Mentally tough.
- View money as a resource and as a way of keeping score, but not as a motivating source.
- Recognize their own limitations.
- Excel in sports but don't care to watch sports events.
- Are successful and satisfied as "doers" rather than as managers or planners.
- Are not big risk takers but are realistic gamblers.

- Will continue to start up new ventures even after they have achieved great success.
- Have little need for group affiliations.
- Have an intensity that can wreck their family life.
- Have the courage to surround themselves with strong people without bruising their own egos.

The Spirit of Entrepreneurship

Very few people will perfectly fit the previously mentioned psychological portrait. In fact, some persons may match only half of the characteristics and yet become successful entrepreneurs. What then is the "bottom line" that all enterpreneurs must possess? Many authorities believe that the energy and spirit of the entrepreneur is the key factor. Nolan Bushnell, the founder of Atari video games put it even more directly.

> The critical ingredient is getting off your ass and doing something. A lot of people have ideas, but there are few who decide to do something about them now. Not tomorrow, not next week, but today (Merwin, 1981, p. 60).

It may be that there is a "window" in life for most people when the time is right to break away from an organization and start their own enterprise. This is a time when the spirit of entrepreneurship overlaps competence and experience. At too young an age a person may have enthusiasm but lack business experience and self-confidence. By the early forties however, this person is usually embedded in a career and facing many family and financial commitments. Even though the experience factor exists, the entrepreneurial spirit may be lost, and it is too late to break away into a new venture. On the other hand, once a person becomes a successful entrepreneur, the spirit can be rekindled with each new venture. Some entrepreneurs are still putting deals together at the age of 80.

Entrepreneurs Exam

It may be fun to test yourself with an entrepreneurs exam. The self-scored exam at the conclusion of this chapter was adapted from a similar test developed by Van Voorhis (1981). It is based on characteristics believed to exist for the typical entrepreneur. Don't despair however if you fall short on this test. It is not meant to predict your future, but to show how you compare to the generic entrepreneur. The real test will come later, and it won't be from a textbook.

Four Faces of the Entrepreneur

The mere presence of various characteristics does not guarantee that a person will become a successful entrepreneur. There needs to be some sense of order and timing if a person is to make the most of those entrepreneurial characteristics. Von Oech (1986) has suggested just such an approach when he analyzed the four roles of the creative process.

According to this concept, the most successful person has the mental flexibility to exercise all four roles: the explorer, the artist, the judge, and the warrior. Each of these roles within an entrepreneur is presented here.

The Explorer pokes around into unknown areas for ideas. This can include a look at outside fields of interest, or it could be an indepth examination of whatever is right in front of our nose. The explorer enjoys the search.

The Artist transforms what the explorer finds into a new idea that has possibilities. An imaginative artist asks a lot of "what if" type questions, then answers the questions.

The Judge evaluates the new idea from the artist and may modify it. Questions the judge asks involve the market, the cost, the time required to implement the idea, the resources available, and the chance of success. It is important for the judge to strike down the ideas that are not well founded.

The Warrior goes to battle for the ideas that the judge approves and does whatever it takes to implement the idea. The warrior must be motivated, have passion for the idea, and be ready to fight a long time.

Each of these "four faces" depend upon different entrepreneurial characteristics. For best results, there needs to be a balance between the four. One weak face can ruin the entrepreneur. For example, if the entrepreneur is not creative, they won't see opportunities, and their "artist" will not come up with many ideas for their "judge" personality to consider. On the other hand, if the entrepreneur has lots of ideas but is not analytical and realistic, then their "judge" will approve too many losers. In turn, the "warrior" within the entrepreneur will expend resources foolishly. Lastly, if an entrepreneur does not have energy and determination, the "warrior" personality will not succeed in bringing a feasible idea to the market.

The key idea of this "four faces" concept is that the entrepreneur needs to utilize the positive characteristics in an orderly, timely, and balanced manner. It takes all four faces to succeed unless there is help available. For example, an entrepreneur might be an excellent explorer, artist, and warrior, but lack the experience of the judge. It would be advisable therefore, to find a partner who is well seasoned, analytical, and realistic to help mold and modify the entrepreneur's ideas into a workable business concept. In another scenario, a manager could be an excellent judge and warrior who counts upon a focus group or "think tank" of business associates to come up with the new ideas.

INTRAPRENEURS

Not everyone can break away from an organization and an established career to become an entrepreneur. For many people, the risks are simply too great. Why then can't a person act in an entrepreneurial manner within an organization? The answer is that this happens frequently under the right circumstances.

Energetic management consultant Gifford Pinchot III calls the process "intrapreneurship." Pinchot (1985, p. ix) defines intrapreneurs as:

> any of the dreamers who 'do'. Those who take hands-on responsibility for creating innovation of any kind within an organization. The intrapreneur may be the creator or inventor, but is always the dreamer who figures out how to turn an idea into a profitable reality.

There are actually advantages to working within an organization as an intrapreneur. Existing companies or agencies have financial resources, business skills, people you can trust, physical resources, and marketing systems. On the other hand, a large organization can also be an overly bureaucratic structure with regulations that inhibit creativity.

The intrapreneur, therefore, must usually begin a project alone and develop the idea to the point where it can be shared and scrutinized by a tight network of allies. If the support of allies can be won, the next phase is to bootleg the resources needed to develop the project to a prototype or trial stage. This means unpaid overtime hours for all concerned, and the "borrowing" of supplies, equipment, or other resources from existing budgeted functions. Finally, there is the "formal stage" where the intrapreneurial project can stand on its own and win approval and funding from the organization.

Barriers to Intrapreneurs

It is important to identify the barriers that intrapreneurs must face. Some of these barriers can be found in almost any organization, but they are particularly prevalent in large bureaucratic companies and in government. Barriers identified by Benest (1986) include:

The Zero Risk Ethic. Some organizations are afraid to take any risks. This may be overcome by exploiting the "forgiveness factor." In a bureaucracy it is easier for an intrapreneur to be forgiven, after the fact for action taken, than to get prior approval for the action.

Insufficient Research and Development Funding. This is typical of government and of businesses that are overconfident and comfortable with past success.

Lack of Excess Production Capacity. Many people are so fully scheduled in their jobs that they have no time left over to take on any intrapreneurial projects.

Lack of Incentives. Many organizations, particularly government, do not provide sufficient incentives for intrapreneurs.

Overburdening Hierarchy. Too many layers of hierarchy slow down decision making and the flow of information throughout the organization.

Over-Emphasis on Accountability. Auditors and accountant types can create systems of regulations, procedures, and controls that stifle the flexibility and responsiveness needed by intrapreneurs.

Keys to Intrapreneurship

In the face of so many barriers to intrapreneurship, is there really much chance to be entrepreneurial within your organization? The answer, according to Pinchot (1985) is a resounding "yes." Keys to successful intrapreneurship include the following: a good idea, time to develop the idea, a business plan, a sponsor, and a rewards system.

A good intrapreneurial idea meets three kinds of needs: customers, corporations, and intrapreneurs. Consider projected margins, proprietory advantage, and "fit" within corporate strategy. It must be an idea that customers will purchase, or an idea that improves the desirability of an existing product/service. This idea must also fit within the corporation's overall philosophy, resources, and strategies. It must also provide profits or savings that are acceptable. Finally, the idea must be one that the intrapreneur finds interesting and personally compatible.

Time to develop the idea is scarce in many organizations, but some companies such as 3M expect employees to pirate 15 percent of their time to work on innovations.

A brief business plan should demonstrate that the idea has been thoroughly researched. The business plan or feasibility study will be covered in greater detail in Chapter 4.

Sponsors are protectors of intrapreneurs. A higher level executive in the organization can help pirate resources for the intrapreneur and help buffer the intrapreneur from political attacks.

Rewards of some type are essential to intrapreneurs. If financial rewards are not possible, the employer might consider travel to conferences, public and peer recognition, and "intracapital" (the freedom and funding to work on future projects) as incentives. Figure 2-1 presents the "Intrapreneur's Ten Commandments," which are rather light-hearted but generally true guidelines for intrapreneurs.

Figure 2-1
THE INTRAPRENEUR'S TEN COMMANDMENTS

1. Come to work each day willing to be fired.
2. Circumvent any orders aimed at stopping your dream.
3. Do any job needed to make your project work, regardless of your job description.
4. Find people to help you.
5. Follow your intuition about the people you choose and work only with the best.
6. Work underground as long as you can--publicity triggers the "corporate immune mechanism."
7. Never bet on a race unless you are running in it.
8. Remember it is easier to ask for forgiveness than for permission.
9. Be true to your goals, but be realistic about the ways to achieve them.
10. Honor your sponsors.

Source: Pinchot (1985).

SYSTEMATIC ENTREPRENEURSHIP AND SOURCES FOR INNOVATION

Entrepreneurs and intrapreneurs don't just pull successful ideas out of thin air. They are usually very familiar with a certain industry and find ways to improve that industry's products or services. According to a survey by the National Federation of Independent Business, 60 percent of entrepreneurs get their ideas from their experience on a prior job or from an area of strong personal interest. An entrepreneur may also understand a particular market segment very well and create products or services to fulfill unmet needs. Another approach is that the entrepreneur correctly anticipates social, demographic, or economic changes that lead to opportunities.

In all three of the above situations, innovation occurs. We can define innovation as any act that endows resources with new capacity to create wealth. A common thread is that the entrepreneur (for simplicity, we will include intrapreneurs when we speak of entrepreneurs) is closely in touch with his environment. Drucker (1985) suggests that the successful entrepreneur monitors the environment, and engages in "systematic innovation." This means a purposeful and organized search for changes in the environment and then a systematic analysis of the opportunities that such changes may offer. Drucker has further suggested eight sources for innovation. These sources are presented in descending order of reliability and predictability. It is important to note that the first four sources of innovation (the unexpected, incongruities, process needs, and industry/market structure) are internal oriented. That is, a person working within a given industry would be in the best position to observe these opportunities. On the other hand, the last four types (demographics, changes in perception, new knowledge, and the bright idea) are all external oriented. As such, industry outsiders can capitalize on these opportunities.

Source 1: The Unexpected

The unexpected success or the unexpected failure of a company's products or services can point to new opportunities. No other area offers richer opportunity, because it is less risky and the pursuit is less arduous. This is because a company usually has its structure and resources in place sufficiently to capitalize on this type of innovation. Yet, this method of innovation is often neglected because it may not be seen, even by insiders.

For example, ten years ago the manager of a sporting goods store in Texas carried a small line of ski equipment, mainly as a convenience to some of his regular customers. Over the years, his ski equipment sales doubled, but he did not really notice the change and did not increase his line. Meanwhile, another store manager monitored his sales more carefully. "Why would ski sales in Texas increase?" he asked. From customers he learned that cheap air fares had made it easy for Texans to reach Colorado. This manager increased his line of ski equipment each year until he became the "ski center" for miles around. The unexpected success of this product line eventually contributed to a huge increase in profitability.

In another example, tackle football became a popular game for military play since it was a form of mock warfare. However, during World War II, priorities on leather, rubber, and wool made it difficult to acquire protective equipment. Tackle games were tried anyway, often with disastrous results. After a forty minute game at Fort McCelland, Alabama, between two companies with practically no equipment, there were 23 men on sick/injury report the next day. Thus, out of the necessity to keep the soldiers healthy, touch football became the "new Army game" and received its biggest boost in popularity (Grombach, 1958). The sport is now a regular offering in community recreation programs and campus intramurals.

The key aspect of this source of innovation is that the entrepreneur must become aware of the unexpected occurence. Then, action must be taken to capitalize upon the circumstances.

Source 2: Incongruities

An incongruity is a discrepancy or a dissonance between an existing situation and "what ought to be." There is an underlying fault that may not manifest itself in figures or reports. If the entrepreneur discovers the incongruity, it can be exploited with a new product or service or by trying a new approach with an existing product or service.

A city in Virginia conducted an extensive youth sports program. In the autumn, this program did not include soccer, but there was a tackle football program with 65 teams. This football program was very expensive and the participant fees did not come close to covering the cost. Meanwhile, a community survey showed virtually no interest in soccer. "How could this be?" asked the city recreation supervisor. After all, he reasoned, soccer is a popular and inexpensive youth sport all over the country. True, no one in the city of 110,000 had ever appeared before the advisory board and asked for a soccer program. The recreation supervisor decided to challenge this incongruity by starting a youth soccer league. Within three years there were 72 teams and the program was paying for itself. Throughout this period, football registration did not drop. An incongruity had been met with a new program that found an entirely new market segment.

Source 3: Process Need

This is a task-focused innovation that perfects a process that already exists by replacing a weak link or redesigning an existing process around new knowledge. When this innovation occurs it becomes the "obvious" solution that people just didn't think of. To be successful, the need must be understood, and there must be high consumer receptivity to it.

Movie theaters make most of their profits from concession stand revenues. During sellouts of popular movies, the crowd at the concession stand gets so long that many late comers forego a purchase in order to find seats. One theater manager observed the concession process and found a way to cut service time by 40 percent. First, soft drink service was redesigned to a self serve format. Even if some people abused this approach, the product cost was minimal. Second, all items were priced so that when tax was added, the amount would be $1.00, $1.25, $1.50, or $2.00. This made it much quicker to handle the customer's payment. As a result of these process innovations, more people could be served during the peak periods and concession sales increased.

Source 4: Industry and Market Structures

This source of innovation requires that managers of a company ask themselves: "What is our business?" The idea is to search for a flaw in the basic nature of the industry. This strategy is particularly effective when an industry has been dominated by a few large companies who have become unchallenged and arrogant. An innovative newcomer then gains a foothold in the market with a simple but important change that appeals to customers. If the innovation is successful, it is difficult for the larger companies to change quickly and mobilize for a counterattack.

In its early years, People Express created quite a stir with its no frills flights and super low prices. Their concept also featured low labor costs due to a nonunion structure. For a while, People Express looked very impressive and it had load factors (seat occupancy percentage) that were much higher than the industry average. Eventually however, several other airlines found ways to combat their unions, reduce labor costs, and charge prices that were more competitive with People Express. This resulted in the decline of People Express, because they did not continue to be innovative.

Source 5: Demographics

Of all the externally oriented strategies, innovations based on demographic changes are the clearest, and have the most predictable consequences. Demographic shifts have long lead times and are measured by numerous organizations from whom data is readily available. However, a problem is that other entrepreneurs can have access to the same demographic information. It therefore becomes a question of which entrepreneur best interprets and exploits the demographic shifts.

Club Med founders have exploited the emergence of large numbers of young affluent single adults in the United States and Europe. An exotic, adult version of a summer camp was created for young tourists wanting an organized vacation setting with peers. Now with demographics changing again, Club Med is beginning to market "mini clubs" at selected locations. A mini club features supervised children's programs while parents participate in water sports, tennis, and other adult programs.

Source 6: Changes In Perception

When changes in people's perceptions take place, facts do not change but meanings do. For example, the physiological benefits of exercise have been known for years. However, in past years, staunch adherents to weight lifting or distance running were not considered normal. Now, the perception of fitness has changed. Fitness is now associated with quality of life and social interaction. As a result of this change in perception, many companies that have exploited the fitness industry have done very well in recent years.

There is a major problem with this strategy however. Timing is critical. Nothing is more dangerous than to be premature in exploiting a change of perception. A company can go broke if it puts money into an idea before the market is ready and receptive. On the other hand, it can be equally disastrous to enter a market after it has peaked. The best approach in exploiting a change of perception is to start small and appeal to a very specific market.

Source 7: New Knowledge

Innovations based on new knowledge are the "superstars" of entrepreneurship. Although new knowledge does not have to be scientific or technology based, these have been the glamor areas of recent years. For example, the technology developed by Nolan Bushnell and Atari Corporation helped start the wave of video games. In many cases, it is a convergence of several different kinds of knowledge that results in a success. The airplane, for example, was a convergence of the gasoline engine and modern areodynamics.

An important characteristic of knowledge-based innovation is the long lead time required to bring an idea to the marketplace. This can mean great expense, and if the idea isn't right the first time, the entrepreneur may be out of business. The next entrepreneur, however, may take the failed idea, add a missing ingredient, and be successful.

Another problem is the "receptivity gamble." A knowledge-based innovation may not be what the public wants. The entrepreneur is gambling that the public will be receptive to the idea when it is developed. There is also the problem that some entrepreneurs get infatuated with their own technology, regardless of what the public wants.

For these reasons, knowledge-based innovation is very risky. The risk can be reduced, however, if the strategy is combined with one or more of the other sources of innovation. Some of the classic innovations in the recreation industry that are based on new knowledge/technology include airplane travel, metal skis, polyurethane wheels for skateboards, scuba diving tanks, and video games.

Source 8: The Bright Idea

Seven out of every ten patents filed belong in this category. These are often simple ideas such as zippers or pull tabs on beer cans. Unfortunately, the bright idea is the riskiest and least successful form of innovation. Only one in 500 bright ideas make significant revenue.

Bright ideas are typically unorganized and out of synch with any particular market demand. This is not a strategy upon which an entrepreneur should focus. However, society does need those rare one in 500 ideas that make it big.

ENTREPRENEURIAL STRATEGIES

Once an entrepreneurial innovation has occurred, it needs to be brought to the market place. Drucker (1985) has suggested four nonmutually exclusive entrepreneurial strategies: a) fustest with the mostest; b) hit'em where they ain't, c) ecological niches, and d) changing values and characteristics.

Fustest With the Mostest

This strategy aims at leadership and dominance of a new market and is considered to be the entrepreneurial strategy "par excellence." The entrepreneur basically tries to capture an entire market by being first on the scene with an innovation. For several years, Head Skis held this advantage when they pioneered metal skis in an era of wooden skis.

Entrepreneurs using this strategy must continue to research and innovate if they are to fight off competition. If they set prices too high, then even more competitors will be encouraged to enter the market. And, like a moon shot, this strategy must be right on target during development or it will be way off by the time a huge promotional program is launched.

The "fustest with the mostest" strategy will fail more often than it will succeed and should be used only for major innovations. If it is successful, it is highly rewarding, but overall, it is not the dominant strategy for marketing an innovation.

Hit'em Where They Ain't

This strategy is based on the assumption that "fustest with the mostest" will fail more often than it will succeed. An entrepreneur will wait until someone else has established something new but has not acheived the ultimate design. The entrepreneur then develops the idea one step better and captures the market.

Several large water theme parks have used this strategy, by expanding upon the small water slide concept of earlier years. Even though the early water slides were fun, it was soon discovered that people prefer a larger attraction where a family can spend a whole day.

Similarly, a large company may be first on the scene with a product and try to "cream the market" with high prices. A newcomer could simplify or modify the idea, offer it at a lower price, and steal part of the market away. Some discount hotel chains have done this in high priced resort areas. They offer basic accommodations for the budget-minded tourist and gain excellent occupancy rates.

Ecological Niches

This strategy aims at control or practical monopoly in a small segment of a market. It may be so inconspicuous that no one tries to compete. An ecological niche may be based upon a specialty skill, product, or service. An example is a ski tuning service that picks up tourist's skis at Salt Lake City hotels at night and returns them freshly waxed the next morning. The ecological niche can also be based upon a specific market. Thomas Cook and American Express had a monopoly on the travelers checks used by middle class tourists for many years. The problem with the ecological niche strategy is that it cannot sustain full control if the specialty market grows to become a mass market. New competitors enter the picture when volume and profit margins grow. This strategy, however, is an excellent one for an entrepreneur with a special service and/or a low overhead operation. The key is to find that unmet ecological niche and then serve it well.

Changing Value and Characteristics

This strategy involves converting an established product or service into something new by changing its utility. In a sense, a new customer is created. Timeshare resorts capitalize on this and attract consumers who generally could not afford their own vacation home. Timesharing offers the security of ownership and relatively fixed prices with the flexibility of trading for different locations. To capitalize on this entrepreneurial strategy, it is critical to know the market and know what the consumer values.

ENTREPRENEURSHIP IN SERVICE INSTITUTIONS

Service institutions such as public park and recreation departments need to be just as innovative and entrepreneurial as a private business is. The problem is that service institutions often have cumbersome structures, procedures, and traditions that are greater barriers than are found in even the most bureaucratic of private companies. Drucker (1985) suggested several specific obstacles that many service institutions face.

- They are dependent on a multitude of constituents and find it difficult to focus on specific market segments.
- Service institutions exist to "do good" for their community and see their mission as moral rather than as economic (and subject to cost/benefit justification).
- They always want to do more of the same and resist abandoning anything. The demand to innovate is perceived as an attack on their basic service commitments. Labor unions almost always fight innovation.
- Service institutions have budgets that have been appropriated by a higher authority (city council, United Way, etc.) rather than budgets based upon their results (i.e., revenues).

Entrepreneurial Policies for Service Institutions

In spite of the barriers mentioned, there is hope for entrepreneurism in service institutions. The key is to develop entrepreneurial philosophies and policies that will guide the operation of the service institution. These policies, as adapted from Drucker (1985) are presented here. In addition, Figure 2-2 illustrates several practical "Do's and Dont's" for innovations, which are applicable to service institutions and to private enterprises.

- Have a clear definition of the organization's mission. Programs and projects must be considered as temporary strategies to fulfill the mission.
- Have realistic statements of goals. It is impossible, for most practical

purposes, to serve all the recreation needs of all the residents or constituents.

- The failure to achieve objectives must be considered as an indication that the objectives could be wrong. They may need modification or elimination. It is not rational to throw more money at a failure time after time.
- Build policies and procedures to search for opportunity. View change as an opportunity, not as a threat.
- Consider the privatization (contracting out) of facilities, programs, or services if they cannot be managed efficiently and effectively by the institution.

Assistance for Entrepreneurship in Recreation Service Organizations

Since many recreation professionals do not have entrepreneurial backgrounds, it may be advisable for them to seek assistance. For general business advice, any office of the Small Business Administration can help, as can the business school of almost any university. Consultation is also available in many communities through local chapters of the Service Corps of Retired Executives or the Active Corps of Executives. Both organizations provide consultation for free or for low fees.

Figure 2-2
DO'S AND DON'TS OF INNOVATION

Do's
1. Analyze the opportunities rather than guess. Study demographics, social trends, technology changes, economic conditions, etc.
2. Innovation is conceptual and perceptual, so go out into the community and look, listen, and ask questions.
3. Strive to be simple and focused.
4. Start small.
5. Aim at market leadership, but not necessarily to become a big business. Small ecological niches are okay too.

Don'ts
1. Don't try to be too clever because most products and services serve ordinary people.
2. Don't diversify, splinter off, or try to be too many different things.
3. Don't innovate for the future because it is too difficult to predict. Innovate for needs that are known today.

Source: Drucker (1985).

SUMMARY

People hold many misconceptions about entrepreneurs; that they are con-men, hucksters, and gamblers who dropped out of school but got lucky with a business venture. Research, however, supports a much different profile. The entrepreneur is more likely to be an honest, well educated individual who wants to create something unique on his own and is willing to work very hard to do it. While entrepreneurs are not big risk takers, they are realistic gamblers if the odds are in their favor. Primarily they are "doers" who make things happen, but who study situations very carefully. A successful entrepreneur must be an explorer of ideas, an artist for developing the idea, an unbiased judge of the idea, and a warrior who fights for the idea.

Intrapreneurs are persons who are entrepreneurial within an organization. The intrapreneur faces additional barriers, but has some additional assets to work with. Most importantly, an intrapreneur needs freedom, a trusting sponsor, and a system of rewards.

Systematic entrepreneurship is the organized search for changes in the environment that will present opportunities. Drucker (1985) suggests eight strategies that are sources of innovation for the systematic entrepreneur: the unexpected, incongruities, process needs, industry and market structures, demographics, changes in perception, new knowledge, and the bright idea. Drucker further suggests entrepreneurial strategies to bring the innovations to market: fustest with the mostest, hit'em where they ain't, ecological niches, and changing values and characteristics.

This chapter has explored the nature of the entrepreneur and the intrapreneur. The next chapter will explore the nature of the arena, commercial recreation, where these entrepreneurs will battle.

Recreation service institutions face certain barriers, but can still become innovative and entrepreneurial. The key is to develop philosophies and policies that allow the organization to have "entrepreneurial elbow room" rather than to be restricted by bureaucracy. A variety of consultation services and publications can provide assistance for the recreation entrepreneur.

STUDY QUESTIONS

1. How does knowledge of entrepreneurship aid the aspiring leisure business professional?
2. Describe a "typical" enterpreneur.
3. What are the four faces of the entrepreneur?
4. What is an intrapreneur, and how does that individual differ from an entrepreneur?
5. What barriers exist in corporations to intrapreneurial innovations?
6. How can innovation occur?
7. What are eight sources of innovation?

PROJECT IDEAS

1. Name and discuss five persons who fit the entrepreneurial psychological portrait.
2. Review the intrapreneur's ten commandments. How well do you fit these?
3. Create an example for each of Drucker's entrepreneurial strategies.

SPOTLIGHT ON: Jazzercise Founder Judi Missett

Judi Sheppard Missett grew up in Red Oak, Iowa, watching her father work two jobs to put food on the table. This unspoiled upbringing taught her the value of hard work, yet she always had dreams and an imagination.

In the late 1960s Missett taught professional jazz dancing in Chicago. Appropriately, she taught a rigorous and disciplined class, but the student drop-out rate was high. Judi noticed that students came to class for fun and exercise, so she came up with the concept of "Jazzercize," a mixture of jazz dance and exercise. After moving to San Diego in 1972, Missett single-handedly launched a jazzercise movement at YMCAs and community centers. For five years, she taught up to 20 classes a week. Satisfied students helped the business expand, and former students opened franchised classes out of state. However, only one out of eight franchise applicants is accepted by Missett's four-member screening board.

Today, Missett, in her early 40's, has 3000 franchised instructors, 350,000 students, and a net worth of $4 million. Her records and video tapes are million copy sellers, and she is establishing a line of exercise clothes. Missett is not comfortable in a millionaire's role however. She still teaches five classes a week and choreographs all Jazzercise workouts. Her husband, Jack, produces videos of her new dance routines to sell to franchises. They don't flaunt their wealth. The Missetts drive a Honda and a Jeep, and their teenage daughter attends public schools.

Judi Missett believes that dreams can come true, but "you first must be imaginative enough to dream dreams." She also believes that you need "patience, perseverance, and guts to work your derriere off and make it happen" (Dworkin, 1986).

Chapter 2 Appendix
ENTREPRENEUR QUIZ

For the following questions please circle the answer that best describes your feelings, desires, or characteristics. Use the following scale for your responses:

SA = Strongly Agree   A = Agree
N = Neutral   D = Disagree
SD = Strongly Disagree

		SA	A	N	D	SD
1.	My parents are employed as managers or in professional occupations.	1	2	3	4	5
2.	At least one of my parents always worked for himself/herself.	1	2	3	4	5
3.	I like to be conservative.	1	2	3	4	5
4.	If I like an idea I never lack motivation.	1	2	3	4	5
5.	I do not see myself as a leader.	1	2	3	4	5
6.	I am always able to work on several tasks at the same time.	1	2	3	4	5
7.	I always accept "no" as the final answer to my ideas.	1	2	3	4	5
8.	I am a creative person.	1	2	3	4	5
9.	I am interested in creating something that is uniquely mine.	1	2	3	4	5
10.	I don't care if others think I am honest and fair.	1	2	3	4	5
11.	I find myself continually looking for good ideas.	1	2	3	4	5
12.	I am able to be honest with myself.	1	2	3	4	5
13.	I am more concerned with achievement than wealth.	1	2	3	4	5
14.	I have no limitations.	1	2	3	4	5
15.	I enjoy watching sporting events.	1	2	3	4	5
16.	I enjoy belonging to many groups.	1	2	3	4	5
17.	When I am working on something I enjoy, I forget about everything else, even time.	1	2	3	4	5
18.	My friends are always the smartest people I can find.	1	2	3	4	5
19.	I love to take big risks.	1	2	3	4	5
20.	I have never excelled in sports.	1	2	3	4	5
21.	I have always been aware of my own limitations.	1	2	3	4	5
22.	In general I am very optimistic.	1	2	3	4	5
23.	When I feel I am right I can usually convince others of my opinion.	1	2	3	4	5

24.	I enjoy taking orders from people in authority.	1	2	3	4	5
25.	My career experience has always been in small business (under 100 employees).	1	2	3	4	5
26.	I feel that I work hard and with intelligence on any project that I undertake.	1	2	3	4	5
27.	In every business situation I like to know who is in charge.	1	2	3	4	5
28.	When I play a competitive sport I am concerned only about winning and losing.	1	2	3	4	5

SCORING

Add up the response number you circled for each of the following questions: 1, 2, 4, 6, 8, 9, 11, 12, 13, 17, 18, 21, 22, 23, 25, 26, and 27.

For each of the remaining questions, 3, 5, 7, 10, 14, 15, 16, 19, 20, 24, and 28, subtract the number you circled from six and add the answers together.

Add up the two scores to find your entrepreneurial score. To gain an indication of your entrepreneurial ability, compare your score to the interpretations below.

28 to 56	Good chance to become an entrepreneur
57 to 84	Fair entrepreneurial potential
85 to 112	Marginal entrepreneurial potential
113 to 140	Keep working for a large company.

Test Developed by Taylor Ellis, Ph.D. and M.B.A., University of Utah, 1987.

REFERENCES

Benest, F. "New Entrepreneurship for Leisure Agencies." Annual Conference of the National Recreation and Parks Association, Anaheim, California, October, 1986.

Berger, F., and Bronson, C. "Entrepreneurship in the Hospitality Industry: A Psychological Portrait." *The Cornell Hotel and Restaurant Administration Quarterly*, August, 1981, pp. 52-56.

Drucker, P.F. *Innovation and Entrepreneurship*. New York: Harper & Row Publishers, 1985.

Dworkin, P. "Putting the Muscle to Music." *U.S. News and World Report*, January 13, 1986, pp. 44-45.

Gregory, P. "The Entrepreneurial Spirit." *Courier*. October 1986, p. 147.

Grombach, J.V. *Touch Football*. New York: The Ronald Press Company, 1958.

Hammond, S. "The Ups and Downs of Entrepreneurship." *BYU Today*, October 1986, pp. 38-42.

Mancuso, J. *The Entrepreneur's Handbook* (volume 2). Worcester, MA: Artech House, 1974.

38

Merwin, J. "Have You Got What It Takes." *Forbes*, August 3, 1981, pp. 60-64.

Princhot, G. *Intrapreneuring: Why You Don't Have to Leave the Corporation to Become an Entrepreneur.* New York: Harper & Row, 1985.

Van Voorhis, K.R. *Entrepreneurship and Small Business Management.* Boston: Allyn and Bacon, Inc., 1980.

Von Oech, R. *A Kick in the Seat of the Pants* (tape). Menlo Park, CA: Tape Data Media, Inc., 1986.

Chapter 3

THE NATURE OF COMMERCIAL RECREATION

The entrepreneur who desires to start a new venture in commercial recreation may have had previous business experience. If so, the entrepreneur will find that there are similarities between commercial recreation and other types of business. There are however, many important differences, and the entrepreneur must understand both the similarities and the differences in order to be successful. In short, the entrepreneur must understand the basic nature of commercial recreation. This includes understanding the problems of the industry, barriers to people's participation, and strategies to overcome those problems and barriers. In addition, the entrepreneur must understand certain economic, psychological, and consumer behavior concepts related to commercial recreation. This chapter will examine these concepts in order to reach a basic understanding of the nature of commercial recreation. It must be emphasized that this chapter deals with general concepts and should not be substituted for more in-depth coursework or study in business related subjects. Specific applications of these concepts to various types of commercial recreation can differ, and future chapters will investigate the many types of commercial recreation in greater depth.

PROBLEMS IN COMMERCIAL RECREATION

It is well known that many businesses fail in their first two years. Even worse, over a ten-year period, it is estimated that 81 percent of all new businesses fail (Van Voorhis, 1980). The failure rate in commercial recreation businesses may be even higher.

There are several underlying problems in the commercial recreation industry that contribute to the difficulty in operating a successful venture. First is the fact that commercial recreation is dependent upon discretionary income. This is compounded by the seasonal nature of many recreation industries. Further, the seasons may have cyclical periods of good and bad years. Even within a good season, there are intermittent flurries of activity and offsetting slow periods. These and other problems will be examined in this section.

Dependence on Discretionary Income

Discretionary income is the money available to households after all basic, everyday expenditures have been made. This money may be saved or it may be spent for nonessentials such as jewelry, education, or recreation. Herein lies the problem. Although some people regard recreation as a necessity, expenditure of one's income for recreation can be deferred more easily than can expenditures for food or housing. Fortunately, Americans are relatively better off today, in terms of income, than they have ever been (Malabre, 1986) and are spending more for recreation.

There are, however, periods of time when the economy sags and people restrain their leisure spending (motion pictures and alcohol may be exceptions). The effects of an economic downturn can be quite severe in certain locales. For example, in the late 1970s and early 1980s, the steel and auto producing areas in Michigan, Ohio, and western Pennsylvania were in depression conditions. In the middle 1980s, the farm belt and oil producing states suffered their own regional recessions, while the east and west coasts flourished (Alm & Deutschman, 1986). In all such difficult economic times, a commercial recreation business may find it difficult to survive if it is dependent upon local clientele.

Substitution. A problem associated with discretionary products and services is that they are subject to substitution. This refers to the extent to which recreation activities can be interchanged in order to satisfy the user's motives, wishes, and desires (Stankey, 1977). Consumers may substitute products/services in order to try something new, different, cheaper, safer, better, or more convenient. Some people, however, are hard-core enthusiasts for certain activities and are not likely to substitute unless the price or availability changes dramatically. Expenditures for necessities, on the other hand, are less subject to substitution.

Who Has It? There is a possible misconception that the young urban professionals (yuppies) are the target market with the most discretionary income. According to studies conducted by the Consumer Research Center (1986), that honor goes to professional, preretirement age adults. After-tax income tends to rise to a peak with the 45-49 age group, then decline. However, due to the absence of children in the household, per capita income is actually greater among persons age 55 to 64. This category is dominated by adults who are near the peak of their earning years and have fewer children in a home where the mortgage is mostly paid off.

Additional statistics from the Consumer Research Center indicate that discretionary income is higher per capita in one and two person households. Further, persons with higher education and persons in professional and managerial occupations tend to have greater discretionary income. In these statistical categories, the "yuppie" as well as the professional, preretirement adult, stand as the favored markets for commercial recreation. It must be remembered, however, that these groups are not the majority of the U.S. population. The majority of the population, although better off than in previous years, still struggles to have discretionary income. With periodic recessions, regional economic problems, and substitution of purchases, the recreation industry is not as stable as other industries, due to the dependence on discretionary income.

Seasonal Nature of Recreation

Many commercial recreation businesses have a seasonal orientation. This is particularly true if the business is climate or natural resource oriented, such as a beach resort, ski resort, or river rafting company. A seasonal orientation also occurs if a business sells products such as sporting goods, toys, or tourist gifts. Some businesses such as amusement parks, beach resorts, and summer camps are affected by the seasonal nature of the public school system. When school is in session, young families do not vacation, and teens are less available for employment. Even businesses that do not have climate restrictions have peak seasons and off seasons. For example, motion picture theaters do well at Christmas and in early summer. Health Clubs often have strong winter seasons as substitution activity for the things people cannot do outside. Figure 3-1 (Anderson, 1985, 1986) illustrates some of the high and low seasons in the recreation industry.

Figure 3-1
Examples of Seasonality in the Recreation Industry

Type Facility	High Season	Low Season
Campgrounds/Trailer Parks	May-Aug.	Nov.-Dec.
Multipurpose Health & Athletic Clubs	October-March	July-Aug.
Racquet/Tennis Clubs	Nov.-March	May
Public Golf Course (Nonmunicipal)	May-Sept.	Nov.-Feb.
Resort Hotel/Motel	June-Aug.	Nov.-Jan.
Theme/Amusement Parks	May-Aug.	Nov.-March
Private Golf/Country Club	April-Sept.	Jan.-Feb.
Sport/Recreation Camps	June-Aug.	Nov.-March
Zoos	April-Sept.	Nov.-Feb.

Adapted from Anderson, (1985, 1986).

There are numerous problems created by a seasonal fluctuation in business. It is very expensive to keep a facility open, and expenses such as utilities and labor may not be balanced by off season revenue. Even if a facility closes for the off season, there are probably fixed expenses for rent or mortgage, insurance, and administrative overhead. Management's main concern then is cash flow. If the revenues drop below expenses, is there enough previous revenue to carry the business through? The alternative may be to take out a short-term loan.

Operation of a seasonal business has its problems even during the busy season. Employees may have to be imported from other areas and provided with housing. Transportation into the area during periods of bad weather must be reliable enough so that customers can get in and out.

Amenities related to a visitors comfort, such as air conditioning, heating, and entertainment, must function flawlessly.

Increasingly, commercial recreation businesses are attempting to create a year round market for their product/service. This may be achieved by carrying different product lines (example: tennis apparel in summer and ski apparel in winter), reducing prices, conducting major special events, or by expanding facilities for different purposes. Stratton Mountain, a resort in Vermont, invested $60 million to make its facilities attractive to year round users, especially for the convention and business meeting trade (Barbati, 1985). Recent research shows that tourists surveyed at different times and seasons of the year desire different combinations of amenities, benefits, and services (Calantone and Johar, 1984). This means that advertising for off-season business may have to reach a variety of target markets.

Cyclical Nature and Unpredictable Variations

Recreational businesses, whether seasonal or not, have cycles of business activity in which participation increases or decreases over time. In some cases, these cycles occur very gradually, and it is relatively easy to manage a business over a long period of sustained growth or to diversify a business during a long and gradual decline. The problem comes when the cycles occur rapidly and/or unexpectedly or when unpredicted variations occur. Cycles can be related to weather or public interest.

Weather in some locales runs in cycles, which can play havoc with commercial recreation. Eastern and Western ski resorts have been hurt several times by lack of snowfall. Artificial snowmaking has helped neutralize this problem. Droughts, hurricanes, rains, jellyfish, mosquitos, and other natural phenomena periodically hurt various types of tourism and commercial recreation.

The public's interest can be tricky to predict. Some recreation products, such as superballs and Rubic's cubes have been relatively short-lived fads, while frisbees and skateboards have had multi-year success. Sports apparel styles can also have short- or long-term cycles. Businesses can be hurt if they are too heavily committed to a product or service during a period of rapid decline.

For whatever reason they occur, cycles of activity can catch the commercial recreation manager off-guard. This compounds the difficulty of achieving success.

Intermittent Nature

Even during peak season, a commercial recreation business is likely to have intermittent periods of heavy and light participation. These periods coincide with certain days of the month, days of the week, and hours of the day.

Paydays in blue collar communities and towns with military bases are often followed by a flurry of discretionary spending. Similarly, money is more available in urban core cities and in retirement communities following the receipt of monthly welfare and social security checks.

Weekends account for more than half of the volume of some commercial recreation businesses. This is mostly due to the standard Monday thru Friday work and school week. Holidays can be peak periods of activity for resorts, but can also be days when some retail stores, restaurants, and local attractions are closed.

Many commercial recreation businesses have busy periods and slow periods during each day. Racquetball and sports clubs for example, typically have good business in the early morning, at lunch time, and during prime-time hours, 5:00 PM till 10:00 PM. On the other hand, movie theaters seldom even bother to open until late afternoon, except for special Saturday matinees.

The intermittent nature of commercial recreation can cause management difficulties. If the busy and slack periods alternate throughout the day, most facilities will have to keep utilities operating constantly. A constant level of staff, however, could be wasted in slow hours or overwhelmed in busy hours. Some businesses simply forsake the slack period and open only for the peak times. This strategy could give a new competitor the opportunity to gain a foothold in the business by catering to the off-peak periods, if it could be done cost effectively.

Failure is rather common in the commercial recreation industry, as evidenced by this business for sale near Yellowstone Park.
(Photo: John Crossley)

Competitive Climate—A Zero Sum Market

The theory of the zero sum market is as follows: In a "constant economy," gains of market share (percent of the market controlled by a specific company) by any enterprise must be offset by similar losses of market share by the other enterprises.

Let's assume that the demand for sporting goods in Smithville is relatively constant (i.e., constant economy). The overall economic base

44

of the community is neither growing nor declining, and people are spending the same amount for sporting goods each year. Store D decides to expand its product line and compete directly with the three larger stores in town. After three years, store D has captured 3 percent of the market from store A, and 1 percent from each of stores B and store C. There was no effect on store E that specialized in Scuba equipment (the only store in town to do so). While a 5 percent overall market share gain may not sound like much, it represents a 50 percent sales increase for store D.

The zero sum market theory illustrates the cruel realities of a tough competitive climate. Gains are made only at the expense of one's competitors. This is why a commercial recreation business must fight so hard to retain its market share. In order to retain its core of regular customers and attract new ones, the commercial recreation business must differentiate its product/service from competitors, offer value for the dollar, and provide excellent service.

If an economy is growing, however, the zero sum market theory is less relevant. Growth of discretionary spending in a given area can be the result of increases in population, increases in income, or decreases in taxes or other expenses. In addition, the market for a particular type of product/service can grow due to increased interest. This illustrates the importance of locating a commercial recreation business in an area where the economy is healthy and growing and being in an industry that is growing.

Figure 3-2
Example of Zero Sum Market

Market Share Before "D" Expansion (Constant Economy)	Market Share After "D" Expansion (Constant Economy)
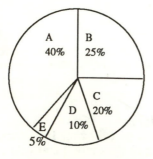	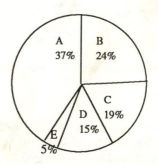

Gains = 5% Market Share
Losses = 5% Market Share
Sum   = 0

ECONOMIC AND POLITICAL PROBLEMS

In addition to the problems previously discussed, there are economic and political problems that can occur in the recreation industry. These problems present difficulties for some types of commercial recreation businesses and opportunities for others. Problems include inflation and interest rates, energy shortages, insurance, and terrorist activities.

Inflation and Interest Rates

In the late 1970s and early 80s, inflation was in the double digits. These high inflation rates caused certain expenses (particularly gasoline, fuel oil, construction materials, and utilities) to increase dramatically. This makes it difficult for a manager to project expenses and to set prices that will adequately cover those expenses. Some commercial recreation businesses such as theme parks, ski areas, and resorts publish their season prices far in advance. Inflation makes this a risky proposition. Since 1982, inflation has not been much of a problem, but the monster could raise its oily head again.

Interest rates charged by banks and other lending institutions were in the high double digits in the early 1980s. High interest rates make it difficult for consumers to finance the purchase of a recreational vehicle, a motor boat, or a vacation home. Also, high interest rates make it very expensive to borrow money to start a business or to finance an expansion. It also becomes very expensive to take out a short-term loan to cover negative cash flow during the off season. Although interest rates have come down significantly, they are still relatively high. During the peak years of double digit inflation (1979-80), the prime rate of interest charged by banks was just a little more than the rate of inflation. Now, however, interest rates are about twice as high as inflation (Council of Economic Advisors, 1987). This means that it is still relatively expensive to borrow money to start or expand a business, or to carry the business through an off-season. However, if a recreation business is generating excess revenues, then short term investing can yield high returns relative to the current level of inflation.

Energy Shortages

The days of Arab oil embargos and sky high fuel prices are behind us—or are they? The earth has a limited supply of gas and oil, and it is probably just a matter of time before there are shortages. We have bought time with more fuel efficient airplanes and autos, but we have not really made a full commitment to alternative energy sources or to conservation of energy.

During an energy crisis such as the one in 1979, the big losers seem to be the tourist attractions in remote areas. For example, attendance at National Park Service areas in Arizona, Colorado, Nevada, Utah, Wyoming, and South Dakota in 1979 were down by an average of 16.4 percent (Goeldner and Duea, 1984). On the other hand, some local and regional attractions picked up business from people who substituted local trips for longer vacations. Six Flags Over Texas installed gasoline pumps and promised customers within a certain radius that they could buy enough gas to get home.

The Insurance Dilemma

Howard and Crompton (1980) have stated that we live in an era when people are reluctant to take responsibility for their own actions. If anything goes wrong, some people want to sue. An oversupply of attorneys gladly accommodate the fortune seekers. All too frequently the claimants are rewarded by million dollar verdicts or settlements.

In recent years, insurance premiums for commercial recreation have sky rocketed. One year, Snowbird Ski and Summer Resort in Utah had a premium increase of 25 percent and their coverage was reduced 75 percent. In addition their deductible amount was raised 300 percent (Hansell, 1985). Other types of commercial recreation are even less fortunate and are not able to get insurance at all. In 1985, Utah's entire $30 million whitewater river tour industry had its insurance canceled. The National Park Service, the Forest Service, and the Bureau of Land Management require proof of insurance before river permits are issued. Only after extensive negotiations, right before the start of the season, did an insurance company agree to underwrite the 16 companies involved (Rolly, 1986).

Terrorist Activities

While terrorist activities have not been extensive within the United States, foreign travel has been affected. According to an ASTA (American Society of Travel Agents) survey of 1800 travel agents, 98 percent say that terrorism has affected where their clients go. Destinations in Europe were particularly affected after a rash of terrorist activities in 1985 and 1986. As a result, American travel to Europe was down 20-25 percent during the summer of 1986. There were a large number of group cancellations, but eventually travel began to recover (Zigli, 1986). In past years, crime and racial problems have been deterrents to travelers to the Middle East, Mexico, and the Carribean. Some people even refrain from travel to New York City due to its reputation for crime.

When people decline to travel to a given location, they often substitute by engaging in more local recreation or traveling to alternate destinations. In the summer of 1986, American travel within the United States was up by five percent (Toohey, 1986). In addition, travel to Canada and the Carribean increased, as did bookings on cruise ships.

BARRIERS TO PARTICIPATION

The previous sections have explained a multitude of problems that affect the commercial recreation industry. Wait, there are more! There is an entirely separate set of problems dealing with the participants themselves. These are the barriers to participation, which cause customers to visit the commercial recreation business less often or not at all. McIntosh and Goeldner (1984), Epperson (1977), and others have offered the following barriers to travel and to recreation in general.

Expense is typically given as one of the top two barriers. This is particularly a problem with low income groups, large families, and senior citizens on fixed incomes.

Lack of Time is the second of the two most common barriers. Business persons and professionals typically offer this as a barrier to their participation.

Physical Condition, depending upon the activity, can be a significant barrier to persons with disabilities or health problems.

Family Status limits participation by adults and families with small children. Recently, the large number of single women with children has been observed as a related trend.

Lack of Interest is a barrier that affects everyone for one recreation pursuit or another. However, some people say they have a lack of interest when another barrier is actually the real problem.

Lack of Skills restricts many people from attempting an activity they might otherwise enjoy.

Lack of Companions, particularly for travel, is a significant barrier for some single people, and many senior citizens.

Lack of Knowledge about what is available is a surprising but common barrier in our complex society.

Lack of Safety whether traveling in foreign countries or in your own hometown will deter people from participation. Even if safety is no longer a problem in a given area, the negative perception and reputation of an area might linger for years.

Lack of Transportation particularly for day-to-day recreation pursuits, is a barrier to urban and rural people alike. If people have the financial resources and plan properly, this should not be a problem unless there is a deficiency in the transportation network.

Witt and Goodale (1982) found that some barriers are more of a problem during the child-rearing years of the family life cycle. For example, free time for parents declines sharply when school-age children must be chauffeured to community activities and meal times juggled for diverse schedules. Conversely, other barriers are less of a problem during these years. School-age children often serve as initiators of neighborhood contact and as sources of information about community events.

STRATEGIES TO OVERCOME PROBLEMS AND BARRIERS

Other than basic informational value, what was the purpose of presenting the numerous problems and barriers in the previous three sections? The reason is that the commercial recreation manager must understand these problems and barriers and must find a way to overcome them. This section will present a variety of generic barriers that commercial recreation managers might consider. Later chapters focus on specific industries and will examine selected strategies in great depth.

Problem/Barrier	Possible Strategies

Discretionary Expense and Cost

1. Give discounts for youth, senior citizens, families, and off-peak periods.
2. Give group rates.
3. Give season passes, annual memberships.
4. Allow credit purchase—Visa, American Express, etc.
5. Emphasize value of the investment and value/quality for the dollar.

Expln.

Seasonal, Cyclical, and Intermittent Nature

Aren't these the same?

1. Provide year round facilities—air-supported bubbles, snowmaking, indoor stadiums, etc.
2. Diversify facilities in off season.
3. Diversify off season programs.
4. Have special events in off-peak periods.
6. Seek different market (conventions, meetings, etc.) for off season.
7. Reduce variable expenses.
8. Reduce hours.
9. Close in off season.
10. Seek higher return on investment in order to build reserves.
11. Obtain short-term loans.
12. Sell unused space or assets.
13. Rent out unused space in off season.
14. Diversify retail product line.

Exph

How?

Competition and Substitution of Product/Service

1. Diversify offerings in order to retain clients.
2. Locate in area of econmic health and growth.
3. Differentiate product/service from those of competitors.
4. Emphasize value for the dollar.
5. Provide extraordinary service and personal attention.

Example!

Inflation

1. Purchase supplies and equipment subject to cost increases in advance.
2. Lock in prices from regular vendors through contacts.
3. List your own prices as a range and/or "subject to change."

Exph

Transportation Shortage and Energy Crisis

1. Give group travel packages.
2. Provide fuel for return trip.
3. Have shuttle busses.
4. Make cooperative agreements with airlines and bus lines.

Insurance Dilemma

1. Plan to pay more. *? Ridiculous ?*
2. Increase deductible limits.
3. Reduce coverage.

| | 4. | Create industry-wide insurance pool. |
| | 5. | Risk management program. |

Crime, Safety and	1.	Promote your good safety record.
Terrorism	2.	Increase security.
	3.	Arrange for insurance that participants can purchase.

Participants	1.	Emphasize closeness and convenience.
Lack Time	2.	Increase hours of operation to accommodate people with unusual schedules.
	3.	Provide time-saving amenities—locker rooms, eating and lodging facilities on site, etc.
	4.	Provide local ground transportation, shuttles, airport pickup, etc.
	5.	Develop programs and packages for long weekends.

Participants Lack	1.	Improve accessibility for physically handicapped.
Skills and/or	2.	Provide beginner level equipment and facilities.
Physical Ability	3.	Develop "first time" packages at discount price.
	4.	Provide group or individual instruction.

Participant's	1.	Provide day care program.
Family Stage	2.	Provide special activities for children.
	3.	Provide programs and facilities that allow the entire family to participate.
	4.	Give special rates for families.

Participant's Lack	1.	Provide information about facility and program.
of Interest or Knowledge	2.	Give trial or "first times" packages.
	3.	Use advertising that stresses attractiveness of area, programs, etc.
	4.	Have personalized contact with prospective participants

Participant Lacks	1.	Have open houses, mixers, and special events to create social interaction.
Companions	2.	Provide dorm style or hostel accommodations.
	3.	Have group travel programs.
	4.	Give single supplement rates.
	5.	Provide travel companion matching service.

The above strategies are all possibilities. As such, each has advantages and disadvantages. It is up to each commercial recreation manager to understand the problems and barriers of their particular industry and to adapt strategies that bring success.

ECONOMIC CONCEPTS RELATED TO COMMERCIAL RECREATION

The commercial recreation manager will probably be more effective if she has an understanding of general economic concepts related to the business. This section will present a variety of these concepts. It must be emphasized that these concepts are presented in a general context and should not replace further study of micro-economics, finance, or management.

Supply and Demand

As defined by economists, *demand* is the quantity of a product or service that consumers will buy at a given price at a given point in time. Factors influencing demand include price, price of related goods, consumer income, tastes and preferences, and advertising (Ellerbrock, 1980). Generally, people buy more of a product/service at a lower price than at a higher price. Demand for a given product/service may also increase when the price of a competitor's product/service increases significantly. In addition, demand may be stimulated by higher income, by effective advertising, and by social changes that make a product/service more desirable. An example of the latter is the growth of health clubs as a result of society's interest in fitness.

Supply is the quantity of a product or service that is willingly provided by a business for a given price at a given time. Sellers typically are willing to supply larger quantities at higher prices than at lower prices.

Equilibrium is the price and quantity where the willingness of the seller to provide the product/service matches the willingness of the consumer to make the purchase (Spencer, 1980). In a free market, prices tend to drift toward equilibrium because of competition by sellers and because of buyer willingness to substitute if prices are too high.

Price Elasticity

Elasticity is the ratio of the percentage change in quantity of a product/service demanded in response to a change in price. If there is a large change in price, but a small change in demand, the demand is considered to be "relatively inelastic." This is illustrated in Figure 3-3, for gasoline, which was found to have relatively inelastic demand during the last energy crisis. People would pay higher prices because they generally felt that they had to have gasoline. This inelastic demand is often a characteristic for the purchase of necessities. In Figure 3-3, price increased about 40 percent (from P_1 to P_2) while demand decreased only about 20 percent (from Q_1 to Q_2).

If there is a small change in price but a large change in demand the demand is considered to be "relatively elastic." This is illustrated in Figure 3-4 for aerobics class registration. As the price increased about 30 percent (from P_1 to P_2), demand decreased about 40 percent (from Q_1 to Q_2). As with other nonnecessities and luxuries, people can go without aerobics class if the price is too high or they can take their business elsewhere (substitution).

Elasticity can also apply with price reductions. Suppose a 20 percent price reduction brought in 50 percent more customers. This would be the strategy behind certain discount prices. It is hoped that, although profit margins may be less, the increased volume would more than compensate. An example is the pricing of resort hotel rooms in the off season.

It is critically important for the commercial recreation manager to understand supply, demand, and elasticity. They must know if their industry tends to be relatively elastic or relatively inelastic. They must also know how particular market segments respond. For example, many

Figure 3-3
Example of Inelastic Demand—Gasoline

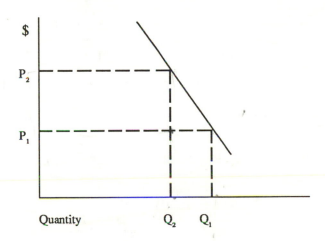

Figure 3-4
Example of Elastic Demand—Aerobics Class

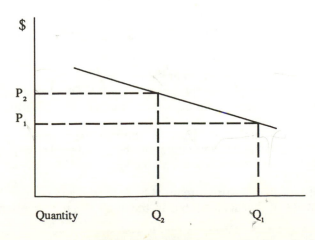

ski resorts charge premium prices to upscale vacationers during Christmas holidays. Space is limited, demand at the holidays is relatively inelastic, and the resorts fill up with "high rollers." On the other hand, weekdays in January and February may have a light quantity of tourists, but have a respectable volume of local skiers using discount passes. For any product or service, demand may be inelastic for one market segment but elastic for another. The commercial recreation manager must understand the demand for the particular industry and make wise decisions accordingly.

Systemstructure

Systemstructure refers to a variety of systems that provide the basic framework of support for a commercial recreation enterprise. Elements of systemstructure include "infrastructure" (developments on or below ground), "superstructure" (developments above ground), and other support systems. Although usually associated with resort development, the concept is equally important to all other types of commercial recreation. If the systemstructure is not in place, the business will not be able to operate properly, if at all. The various components of systemstructure are detailed below.

Transportation System. Customers, employees, and suppliers must be able to get to the commercial recreation enterprise. This requires interstate highways, state and local roads, access roads, airports and airlines, buslines, railroad transportation, taxis and other ground transfers.

Utility Systems. This includes electricity, gas lines, water and sewage systems, garbage pick up, and telephone service.

Public Services. These provide stability and security for the commercial enterprise. Included are police and fire departments, local government management and planning, public schools, and local parks.

Local Services Network. Certain services are necessary to keep the commercial recreation enterprise operating. These include suppliers and vendors, maintenance and repair shops, trades (electrical, plumbing, etc.) contractors, and a reliable local labor force.

Marketing and Media Network. In order to support the promotional functions of the business, there needs to be television and radio stations, newspapers, roadside advertising, printing companies, advertising agencies, and market research companies.

Related Amenities. Certain types of commercial recreation enterprises need other recreation amenities in order to provide a tourist/customer with a complete experience. These related amenities may include hotels, restaurants, retail shops, tour guides, gasoline service stations, and parking facilities.

A key concept is that an infrastructure must be in harmony with its natural environment. All development should minimize negative impacts on the land and water resources, the vegetation, and the wildlife of an area.

In addition, an infrastructure must be balanced and compatible with all its elements. If this does not occur, the quality of the experience and/

or the local economy will suffer. For example, Ocean City, Maryland, has a winter population of about 7,000, but in the summer this swells to 400,000. Although the city has hotels and beach houses to accommodate this surge, the roads are choked and the water and sanitation systems are overburdened. The 1981 Ocean City municipal budget was $500,000 in the red (Wiessler, 1982).

Another problem with infrastructure is that it may cost a commercial recreation enterprise extra. It is not unusual, for example, for a campground to spend heavily to bring utilities into a remote location or for a resort to build housing for scarce seasonal employees.

Critical Mass Concept

A commercial recreation enterprise must achieve a certain "critical mass" at each stage of its development in order to optimize the experience for the participant and optimize the return on investment for owners. This ideal size is reflected by several characteristics.

1. It is the optimal size for the best recreation experience. If a facility is too small for market demand, it can become overcrowded. On the other hand, if a facility is overbuilt it will not have an attractive atmosphere. Part of the total experience of a theme park, dance hall, or health club is the color, noise and interaction with a crowd. Optimal size, therefore, is big enough to alleviate overcrowding, but small enough for crowd atmosphere.

2. It is large enough to create a desired length of stay for visitors. Most theme park managers know that if participants stay four or five hours, they are likely to purchase food and beverages. Similarly, an entire resort community should strive to develop a total package of amenities that will keep visitors entertained for a week or more.

3. It is big enough and varied enough to keep participants coming back. Members of single purpose aerobic dance studios or racquetball centers often switch memberships when their interest changes. Members of larger, multipurpose sports clubs can simply change activities within the same facility. Similarly, people have foresaken the small water flume slide facilities in favor of larger water theme parks.

4. It is balanced in terms of optimal cash flow. A facility that is overbuilt will have large expenses for buildings and equipment that are underutilized. On the other hand, if a facility is too small, it may not realize its full potential, and customers will leave due to overcrowdness.

The difficult problem with critical mass is that it must be viewed within a seasonal context. A facility may be too small for the peak season, but too large for the off season. The best strategy is to plan for the optimal combination of peak and off-peak volume in light of the expenses involved.

In Figure 3-5, the smaller resort is closer to having an optimal critical mass than is the large resort. Even though the large resort operates at a lower cost per room/night (due to economies of scale and control of the cost of unused rooms), it has a much lower occupancy rate and barely makes a profit. At the present rate of demand, the smaller resort is making better use of its facilities and generates the better overall profit. If however, demand increases significantly, the larger resort will improve its profit picture.

Figure 3-5
Critical Mass Comparison of Two Resorts

Room Demand	Room/Nights Sold	
	100 Room Resort	200 Room Resort
3 months = 200 per night	9,000	18,000
6 months = 100 per night	18,000	18,000
3 months = 50 per night	4,500	4,500
Total Room Night Sales	31,500	40,500
Room Inventory	36,000	72,000
Occupancy Rate	87.5%	56.3%
Revenues at $50	$1,575,000	$2,025,000
Expenses	$1,368,000	$2,016,000
	(at $38 room/night)	(at $28 room/night)
Profits	$207,000	$9,000

Phased Development. A commercial recreation enterprise can solve some of its problems related to critical mass by having a phased development. In its early stages, the business may start off at less than its ultimate future size. As participation materializes, the business can expand. Recreation enterprises should plan for this by retaining area or access to additional area for future use. Disneyworld is an excellent example of a huge resort and entertainment complex developed in phases over many years.

Gravity Effect

Planners and economists (Gold, 1980, and King, 1977) have used "gravity models" to predict the amount of travel from a particular origin to a particular destination and to estimate the economic activity involved. A gravity model establishes a mathematical relationship between the location of the population, frequency of visits to a given recreation site, and competing attractions.

The gravity effect however, is a nonquantitative simplification of the gravity model, which helps explain the pull exerted by a major recreation attraction. Scientifically speaking, gravity is the pull or attraction exerted by a large mass. The greater the mass, the greater is the pull. The gravity effect of a recreation area works much the same way. Large recreation areas such as New York's Broadway or Disneyworld exert great attraction to millions of visitors from around the world. Smaller attractions have their own significant, yet smaller gravity effect.

The significance of the gravity effect is its influence on the location and marketing efforts of businesses. Major recreation attractions that exert a gravity effect often have the characteristics illustrated below.

Clustering of Similar Businesses. Rather than discouraging competition, an area exerting a gravity effect will encourage the location of similar businesses. Most cities have a major street that is the location of numerous auto dealers. Customers gravitate to this area because of convenience, variety, and quantity. Similarly, many cities have their own entertainment districts and "restaurant rows." People are drawn to these areas because of a collective attraction.

The central Florida area around Disneyworld has become a huge tourist destination with numerous attractions. People come for one or two weeks because there are so many different things to do. Another location, the historic Stockyards area of Fort Worth, Texas, has over a dozen restaurant and saloons. This draws people for an extended evening of dining, bar-hopping, and western dancing.

Cooperative Advertising. Once a cluster of recreation attractions has gained a collective reputation, it becomes cost effective to do a certain amount of cooperative advertising. The theory is that if more people are drawn to the overall area, then all the attractions will benefit. Cooperative advertising can be a cost effective approach for advertising to a larger audience using more expensive media. Ski areas in Summit County, Colorado, Lake Tahoe, and Utah are active in cooperative promotions.

Location of Supporting Amenities. An area that has become a major attraction will be a popular location for related businesses. Most major shopping malls feature a couple of "magnet" or "anchor" stores, such as Sears, Penney's, or Nordstroms, strategically located at either ends of the mall. These stores attract a large number of customers, therefore shops for clothes, toys, records, and books will strive to locate near the magnets in order to benefit from passing traffic. Similarly, fast food restaurants, gas stations, motels, and souvenir shops are drawn to locations near major recreation attractions. Often, these small businesses will advertise on the basis of their proximity to the major attraction (i.e., "just two blocks from Disneyland").

Location of En-Route Attractions. If a manager knows where the primary markets are for a major recreation attraction, some determination can be made as to the travel routes most frequently used. It therefore becomes a good strategy to locate secondary recreation attractions and amenities along these prime travel routes. Motels, campgrounds, restaurants, roadside attractions and souvenir stands are common within a day's drive from major attractions. Marketing of these businesses may take advantage of the gravity effect. For example, Wall Drug in Wall,

South Dakota, promotes itself as a tourist attraction for people who are en route to Mount Rushmore. The huge drugstore complex includes giftshops, entertainment, and souvenirs and it advertises all over the world.

Commercial recreation managers need to understand whether or not a given attraction exerts a significant gravity effect. Further, they need to know where the markets come from and what related amenities would be attractive.

Multiplier Factor

The multiplier factor refers to the number of times an "outside" (or tourist dollar) "turns over" (is respent), in a local economy. For example, a skier purchases a lift ticket for $20, and a portion of that amount goes to pay the wages of the lift operators. The lift operator spends part of her money on groceries, and the grocer uses the money to pay part of his rent. The landlord goes out to dinner and spends it for steaks that were shipped in from Kansas City. The cycle stops here since the money is lost to the local economy. This last transaction is called "leakage" from the economy. Leakage occurs whenever money is spent on goods or services imported from outside the local community. (McIntosh and Goeldner, 1984).

The importance of the multiplier factor is that it measures how important tourism really is to an area. The higher the multiplier, the higher the impact of tourism on the local economy. In Las Vegas, the multiplier factor as measured through a complex survey process, was 1.87 for 1985. Using this multiplier, the impact of visitors spending $6.9 billion equals a $12.9 billion economic contribution to the Las Vegas area economy (Ralenkotter, 1986).

Although some communities claim multiplier factors of five or more, there is little evidence of multipliers higher than 1.9 (Crompton and Richardson, 1986; Hudman, 1980). It is important to realize that communities with low multiplier factors may not benefit from tourism as much as they might think. In such cases, the negative aspects of tourism may outweigh the economic benefits. Hawaii, for example, has a lot of tourism, but a low multiplier due to high leakage. With congestion, high real estate prices, and loss of local culture, many people feel that Hawaii is actually worse off because of tourism.

The communities with the highest multiplier factors are those that are relatively self-sufficient, that is, having local labor, agriculture, manufacturing, food processing, and so on. Here, less leakage occurs for imported products or services. In such communities, tourism has its most positive economic impacts. However, communities must be realistic about their multiplier factor in order to truly evaluate the importance of tourism.

Repeat Visitor Concept (80/20 Principle)

According to the so called "80/20 rule," 20 percent of the customers of some businesses account for 80 percent of the product consumption or participation (Mullins, 1983). Although the figures may differ in various businesses, the principle is the same: repeat visitors are the heart of a company's revenue. McKenzie (1983, p. 10) puts it another way:

The only reason to be in business is for repeat business; and if you aren't in business for repeat business, pretty soon you won't be in business.

McKenzie further points out that in some resorts, it costs four times as much in advertising to bring in a new customer as it does to get a past customer to return. In addition, in some markets, 80 percent of new customers come because of a referral from an old customer. The primary way to get repeat business is to make a promise of a certain quality experience and then live up to or exceed that promise. For recreation services, when price between competitors is about equal, participants will choose on the basis of friendliness, cleanliness, and service.

The importance of this principle lies in the implication that it is worth it to "go the extra mile" for the customer. It is worth it to spend the extra dollars to maintain an attractive atmosphere, provide quality products and services, and be concerned with meeting the customers expectations. This is critical, particularly in local recreation establishments such as sports clubs, restaurants, night clubs, and retail shops. The local resident is in a position to come back again and again. Similarly, in resort areas such as Las Vegas, about 81 percent of the visitors have been there previously (Dandurand, 1986). With some resorts and theme parks, however, this may not be the case, but word of mouth evaluation creates the same effect.

Maximizing vs. Optimizing

Meeting the expectations of the customer should not be confused with "maximizing", that is, providing the best possible product or service at all times. Perfection is very expensive to provide and would often exceed the tastes and resources of the target market. It is more realistic to "optimize" the product or service. That is, to offer the level of quality that meets or somewhat exceeds the expectations of the customer. Few customers will desire to pay a lot more for benefits that are in excess of what they seek. Rather, they would prefer to pay a more modest amount and receive the benefits that are most important to them. The optimal product or service, therefore, is one providing value for the dollar while meeting the customers expectations. This is entirely consistent with the repeat visitor concept previously mentioned.

CONSUMER BEHAVIOR AND PSYCHOLOGICAL CONCEPTS

Although the recreation manager must understand the various economic concepts and problems related to commercial recreation, this is not enough. The recreation manager must also understand consumer behavior and psychological concepts related to commercial recreation. This section will present a brief overview of the motivations for leisure, determinants of leisure activity, recreation in three life courses, and the diffusion curve of purchasing behavior. It must be emphasized that this general overview should not replace further study or coursework in leisure behavior. It should also be noted that specific content related to consumer behavior in various types of commercial recreation is presented in later chapters, especially the chapter devoted to travel and tourism.

Determinants of Leisure Activity

An individual's leisure behavior begins with the family. According to Kelly (1982) there is considerable evidence that leisure interests and competencies are developed within the family. Although people do learn new leisure activities, about half of a person's favorite activities begin in their childhood years (Kelly, 1974). The major determinants of leisure choice have traditionally been thought to be income, occupation, education, age, sex, and urbanization. However, adult leisure behavior is now thought to be much less predictable than was once thought. It does appear that most recreation occurs as a group activity, either family or social group. However, leisure changes can occur at major life cycle points such as going to college, changing residence, marriage, birth of children, or death of spouse.

Motivations for Leisure

There are a number of motivators for one's choice of recreation (McIntosh and Goeldner, 1984; Epperson, 1977; Crandall, 1980). These include:

Relaxation	Family interaction
Status needs	Self-actualization
Courtship	Health and fitness
Socialization	Skill development
Risks and thrills	Accomplishment and recognition
Self-image	Environmental contact
Escape	Achievement, challenges and competition
Creativity	Social contact

Commercial recreation managers must realize that different people will choose to participate in a given activity for different reasons. Experience in the field, plus market research, may help the manager determine which market segments seek which benefits. It is then up to the manager to be sure that the facility, product, or service delivers those benefits. This, of course, is easier said than done.

Recreation in Three Life Courses

Kelly (1985) has identified three main periods of the family's life course. Each period presents implications for the development and marketing of commercial recreation.

The Preparation Period covers the first third of the 75-year life span. Much of this period is oriented toward the socialization process; learning

roles, values, and social skills. Recreation characteristics are as follows:
- Crib toys, sex differentiated toys, sports equipment, games, costumes, and books are purchased for play with peers and family.
- Television captures the largest number of at home leisure hours for children.
- Sports and arts are introduced through school and/or neighborhood opportunities.
- Family vacations are a special time for travel, usually by auto.
- Teen activities evolve around sexual and work-related identities in places where teens can meet away from adult supervision: concerts, shopping malls, fast food restaurants, etc.
- College campuses provide an important leisure environment where clothing, cars, and music are part of a very expressive period.
- Recreation environments provide many of the places and activities for male/female interaction and dating.

The Establishment Period begins when people leave school, take fulltime employment, marry, and have children. Recreation does not stop, but it takes on a different context.
- More leisure takes place at home.
- Prior to the arrival of children, young adults comprise a major market for recreation and travel.
- With the birth of children, family recreation revolves around the children. Time and costs are very important.
- Leisure goods may be purchased for status symbolism.
- Mid-life adults may seek some demonstration of performance that shows success.
- As children leave home, parents seek some compensatory recreation investment such as travel.

The Reintegration Period, the last 25 years, is characterized by an attempt to achieve some integration of investments, relationships, and meanings. Leisure may change, and old interests are often renewed.
- Availability of time and financial resources allow for purchase of "big ticket" items such as boats, second homes, campers, and major trips.
- Concern with health leads some people to return to regular physical activities.
- Two-income adults dine out and entertain more often.
- In-home recreation becomes more important because of available time. This includes reading, gardening, hobbies, and social interaction.
- The loss of a marriage partner causes the rebuilding of social contexts, and leisure becomes even more important to express identity.

The commercial recreation manager must understand the needs of people at each stage or period of the life course. Then, products/services can be developed and marketed to fulfill these needs and expectations.

The Diffusion Curve

The diffusion process is the process by which innovations (new or different products or services) are spread to members of a social system. A diffusion curve, Figure 3-6, illustrates how innovations are adopted by various types of people over time. The time period could be very short or it could be many years. Consumer behavior researchers (Hawkins, Coney, and Best, 1980) have described the characteristics of the various classifications of adopters.

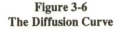

Figure 3-6
The Diffusion Curve

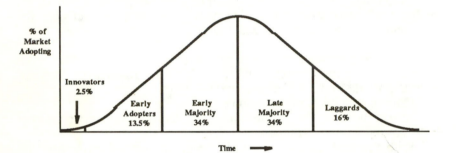

Innovators are adventuresome risk takers. They are typically younger, better educated, and more socially mobile than the other groups. Innovators make extensive use of commercial media in making their purchase decisions. They are also capable of absorbing the financial or social costs (embarrassment about a dumb purchase) if the new product/service is unsuccessful.

Early Adopters are opinion leaders in local reference groups; they are also successful, well educated, and somewhat younger than other groups except innovators. The early adopters are willing to take calculated risks on products/services, but they are also concerned with failure.

The Early Majority are cautious. They adopt a product/service earlier than most of the market, but only after it has proven to be successful. These persons are socially active but seldom opinion leaders. They are somewhat older, somewhat less educated, and less socially mobile than the two previous groups. The early majority rely more on interpersonal sources of information.

The Late Majority are skeptical about new products/services. They tend to respond more to social pressures than to advertising to adopt an innovation. They also try new products/services when there is a decrease in availability of their previous choice of products/services. The late majority are typically older, with less social status and less mobility.

Laggards are locally oriented persons who engage in limited social interaction. They are relatively dogmatic and oriented toward the past. They are the last in a market segment to buy the product/service.

It is important to note that these characteristics are generalizations for the entire spectrum of products and services. The market for any particular product/service might, in reality, be comprised only of persons from the first three categories. For example, some people will never be in the market for para-sailing or vacations to Margaritaville. A modified diffusion curve could be developed for any particular product/service for any given target market.

SUMMARY

The entrepreneur must understand the basic nature of commercial recreation in order to cope with problems to be faced in managing the business. Specifically, the manager must understand that commercial recreation is dependent upon discretionary income and know who has it and how they spend it. Commercial recreation is often cyclical, seasonal, and intermittent in nature. Strategies must be devised to overcome these problems in a competitive environment. Additional problems to be faced may include inflation and interest rates, energy shortages, insurance costs, terriorism and crime, and personal barriers of participants. Barriers can include expense, transportation, lack of time, health, family status, lack of skills, interests, lack of comparison, and safety concerns. Again, Commercial recreation managers must overcome these barriers in order to operate successfully.

Commercial recreation managers will probably be more effective if they have an understanding of general economic concepts related to the business. These include supply and demand, price elasticity, System-structure development, critical mass concept, gravity effects, multiplier factors, and the repeat visitor concept.

Even when economic conditions are relatively stable, people's consumer behavior can change. People's motivations for leisure differ, and their needs change over different periods of the life course. Further, within any market, products and services diffuse, or are accepted into society, at different rates. Once again, the commercial recreation manager must have an understanding of these phenomena and develop strategies to bring success.

STUDY QUESTIONS

1. What is substitution?
2. How does the seasonal nature of recreation affect the commercial business?
3. When business goes through a cyclic change what dangers exist? Use examples.
4. In a zero sum market, how are gains made?
5. What economic problems affect commercial recreation business.
6. Cite five barriers to participation in leisure pursuits.

62

7. Explain five economic concepts affecting commercial recreation business.
8. Name the three life courses and explain their affect on recreation participation.

PROJECT IDEAS

1. Compare the nature of two different commercial recreation businesses in terms of seasonality, cycles, dependence on discretionary income, opportunities for substitution, and competition in the area.
2. Select a type of commercial recreation industry and examine how economic and political problems have effected it.
3. Trace your family's life course and recreation choices of each generation. Compare how activities and opportunities have changed from one generation to the next.

SPOTLIGHT ON: Boardwalk's Shattered Dreams

In June 1977, the State of New Jersey passed the Casino Control Act, legalizing gambling for Atlantic City. The poor people of Atlantic City literally danced in the streets that night. They expected the influx of casino construction and tourist trade to bring an instant prosperity to their city, to rejuvenate the deteriorating "Grande Dame" of eastern seaside resorts. Instead, within a few years, the people of Atlantic City were bemoaning their fate. Property taxes and water, sewer, and utility bills soared along with street crimes, prostitution and drug abuse. Thousands were forced out of their homes and out of town. Thousands more now live like gypsies, moving around between cheap apartments two steps ahead of land speculators. Crime is up, education is poor, there are no movie theaters, no shopping, not much of an airport, and skyrocketing land prices have made the construction of low to middle income housing virtually impossible. One authority calls it a "war zone", a "lurid mix of glitz and trash, with tattoo parlors, pawn shops, and diners crouched beneath the sleek shadows of the casio hotels" (Reed, 1987, p. 61).

What went wrong in Atlantic City? It certainly wasn't the number of visitors. Atlantic City has become the number one tourist destination in the country, attracting 30 million visitors a year, 7 million more than Disneyworld. The problem actually has three aspects: a low to middle income market, a deficient system-structure, and a conflict between the casinos and the local government.

About 60 million people live within a day's drive of Atlantic City, and driving is how most of the gamblers arrive. Over 12 million of the 30 million visitors are hustled into town on junket busses. People are picked up on street corners in Philadelphia, New York, and Newark and include many poor and lower middle income seniors who cannot afford to lose money. Visitors stay an average of only six hours. They don't need hotel rooms or much food or entertainment. All they care about are the slot machines, gaming tables, and a bargain lunch. They are cautioned not to leave the casinos because the city is a high crime area. Overall, the per-capita spending of these tourists is much less than tourists at Las Vegas and many other resorts.

The second problem is the unbalanced systemstructure, and it is a classic "catch 22" situation. Atlantic City has lacked a major convention center to attract the large groups that make Las Vegas a year round attraction. Without a convention center, investors are reluctant to build hotels, but without adequate hotel rooms, a convention center cannot be justified. To compound problems, major airlines are reluctant to schedule many flights to Atlantic City until it has sufficient hotel space and convention facilities. There are other systemstructure problems as well. The water and sewer system has deteriorated, streets are congested, buildings abandoned, 90 percent of the city's businesses have closed, and there are a limited variety of recreation opportunities.

The third problem area is the running battle between casino operators and government regulators. It costs about 40 percent more to operate a casino in Atlantic City than in Las Vegas. Casinos pay up to $4 million for their license investigation and they must pay for a long and expensive investigation of each new employee. In addition, casinos pay 8 percent of their gross win to the state and then pay income tax too! Unfortunately, Atlantic City does not receive a direct benefit from the casino tax, which is used to fund a variety of social programs statewide. The state also regulates many aspects of the casino games, limiting play varieties and thus costing the casinos millions. While the casino operators moan about overregulation, residents of Atlantic City justifiably argue that the casinos have not improved the town.

So, is there hope for Atlantic City? Maybe there is, if the problems of market, systemstructure, and regulation can be solved. There is some evidence that progress is being made. The Showboat hotel/casino is trying to reach a family clientele by offering bowling lanes, and the Tropicana is adding a two-acre indoor theme park. A new casino, the Carnival Club, will be family oriented with a skating rink, a carnival midway, and other recreation offerings. One casino owner, Donald Trump, has promised to build low and middle income housing. A convention center may also be on the horizon. These changes could make Atlantic City more of a destination resort and bring some prosperity and civic improvements. Until then, life on the Boardwalk is more seedy than glamorous. In the words of one local merchant its just a "dump with casinos."

Sources: Reed (1987), Demaris (1986), *Leisure Industry Digest*, (March 1986), October 1986, Reese and Taylor, (1981), *Business Week*, (1981).

REFERENCES

Alm, R., and Duetschman, A. "The Bicoastal Economy: Can the Center Hold?" *U.S. News and World Report,* July 28, 1986, p. 18.

Anderson, B. (editor). *Managed Recreation Research Report.* Minneapolis; Lakewood Publications, 1985 and 1986.

Barbati, C. "Meetings at Mountain Resorts." *Meetings and Conventions,* February, 1985, p. 87.

Business Week. "Atlantic City Gambling Loses Its Glow." January 26, 1981.

64

Calantone, R., and Johar, J. "Seasonal Segmentation of the Tourism Market Using a Benefit Segmentation Framework." *Journal of Travel Research*, Fall, 1984, pp. 14-23.

Consumer Research Center. *A Marketer's Guide to Discretionary Income*. New York: Consumer Research Center and the U.S. Bureau of the Census, 1986.

Council of Economic Advisors. *Economic Indicators: August 1987*. Washington, D.C.: U.S. Government Printing Office, 1987.

Crandall, R. "Motivation For Leisure." *Journal of Leisure Research*, Volume 1, 1980. pp. 45-54.

Crompton, J., and Richardson, R. "The Tourism Connection." *Parks and Recreation*, October, 1986, pp. 38-44; 67.

Dandurand, L. *Las Vegas Visitor Profile Study*. Las Vegas, Nevada: Las Vegas Convention and Visitors Authority, First, Second, and Third Quarter, 1986.

Demaris, O. "Why Casino Gambling is a Bad Bet." *Parade Magazine,* May 11, 1986. pp. 12-14.

Ellerbrock, M. *Fundamentals of Recreation Demand Analysis*. A technical report published by the College of Forest and Recreation Resources, Clemson University, 1980.

Epperson, A. *Private and Commercial Recreation: A Text and Reference*. New York: John Wiley & Sons, Inc., 1977.

Goeldner, C., and Duea, K. *1984 Travel Trends in the U.S. and Canada*. Boulder, CO.: Travel and Tourism Research Association and the University of Colorado, 1984.

Gold, S. *Recreation Planning and Design*. New York: McGraw-Hill Book Company, 1980.

Hansell, C. "Soaring Insurance Costs Mean Higher Lift Rates at Ski Resorts." *Salt Lake Tribune*, November 27, 1985, p. D1.

Hawkins, D., Coney, K., and Best, R. *Consumer Behavior: Implications for Marketing Strategy*. Dallas: Business Publications, Inc., 1980.

Howard, D., and Crompton, J. *Financing, Managing and Marketing Recreation and Park Resources*. Dubuque, Iowa: Wm. C. Brown Company, 1980.

Hudman, L. *Tourism: A Shrinking World*. Columbus, Ohio: Grid Publishing, Inc., 1980.

Kelly, J. "Socialization Toward Leisure: A Developmental Approach." *Journal of Leisure Research*, 1974, pp. 181-193.

Kelly, J. *Leisure*. Englewood Cliffs, New Jersey: Prentice-Hall, Inc. 1982.

Kelly, J. *Recreation Business*. New York: John Wiley and Sons, 1985.

King, W. "The Use of Gravity-Potential Models for Outdoor Recreation Benefit Estimation." *Outdoor Recreation Advances in Application of Economics*. Washington, DC: U.S. Department of Agriculture, 1977, pp. 188-120.

Leisure Industry Digest. Content from issues November 14, 1986; March 31, 1986; October 31, 1986.

Lewis, R. "Policy Formation and Planning For Outdoor Recreation Facilities." *Outdoor Recreation: Advances in Application of Economics*. Washington, DC.: U.S. Department of Agriculture, 1977, p. 62-69.

Lundberg, D. *The Tourist Business* (3rd Edition). Boston: CBI Publishing Company, Inc., 1976.

Malabre, A. "Despite Big Problems, U.S. Economy Seems Surprisingly Healthy." *Wall Street Journal*, June 2, 1986, p. 1.

McIntosh, R., and Goeldner, C. *Tourism: Principles, Practices, Philosophy* (4th Edition). New York: John Wiley & Sons, 1984.

McKenzie, B. "Repeat Business--New Dealing For Dollars." *Recreation, Sports, and Leisure,* July, 1983, pp. 10-14.

Mullins, B. *Sport Marketing, Promotion and Public Relations.* Amherst, Massachusetts: National Sports Management, Inc., 1983.

Ralenkotter, R. (editor). *Marketing Bulletin: 1985 Summary.* Las Vegas, Nevada: Las Vegas Convention and Visitors Authority, 1986.

Reed, J. "Battle Royal on the Old Boardwalk." *U.S. News and World Report,* April 27, 1987.

Reese, M., and Taylor, J. "Atlantic City Craps Out." *Newsweek,* August 31, 1981.

Rolly, P. "Insurance Firms Rescue River Runners by Agreeing to Write Liability Policies." *Salt Lake Tribune,* March 6, 1986, p. C1.

Spencer, M. *Contemporary Microeconomics* (4th Edition). New York: Worth Publishers, Inc., 1980.

Stankey, G. "Some Social Concepts for Outdoor Recreation Planning." *Outdoor Recreation Advances in Application of Economics.* Washington, D.C.: U.S. Department of Agriculture, 1977, p. 154-161.

Toohey, W. "Travel in U.S. is Up by 5%, Industry Says." *Salt Lake Tribune,* August 2, 1986, p. B11.

Van Voorhis, K. *Entrepreneurship and Small Business Management.* Boston: Allyn and Bacon, Inc., 1980.

Wiessler, D. "How Cities of Summer Deal With the Throngs." *U.S. News and World Report.* August 30, 1982, pp. 50-52.

Witt, P., and Goodale, T. "Stress, Leisure and the Family." *Recreation Research Review,* October, 1982.

Zigli, B. "Terrorism Fears: Agents Fight Back." *U.S.A. Today,* June 19, 1986, p. 4D.

PART II

INITIATING AND MANAGING COMMERCIAL RECREATION

CHAPTER 4

STARTING THE COMMERCIAL RECREATION ENTERPRISE

There are many tasks and responsibilities to be carried out when initiating a commercial recreation business. First, there must be a concept that meets a market need. Next, there should be a feasibility study to assess the concept, locations, management, and financial aspects. Finally, financing for the venture must be found.

The overall business can be visualized as a table with four supporting legs: a sound concept, a good location, adequate financing, and experienced management (see Figure 4-1). The business will be most stable when all four legs are firm and proven. If one of the legs is not up to par, the business can still stand, but it will be shaky and the other three legs could be pressured into a fatal level of stress. If two of the legs are shaky, forget it and get everything valuable off that table!

This chapter will consider all these aspects of starting the commercial recreation enterprise.

BASIS FOR STARTING THE BUSINESS

A successful commercial recreation business must be based on a sound concept that meets the needs of the market. It may meet the needs of an established market or it may be based on the creation of a new market. Development of the new product/service must be timed to fit within an opportune stage of the industry lifecycle. Finally, the business must develop an image and a market platform that differentiates it from its competitors. First, however, there must be an analysis of the rewards and risks of going into business.

Rewards and Risks of Starting Your Own Business

Most everyone has thought at one time or another about starting their own business. There are, of course, numerous rewards and risks. Each

Figure 4-1
Four Criteria for Success

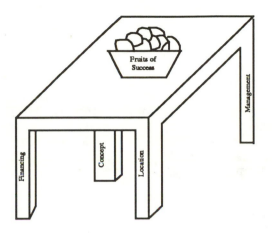

person must evaluate for themselves whether or not the rewards are adequate motivation or the risks sufficient barriers. Rewards include the following (Van Voorhis, 1980):

- Personal Satisfaction—from providing a product/service that is well received.
- Independence—making your own decision.
- Profits—leading to a higher standard of living.
- Power and Influence—proving one's ability.
- Use of Accumulated Capital—making better use of your personal assets.
- Application of Skills and Background—trying out your training and skills, which may be blocked in other areas of employment.
- Security—having the future of your employment in your own hands, rather than at the discretion of others.
- Get Out of a Rut—escaping boredom, routine or frustration with the status quo.

There are of course, negative aspects and risks of starting a business. These include the following:

- Financial Losses—if the business fails.
- Loss of Friends and Family—when pressures of the business interfere with personal life.
- Anguish Over Uncertainty—when fluctuations of business conditions are beyond your control.
- Time and Effort—when constant demands are made on your time.
- Straining of Values—when success may depend on compromise of personal values.

- Demands Above Expertise—when you can't know everything, do you guess or trust "experts" you may hire?
- Growth Dilemmas—when the business grows, can you still be in touch with all phases of the operation?

Business Failure Record

Although many businesses are successful, more are failures. The most frequent reason for business failure is the manager's incompetence. This is followed by the manager's lacking experience or having unbalanced experience (Dun and Bradstreet, 1981). An example of unbalanced experience is the accountant who starts a fitness center without a solid knowledge of the fitness industry or a background in marketing. As related specifically to the business, the most frequent problems include poor location, inadequate sales, high operating expense, lack of sufficient working capital, and basic competitive weakness of your product/service.

The Business Concept

One key to avoiding business failure is to have a sound business concept; based upon a strategy that is expected to succeed. The eight "sources of innovation" suggested in Chapter 2 would be examples of such strategies. These concepts require the entrepreneur to engage in a systematic search of the environment in order to discover opportunities. There are several tips that will help this search for business concepts to be more realistic and successful. Consider areas of business in which you have past work experience, education, and expertise, and areas in which the products or services parallel your personal leisure interests. Consider areas of business that serve market segments you are very familiar with. Avoid business concepts that are beyond your financial resources or your proven ability to attract financial resources. Finally, avoid the temptation to be a "crusader" for a leisure activity or social cause that is of high personal interest but low business potential.

Established vs. Created Market. A factor in the development of the business concept is the decision whether the business is to serve an established market or a created market. An established market is one in which participation already exists in your geographic area. This is an advantage because both the supply and the demand can be measured. A business built on serving an established market hopes competition cannot meet all the demand, or that demand can be stimulated. Another strategy is that the new business can successfully differentiate its product/service and gain a share of the market (Kelly, 1985).

A created market is one that does not currently exist, but that the new business hopes to initiate. It is difficult to assess if the market will materialize, but if the new product/service capitalizes on a latent demand, it could be an excellent opportunity. For example, fifteen years ago few people would have anticipated the huge demand for water theme parks which have since become very successful in many locations.

Life Cycle of the Industry. Another important consideration for a new business is the life cycle of the industry. Ideally, a new business would enter a market at the introductory or "take-off" stages and grow along with the overall industry. During this period, it would have a decent chance to gain a loyal following of repeat customers. If, however, a company enters a market too late, there may be little growth left in the overall industry. Then it would have to fight to take customers away from other businesses.

Competitive Differentiation

The new business must find a way to differentiate itself from its competitors. If no basis of difference can be found, the company has no competitive advantage and no reason to expect customers.

The most successful way to differentiate is to provide whatever makes the most difference in the eyes of the consumer. This of course varies with every product/service or market. Some ways to differentiate a business are as follows:

- Price—lower or higher. Special prices for children, off season, etc.
- Quality—higher or lower depending upon market preference.
- Consistency—reliable quality time after time.
- Features—more or different features and/or amenities and variety of selections.
- Clientele—customers/participants who would enjoy interaction.
- Location—number of locations, access, convenience, ground transportation to location.
- Time—hours of operation, length of season, etc.
- Credit—availability of credit purchase, credit cards, lay-a-ways.
- Service—personal attention, repairs, etc.
- Packaging and Atmosphere—the physical presentation and atmosphere including appearance, cleanliness, use of color, smell, sounds, etc.

Image and Market Platform

A commercial recreation business has an image whether or not the manager is aware of it. The way that people think about the business will be influenced by the way a business differentiates itself from competitors. Its promotional efforts, physical layout, and courtesy of staff will also effect the image. Will a sporting goods store focus on a few special sports, offering depth in the product line and expert service? Or will it be a discount store with a few choices available in a wide breath of sports? A business can and must control its image, and that image should be planned from the very outset. In some cases, "instant image" can be purchased by affiliating with a well known franchise operation. In any case, the desired company image helps to focus efforts and develop a marketing strategy.

The market platform is a concise summary of the key elements of the corporate image and competitive difference. It is the basic business premise and the sales promise to the customer. Often, the market platform is reflected in songs, sales jingles, and other promotions. For example, the Barnam and Bailey Circus promoted itself as the "Greatest

Show on Earth." The Utah Travel Council promises "the greatest snow on earth" to visitors who ski at Utah resorts. Club Med promotes itself as the "antidote to civilization" and leaves it somewhat up to your imagination to decide what you want that to mean.

Issues of Scale

What is the optimal size for a commercial recreation business? There is no easy answer, because it depends on the background and objectives of the owners, the market areas, and the type of recreation industry involved. Some of the advantages of a small business include lower overhead costs, product/service specialization, flexibility in managing the business, ease of starting, closeness to employees and customers, and the profit incentive of direct ownership.

There are, of course, possible disadvantages in small scale business. These include competition from larger companies, less service from suppliers, overlap of personal and business relationships, and the inability to take advantage of economies of scale (Kelly, 1985; Van Voorhis, 1980).

For most commercial recreation entrepreneurs, starting small is the only choice available. However, through franchise operations and other alternatives, the advantages of a larger operation may be achieved. These will be discussed later in this chapter.

THE FEASIBILITY STUDY

A second major task in starting a commercial recreation business is to develop a realistic feasibility study. This is a document that provides a comprehensive analysis to determine if a specific project has potential for reaching its financial goals. The project may be a new product/service at a present location, a move to a new location, or the creation of a new business. Since the latter type is the most involved, it will be the focus of this section. Feasibility studies for the other types of projects may follow the same process but be shorter in length, since an existing business is involved.

A feasibility study cannot determine the final outcome with total certainty. There are too many variables, assumptions, and unknowns for that to occur. Rather, a feasibility study can help the entrepreneur to see the project in a more objective light. In Figure 4-2, the entrepreneur will never reach "absolute certainty," but if she can reach "enlightened uncertainty," then the risks will be reduced. By conducting a systematic analysis and a reasonable market projection, the entrepreneur may make intelligent decisions about the business. The feasibility study therefore acts as a road map to help guide this effort.

There are four specific purposes of a feasibility study (Haralson, 1986):

1. To Establish Feasibility—deciding whether or not a project will realize a return on the investment.

Figure 4-2
Purpose of a Feasibility Study

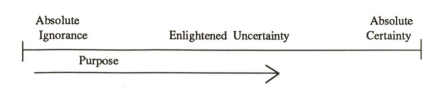

2. To Formulate the Optimum Concept—finding the best facilities, location, scale, and market orientation for success.
3. To Assist in Establishing Management and Marketing Guidelines—deciding useful operational strategies.
4. To Assist in Obtaining Funding—creating a document that lenders and investors can study.

The feasibility study may be prepared in-house or by contracting a consulting firm. If the entrepreneur undertakes the in-house approach, it should cost less, be more sensitive to the local community, and be used more. Counter arguments for this approach are that the in-house researcher may not be qualified, may not be objective, and may not have time to do a thorough job. Another problem is that the results of an in-house study may be viewed with less credibility when a loan is sought. These pros and cons can be reversed when considering the outside consultant (Kelsey and Gray, 1985).

It is probably true that the more money involved in the project, the more the project is studied. But is the effort really worth it? Hills (1985) surveyed 16 venture capital firms to determine their perspective of business plans and feasibility studies that were submitted in request of financing. Overall, the venture capitalists felt that feasibility studies were quite valuable and that new business failure rates could be reduced significantly through improved analysis. But they also believed that the feasibility studies tended to greatly overstate market demand.

Prior to starting the feasibility study it is necessary to gather a variety of data. Figure 4-3 provides a variety of sources for data, much of which can be found at major libraries and community agencies. It is difficult, however, to obtain data for small or specialized industries such as hang gliding, batting cage operations, and ski rental shops. For such industries it helps to have inside information gained from past employment in that industry.

It should be noted that there are two schools of thought regarding feasibility studies. One approach is that a feasibility study should be a comprehensive and detailed document of sufficient length to cover all aspects of the business. The second approach is that it should be a 20 to 30 page business plan giving only the most essential information. This business plan is used to gain the interest of investors. If interest is

Figure 4-3
Sources of Information For Feasibility Studies

General Sources:

- Encyclopedia of Business Information Sources—data sources, periodicals, associations, etc., listed by type of business.
- Frost and Sullivan Reports—lengthy, indepth industry reports.
- Standard and Poors Industry Surveys—review of major industries.
- U.S. Industrial Outlook— projections in 250 Standard Industrial Code categories.
- Gale's Encyclopedia of Associations—trade association addresses.
- Monthly Catalog of U.S. Government Publications.
- Funk and Scott Index—content of 750 publications by SIC codes covered.
- Business Periodicals Index—160 publications covered.
- Wall Street Journal Index.
- Trade Publications—Check specific association.

Corporation Data: Information about specific corporations

- Standard and Poors Register of Corporations by SIC code.
- Directory of Corporate Affiliations—subsidiary list.
- Value Line—corporation reports.
- Stock Reports Index—corporation reports.
- Moody's Industrial Manual—corporation reports.

Industry Financial Data:

- Dunn & Bradstreet's Key Business Ratios.
- Robert Morris Agency Annual Statement Studies.
- Almanac of Business and Industrial Financial Ratios.
- Dun & Bradstreet's Cost of Doing Business.
- Bank of America Small Business Reporter.
- Accounting Corporation of America—barometer of Small Business.
- Trade association publications—annual reports, member surveys, and technical aids. Check with applicable trade associations.

Market Information:

- Coles Directory—index of demographics and buying power by local census tracts.
- Survey of Buying Power—by *Sales Management* magazine.
- U.S. Travel Data Center Annual Report.
- Statistical Abstract of the U.S.—by Bureau of the Census.
- County and City Data Book—by Bureau of the Census.
- Donnelley Demographics—database file with product usage by 47 types of lifestyles.
- Market Research Companies—contracted for specific studies.

Federal Government Sources:

- Small Business Administration—publications and advice.
- Internal Revenue Service—tax requirements.
- Occupational Health and Safety Administration.
- Department of Labor—labor regulations.
- Securities and Exchange Commission—stock issue regulations.
- U.S. Geological Survey—topographic maps.

State and Local Government:

- Secretary of State—incorporation requirements.
- State Tax Commission.
- Department of Business Regulations.
- Industrial Development Office.
- State Travel Council or Tourism Office.
- State Parks, Recreation, and/or National Resources—statewide demand surveys.
- Department of Transportation—traffic counts.
- City and County Planning Departments—demographic and other data.
- City and County Regulatory Agencies—health, zoning, etc.
- Utility Companies—demographic data, utility costs, etc.

Other Local Sources:

- Competitors—check their products, services, prices, etc.
- Local Newspapers—marketing department data.
- University Research Centers.
- Banks—demographic data.
- Chamber of Commerce—local business data.
- Present Customers—survey them.
- Customer Data—from license plates, telephone numbers, zip codes, etc.
- Similar businesses—Noncompetitors in other cities may provide financial and market data.

---

generated, then the more complete feasibility study is developed. The remainder of this section will present the elements of a recreation feasibility study based on various formats suggested by several authorities (Haralson, 1986; Bullaro and Edginton, 1986; Kelsey and Gray, 1985; and Fails, 1985). The approach presented here represents the comprehensive feasibility study.

The Cover Letter

In business letter form, a cover letter is delivered with the feasibility study, but not actually between the covers of the document. The cover letter gives the basic recommendation of the feasibility study and support for that recommendation, including the key items from the market analysis. Also included are any assumptions (the economy, interest

74

rates, energy availability, etc.) which are necessary to support the recommendation.

Chapter I: Description of the Business

The first chapter sets the stage of the feasibility study. It presents the business concept (as previously discussed), including a description of the product/services, competitive differentiation, historical background of the industry, and current status of the industry. Also included is an exploration of the legal form of organization of the business.

Each legal form of organization (proprietorship, partnership, or corporation) has its advantages and disadvantages. The one that should be selected depends upon a variety of circumstances including your financial condition, type of business, number of employers, risk involved, and tax situation. The following comparison outlines some of the characteristics of the most popular forms of doing business (Harmon, 1979; Bullaro and Edginton, 1986; Hazard, 1984).

Sole Proprietorship. This is a business enterprise owned and operated by one person. It is the simplest and least costly form for an individual to start. The company name and purpose is simply registered at the county courthouse. The Internal Revenue Service will require forms for employee withholding tax, social security, workmens compensation, and so on. As with all other forms of organization, there may also be a city or county business license to purchase, bonds to cover liability on sales tax collection, and special licenses for certain purposes. The owner is personally responsible for all debts, taxes, and legal liabilities but is entitled to all net profits. The business income or loss is reflected on the proprietor's personal tax return. Outside financing for a proprietorship may be difficult to attain, and the owner generally has to rely on their own resources and management expertise. Growth is tied exclusively to the owner, who has complete authority over the business. If the owner dies or is incapacitated, this form of business is less likely than other forms to be perpetuated.

General Partnership. This is an association of two or more persons as co-owners. There should be an "Articles of Co-Partnership" (in writing and filed with the state) that details the financial commitments, distribution of profits or losses, and any other significant agreement. All partners have unlimited liability, as in a proprietorship, and all profits or losses are similarly reflected on the individual's tax return. There is, however, more growth potential in this form due to the combined resources and management abilities of the partners. The partnership may terminate with the death or withdrawal of any partner.

Limited Partnership. This is similar to a general partnership, except there are two classes of partners. General partners act as officers of the company and have unlimited personal liability. Limited partners invest money or property, but do not share in the management of the company. They are liable only up to the amount of their investment. Amounts invested, distribution of profits, and other agreements must be covered in the written "Articles of Partnership" filed with the state. A limited partnership has more growth potential since the resources of many limited partners are available. Profits again are taxed as individual income. In past years, losses (actual losses or paper losses due to depreciation) could offset ordinary income, so limited partnerships were excellent tax shelters. Now, however, limited partnership losses may be used only to offset gains in other partnerships and may not offset ordinary income.

Corporation. This is a separate legal and taxable entity that usually relieves the owners of liability. It is the most complex legal organization to form and requires "Articles of Incorporation" to be filed with the state, listing the powers of officers, intent of the corporation, classes or types of owners, means of perpetuation, and other aspects. Filing fees and opening taxes are expensive, and the process usually requires help from an attorney. To operate interstate, the corporation must pay fees, taxes, and filing costs in the other states as well. Stockholders are not individually liable for the firm's debts, but share in the profits or losses according to their proportion of ownership. This is usually the best organizational form for raising large sums of money, since numerous stockholders or "owners" may buy in and sell out with relative ease. Corporate profits are taxed first, and then if the corporation decides to distribute earnings to its stockholders, the dividends are taxed again at the individual level. Managers may be hired and fired by the owners, usually through the corporation's elected board of directors. The corporation lives on when owners or managers die or leave the firm.

Subchapter S Corporation. This is a regular corporation with limited stockholder liability, but its profits are taxed like a partnership. There is no corporate tax, but stockholders report profits as ordinary income on their taxes. A Subchapter S Corporation can have no more than 35 stockholders, all holding the same class of stock (no preferred shares). This form of organization has many of the legal advantages of both the corporation and the partnership. The business, however, is restricted to one primary area of endeavor, such as retailing, manufacturing, or land development. This form is very popular among small businesses where the owners desire the legal protection of the corporation but the flexibility and tax treatment of the partnership.

Chapter II: Regulatory and Risk Analysis

After completing this section of the feasibility study it will be clearly evident that the U.S. is no longer a simple place to live. As frustrating as it may be, it is essential to find out what regulations must be complied with, what licenses obtained, and what insurance purchased. The cost of each must also be reflected when business start-up expenses are estimated. Regulations, taxes and licenses will vary for different lines of business and from state to state. Agencies such as the Internal Revenue Service and the Small Business Administration periodically conduct workshops to assist new businesses in meeting their obligations.

Figure 4-4 lists many of the regulations, taxes, and licenses that may be required of a commercial recreation enterprise (Coopers and Lybrand, 1983).

Figure 4-4
Regulations, Taxes, and Licenses

Regulations
- Federal Minimum Wage Laws—Department of Labor
- Worksite Safety Laws—Occupational Safety and Health Administration (OSHA)
- Employee's Identification Numbers—IRS
- Employee Withholding Allowance Certificates—IRS
- Wage and Tax Statements—IRS
- Statements of Periodic Annuities and Pensions—IRS
- Equal Opportunity Laws—Department of Labor
- Land Use Regulations—Environmental Protection Agency (EPA)
- Employer's Withholding Tax Forms—IRS
- Health Regulations—State and County Health Department
- Zoning Regulations—City and County Government
- Building Codes—State and Local Government

Taxes
- Franchise and Income Tax—IRS, State and Local Government
- Sales Tax—State Government
- Property Tax—City and County Government
- Self-Employment Tax—IRS
- Unemployment Insurance—IRS
- Workmans Compensation Insurance—State Insurance Commission

Licenses
- State License Fees
- City or County Business Licenses
- State Trade Name Certificates
- Construction Permit Fees
- Motor Vehicle License and Inspection Fees

In addition, depending upon the state, special licenses or permits may be required for:

Outdoor Advertising Signs	Masseurs and Masseuses
Amusement Devices	Milk Vending Machines
Beer Sales	Musical Devices
Billiard and Pool Tables	Photographer Service
Bowling Lanes	Private Clubs
Burglar Alarms	Professional Dancers
Card Clubs	Public Dances
Catering Service	Restaurants
Childcare Center	Rooming House
Cigar and Tobacco Sales	Service Station Pumps
Dance Halls	Shooting Galleries
Dance Studios	Vending Machines

Film Exchange	Skating Rinks
Golf Courses	Soft Drink Fountains
Ice Cream Vending Machines	Special Transporation Vehicles
Liquor Consumption	Theaters
Live Music Entertainment	Vehicle Rental

Insurance. Adequate insurance coverage is a prerequisite for most loans or other financing, for rent or lease agreements, for purchase of vehicles, and for carrying the products of certain suppliers. It is commonplace now to carry policies offering a million dollars or more in coverage. Particularly, if a company engages in any type of risky activity (practically everything in the eyes of attorneys) or holds significant assets, it is imperative to be adequately insured. Some common types of insurance are:

- Fire Insurance—on structure and property within
- Liability Insurance—for company, personal coverage, and employees
- Automobile Insurance—for all employees and subcontractors
- Business Interruption Insurance—for fixed expenses if shut down temporarily
- Crime Insurance—for burglary, destruction, theft by employees
- Glass Insurance—for plate glass windows and displays
- Rent Insurance—in case lease property becomes unusable
- Group Life Insurance—for employees
- Group Health Insurance—for employees
- Disability Insurance—for employees
- Key Employee Insurance—for loss of a key employee

Risk Management. It is important that the commercial recreation manager identify the risks inherent in the business and establish management procedures to minimize those risks. Regular facility inspections, preventive maintenance, crowd control, and adequate supervision are essential steps to take. Insurance should be purchased to cover the largest potential loss exposures, and as funds are available, lower priority areas can be covered. All insurance programs should be reviewed periodically to be sure that coverage is adequate. Risk management strategies are covered in greater detail in Chapter 6 of this text.

Chapter III: Location Analysis

Selecting a location for the commercial recreation business is a two step process (Kelly, 1985; Guadagnolo, 1986). First, a general area is selected, and then a specific site within that area is chosen.

Selection of the general area should be based on the overall market potential of the metropolitan area or the trading area involved. In reality, some people starting a small business decide that they want to live in Tallahassee, Denton, or Sacramento, and this step of the location process is over! Notwithstanding these local loyalties, the general area selection should be based on several key factors:

- Overall Demograhics—population, growth, income, age, occupations, education, and cultural backgrounds of the desired target market.
- Community Environment—employee availability, competition, transportation availability, insurance rates, community character, local ordinances, climate.
- Business Environment—tax rates, real estate costs and availability, business trends, cooperation of government.

Selection of a specific site should be based upon its attractiveness to customers and its cost effectiveness to manage. A checklist of these factors is provided in Figure 4-5 (Van Voorhis, 1980; Davidson, 1981; Weber, 1981; Kelsey and Gray, 1985).

Figure 4-5
Site Selection Checklist

Auto and pedestrian traffic flow volume	Visibility
Accessibility and turn lanes into location	Signs and storefront design
Proximity to airports, bus lines, etc.	Community attractions
Nearby business compatability	Adequate parking
Community attractiveness and safety	Vistas from the site
Access for handicapped persons	Space for future expansion
Attractiveness of facility and grounds	Proximity to labor source
Utility availability and cost	Zoning regulations
Physical suitability of facilities	Fire and police protection
Proximity to suppliers and vendors	Delivery access
Cost to purchase or lease facilities	Storage facilities
Topography of site - slope and soil types	Vegetation types and tolerance
Risk of floods, landslides, earthquakes	Wildlife compatability

Depending upon the type of business, certain site selection criteria may be more important than others. For example, sports apparel shops, record stores, and many restaurants need sites with high visibility, high pass-by traffic flow, and easy access. On the other hand, specialty businesses such as expedition outfitters, scuba shops, racquet clubs, and boat dealers do not need to pay top dollar rents for locations that draw a pass-by crowd. For other types of businesses, such as cross-country ski touring centers, hunting lodges, and fishing camps, the natural features of the site are of prime importance. The key to site selection therefore begins with a realistic analysis of the criteria needed for success.

Chapter IV: Management Analysis

This section is devoted to an explanation of how the project will be managed. The primary components are: organization, staffing, and major operational considerations. When the business actually starts, this section should be expanded into a complete policy and procedure manual for the organization.

Organization. A variety of considerations include:
- Define the major areas of responsibility in operating the project.
- Who in management will be responsible for each area.
- Develop summary job descriptions for key personnel.
- What secondary level tasks and duties must be accomplished to carry out the business.
- Determine the number and types of personnel to accomplish the work of the business.
- Develop an organizational chart.

Staffing. After completion of the organizational concept, consider staffing details:
- Specific skills, expertise, and certification required of the various personnel throughout the system.
- Availability of such personnel in the local labor force.
- Compensation and benefits required to draw good personnel.
- Employee housing or transportation if necessary.
- Orientation and training programs.
- Employee incentive programs.

Major Operational Considerations. This includes attention to special areas of the operation such as:
- Particularly significant aspects of programs or services, such as special instructional methods, and service philosophy.
- Use of other organization's facilities through contract, joint-use agreements, trade-offs, etc.
- Use of special equipment, back up equipment, and preventive maintenance.
- Use of subcontracted services—what vendors and alternates are available.
- Facility maintenance scheduling and allowable down time.

Chapter V: Market Analysis

Market analysis is an organized way to find objective answers for questions that every commercial recreation manager must ask in order to succeed. Questions include: Who are the customers? How often and how much do they purchase? How do competitors differ? How much market share can be captured?

Market research helps reduce business risks, spot problems, and identify opportunities. Large corporations hire researchers to discover what is going on in the mass market. Small business managers, on the other hand, are usually closer to this market and have a better "feel" for the market. That "feel" may be biased, however, so small business managers also need to engage in objective analysis (Laumer, Harris, and Guffey, 1981). Market analysis includes segmentation of the market, analysis of competitors, product/service positioning, and projections of market demand.

Market Segmentation. A market segment is a group of people with some common characteristics that make a difference in their purchasing behavior. According to Howard and Crompton (1980), market segments can be based on socio- demographics (age, sex, family stage, income, education, occupation, race, social affiliation) behavioral characteristics (benefits sought, level of use, level of skill, psychographic profile) or geographic characteristics (place of residence, location of facility).

It is essential that the commercial recreation manager know what market segments to focus on. Otherwise the efforts of the business will be wasted on people who have little likelihood of becoming customers. The market segment the business decides to focus on is called the "target market" and may be a very specific or a very general group. For example, an outdoor adventure specialty store may focus on a market that is age 20-35 years, predominantly male, well educated, upper middle income, and oriented toward outdoor activities and risk. On the other hand, a water theme park may focus on preteens, teens, and families of middle to upper income range.

Competition Analysis. Most competition is either brand competition or product competition. If you are the manager of a Plitt/Cineplex movie theater, the brand competitors would be the other theaters operated by Mann, United Artists, or various independents. You also have product line competition when people choose to bowl, skate, play softball, or go to an amusement park instead of going to a movie.

Against product competition, the commercial recreation manager must promote the overall quality of the product/service, the positive experience that it will provide, and the value for the dollar. Sometimes professional and trade associations help do this for an entire industry. For example, the PGA (Professional Golfers Association) has promoted the overall game of golf through tournaments, books, films, workshops, clinics, and advertisements.

For brand competition, it may be necessary to undertake a detailed analysis of the competition. Questions to be answered include: How many competitors are there? How big are competitors? How strongly entrenched are they? Where is the heaviest competition located? What are their successful sales points? What are their weaknesses? What competitive edge can you offer? (Van Voorhis, 1980).

Marketing Positioning. Market positioning is a decision process that helps decide the best product/service niche and marketing strategy for a given business. The process is based on three considerations: internal analysis (including available resources, organizational constraints, the company's philosophy and values), market segment benefit analysis, and competitive analysis (Wolff, 1986). According to Lewis (1981), the most important element is the market segment analysis. This is an analysis of the benefits that the market segment values most in the particular product/service. The company is then able to position the product/service in an attempt to satisfy the customer's expectation of benefits. Second priority is to differentiate the business on the basis of the competitive analysis.

In Figure 4-6, market positioning for a retail sporting goods store is illustrated. In this case, the most important market considerations were price and variety of selection. Using this criteria, the various stores could be identified as specialty shops or full line stores or as discount versus full price stores. For this situation, it was decided that a discount ski shop would fill a special niche in this community. The shop would, however, have to develop a good off-season strategy such as a complementary product line in tennis and water sports.

Figure 4-6
Market Positioning for Sporting Goods

High Price

D (Skis)	C (Outdoor Speciality)	B (Independent Full Line Store)
	E (Scuba & Tennis)	I (Ski & Tennis & Windsurfing)	F (National Full Line Chain)

I
(Bikes)

Speciality Store ————————————————— Full Line Store

Targeted
Niche:

Discount Ski
Shop

G
(Outdoor
Discount)

H
(National Discount
Chain)

A
(Discount Team and
Outdoor Sports)

Low Price

Letters represent market position of existing competitors
(type speciality in parenthesis)

Demand Projection. Probably the most difficult part of the market analysis and the entire feasibility study is the projection of demand for a given product or service. No matter what method is used to project demand, there are assumptions and weaknesses inherent in the process. There are many different approaches to projecting demand (Rosenthal, Loomis, and Peterson, 1984; Haralson, 1986; Van Voorhis, 1980; McIntosh and Goeldner, 1984; Yesawich, 1984; and Gold, 1980), which are summarized in this section.

- *Application of Standards*—This is a simple approach and one often suggested by optimistic trade associations. An experience-based criteria is established in which a certain population figure can supposedly support a given type of business. For example, if a particular trade association suggested a standard of one retail store per 20,000 population, then a community of 80,000 should supposedly support four stores. It should be obvious that this approach is a rough approximation that may not work in every locale.

- *Comparable Project Methods*—An existing recreation business in an area of similar demographics is compared to the project under study. Participation rates are then transposed to the new location. Although the figures may be adjusted to account for variance in competitors, demographics, and so on, the reliability of this method depends upon how comparable the circumstances are. This method has frequent application among franchisers and large chains with enough outlets to have comparable data for many situations.

- *Trend Analysis*—When there is a history of demand data (for example, number of tourist arrivals at a given destination) then demand for future years can be projected. Depending upon the number of variables that have major impact on the demand, a trend line can be extrapolated (using simple or multiple regression techniques) that projects future use. Use caution in extending the trend line too far into the future. Figure 4-7 illustrates this procedure.

Figure 4-7
Trend Analysis Example

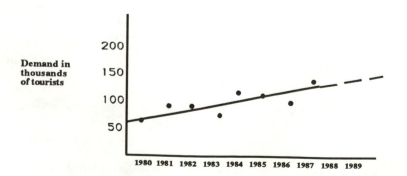

Estimated 160,000 tourist arrivals in 2 years future

- *Participation Rate Projection*—Surveys are often taken by planning agencies and market research companies to determine the consumer behavior pattern for various products/services. Participation or usage rates can be broken down by various market segment categories such as age, income, residence, and location. It is best when the surveys reflect actual participation rather than anticipated participation. The appropriate participation rates can then be applied to the market population of the project under study to yield expected participation. For example, if a national market survey finds that five percent of adult Americans belong to private tennis clubs, and your city has 100,000 adults, then it may be projected that there are 5000 potential tennis club members in your city. Caution must be exercised, however, when using national or regional participation rates to estimate demand rates for a local business. There could be a huge difference between a data-based projection and local reality. If the new business is a major investment, companies usually find it is worth the expense to contract for market research within the specific market area. The "travel cost model" or "gravity model" approaches to forecasting demand are basically variations of the participation rate approach, in which major considerations are given to the distance factor (distance from origin to destination) and competition.

Which method should be used to estimate demand? It would be wisest to use more than one method to establish a likely range or average. It is important to remember that the tendency is to estimate demand too high.

Determination of Market Share. Once demand for a product/service in a given area is estimated, it cannot be assumed that the new business will capture the market. This would only occur if the business was the first in the area to provide that product/service. It is more likely that the new business will have to fight it out with existing competitors to gain any respectable share of the market.

Yesawich (1984) suggests that your expected market share can be calculated by dividing your capacity for business by the total capacity in the area. For example, if your resort had 200 rooms and your competitors had 800 rooms, then your expected share would be 20 percent of the 1000 room market.

It is however, unreasonable to expect a new business to gain its expected market share immediately. Instead, its fair share of the market should be estimated by factoring the expected share downwards. If the overall market is booming (evidenced by waiting lines, unmet demand, and high prices), and if the new business is truly competitive, then it may not have to factor down very much. On the other hand, if the overall market is saturated or stagnant (evidenced by excess supply, price discounts, and business failures) then the initial fair share may be 50 percent or less of the expected.

Chapter VI: Financial Analysis
The financial analysis section builds upon the content of all the

previous sections of the feasibility study. The concept, operating structure and location of the business will help determine the costs involved in starting and continuing the enterprise. Revenue projections build upon the market analysis.

There is one "golden rule" for the financial analysis section: be liberal in estimating expenses and be conservative in estimating revenues. Another approach often taken is to create three scenarios (optimistic, realistic, and pessimistic) for the operating costs, revenue projections, and financial statements. This helps establish a range for the potential profits or losses. Projections need to be developed for the start up costs, the operating costs, and revenues. Then the figures must be organized and displayed on several types of financial statements.

Start-Up Costs. Include the expenses to initiate the business, to finance capital facilities and equipment, and to cover pre-opening costs. It is a major mistake to underestimate these expenses, because the business must get off to a solid start. There are, however, some legitimate corners that can be cut. For example, facilities and equipment can be leased instead of purchased. Typical start-up costs (Bullaro & Edington, 1986; Bangs & Osgood, 1981) include:

- Business Initiation Expenses—Legal and professional consultants Insurance, Incorporation expenses, Tax deposits, Licenses and permits, Cost of obtaining loans

- Capital Expenses—Land and buildings, Equipment, vehicles, machinery, Remodeling and decorations, Fixtures, displays, signs

- Pre-Opening Operations (for 1-3 months as necessary—Salary for owner/manager, Utility deposits & installation, Salary for key employees, Utilities and telephone, Staff training costs, Supplies and equipment, Initial inventory purchase, Maintenance expense, Advertising, Cash reserves, 10%

Operating Costs should be estimated for 12 monthly periods. Most organizations group their expenses into the following categories: cost of goods sold, personnel (including benefits), contractual services (including rent), equipment and supplies, taxes and licenses, debt service (paying on loans) and depreciation (expensing of certain capital assets). There are, of course, many sub-categories possible within each of the expense groups. For the feasibility study it is best to estimate the expenses for at least three years.

In many commercial recreation businesses, the expenses occur at irregular intervals throughout the year. For example, in the water theme park, certain expenses occur during the off season, but most of the expenses occur during the months May to September. Therefore, the commercial recreation manager cannot simply distribute the estimated expenses evenly throughout the 12 months. Again, it should be emphasized that it is safest to estimate expenses liberally.

Revenue Projections also should be made for 12 monthly periods. Categories for revenues are not as standardized as with expenses, because the source of revenues vary greatly according to the type of businesses. Generally, the bulk of revenues come from the sale of products and/or services, but there may also be income from rents, leases, earned interest, or other sources. An example of revenue projections is illustrated in Figure 4-8. As with the estimates of costs, revenue projections should be made for three years. The revenue projections for years two and three should similarly be based on conservative growth.

Revenue projections are often based on the average per capita expenditure of the numbers of customers estimated in the demand analysis section. The "per cap" figure may be based on known industry averages, figures from a comparable business, or the experienced judgment of the manager. After a year's operation, the "per caps" estimate for the second and third year may be revised. In certain types of commercial recreation businesses, there is a high percentage of revenue generated through preseason or advance sales.

Financial Pro-Formas. In addition to the Pro Forma Profit and Loss Statement (monthly, for one year, quarterly, for three years), three other types of pro formas should be shown in the feasibility study.

- Pro-Forma Cash Flow Statement—monthly for one year, quarterly for three years (see example in Chapter 5).
- Balance Sheet—showing assets, liabilities and owners equity at the end of each year. (See example in Chapter 5.)
- Break Even Analysis—showing the quantity of sales necessary to break even during a period of time, usually monthly (See example in Chapter 5.)

Chapter VII: Feasibility Recommendation

Based upon the financial analysis and consideration of the risks and assumptions involved, a decision can be made regarding the future of the project. Four basic decisions can be made: (1) to proceed with the project contingent upon funding, (2) to amend the project and seek funding, (3) to amend the basic concept and conduct a new feasibility study, or (4) to terminate the project. These decisions can be made on the basis of the expected return on investment (net profits divided by owner equity) to the owners. This is where the three scenarios (optimistic, realistic, pessimistic) come into play. By estimating the return on investment according to the three scenarios, a range of potential opportunity can be visualized. Figure 4-9 illustrates the comparative opportunity presented by four hypothetical businesses. Based on this comparative analysis, it would appear that the low overhead mobile ski tune service would appear to be the best opportunity.

Figure 4-8
Pro Forma Profit and Loss Statement
Midvale Water Slides Inc.

	Jan	Feb	Mar	Apr	May	June	July	Aug	Sept	Oct	Nov	Dec	TOTAL
Retail Sales				0	400	4,285	7,815	5,554	160				18,214
Less cost of goods				2,000	3,000	3,000	1,000						9,000
Gross Margin on Sales				-2,000	-2,600	1,285	6,815	5,554	160				9,214
Admissions					8,283	69,823	111,632	76,786	3,000				269,524
Group Sales					160	4,100	13,100	6,100					23,460
Season Passes					10,000	15,000	5,000						30,000
Concession Lease					400	7,000	9,281	7,000	300				23,981
Total Revenues				-2,000	16,243	97,208	145,828	95,440	3,460				356,179
Operating Expenses													
Salaries			1,000	2,196	8,000	32,000	33,830	33,829	10,000	1,000			121,855
Payroll Taxes/Bene.			88	191	696	2,800	2,960	2,960	880	88			10,663
Pool Chemicals				1,500	1,859	500	500	500					4,859
Maint. Supplies				3,000	4,938	1,000	1,000	1,000					10,938
Office Supplies			1,000	1,500	2,470	800	800	800	200				7,570
Postage			100	100	100	100	100	50	50				600
Telephone	74	74	74	74	232	371	371	384	191	74	74	74	2,067
Advertising				5,350	15,000	8,000	8,000	3,000	500				39,850
Utilities	886	886	886	886	1,493	7,536	12,152	11,832	1,324	886	886	886	40,539
Insurance	2,035	2,035	2,036	2,035	2,035	2,036	2,035	2,035	2,036	2,035	2,035	2,036	24,424
Total Operating Exp.	2,995	2,995	5,184	16,832	36,823	55,143	61,748	56,390	15,181	4,083	2,995	2,996	263,365
Sales Tax				90	800	4,800	7,200	4,700	160				17,750
Property Tax											20,028		20,028
Total All Expenses	2,995	2,995	5,184	16,922	37,623	59,943	68,948	61,090	15,341	4,083	23,023	2,996	301,143
Net Pre-Tax Profit	-2,995	-2,995	-5,184	-18,922	-21,380	37,265	76,880	34,350	-11,881	-4,083	-23,023	-2,996	55,036

Figure 4-9
Comparative Feasibility Analysis

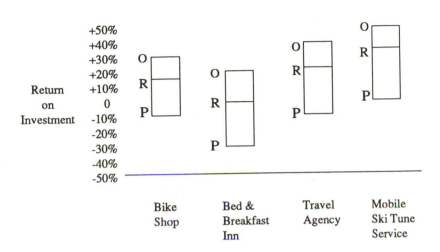

O = Optimistic Scenario R = Realistic Scenario P = Pessimistic Scenario

Note: All figures hypothetical.

FINANCING THE VENTURE

After completing the feasibility study, a third step must be taken to start the business. The entrepreneur must secure adequate financing for the venture. Occasionally the entrepreneur will have enough personal resources, but usually, additional funds are needed. Any financial source will want to know the answer to four key questions (Guadagnolo, 1986): Exactly how much money is needed? How will the money be used? How and when will the investment be repaid? Can you afford the cost of the financing?

The entrepreneur must understand the advantages and disadvantages of borrowing and/or using other people's money. In addition, the entrepreneur must be credit worthy and know what sources of financing are possible. This section will explore those topics.

Advantages and Disadvantages of External Funding

As with everything in business, there are advantages and disadvantages in using nonpersonal financial sources. Advantages include the following:

- You can start the business now, when the opportunity exists. Ten years from now you may have saved enough to start, but someone else may have met the market demand.

- You can start with a larger financial base, which could mean opportunity for greater profits and a greater return on your "leveraged" (borrowed) investment.
- You can distribute part of the risk to others, particularly to investors.
- Persons who provide financial assistance want you to succeed in order to protect their investment. Often, these persons will provide expertise, assistance, and contacts that can be very valuable to the success of the business.

Disadvantages include the following:

- There is a cost of financing. You either have to pay back loans with interest or you have to share the profits with the investors.
- There is personal liability for failure. If you default on a loan, personal assets may be taken. If you fail your co-owners, you may never get another chance.
- Some of the advice given by investors may be conflicting, wrong, untimely, or unwanted.
- Your own business is a commitment that is difficult to walk away from. A salaried employee on the other hand can easily change jobs.
- There is pressure to succeed because of the consequences of failure. This pressure can wreck a person's health and family life.

The C's of Credit

Lenders and investors consider a wide variety of factors when making a decision regarding the financing of a new venture. These factors can be called the "C's of credit." Most if not all of these C's must be present in order to secure financing (Andrew, 1984).

- Character—includes the borrowers integrity, personal background, and desire to fulfill the obligation.
- Capacity—the experience and ability to operate the business efficiently and profitably.
- Capital—the current worth of the business, which could be marshalled to repay the debt.
- Collateral—the personal assets that could be converted into cash to repay the debt.
- Concept—the overall soundness of the business concept and plan of operation.
- Conditions—the overall economic conditions in the area including interest rates, recent failures, recession vs. growth economy, etc.
- Contingencies—alternate plans for utilizing the assets of the business if the initial plan fails.
- Competition—likelihood of gaining and retaining an adequate market share from competitors.
- Circumstances—any special circumstances that could affect future success of the business; for example, political or social uncertainties.

Financial Sources

There are three primary approaches to financing a new business: personal sources, debt financing, and equity financing. Each has its purposes, advantages, and disadvantages.

Personal Sources include savings, property, and assistance from relatives and friends. In order to secure debt or equity financing it will probably be necessary to have at least 10 percent and perhaps as much as 60 percent of the start-up cost backed by personal sources. It is not uncommon for entrepreneurs to take out a second mortgage on their home in order to raise this money.

There is a hidden danger when approaching relatives and friends for money. Will the money be given solely because of the relationship or because it is a good business proposition? It would be a mistake for relatives or friends to toss away money on a weak project just because of a special relationship. Many friendships and families have been wrecked because of business ventures that have gone sour.

Debt Financing is the securing of money through a loan. In addition to funding a business start-up, debt financing can also be used to fund an expansion, provide working capital (cash needed to keep the business going), or purchase equipment, supplies, or resale goods. Terms of loans vary according to the type of business involved, but are usually at least one to five percent over the prime rate, which is the interest rate that lenders charge their largest corporate accounts or other preferred clients. Sources of debt financing include banks, commercial finance companies, life insurance companies, savings and loan institutions, suppliers and vendors (trade credit), and the government (Coopers and Lybrand, 1983; Johnson, 1986; Bullaro and Edginton, 1986; Eyster, 1983; and Guadagnolo, 1986).

- Banks—offer all types of loans; short-term loans, inventory financing, equipment loans, and long-term loans. Banks offer some of the best loan rates, usually one to three percent over prime, and provide auxilliary services such as cash management advice, credit checking, and deposit services. It is a good idea to arrange in advance for a short-term line of credit to meet unexpected cash flow problems. Unfortunately, banks are the most conservative lending sources and often turn down recreation ventures.

- Commercial Finance Companies—lend money to companies that do not qualify for standard loans made by commercial banks. Finance companies generally make loans against the value of three types of assets: accounts receivable, inventories, and facilities and equipment. Because they accept higher risk projects, interest rates are usually higher than with a bank.

- Savings and Loan Associations—may provide loans for real estate financing for about 75 percent of the property's value. Interest rates are similar to commercial finance companies.

- Insurance Companies—allow policy holders to borrow against the paid-up cash value of the individual's life insurance. Interest rates are very good; lower than bank's because there is less risk involved.

- Trade Credit—occurs when a supplier of retail goods sends merchandise to a retail store and bills the store at a later date, usually 30-60 days. It may be in the supplier's best interest to encourage the use of its products by allowing no interest or extremely low interest credit.

- Equipment Financing, Rentals and Leases—are usually available from dealers of major equipment and vehicles. Rental payments can usually be applied to the later purchase of the equipment.

- Government Loans—can be obtained from the U.S. Small Business Administration (SBA), which guarantees up to 90 percent of certain loans made by a local bank but approved by SBA. In case of default, the SBA repurchases the loan. Due to this low risk, interest rates are only about two percent over prime. In order to qualify for an SBA guaranteed loan, the proposal must have been denied previously by a bank or other commercial lender. Occasionally, states and cities also provide loans to stimulate business.

- Small Business Investment Companies (SBIC)—are privately owned, profit-oriented companies chartered by the state. SBICs are eligible for low interest federal loans and use these funds to invest in small businesses.

Equity Financing requires that the entrepreneur give up a portion of ownership in return for the funds to start the business. Sources of equity financing include limited partners, venture capital firms, SBICs, and public stock offerings (Coopers and Lybrand, 1983; Cohen, 1985; Steward, 1983; Deloitte, Haskins and Sells; Hosmer, 1978; and Rebello, 1986).

Tremendous capital investment is needed to start a major resort with modern lodging and recreation amenities.
(Photo: Courtesy of Marriott's Tan-Tar-A Resort)

- Limited Partnerships—allow the entrepreneur, as the general partner, to attract funds for start-ups. The contribution of capital by limited partners and the distribution of profits is spelled out in advance in the articles of partnership filed with the state. Limited partnerships can often be arranged through local asset management companies and financial consulting firms.

- Venture Capital Firms—are interested in buying into companies that demonstrate excellent prospects for future earnings growth. Venture capital firms typically look for a return of three to five times their investment within five to seven years or as much as 50 percent a year. Even though many start-up companies will fail to earn this much, the venture capitalists hope that one big winner will make up for several losers. Most venture firms do not seek a position of more than 40 percent ownership in a company because they want the primary owner to have incentive to keep building the business. Usually, venture capital firms are not interested in projects requiring less than $250,000 because the cost of investigating a proposal could almost equal the profit potential in a very small company.

- Small Business Investment Companies—are often interested in an equity position in a new company. There are about 500 SBICs licensed by the SBA. The maximum SBIC investment in any single firm cannot exceed 20 percent of the firms assets, although several SBICs may join together to finance a company.

- Public Stock Offerings—allow part of the ownership of a company to be sold to the public. The sale of the stock is arranged through an underwriter/stockbroker who specializes in this service in return for a sales commission. Offerings over $5 million require a myriad of compliances with the Securities and Exchange Commission (SEC). For 53 offerings less than $5 million, the rules and regulations are much less stringent. Seven states (New York, New Jersey, Florida, Illinois, Colorado, Nevada, and Utah) have relatively weak securities laws and are considered stock fraud havens. The success of a small stock offering may depend more on the ability of the underwriter/broker to sell the stock than on the legitimacy of the business concept.

ALTERNATIVES IN STARTING A NEW BUSINESS

There is no one best way to start a new commercial recreation business. Rather, there are many alternatives. The previous section presented the three basic financial approaches: personal resources, debt financing, or equity financing. There are, however, several variations that can build upon any of the financial or legal structural approaches. These alternatives are franchises, purchase of an existing business, auxillary service at an existing business, small business incubators, and public/commercial cooperative ventures.

Franchises

A franchise agreement permits the buyer/operator (the franchisee) to sell the products or services of the seller or franchisor (Bullaro and Edginton, 1986). In the most popular type of franchise arrangement, the franchisee pays an initial fee (which can range from $1,000 to $1,000,000) and a continuing royalty and may be required to purchase the wholesale product from the franchisor. The royalty is typically between one and ten percent of gross sales. In return, the franchisor allows the use of the product, trademark, and image, and provides management assistance such as market research, marketing strategy, promotions and national advertising, operating manuals, standards, quality control, and possibly some financing.

Franchising is a good way for an entrepreneur to get started in a business where most of the mistakes have already been made and corrected by the franchisor. Franchising is also an advantage to established companies because it is a fast, cheap way to expand. There are, of course, some problems with franchising: the franchisor's services may not be high quality or worth the royalty fees involved. The franchisor could become overly aggressive in awarding franchises and saturate the market. Also, the franchisee/operator may feel somewhat constricted due to the regulations, policies, procedures, and controls required by the franchisor.

Overall, franchising is a very successful concept. Only about five percent of new franchises fail in their first two years. There are about 2000 different franchise companies in the United States, with about 478,000 outlets. Expansion is very rapid. McDonald's, for example, opens a new outlet somewhere in the world every 15 hours. Franchises account for about $576 billion in sales annually, which is one third of all retail sales (Battle, 1986). One of the key reasons for success of franchises is the consistency of the product. Consumers always know what they are going to get when they eat at McDonalds or stay at a Sheraton. Franchise opportunity information can be found in the "business opportunities" section of newspaper classified ads, various bookstore and newstand publications, and from the Small Business Administration.

Some franchise "opportunities" are outright scams designed to take your initial franchise fee. To evaluate a franchise opportunity, there are several factors to be considered (Van Voorhis, 1980; Kelly, 1985).

- The company—its history, reputation, experience, honesty, networth, past success, rate of failures.
- The product—quality, market advantages, value for the dollar, availability, durability, purchasing requirements, etc.
- Location—quantity and quality of areas available, protection of exclusive or territory rights, assistance in selecting a location.
- Assistance—quality and value of assistance in training, operational procedures, financial procedures, inventory control, market research, promotion, advertising, financial help.
- Control—exact terms of initial payment and ongoing royalties, re-

strictions in the conduct of business, product requirements, quotas and terms for ending the franchise.

Buying An Existing Business

The purchase of an existing business is much like the purchase of a used car. Initially, it could look sharp and appear to be running smoothly, but it could turn out to be a lemon. Therefore, it is essential that there be a thorough feasibility study conducted, just as with a new business location. There is a difference however, because with an existing business, there should be plenty of existing records and data to analyze: sales and market data, financial reports, inventory records, and so on. If after careful review, it turns out that there are discrepancies or misrepresentations in any of the data, regard this as a warning sign. Other aspects to check carefully include: condition of the facility and equipment, employee qualifications and productivity, all contracts and legal aspects (leases, debts, loans, titles, zoning, unsettled lawsuits, etc.), customer relations, and the seller's reasons for leaving the business (Bullaro and Edgington, 1986). According to Van Voorhis (1980) there are many advantages in buying an existing business, such as:

- Less uncertainty about market demand.
- No "lag time" in receiving returns on investment.
- Known capabilities of facilities, equipment, and personnel.
- Established sources of supplies.
- Easier financing if the business has a good track record.
- Less time, effort, and pressure as compared to a start-up.
- Opportunity to purchase the business at a low price.

There are of course disadvantages with this approach, including:

- Compromise of the purchaser's goals to match the existing business.
- Existing customers may leave.
- Poor selection or quality of goods/services that are currently offered.
- Inadequate or deteriorated facilities and/or equipment.
- Poor customer relations that linger on from the previous owner.
- Questionable policies and practices that may be difficult to change.
- The apparent bargain (business purchase price) could be overpriced.
- Legal problems with property, lease, contracts, or lawsuits.

Small Business Incubators

Another approach is to start a business through a small business incubator. These are facilities and organizations where fledgling businesses share space and office services while receiving management help and occasionally, financial help. The idea is that the environment will improve the chance of success.

There are over 100 small business incubators existing nationwide (Witkin, 1985). While most are manufacturers or technology firms, there is opportunity for service-based companies. The incubator provides favorable rents, tie-ins with venture capital, secretaries, phone service, computers, copiers, conference rooms, and maintenance. The sharing of services help the small company to lower its operating costs. Not surprisingly, the success rate of incubator-based firms is higher than average. Some types of commercial recreation enterprises that have flourished in the incubator concept include a resort property broker, a party and contract recreation service, and a sportswear importer/wholesaler.

Auxiliary Service at Existing Business

There are many opportunities for an entrepreneur to establish an auxiliary service at an existing business location. These arrangements are good for small specialty services that can operate with low overhead. In almost every case there is a contractual agreement between the entrepreneur and the existing business. It is also important that the service be compatible with and complementary to the primary business. Some examples of auxiliary services are:

- Contracted sailing instructor at a private marina.
- Guide service at a mountain resort.
- Mobile specialty food vendor at an amusement park.
- Ski tune/repair service at a sporting goods store.

Auxiliary services such as these are attractions to a business that wants to expand its services but lacks the knowledge or inclination to do it themselves. It is a good way to expand at little or no risk. The additional service can be a way to differentiate from competitors and draw new business.

From the entrepreneur's standpoint, this approach is a good way to reduce overhead, since the existing business provides the facility and most of the advertising. The auxilary service capitalizes upon the customers who are already drawn to the existing business. Of course, the auxiliary service will probably have to pay a minimum monthly guarantee and a percentage of gross sales.

Public-Commercial Cooperative Venture

Due to budget crises in recent years, many public park and recreation agencies have turned to private enterprise in order to expand services. There are many types of public-commerical cooperative ventures, and in most cases, the public agency will want to contract with a proven company. There are, however, opportunities for entrepreneurs to bid successfully for small but potentially profitable contracted services. Examples include paddle boat rentals, contracted tennis pro, food and beverage concessions, mobile skate rental, umbrella and beach raft rental, and imprinted t-shirt concession.

The advantages of public-commercial cooperative ventures are very much the same as with the auxiliary services mentioned in the previous section. Similarly, the private contractor usually has to pay a monthly guarantee fee and a percentage of gross sales.

SUMMARY

A new business must begin with a sound concept. It could be an improvement, an innovation, or an invention that is designed to serve an existing or a created market. It is critical that the new product or service enter the market at an early growth stage of the lifecycle of the industry. Differentiation of the product/service from other competitors is also critical for success. As part of the development of the business concept, there must be consideration of the desired image, the marketing platform, and the scale or size of the enterprise.

A feasibility study builds upon the initial business concept. Generally, the more money involved in the new business, the more effort will go into the feasibility study. While a feasibility study cannot eliminate all doubt regarding the future of the enterprise, it can illuminate many of the uncertainties. The feasibility study includes a description of the business (including legal organization), a regulatory, and risk analysis, a location analysis, a management analysis, a market analysis, a financial analysis, and finally, a recommendation.

The entrepreneur needs to understand the advantages and disadvantages of outside financing for the new venture and have a knowledge of various financial sources. In addition to personal resources, the entrepreneur may seek debt financing (loans from banks, finance companies, savings and loan associations, insurance companies, trade suppliers, and the government) or equity financing (limited partnerships, venture capital firms, small business investment companies, and public stock offerings).

There are alternatives in starting a new business. These include franchises, purchase of an existing business, small business incubators, auxiliary services at existing businesses, and cooperative ventures with public park and recreation departments.

STUDY QUESTIONS

1. Outline the key considerations in developing a sound business concept for a commerical recreation enterprise.
2. What major decisions affect a business concept once developed?
3. Describe the purposes of a feasibility study.
4. How does one go about securing primary and secondary information in the first step of a feasibility analysis?
5. List and describe the types of decisions that are determined by a feasibility study.
6. What is market positioning?
7. Explain some of the more sound methods of projecting demand for a business.
8. What are some advantages and disadvantages of external funding of a business venture?
9. What are the chief considerations in gaining credit for a business?
10. Describe several sources of financing a business.
11. What are some creative alternatives to funding a business?

PROJECT IDEAS

1. Write a business concept you may have for a commercial recreation venture.
2. Go to the library and find five sources of information for a potential business of your choice. Cite references and state the contribution of this information to making a potential decision about going into business.
3. Invite a bank commercial loan officer to your class and have him/her critique your business concept.
4. Locate the Franchise Opportunities Handbook in your library. Write to a Commercial Recreation franchisor and request information about the franchise.

SPOTLIGHT: YOU CAN'T DO START-UPS BY THE BOOK

Craig Rausch is a financial consultant for Arthur Anderson, Inc. Each year he reviews hundreds of feasibility studies from entrepreneurs who seek financing for start-up ventures. Through his experience, Rausch has made some observations about business start-ups that differ from the conventional advice expounded in business periodicals and texts. In a nutshell, Rausch advises that "you don't do start-ups by the book." Each start-up is different, and Rausch finds fault with many of the key people involved in start-ups. His "gripes" are primarily with accountants, attorneys, and venture capitalists.

Accountants are often used by venture capitalists to analyze feasibility studies. The accountants "model" or compare the financial ratios of the proposed project with standards for similar businesses in the same geographic area. According to Rausch, the accountants are too narrow minded in their analysis, because most start-ups cannot realistically achieve the model numbers. In addition, there are no models that apply for many types of new ventures.

According to Rausch, entrepreneurs "spend enormous amounts of time and money with lawyers, and two years later wonder why." This is because entrepreneurs tend to overuse lawyers, especially at the first stages of the business start-up. Rausch recommends not to use lawyers for conceptual matters, but only for legal detail work. For example, when negotiating any deal, reach agreement on the principles, then turn it over to the lawyer to write the contract.

Rausch also has little good to say about venture capital firms. Venture capitalists waste time by taking forever to study proposals, often wanting more details and market studies. In addition, they "suck blood" in the percentage of equity they want in relation to the amount of financing they supply. Rausch feels that there are better ways to seek financing.

For entrepreneurs seeking start-up capital for a small business, Rausch suggests looking for local investors. A typical profile would be the suggested professional who has $100,000 in a money market fund while looking for something new to invest in. These people often contact tax consultants and asset management firms for ideas regarding investments. Rausch suggests selling your concept to these advisors who in turn sell the concept to the local investors.

Regarding the feasibility study itself, the main reason it should be done is to serve as a business plan for the entrepreneur. If it doesn't meet this purpose, it will have little value in securing outside financing.

Lastly, Rausch suggests that the entrepreneur bail out of the company before it gets too big. This target might be 10 times the initial investment in four to five years. Rausch just doesn't have much confidence in the ability of entrepreneurs to manage an established business. Entrepreneurs are different types of people who are happiest and at their best when starting new ventures, not mired down in day-to-day management (Rausch, 1986).

REFERENCES

Andrew, W. "Lender's Perspective: The Key to Successful Borrowing" *The Cornell Hotel and Restaurant Administration Quarterly*, February, 1984, pp. 37-43.

Bangs, D., and Osgood, W. *Business Planning Guide*. Portsmouth, New Hampshire: Upstart Publishing Company, 1981.

Battle, D. "The Great American Franchise Extravaganza." *U.S. News and World Report*, July 28, 1986, pp. 36-37.

Bullaro, J., and Edginton, C. *Commercial Leisure Services*. New York: Macmillan Publishing Company, 1986.

Cohen, R. "Utah Among Penny Stock Fraud Havens." *Salt Lake Tribune*, February 3, 1985, p. F1.

Coopers and Lybrand, Inc. *Doing Business in Utah*. Salt Lake City, Utah: First Interstate Bank of Utah, 1983.

Davidson, J. *Store Location: Little Things Mean A Lot*. Washington, DC: U.S. Small Business Administration, 1981.

Deloitte, Haskins, & Sells. *Raising Venture Capital*. New York: Deloitte, Haskins, & Sells, no date.

Drucker, P. *Innovation and Entrepreneurship*. New York: Harper & Row Publishers, 1985.

Dun and Bradstreet. *The Business Failure Record*. New York: Dun and Bradstreet Business Economics Department, 1981.

Eyster, J. "Creative Debt-Financing Vehicles." *The Cornell Hotel and Restaurant Administration Quarterly*, May, 1983, pp. 28-35.

Fails, B. "The Feasibility Study Process." Presentation at the annual conference of the *Resort and Commercial Recreation Association*, Phoenix, Arizona, January, 1985.

Gold, S. Recreation *Planning and Design*. New York: McGraw-Hill Book Company, 1980.

Goretsky, M. "A Marketing Audit: Your First Step in Planning." *Destinations*, December, 1984, pp. 74-75.

Guadagnolo, F. "Entrepreneurship." In *Private and Commercial Recreation* (A. Epperson, editor). State College, Pennsylvania: Venture Publishing, Inc., 1986.

Haralson, W. "The Economic Feasibility Study." *In Private and Commercial Recreation* (A. Epperson, Editor). State College, Pennsylvania: Venture Publishing, Inc., 1986.

98

Harmon, P. *Small Business Management*. New York: D. Van Nostrand Company, 1979.

Hazard, J. "Going Into Business For Yourself?" *U.S. News and World Report*, September 3, 1984.

Hills, G. "Market Analysis in the Business Plan: Venture Capitalist's Percpetions." *Journal of Small Business Management*, January, 1985, pp. 38-46.

Hosmer, L. *A Venture Capital Primer for Small Business*. Washington, D.C.: U.S. Small Business Administration, 1978.

Howard, D., and Crompton, J. *Financing, Managing and Marketing Recreation and Park Resources*. Dubuque, Iowa: Wm. C. Brown Company, 1980.

Johnson, H. "SBA Talk." *USA Today*, February 10, 1986, p. 4E.

Kelly, J. *Recreation Business*. New York: John Wiley & Sons, 1985.

Kelsey, C., and Gray, H. *The Feasibility Study Process for Parks and Recreation*. Reston, Virginia: The American Alliance for Leisure and Recreation, 1985.

Laumer, J., Harris, J., and Guffy, H. *Learning About Your Market*. Washington, D.C.: U.S. Small Business Administration, 1981.

Lewis, R. "The Positioning Statement for Hotels." *The Cornell Hotel and and Restaurant Administration Quarterly*, May, 1981, pp. 51-62.

McIntosh, R., and Goeldner, C. *Tourism: Principles, Practices, Philosophy* (4th Edition). New York: John Wiley & Sons, 1984.

Rausch, C. "You Can't Do Start-Ups By The Book." Presentation for the American Collegiate Entrepreneurs Association, Salt Lake City, Utah, March, 1986.

Rebello, K. "Adept Managers Find Ways to Lure Venture Capital." *USA Today*, February 10, 1986, p. E1.

Rosenthal, D., Loomis, J., and Peterson, E. *The Travel Cost Model: Concepts and Applications*. Fort Collins, Colorado: USDA Forest Service, 1984.

Stewart, M. "Venture Capital and the American Dream." *INC.*, July, 1983, p. 116.

Van Voorhis, K. *Entrepreneurship and Small Business Management*. Boston: Allyn and Bacon, Inc., 1980.

Weber, F. *Locating or Relocating Your Business*. Washington, D.C.: Small Business Administration, 1981.

Witkin, G. "Incubators - New Tool to Aid Small Firms." *U.S. News and World Report*, May 13, 1985, p. BC8.

Wolff, R. "Effective Marketing." In *Private and Commercial Recreation* (A. Epperson, editor). State College, Pennsylvania: Venture Publishing, Inc. 1986.

Yesawich, P. "A Market-Based Approach to Forecasting." *The Cornell Hotel and Restaurant Administration Quarterly*, November, 1984, pp. 47-53.

Chapter 5

FINANCIAL MANAGEMENT

Once a new commercial recreation enterprise has been started it must be managed efficiently and effectively. The two terms should not be confused or used interchangably, because a business can easily fail if it is managed efficiently but not effectively. By the same token, it can fail if managed effectively but not efficiently.

Efficient management implies that whatever is done, it is accomplished with an economy of resources for a maximum of results. For example, in a sporting goods store, this would mean that stock is purchased at the best possible price, that sales are made with the lowest possible ratio of labor costs, and that every dollar spent for advertising reaches the largest possible audience.

Effective management implies that the right things are done to further the objectives of the company. Again, using the sporting goods example, stock purchased would be exactly what customers want to buy. Further, sales staff would give the kind of service that makes customers want to return, and the advertising dollar would be spent reaching the right market segment.

Obviously, the manager should strive for an optimal combination of efficiency and effectiveness. This chapter will be concerned with the efficient and effective management of financial aspects of the commercial recreation business. This will include financial records, financial planning, maximizing profits, pricing strategies, and other financial issues. Operational aspects of management involving facilities, personnel, and programs will be covered in Chapters 6 and 7.

FINANCIAL OBJECTIVES

The first step in financial management is to have clear objectives. Objectives help the manager determine if the company is on course toward financial success. These objectives must be measurable and occur within a specific time frame. Two major objectives, liquidity and profitability, are at the heart of financial management efforts. There also can be numerous secondary objectives that ultimately relate to the primary objectives of liquidity and profitability.

Liquidity

Liquidity is the ability to generate enough cash to pay the bills. This can be measured each month by comparing the total revenues to the total expenses. For a retail operation, any returned merchandise and the cost of all goods sold must be subtracted from the revenues. Expenses comprise all current operating expenses (labor, utilities, advertising, property taxes, etc.) including debt service (mortgage and loan payments). Figure 5-1 shows the basic formula for liquidity.

Figure 5-1
Liquidity Formula Example
(For a Retail Store for one month)

Sales of Merchandise	$22,500
Less: Returned Merchandise	- 300
Net Sales	$22,200
Less: Cost of Goods Sold	$10,200
Margin on Sales	$12,000
Less: Operating Expenses	$ 5,500
Less: Debt Service	2,500
Profit Before Taxes	$ 4,000

Obviously, the objective is to have more revenues than expenses, but this can be very difficult for a new company or a new location. This is why it is necessary to have an adequate cash reserve when starting the business to cover expenses during the initial months when the business is not liquid. The topic of liquidity will be discussed further in the section concerning cash flow.

Profitability

Short-term liquidity is just the first part of a company's financial objective. Ultimately, a company must be profitable in the long term in order to succeed. Without profit, there would be no capital to expand the business or to provide a cushion in times of emergency or slumps in business. Most importantly, if there were no profits, there would be no one interested in investing in the business.

How much profit is sufficient? That answer really depends on the amount of risk involved. The greater the risk, the more profit will be expected. At the very least, a new business must return several percentage points more than is available through relatively secure investments such as U.S. Treasury bills or money market funds. On the other hand, a venture that involves significant risk or that has a short lifecycle may be expected to earn an annual profit that is a 40-50 percent return on investment.

In the case of nonprofit recreation organizations, profit may not be an objective. Usually, it is sufficient that a nonprofit enterprise break even. It is wise, however, to strive for some excess revenue in order to have seed funds to start future projects or as a cushion for emergencies.

Other Financial Objectives

Depending upon the organization, there may be other financial objectives that ultimately relate to liquidity and profitability. Some of these objectives include the following:

- Market Share—the percentage of the overall market for a particular product/service which the business hopes to gain.
- Occupancy Rate, Use Rate, or Load Factor—the percentage of available rooms, court times, or seats by paying customers.
- Labor Factor, Food Factor, or Fuel Factor—the percentage of total costs attributable to specific items such as labor, food, fuel, etc. Some businesses consider these costs to be somewhat controllable and set targets they strive to hold expenses under.

FINANCIAL RECORDS

One of the most important aspects of financial management is the keeping of accurate records. Without accurate financial records, many management decisions have to be made in a void of misinformation. Realistically, financial record keeping is not a very exciting aspect of management, and most managers prefer to spend their time on other tasks. Nevertheless, the commercial recreation manager must understand why financial record keeping is important, know what records to keep, and understand the accounting process.

Reasons To Keep Financial Records

The general reasons for keeping financial records (as well as other types of records) can be categorized into three areas: (1) to meet legal requirements, (2) to safeguard assets, and (3) to help plan and control operations. Specific reasons can overlap those general reasons. For example, keeping records for tax purposes is a legal requirement, but it is also important in planning and controlling the business. According to Epperson (1977) and Harmon (1979), specific reasons for keeping records are as follows:

- To meet requirements for government reports, tax returns, and licenses.
- To determine the current status of the business.
- To measure profitability and performance.
- As data upon which to base forecasts of future performance.
- As evidence in lawsuits.
- As information to present creditors when seeking a loan.
- To inform potential investors or buyers of the company.
- To inform partners, stockholders, board members, or governing authorities.
- To evaluate the results of responsibility that have been delegated to others, and to monitor employee performance.
- To monitor facilities and equipment for preventive maintenance.

Which Records To Keep

A commercial recreation business should keep records for a variety of financial and operational functions (Record Retention Timetable, 1983). Records to be kept include the following:

Income Records—including all original transactions in whatever form the income comes to the business, such as sales slips, cash register tapes, or ticket stubs.

Expense Records—including all current and periodic expenses whether paid by cash or check. Documents include invoices, bills, receipts.

Tax Records—documenting the liability for and payment of income taxes, sales taxes, and property taxes, records of withholding employee income taxes, social security payments, unemployment insurance, and workers compensation.

Payroll Records—including employee timecards and payroll ledgers, commission (if applicable) records, annual leave, sick leave, and compensatory time records.

Mortgage and Debt Records—including payments and record of balance for mortgages, bonds, or other loans.

Regular Financial Statements—including monthly, quarterly and annual profit and loss statements, balance sheets, and cash flow statements.

Other Accounting Records—including accounts receivable ledgers, bank deposits, bank statements, asset depreciation records.

Personnel Records—including employee contracts, accident reports, injury claims, critical incident reports, and evaluations.

Facility and Equipment Records—including inventory records, lease contracts, and preventive maintenance records.

Legal Records—including trademarks, patents and copyrights, contracts, and any legal claims or suits.

Other Administrative Records—including audits, annual reports, board minutes, executive correspondence, bid documents.

The Accounting Process

An essential aspect of financial record keeping is an accounting system. Simply stated, accounting is a process in which a multitude of business data is organized and summarized into a form usable to a manager. If a commercial recreation manager asks to look at this year's revenues, it doesn't do much good to bring a truckload of cash register tapes. If the information from those tapes can be organized into major categories and summarized into monthly totals, then the revenues can be evaluated. The wise manager, however, does not wait long periods before organizing the relevant business data. Instead, the accounting process should be considered as a constant and ongoing process.

The actual accounting process can be viewed in five steps (Harmon, 1979; Bullaro and Edginton, 1986) as illustrated in Figure 5-2. "Documents of Original Entry" such as cash register tapes, ticket stubs, and purchase invoices are totaled each day and recorded in daily journals. Each major category of income and expense is included in the daily journals. Periodically (which may be daily, weekly, or at least monthly), the journal data is transfered to account ledgers. There is a separate ledger kept for each category of asset and liability and financial activity. Each ledger shows the increases and decreases to that account. Monthly or quarterly the balance in each account is shown on one of the primary financial statements, the balance sheet and the income and expense statement (or profit and loss statement). At this point, the data is organized and summarized sufficiently for the manager to use in decisions about the business.

Figure 5-2
The Accounting Process

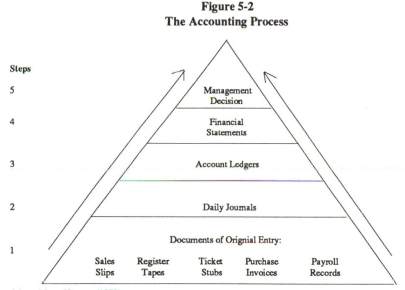

Adapted from Harmon (1979).

Financial Statements

Financial statements are the documents or reports that bring together all the data in the accounting process. Typically, financial statements are developed annually, quarterly, and monthly in order to describe the financial condition of the organization. The income statement (or profit and loss statement), the cash flow statement, and the balance sheet are the three primary financial statements.

The Income Statement summarizes the financial activity of the organization over a specific period of time, usually a month, a quarter, or a year. An example of an income statement is shown in Figure 5-3. It shows all the revenue sources, total revenue, all the operating expenses, total expenses, pretax income, taxes (or tax reserve), and net income. The income statement allows the commercial recreation manager to monitor the firm's performance and compare that performance to its objectives and to performance in previous months.

Figure 5-3
Midvale Sports Club: Income Statement Year to Date (6 months)

	Amount	% Net Sales
Revenue		
Pro Shop Sales	15,500	
Less cost of goods sold	6,200	
Margin on Pro Shop Sales	9,300	5.9
Memberships	100,500	63.9
Court Fees	20,200	12.8
Class Fees	24,800	15.7
Vending Concession (contract)	2,500	1.6
Total Revenues	157,300	
Operating Expenses		
Salaries, Wages, & Benefits	80,300	51.0
Utilities	12,200	7.7
Advertising	8,500	5.4
Insurance	6,400	4.1
Rent	18,000	11.4
Eqiupment and Supplies	1,200	.8
Depreciation	4,000	2.5
Debt Service	3,600	2.2
Miscellaneous	800	.5
Total Operating Expenses	135,000	85.8
Pretax Income	22,300	14.2
Less tax reserve	5,400	3.4
Net Income	16,900	10.7

The Cash Flow Statement is an important planning and control tool for the commercial recreation manager. It shows the difference between revenues and expenses for the monthly (or quarterly) period. The positive or negative cash flow is also shown cumulatively through the statement. This in turn allows the manager to know if it is necessary to borrow additional cash to remain operationally solvent or whether to invest excess cash. The data used for the cash flow statement comes directly from the income statement, with one exception. Depreciation is not considered a cash expenditure on the cash flow statement. Figure 5-4 shows a monthly cash flow statement in which a $10,000 cash advance was available at the beginning of the six-month period. This cushion allows the company to remain liquid through the first several months when the operation actually lost money.

Figure 5-4
Midvale Sports Club: 6-Month Cash Flow Statement

	July	August	Sept	Oct	Nov	Dec	Total
Net Revenues	12,000	18,100	26,200	30,800	34,500	35,700	157,300
Expenses	18,800	18,600	21,200	23,000	24,200	25,200	131,000
Monthly Cash Flow	(6,800)	(500)	5,000	7,800	10,300	10,500	
Cumulative Cash Flow	(6,800)	(7,300)	(2,300)	5,500	15,800	26,300	
Cash at Beginning of Month	10,000	3,200	2,700	7,700	15,500	25,800	
Cash Position at End of Month	3,200	2,700	7,700	15,500	25,800	36,300	

The Balance Sheet shows the financial condition of the organization at a point in time, usually the end of the month, quarter, or year. This information also helps the manager to monitor the firms progress. Various figures from the balance sheet (as well as the income statement) can be compared to industry norms to see if the company is on track. Figure 5-5 shows a balance sheet for a sports club that does not own its building or land. Some terms used in the balance sheet may need explanation (Merrill Lynch, Pierce, Fenner and Smith, Inc., 1979):

- Current Assets—cash and those assets that can be turned into cash in the near future.
- Accounts Receivable—amounts not yet collected from customers that are currently due.
- Fixed Assets—the assets not intended for sale that are used to create, display, or transport the product or service, include land, buildings, machinery and equipment.
- Depreciation—an accounting method used to expense the decline in useful value of a fixed asset due to normal wear, tear, and obsolescence.
- Accounts Payable—the amount the company owes to its regular business creditors from whom it has bought goods or services on open account and to employees for salaries.
- Current Liabilities—debts for regular business operations that will come due in the near future, usually the coming month.
- Long Term Liabilities—debts that are due after one year from the date of the financial report, typically mortgages, bonds, and other major loans.
- Net Worth (or Owner's Equity)—the portion of the business that is owned free and clear of all debts.

The basic formula for the balance sheet is: Assets = Liabilities + Net Worth. Therefore, the total for the left side of the balance sheet must equal the total for the right side. Stated another way the formula is: Assets - Liabilities = Net Worth.

Figure 5-5
Midvale Sports Club: Balance Sheet
December 31, 1986

Assets		Liabilities and Net Worth	
Cash	16,300	Accounts Payable	13,100
Merchandise Inventory	7,000	Taxes Payable	400
Accounts Receivable	17,500	Total Current Liabilities	$13,500
Total Current Assets	$40,800		
		Bank Loan	28,000
Pro Shop Fixtures	1,000	Total Long-Term Liabilties	$28,000
Fitness Equipment	45,000		
Office Equipment	4,000	Total Liabilities	$41,500
Total Fixed Assets	$50,000		
		Total Net Worth	$49,300
Total Assets	$90,800	Total Liabilities and Net Worth	$90,800

*Depreciated Value

Issues In Accounting

Certain issues in accounting should be discussed with the company's financial and accounting advisors (Kelly, 1985). Decisions in these areas could improve the company's operation and profitability.

- Tax advantages of different methods of business organization, accounting, depreciation, inventory evaluation, borrowing, etc.
- Early payment of bills if substantial discounts are involved. In periods of high inflation, it may not be cost effective to pay bills early even if there is a small discount.
- An accounting system that will meet data processing requirements of the future (ie., larger computerized system).

FINANCIAL PLANNING

One of the main purposes of financial records is to provide the commercial recreation manager with information that can be used in planning and decision making. Due to the seasonal, intermittent, and competitive nature of commercial recreation, financial planning is essential. The manager must know the current status of the business and have a plan for where the business is headed. Some of the tools of financial planning are break-even analysis, ratio analysis, cash flow management, tax planning, and budgeting.

Break-Even Analysis

Break-even analysis is a management control device that helps determine how much you must sell in order to cover costs, with no profit and no loss. Profit comes with each unit sold after the break-even point. To figure the break-even point, fixed costs must first be separated from the variable costs.

Fixed costs are those expenses that must be paid regardless of how many customers purchase the product or service. Depending upon the type of business, fixed costs typically include management salaries, property taxes, operating licenses and permits, office equipment, telephone, regular maintenance, most utilities, insurance, rent or mortgage, legal fees, accounting fees, advertising, vehicles, and major equipment.

Variable costs are those expenses that increase or decrease depending upon how many customers use the product or service. Typically, a ratio can be established between the number of customers and the item of expense. For example, a river rafting company may schedule one boatman/guide per five customers, and order food on a basis of $4.00 per person per day. Therefore a group of 25 customers would require five boatman and $100 per day for food. Management tries to control variable expenses by scheduling or committing only enough resources to meet the needs of the customers. Depending upon the type of business, variable expenses may include seasonal and part-time labor, additional maintenance, additional utilities, food, program supplies, retail resale goods.

Figure 5-6 illustrates the break-even point for a river rafting company offering one day float trips on a western river. The company's fixed costs are $2500 per week during its operating season. Its total variable costs are $18.75 per person per trip. Depending upon demand, the company can schedule more staff, order more food, and so on to provide up to eight boats per day.

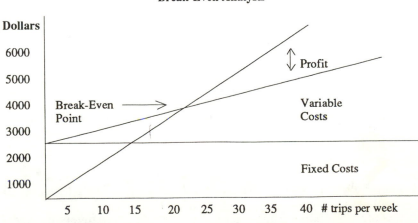

Figure 5-6
Break-Even Analysis

Fixed costs are plotted as a horizontal line since they are constant with volume. Variable costs are plotted on top of the fixed costs at the ratio of $18.75 per person per trip. The revenue line is plotted from the zero point. Customers pay $50 each, with four persons to a boat, or $200 per boat trip. Using the break-even formula below, the break-even point occurs at $4000 or 20 boat trips per week.

$$\text{BE Point} = \frac{\text{Total Fixed Costs}}{1 \text{ minus } \dfrac{\text{Variable cost per unit}}{\text{Revenue per unit}}}$$

$$\text{BE Point} = \frac{2500}{1 \text{ minus } \dfrac{18.75}{50}} = \frac{2500}{1 \text{ minus } .375} = \frac{2500}{.625} = \$4000$$

Using Ratios to Analyze the Business

One of the best ways to analyze the status of the business is through ratio analysis. Meaningful ratios can be created from a variety of data from both the income statement and the balance sheet. These ratios can be compared to similar ratios from past months or years or to industry averages. Financial ratios for a large number of industries can be found in Standard and Poors Industry Surveys, Dunn and Bradstreet Industry Services, Robert Morris Agency Annual Statement Studies, and other sources.

Financial ratios can be classified as debt ratios, liquidity ratios, activity ratios, or profitability ratios. Some of the more important ratios of each type are illustrated below (Gibson and Frishkoff, 1983).

Debt Ratios provide insight into the extent to which a firm is relying on borrowed money, and the ability to pay debts when due.
• Debt to Equity Ratio—total debt compared to the owners equity. If it exceeds 100 percent, then creditors have more invested than the owner does.
• Maturities of Long Term Debt—annual payment of long-term debt compared to the company's earnings before taxes. This measures the company's ability to pay debts based upon its earnings.

Liquidity Ratios show the firms ability to meet its short-term obligations.
• Current Ratio—current assets compared to current liabilities show the ability to pay off current debts from current assets. A common standard is that current assets should be twice current liabilities.
• Quick Ratio—cash plus accounts receivable compared to current liabilities. This shows the ability to pay off current debts without selling inventory.

Activity Ratios show how effectively the business is using its assets in relation to sales.
• Inventory Turnover Ratio—cost of goods sold compared to the aver-

age inventory on hand. This shows how quickly the inventory sells out (turns over) and whether too much inventory is on hand.
- Total Assets Turnover Ratio—net sales compared to total assets show how actively and effectively the assets of the business are being used to generate sales.

Profitability Ratios show the company's ability to earn money.
- Net Profit Margin—net profits compared to net sales show the ability to generate profits from sales. A low rate can be offset by higher volume.
- Return on Investment—Net profits compared to owner's equity shows the ability of the company to earn adequate profits. This rate should be substantially higher than is available through secure investments.

Cash Flow Management

Most commercial recreation businesses have periods during their peak season when revenues generate more cash than is needed to meet expenses. Conversely, during off seasons, expenses usually demand much more cash than revenues can generate. The primary objective of cash flow management is to smooth out these uneven combinations of revenue and expenses. According to Chastain and Cianciolo (1986), businesses are putting increased emphasis on cash flow as a measure of financial health, because cash is an immediate indicator of liquidity.

Throughout the year, there are two primary strategies for improving cash flow: (1) emphasize transactions that increase or accelerate cash inflow and (2) engage in transactions that economize or delay cash payments. Specific strategies (Chastain and Cianciolo, 1986; Deppe, 1983) to accomplish this include the following:

- Tighten customer credit, require cash payment.
- Accelerate billing of credit sales and require prompt payment.
- Sell aging account receivables to collection agencies.
- Deposit revenue the same day that money is received.
- Delay payment of bills until the last possible date that they are due.
- Pay bills within the discount period only if the invoices offer attractive discounts.
- Minimize inventory build-up.
- Reduce investments in idle assets by selling them or leasing them.

In periods when there is excess cash, the common strategy is to invest idle funds. This requires that the manager make accurate projections of expenditures in order to know how much cash is available to invest. The manager must also be familiar with short-term money markets such as bank savings, certifications of deposit, and treasury bills. It is important to consider risk versus yield, and high risk speculative investments are not recommended.

In periods when cash flow is short, the common strategy is to operate off the reserve generated in better times or if that is nonexisting, to take out a short-term loan. The commercial recreation manager needs to keep good relations with a bank or other financial institution in order to have loans available on short notice. Of course, another major strategy is to cut back on operational expenses, particularly in the off season. In these circumstances, the flexibility of a part-time or seasonal labor force is advantageous. Some commercial recreation businesses even close down completely in the off season.

Tax Aspects

In past years, when tax rates were much higher, some business decisions were made primarily because of tax advantages. For example, if a company knew that it was going to finish the year with a $100,000 profit, it might spend the money for new vehicles rather than pay tax on the profits. The expenditure would have yielded a $10,000 investment tax credit, and in later years, the accelerated depreciation of these assets would yield further tax reductions.

Today, the top corporate tax rates have been dropped from well over 50 percent to about 34 percent. In addition, investment tax credits have been repealed, capital gains are now fully taxed, and there are longer periods required for many asset depreciation write-offs. Business entertainment is not even fully deductible anymore (Weiner, 1986).

As a result of these tax changes, most business decisions today should be made on their own merits, not because of tax angles. The commercial recreation manager should still be sure to take whatever tax deductions are available; there just aren't as many now. Further, when trying to raise money through limited partnerships, the enterprise must show its potential for earning income, because limited partnerships are no longer tax shelters for losses and huge tax write-offs.

Budgeting

Note,

A budget is simply a plan of action with price tags attached. It shows everything that is expected to occur in the coming year, with the associated revenues and costs. In this way it is a very important financial planning tool. After the budget is established, it is also a mechanism used to monitor and control expenditures.

The budget process begins with establishing goals and objectives for all units of the organization. Next, it is determined what programs, projects, and tasks will accomplish those objectives. Finally, costs are calculated for the labor, equipment, supplies, and services that are necessary to accomplish those programs, projects, and tasks. A similar sequence based on projected demand, is used to estimate revenues.

The commercial recreation manager needs to guard against the following problems that can occur in budgeting:

- Overbudgeting—Too complex and overly detailed budgets can stymie the flexibility needed to operate the enterprise.
- Budgeting based only on precedent—Budgets should reflect current market conditions not ancient history.

• Budgets as a straight jacket—Budgets are a tool, not an end in themselves; during the year when conditions change, budgets can be
changed too.

PRICING

A key aspect of financial management is the setting of prices. Since
the demand for most recreation products and services is relatively elastic,
the price charged will have a major influence on business volume. This
section will review methods for setting prices and a number of pricing
strategies.

Methods for Setting Prices

Howard and Crompton (1980) have suggested three methods for
setting prices: (1) cost-based pricing, (2) going-rate pricing, and (3)
demand-oriented pricing.

Cost-Based Pricing considers the total of fixed and variable costs
and adds a percentage mark-up to cover profits. This is a safe approach
to assure that the business costs are met, but it does not take into account
the fact that competitors could have much different prices due to different
costs. Also, this method does not account for market pressures.

Going-Rate Pricing is based upon charging what competitors
charge. The problem with this approach is that a competitor could be
making a good profit at a price you cannot offer due to higher costs of
your location.

Demand-Oriented Pricing is based upon what the market segments
are willing to pay. Obviously, this approach could lead to prices that
would yield no profits at all in some situations.

Since all three pricing methods have advantages and disadvantages,
perhaps the best approach is a combination of the three. A business could
use cost-based pricing to set the minimum level of prices. A normal
profit, the opportunity cost for the investors money, could be built in as
a fixed cost. If the business could not be competitive at this level, then
it probably should consider another location or another business. Next,
prices of competitors and market demand should be considered when
adding further mark-up. It may even be possible to have differentiated
prices to allow for market demand at different times. For example,
discount prices may be charged in the off season. Such prices would be
just high enough to cover base expenses.

Pricing Strategies

There are no clear cut pricing strategy "truisms." It seems that for
every pricing strategy used successfully by one manager, there is a
counter argument by another manager. Some of these pro/con arguments
follow.

A. If demand is relatively inelastic, then a price increase may yield more
revenue even though there may be a few less sales. But...

You could lose significant market share if your competitors stay with lower prices.

B. If demand is relatively elastic, a price reduction may generate enough volume to yield increased profits even though the margin on each sale is less. But...
If competitors follow your lead and drop prices too, you could just wind up cutting each other's throats. Consumers love this "healthy competition."

C. "Loss leaders" (low priced specials that bring in new business) can create awareness of your business, bring in new customers, and lead to increased sales of regularly priced goods/services. But...
Some people come only for the loss leaders, and having too many loss leaders cuts deeply into profits.

D. If you have to increase prices, do something to emphasize new value, such as promoting additional benefits, highlighting service, etc. But...
So will competitors.

E. It is better to reduce prices by using discount coupons and promotions than by reducing prices across the board. But...
Too many discount coupons and promotions can be a clerical nightmare and cause confusion and delays at ticket windows and sales counters.

F. It is best to set prices for a brand new product/service low enough to make it very difficult for competitors to enter the market. But...
Low prices become a "reference point" for many customers who later resist price increases.

G. There is no such thing as an obscene profit. But...
If you have huge profit margins, you will soon have many more competitors.

HOW TO INCREASE PROFITS

Every commercial recreation business wants to increase its profits. Opportunities to increase profits can occur at each step of the formula for the income statement.

$$
\begin{array}{r}
\text{Sales} \\
- \underline{\text{Cost of Goods}} \\
\text{Margin on Sales} \\
- \underline{\text{Operating Expenses}} \\
\text{Profits}
\end{array}
$$

This section will consider each step of the income statement and suggest a number of strategies for increasing profits.

Price Increases will improve the margin on sales, provided that the cost of goods remain constant. The increase, however, could be offset by a decrease in sales volume.

Increased Sales Volume can lead to increased profits under several circumstances. First, if the margin on sales and expenses can be held constant, increased sales will always yield greater profits. Second, even if the margin is reduced a little (through discount prices) a large increase in volume can more than compensate. Lastly, increased volume could result in "economies of scale." This means that the expenses to sell a large volume are proportionally lower due to more efficient use of available facilities and labor.

So how is sales volume increased? One possible approach previously mentioned is to reduce price. Another approach is through more effective marketing to bring in more customers. Finally, you might realize increased demand due to demographic changes, the loss of competitors, or changes in public interest.

Improved Purchasing can result in significant savings that in turn yield greater profits. Unfortunately, some commercial recreation managers overlook the many ways in which purchasing may be improved. First, and most important, is to make smart purchases. In a retail situation, this means to purchase the types of products that customers want and in a quantity that will not be left on the shelf occupying valuable sales space. For a tour operator, this means "blocking out" or committing to the right number of rooms in a resort that people want to go to. Obviously, smart purchasing requires a good knowledge of your market, its preferences, and its ability to pay.

Volume purchasing can also save money. One danger, however, is that storage space may cost more than is saved through the volume purchase. Another risk with some types of products, particularly food, is spoilage. One approach to volume purchasing is to form a cooperative purchasing group. Here, several companies, even competitors, pool their purchasing needs in order to get the volume necessary for a price reduction. A bonus advantage is that each company may attain the savings and not have to increase storage space.

Finally, it may be possible to get some products on consignment from the manufacturers. This means that you are billed only for what you sell, and any unsold products can be returned at no penalty. This approach reduces your risk for unsold merchandise. Consignment agreements are often available from small manufacturers who are just starting out with a product line and are eager to find outlets.

Inventory Control can help a company increase sales and save money. It has been estimated that 25 percent of small store business is lost by lack of adequate stock (Cassell, 1986). Further, the cost of carrying stock (sales floor space, storage space, utilities, etc.) often equals 15-25 percent of the inventory cost (Harmon, 1979). Obviously, improvements in either area can increase profits significantly.

Ideally, stock received would go directly onto the sales floor, thus eliminating the need for storage. However, there needs to be some cushion to allow for sales fluctuation. Seasonal variations must also be allowed for. Today, an inventory reorder system is easily facilitated by a computer linked directly into the sales registers.

Reduced Labor Costs can result in great savings for the commercial recreation business. In many service organizations, labor represents 80 percent of the budget. Any savings here would be almost a dollar for dollar improvement in profits. Unfortunately, reducing labor cost is easier said than done, and sometimes labor reductions can come back to haunt you in terms of safety or customer satisfaction. Nevertheless, there are several approaches to reducing labor costs.

- Use of Part-Time and Seasonal Labor—Many jobs can be performed by nonprofessional labor hired on a part-time or seasonal basis. It is relatively easy to increase or decrease the hourly schedules of this labor force in order to meet fluctuations of the business.
- Below Minimum Wage Rates—It is justifiable to pay below the minimum wage in certain circumstances. Camp counselors for example may be given a small weekly salary plus food and lodging. Bellboys, valet parking attendants, tour guides, and waitresses may also receive low wages because of the amount they make in tips.
- Hire Generalists—Employees who can do several jobs can be scheduled where they are needed most. This allows a business to be flexible and responsive to the market.
- Contract Out For Specialists—If tasks requiring specialists (electricians, accountants, lawyers, draftsman, etc.) do not absolutely justify full-time, year round work loads, then do not hire for these positions. Instead, contact out for these specialists, but only when regular staff cannot do the job.
- "Union Busting"—Some companies have been restructured under bankruptcy laws, and in the process, voided costly union contracts. New employees are then hired at more reasonable and competitive pay scales.

Reduced Overhead Costs can greatly reduce overall expenses and thereby contribute to profitability. There are several possible strategies.

- Leasing facilities and equipment could be less expensive than purchasing them, especially if there are high interest payments for a mortgage or other loan.
- Share certain capital assets and overhead expenses with other businesses. As mentioned previously, some small businesses share office space, secretarial service, copy machines, with other enterprises in a small business complex or "incubator."
- Sell off nonproductive assets such as land, buildings, or equipment if they do not contribute profits in proportion to their costs.
- Reduce other overhead costs such as utilities, telephones, maintenance, and advertising, by aggressively monitoring those costs.

Again, this is easier said then done. One executive who spends a million dollars a year on advertising is absolutely positive that half the money is wasted. The problem is, he doesn't know which half!

Financial Controls can help an organization avoid losing money through employee error or dishonesty. It is sad but true that this type of loss occurs much too often. The most important factor in financial control is to assure that there is a subdivision of duties so that no individual handles a transaction from beginning to end. Gray (1986) has suggested ten steps that will increase financial control.

1. Assign someone other than the bookkeeper to receive bank statements and reconcile them.
2. The person who records disbursements should not be authorized to sign checks. Two signatures should be required for all checks.
3. The person signing checks should review, approve, and cancel invoices or other disbursement documents.
4. Disbursements (except for petty cash) should be made by serially numbered checks.
5. Someone other than the bookkeeper should open the mail and list incoming checks.
6. The person opening mail should endorse all checks upon receipt.
7. Someone other than the bookkeeper should authorize write-offs of nonrecoverable accounts receivable.
8. Detailed records of fixed assets should be maintained and periodic inventories taken.
9. Carry fidelity insurance against loss from embezzlement.
10. Monthly financial statements should be prepared in sufficient detail to disclose significant variances from prior months and years.

OTHER FINANCIAL MANAGEMENT ISSUES

Several financial management topics that deserve examination have not previously been covered in this chapter. These topics include auxiliary revenue sources and consumer credit.

Auxiliary Revenue Sources
Most commercial recreation businesses have a primary line of products or services. It is very possible however to have secondary or auxiliary revenue sources that contribute significantly to the overall profit of the business. Often these auxiliary efforts can be conducted with existing personnel or managed contractually. Examples of some common auxiliary sources are provided here.

Alternative Products and Services can complement a company's primary business, particularly in the off season. Examples include:

• Alpine slides and summer concerts at ski resorts.
• Snowmobile sales at a motorcycle dealer.

- Tennis, sailing, or bicycle lines at a ski shop.
- Hunting guide services and lodging at a summer camp.
- Racquetball and fitness activities at a golf or tennis club.

Recreation Programs can generate additional revenue and just as importantly, bring in additional clients. Programs can be conducted by virtually any type of business. Examples include:

- Knitting, painting, or ceramics classes conducted at an arts and crafts shop.
- Trips and tours offered at a resort hotel.
- Fun runs sponsored by a sporting goods store.
- Video game championships held at a video arcade.
- Climbing clubs sponsored by outdoor speciality shops.

Equipment Rental Programs can be a convenient and major revenue producer. Bicycle rentals at Kiawah Island, South Carolina, generated about $400,000 one year. Other examples include video machine and movie rentals at hotels, sports equipment and games rental at resorts, and equipment "demo" rentals at sporting goods stores.

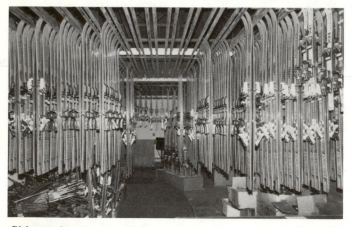

Ski rentals are one way for a sporting goods store to diversify its revenue base. (Photo: John Crossley)

Repair Services can be an auxiliary revenue source and are particularly appropriate for certain types of retail stores, including those selling bicycles, boats, cameras, recreational vehicles, and ski equipment.

Food and Beverage Concessions can be made available to clients in several ways. The organization can self-operate the service and gain potentially good revenue. This however can be a risk and a management headache. Another approach is to contract out the space to a food and beverage concessionaire. This can reduce risk and still yield decent revenue. Finally, a very popular approach is to use vending machines. Again, these can be owned and self-operated or contractually operated by a vendor.

Retail Product Sales, even on a small scale, can be a profitable addition to many service businesses. Almost any business that has a cash register and staff on duty could have retail products for sale. At a sports club, for example, front desk staff who greet members and make court reservations could also sell racquets, balls, sports clothing, health foods and fitness records. Other examples include:

- T-shirts and post cards at a tourist attraction.
- Travel guidebooks at a travel agency.

Video Games may have seen their better days, but they can still bring in some extra revenue at very little risk. Most video game companies will provide the machines, rotate them periodically, service them, and provide 40 to 50 percent of the gross revenue to the host location.

Leased Space can provide revenue for a business that does not want to self-operate a given service. Examples include:

- Pro shops at sports and racquet clubs.
- Small restaurants and retail shops at resorts.
- Travel agency desks at large sporting goods stores.
- Souvenir stands at sports arenas.
- Open space at a resort for cattle grazing or farming.

Consumer Credit

Credit purchases are an important part of many commercial recreation enterprises. For some types of businesses, such as travel agencies and resort hotels, credit purchases may be the bulk of the sales. There are five types of consumer credit (Harmon, 1979).

1. Open (or Charge) Account—Purchases are billed on a regular cycle, usually the first of the month, and the entire amount is due within ten days.
2. Revolving Account—Customers are allowed a fixed amount of credit and each month pay a minimum percent of the unpaid balance, plus interest. Credit cards can be included in this classification.
3. Budget Account—Used for somewhat costly items, an account is established for a set number of months, typically three to six. A down payment is made followed by monthly installments plus interest.
4. Installment Account—Used for high cost items, a down payment is made, and the balance plus interest is paid monthly over one to five years.
5. Bank Debit Card—This is a credit card in which the purchase is charged against an existing deposit balance in a bank or money market account.

Advantages of Extending Consumer Credit. There are many advantages of allowing customers to make purchases using one of the five types of credit (Harmon, 1979; Kelly, 1985). These advantages include:

- Credit frees buying resistance and can lead to increased volume of business.
- Certain types of credit, especially credit cards, make it possible to accept orders by phone or mail.
- Charge customers typically buy higher quality merchandise and have less tendency to wait until there are discount sales.
- Allowing credit can help improve customer loyalty.
- Lists of credit customers are good mailing lists for advertising.
- Significant revenue can be earned from the interest charged on the credit purchases of "big ticket" items.

Disadvantages of Extending Consumer Credit. There are also disadvantages of extending credit, including:

- The receipt of payment is delayed.
- It costs money to investigate the credit worthiness of customers.
- There are risks in extending credit as some customers don't pay up.
- There is extra paperwork for billing and bookkeeping.
- There are service charges involved with some types of credit. Fees for credit card sales average about three percent.

SUMMARY

A commercial recreation enterprise must be managed effectively and efficiently. This means that the right things are done to further the objectives of the company, and done with an economy of resources for a maximum of results. The key objectives are liquidity and long-term profitability. Other more specific objectives may include market share, occupancy rate, management overhead percentage, and labor cost ratios.

The business must keep records in order to meet legal requirements, to safeguard assets, and to plan and control operations. Important records to keep include those for income, expenses, taxes, payroll, long-term debts, personnel, facility and equipment, legal aspects, and regular financial statements.

Accounting is a process in which business data is organized and summarized into a form where it can be useful to a manager. It is a five step process in which documents of original entry are consolidated into journals, then ledgers, then financial statements. The primary financial statements are the income statement, the cash flow statement, and the balance sheet. These financial statements are important aids in managerial decision making.

Various financial planning tools help the manager know the current status of the business and plan for its future. Break-even analysis determines how much product or service must be sold in a given period of time to cover fixed and variable costs. Ratio analysis permits comparison of different aspects of the business with past periods and with industry standards. There are numerous ratios for analyzing debt, liquidity, activity, and profitability. Cash flow management helps determine when excess cash may be invested, or when a loan is needed to cover expenses. Although tax rates are lower than in past years, it is still important to take advantage of all strategies to reduce tax liability. Finally, budgeting is simply a plan of action with price tags attached. A well planned budget will help the organization meet its objectives and control its expenses.

A key aspect of financial management is the pricing of products and services. Prices may be based on costs, the going rate of competitors, market demand, or a combination of the three. There are many pricing strategies but there are arguments for and against each one.

Every commerical recreation business wants to increase its profits, and there are a variety of ways to do this: increase prices, increase sales volume, reduce purchasing costs, reduce inventory costs, reduce labor costs, reduce overhead costs, improve financial controls, and various combinations of the above. There is however, the potential for strategies to backfire due to inaccurate assessments of market demand or due to improper management.

Auxiliary revenue sources can supplement a company's business and/or diversify the business in the off season. Types of auxiliary sources include alternative products/services, recreation programs, equipment rentals, repair services, food and beverage concessions, retail sales, video games, and leased space.

The availability of consumer credit can be the difference in making a sale or not. Although there are advantages and disadvantages to each type of consumer credit (open account, revolving account, budget account, installment account, and bank debit card) most commercial recreation businesses would probably benefit by allowing some type of credit, especially the use of credit cards.

STUDY QUESTIONS

1. Describe the importance of liquidity and profitability in a commercial recreation business. Which is the short-term need?
2. Explain five reasons to keep good financial records in a commercial recreation business.
3. Differentiate between an income statement, a cash flow statement, and a balance sheet.
4. In a break-even analysis what is the difference between fixed and variable costs?
5. List and describe some common ratios that are used in analyzing a commercial recreation business.
6. How should price be set for a commercial recreation service?
7. Explain five ways of maximizing profits in a commercial recreation venture.
8. What is the difference between a capital intensive business and a less capital intensive business? Cite an example of each.

PROJECT IDEAS

1. Using the Robert Morris Agency (RMA) Annual Statement Studies or other source of financial ratios, compare several different types of

commercial recreation. Discuss reasons why the ratios differ between several industries.

2. With the cooperation of a local commercial recreation enterprise, track a single financial transaction (utility bill, entrance ticket receipt, etc.) through the accounting system.

3. Compare three different commercial recreation enterprises: a sporting goods store, a river rafting company, and a theme park. Discuss the probable key points for maximizing profits in each industry.

SPOTLIGHT ON: Financial and Entrepreneurial Management in Public Recreation

Sound financial management is just as important for public recreation agencies as it is for commercial recreation business. Similarly, an entrepreneurial spirit should not be limited to private enterprise. Public recreation managers also need to act as entrepreneurs in order to discover unmet needs and develop programs to match the opportunity. This spotlight will introduce four public parks and recreation departments in southern California that are examples of good financial and entrepreneurial management.

Conejo Recreation and Park District (Thousand Oaks, California)

The banner in Harvey Roth's office reads: "In order to find the edge, you must risk going over the edge." This is the spirit that Roth, Recreation and Community Services Administrator, brings to the Conejo District. Each member of the recreation staff is expected to work at least part of the time in an "area of discomfort," which will cause the person to stretch their ability and expand their horizons. One way to accomplish this is to have staff become involved in community organizations other than the recreation department. In the Conejo District, every community organization has at least one recreation staffer among its members. The fruits of this approach are evident in the large number of recreation programs that are co-sponsored or hosted by community groups. This approach yields obvious financial savings and allows the department to initiate a wide range of other programs that are highly self-sustaining through fees. Innovative programs include "Park and Ride" service to Hollywood Bowl concerts and three-day trips for teens to Catalina Island, a beach resort offshore from Los Angeles (Roth, 1986).

San Bernadino County (California) Regional Parks

One of the most financially aggressive departments in the country is the San Bernadino County Regional Parks Department. This department serves one of the geographically largest counties in the country, stretching 195 miles from the Los Angeles area to the Arizona border. There are a variety of regional parks administered by the department, and many of the parks feature special facilities operated by contracted concessionnaires. There are over 50 leases covering such diverse facilities as a marina, OHV park, gun club, equestrian center, golf course, softball complex, camp, restaurants, snack bars, and an entire western town theme park. These contracts provide a combination of payments (annual guarantees and percentage of gross revenues) that bring the county as much as $70,000 per concession lease. Overall, the lease revenues, park admission fees, and other park fees cover about 70 percent of the $4 million budget. This revenue production is about three times higher than the national average for public park self-sufficiency. If it were not for the entrepreneurial management, traditional tax revenue would not be able to finance the wide range of facilities available in the San Bernadino County Regional Parks (Newcomb, 1986).

City of Los Angeles Department of Recreation and Parks

The City of Los Angeles Department of Recreation and Parks generates over $17 million a year through fees and charges, lease revenues, and concessions. There are several financial management approaches and techniques that help achieve this success.

Fees and charges are administered through a well organized system. There is an 81-page schedule of fees that details all rates, deposits, reservation procedures, and requirements for security, insurance, and so on. Policies cover typical programs and facilities plus bandshells, garden plots, road races, wedding receptions, carnivals, stadium parking, movie filming, and other innovative revenue sources. Revolving funds are utilized throughout the department to keep revenues within the division that generates the money. In some cases, however, part of the revenues are channeled to the department office to help cover overhead costs. For example, 15 percent plus $1.25 per person of the revenue from self-supporting instructional classes goes toward department overhead.

Under another approach, "class permits" are issued to approved instructors who arrange their own class programs. The instructors are motivated to promote the classes and generate repeat business because they get to keep 75 percent of the class fees (Sessinghaus, 1986).

Anaheim Parks, Recreation, and Community Services

Anaheim, California, prides itself in being the "Leading Edge City." the Parks, Recreation, and Community Services Department similarly takes pride in contributing to a high quality of life. For example, recreation classes are set with low maximum enrollments in order to keep instructor-participant ratios low enough to ensure a quality experience. They also set class minimum low in order to assure that most classes "make."

The department has established a "Revolving Opportunity Fund" that encourages innovative ideas that have high benefit-cost ratios. Under this program, a portion of generated revenue is channeled into a special fund. The fund provides seed money to start new projects having potential to generate more revenue or improve productivity. Park and Recreation staff identified and prioritized over 120 potential uses of the Revolving Opportunity Fund (Kolin, 1986).

REFERENCES

Berman, B., and Evans, J. *Retail Management: A Strategic Approach*. New York: MacMillian, 1979.

Bullaro, J., and Edginton, C. *Commercial Leisure Services*. New York: Macmillan Publishing Company, 1986.

Cassell, D. "Retail: Profiting by the Numbers." *Fitness Management*. November/December, 1986, pp. 26; 51.

Chastain, C., and Cianciolo, S. "Strategies in Cash Flow Management." *Business Horizons*, May-June, 1986, pp. 65-73.

Deppe, T. *Management Strategies in Financing Parks and Recreation*. New York: John Wiley & Sons, 1983.

Epperson, A. *Private and Commercial Recreation: A Text and Reference*. New York: John Wiley & Sons, 1977.

Gibson, C., and Frishkoff, P. *Financial Statement Analysis* (2nd Edition). Boston, MA: Kent Publishing Company, 1983.

Gray, R. from "How To Prevent Fraud In A Small Association" cited in *Commercial Leisure Services* (by Bullaro and Edginton). New York: Macmillan Publishing Company, 1986.

Harmon, P. *Small Business Management*. New York: D. Van Nostrand Company, 1979.

Howard, D., and Crompton, J. *Financing, Managing and Marketing Recreation and Park Resources*. Dubuque, Iowa: Wm. C. Brown Company, 1980.

Kelly, J. *Recreation Business*. New York: John Wiley & Sons, 1985.

Kolin, J., Recreation Superintendent, City of Anaheim Parks, Recreation, and Community Services Department, Anaheim, California, Personal Interview, September, 1986.

Merrill Lynch. *How To Read A Financial Report*. New York. Pierce, Fenner, and Smith, Inc. 1979.

Newcomb, G., Chief of Administration, San Bernardino Regional Parks Department, San Bernardino, California, Person, Interview, September, 1986.

Record Retention Timetable. New York: Electric Wastebasket Corporation, 1983.

Roth, H., Recreation and Community Service Administrator, Conejo Recreation and Park District, Thousand Oaks, California, Personal Interview, September, 1986.

Sessinghaus, R., Supervisor of Administrative Services, Valley Region, Los Angeles Department of Parks and Recreation, Van Nuys, California, Personal Interview, September, 1986.

Weiner, L. "Playing To Win By The New Tax Rules." *U.S. News and World Report*, September 1, 1986, pp. 49-50.

Chapter 6

OPERATIONS MANAGEMENT

Operations management as defined in most commercial recreation enterprises involves the day-to-day management of facilities and programs, supervision of front-line personnel (employees who interact with the public), and maintenance of positive guest relations. In this chapter we will also examine overall management theory, personnel management, marketing, risk management, and computer uses. Indepth coverage of any of these topics warrants an entire text, which of course, is impossible here. Therefore, this chapter will not attempt to duplicate the content typically covered in separate courses or texts in management theory, personnel management, marketing, etc. Instead, this chapter will present an overview of operations management and cover select topics that are unique to commercial recreation and/or deserving of special attention.

OVERVIEW OF OPERATIONS MANAGEMENT

The traditional view of management is often expressed by scholarly theorists through some acronym such as POSDCORB (Planning, Organizing, Staffing, Directing, Coordinating, Reporting, and Budgeting). This concept however, seems rather artificial. When a manager is up to his neck in "alligators", fighting ten things at once, is he planning, organizing, directing, or coordinating? Management authority Henry Mintzberg (1984) suggests that there are many myths concerning management: that the manager is a reflective, systematic planner; that the manager needs aggregated information from a formal information system; and that management is a science.

The facts of the matter, according to Mintzberg are:

- Managers work at an unrelenting pace, are action oriented, and dislike reflective activities.
- Managers favor verbal communication and engage in an unending variety of brief unscheduled interchanges of information.
- Managers process much information and then make most decisions based on judgment and intuition.

In this hurried environment, the manager commands the most information and resources and through the force of her leadership, gives direction to the organization.

Hurst (1977) puts the role of commercial recreation management into a similar and realistic perspective. According to Hurst, the prime role of the manager is to personally "make something happen as a result of your leadership." This requires a commitment to change and improve, even when things have gone well. The good manager constantly asks: "How can I make it even better?"

Going one step further, successful management can be characterized in a number of ways (Epperson, 1986; Hurst, 1977; Drucker, 1985). These characteristics include:

- The manager must set the pace: Be active, interested, and committed.
- The emphasis should be on quality and not just quantity.
- There is no such thing as "can't." Management must find a way to overcome problems.
- The manager must be people centered as well as profit oriented.
- Management must develop compassionate leaders and use supervisors as facilitators, cheerleaders and coaches rather than as cops, watch-dogs, or devils advocates.
- Management must be totally honest.
- Management must get results with people, not through people.
- Every three years, management must review every product, service, process, policy, procedure, and market the business is involved with, eliminate those that are outdated or wasteful, and update the remaining.
- Management must have innovative projects underway at all times. A steady flow of projects at different stages of development will assure that something new is brought to the market on a regular basis.
- Management must do everything possible to keep in touch with the needs of the market. This may include formal surveys, focus groups, informal observation, staff feedback, and industry litera-ture.

PERSONNEL MANAGEMENT

Most commercial recreation businesses involve more than one em-ployee. Therefore, the manager must devote at least some, if not a great deal of their time to the supervision of employees. According to traditional management theory, the work of the organization should be divided into various tasks and specialties, procedures would be written for the "best way" to do each task, and people would be hired and trained to perform each task/slot of the formal organization chart. Communica-tion would flow down from the top and workers would perform rather mechanistically to achieve the previously agreed goals of the organiza-tion.

We now know, however, that the traditional theories did not account for the worker's individuality. In reality, personnel management is possibly the most difficult area of management. Service industries such as recreation are very labor intensive and employees should not be treated too simplistically according to traditional management theory. It is important to recognize that each employee is an individual with their own needs, goals, abilities, and weaknesses.

The success of most recreation businesses depends on the interaction of its personnel with the public. Customers will judge the enterprise on the friendliness, alertness, and performance of its staff. A good manager can make a difference in this area by influencing the attitude and behavior of employees (Epperson, 1977). This section will examine several key aspects of personnel management in a commercial recreation setting.

Hiring, Training, and Compensating Staff

Legendary football coach Paul "Bear" Bryant of Alabama knew that game strategy was not the only key to winning national championships. The key to winning was in recruiting and in developing that talent into the best players they could be. Similarly, any business that finds talented people with good attitude and develops their potential should be a winner. This is so easy to say but so difficult to do!

Hiring. Rather than wait for talent to come to us, we can go out and find it. Recruiting trips to high schools, trade schools, colleges, and professional conferences can generate a large number of interviews where the best candidates can be screened for further consideration. Some employers do not give much consideration to academic grades, but this could be an error. Good grades are earned through intelligence, aptitude, effort, the ability to get along with "the system," or a combination of these characteristics. Any of these characteristics is an asset in one job or another.

It is, of course, standard procedure to examine work experience, references, professional/trade affiliations and certifications when assessing a prospective employee. But what about a person's attitude and personality? References may or may not yield accurate information. Elaborate tests are available, but are too expensive an approach for most commercial recreation businesses. It often boils down to the applicant's "intangibles."

To assess these intangibles, restaurant owner/manager Mike Hurst (1977) works a couple of key questions into each interview. "What's the funniest thing that's ever happened to you?" Hurst asks. He looks for humor, expressive movement, and animation. Hurst wants to hire people with personality, who can laugh at themselves. Later in the interview, Hurst asks, "What's the most significant thing you learned in the last six months?" He wants to hire people who have grown and learned something from their last job, no matter how low the position was.

Occasionally, a person with "superstar" potential will apply for employment when no positions are open at the time. If you do not hire this person, they will leave and find employment elsewhere, possibly with a competitor. If however, there are a number of part-time personnel in your labor force, their schedules can be adjusted and space found for the superstar. Later, this person can be worked in to a regular position. The bottom line is, find a way to hire the superstar when he walks in.

Orientation and Training. Employee orientation programs should be established based upon written job descriptions, company policies, and operating procedures. It is important that the employee understand the overall mission of the organization and how their position is important to the success of the organization. Specific orientation topics should include the history and philosophy of the organization, details regarding the specific job responsibilities, equipment used, employee benefits, and key operational policies regarding emergencies, rain days, guest relations, etc.

Training of employees can be accomplished through a combination of written materials, workbooks, audio visual media, and personal instruction by staff. One popular method of personal instruction, especially for parttime and seasonal employees, is called "shadowing." The new employee basically follows around, or "shadows," an experienced employee and learns the job through first-hand observation and trial.

It is a good idea for the manager to have some part in the training process of all employees. This allows some rapport to be established between management and new employees at the very start. It is also an opportunity for the new employee to be exposed to the service philosophy, energy, and drive of the manager.

McKenzie (1983) suggests that new employees need to be taught the importance of repeat business. They need to understand that the satisfied customer is always the backbone of any organization's success. In order to respond to frequent customer problems and situations, some theme parks develop standard responses for employees to use in given situations. Employees may be encouraged to take part in "scripting sessions" where these responses are created.

Compensation. Fair compensation is generally determined by three factors: federal regulations, market conditions, and company philosophy. The Fair Labor Standards Act (1984) requires that employees be paid a minimum wage ($3.35 per hour in 1988) for the first 40 hours work per week. For employees other than management professionals, time and a half wages must be paid for work over 40 hours. There are exceptions for companies with sales less than $325,000 per year, for public agencies, for seasonal businesses, and for certain jobs that pay tips and/or employee lodging (Feld, 1981).

Beyond minimum wages, competition for skilled labor will help determine prevailing local wage rates. Further, some companies may desire to take a leadership role in wages in order to attract the best employees.

Another consideration related to employee compensation is the provision of employee benefits, which may include the following:

employee insurance programs	profit sharing plans
employee health care programs	employee discounts
retirement fund contribution	child care
sick leave	educational reimbursements
vacation leave	uniform reimbursements
sales commission	professional expenses
performance bonuses	(travel, memberships, etc.)

Courteous personnel are needed to operate revenue facilities such as this tennis center in Los Angeles.
(Photo: Courtesy of the City of Los Angeles Parks and Recreation Department)

Staff Supervision and Motivation

There are many theories regarding employee management and motivation. Textbooks in management and in parks and recreation administration typically examine Maslow's Hierarchy of Needs, Hertzberg's Motivation/Hygiene Theory, and X, Y, and Z Theory Management. Rather than duplicate such content, this section will present a variety of specific suggestions regarding employee supervision, motivation, morale, and incentives (Hurst, 1977; Epperson, 1977; Drucker, 1985).

- Learn employees names and treat them as individuals.
- Don't be afraid to do an employee a favor.
- Remember that employees live up or down to expectations.
- Recognize employees needs and goals that exist outside the workplace, and if possible, help them achieve these goals as well as work-related goals.
- Eliminate dull jobs or combine them with good jobs and learning experiences.
- Don't be afraid of high employee turnover if the people are moving up to better jobs, even outside the organization.
- Develop career paths within the organization.
- Provide opportunities for recognition, praise, achievement, responsibility, and social prestige.
- Show employees that their welfare is closely related to the success of the organization.
- Give employees a true opportunity to contribute to the decisions within the organization.
- In a small organization, let key employees take major responsibilities and grow with the job. Then when the company grows, you have

the base for a management team, rather than having to import new managers.

Part-Time and Seasonal Labor

Almost every commercial recreation business uses part-time and/or seasonal personnel. There are good reasons for this. Many businesses are seasonal in nature and it is impractical to hire many year round employees. There is flexibility in using part-time and seasonal employees whose hours can be increased or decreased as operating conditions warrant. In addition, wages and benefits typically cost less if the work can be performed by less experienced employees.

The use of part-time and seasonal employees presents several distinct problems for the commercial recreation manager. Do the school vacation schedules coincide with the business peak seasons and labor needs? Are there enough employees in the local community, or does a labor force have to be imported? Do the young employees have the maturity, skills, and experience to do an adequate job? Will they burn out by season's end and/or quit early? Many resorts, theme parks, and summer camps face labor shortages in late August and early September when summer employees quit to take two weeks of vacation before returning to school.

There are a number of strategies to help combat these problems:

- Have a higher pay level for returning employees who completed their full season the previous year.
- Have a bonus for employees who complete the full season.
- Hire extra employees to start the season so you have the flexibility to fire those who don't perform up to standards.
- Provide a thorough training program.
- Utilize supervisors who understand and can communicate with the part-time and seasonal employees.
- Diversify the jobs so that the boredom factor is reduced.
- Provide employee housing if labor must be imported from out of state.
- Provide employee transportation if labor must be imported from adjacent communities.
- Provide activity programs for employees in their off-duty hours.
- Plan on "creative scheduling" late in the season when labor is short. Use supervisors and give overtime pay to the best employees remaining.

Unions

In some commercial recreation industries, part of the labor force may be unionized. Managers should be aware of unfair labor practices that are contrary to the National Labor Relations Act (Kohl and Stephens, 1985; Daschler and Ninemeir, 1984). Under this law employers cannot interfere with, restrain, or coerce employees in the exercise of their rights as union members or induce employees to resist unions by offering higher pay, more benefits, or a better job. Neither can an employer allow union membership to influence any personnel decisions including hirings, promotions, and firings. The employer must bargain in good faith with representatives of the employees and provide the union with information it needs to bargain intelligently.

FACILITY MANAGEMENT

Many commercial recreation enterprises have facilities that are worth hundreds of thousands if not millions of dollars. This is particularly true with resort hotels, theme parks, sports clubs, campgrounds, golf and country clubs, and other businesses where the facility is part of the recreation experience. The management of these facilities should therefore be a high priority. This section will examine various aspects of facility management including maintenance, operations, and security, that are of special interest and/or importance in commercial recreation.

Overview of Facility Management

What makes a facility superior, adequate, or inadequate? It basically boils down to two elements (assuming the location is good): design and management. Epperson (1986), Sternloff and Warren (1984), and others have provided several guidelines in this area.

- The facility should be of sufficient size for the people expected to attend and have room for expansion. It is probably less expensive to add on than to relocate.
- The facility should be designed to serve the full needs of the programs and service that will be offered. Too often we see facilities short-changed in storage areas, dressing rooms, sound systems, etc.
- The facility should be designed to be flexible. Use of mobile staging, room dividers, changeable floor surfaces, can increase flexibility.
- The facility should be designed for safety and easy maintenance. This includes provision of fire escapes, sprinkler system, durable furnishings and equipment, choice of floors and floor coverings, types of paint, and access to electrical, plumbing, and other utility systems.
- Facilities should provide the aesthetics and amenities that the participants want. This includes attractive lounges, furnishings, color, and decor; adequate parking, and areas for food and beverage, spectator viewing facilities, and locker rooms.
- Facilities must be maintained in a safe and attractive manner. Participants value safety and cleanliness above most other aspects of their recreation experience.

Facility Maintenance

The ultimate objective of maintenance is to provide a facility that is as close to original condition as possible. This of course is difficult to achieve due to normal wear and tear, participant traffic, and environmental conditions. Realistically then, the objectives should be to:

1. Provide safe, clean, and attractive facilities.

2. Minimize "down time" (unplanned shut downs) of equipment and facilities.
3. Minimize normal deterioration of facilities.
4. Renovate, replace, or rejuvenate facilities when needed.

The importance of good facility maintenance must not be underestimated. Customers will take their business elsewhere if they perceive facilities to be unsafe or unclean compared to competitors. Industry leaders such as Disney have recognized this and made maintenance a keystone of their philosophy.

Unfortunately, some commercial recreation managers and a large number of college students in recreation underestimate the sophistication of modern maintenance. Good maintenance today requires employees who can handle sophisticated equipment, become certified in handling certain chemicals, understand basic landscaping, have fundamental skills in the "trades" (painting, plumbing, carpentry, etc.), be able to supervise seasonal employees, and be competent in public relations.

Due to the importance of safety and public relations, several aspects of maintenance deserve special attention in the commercial recreation setting (Newman, 1980; Veiders, 1979). These practical ideas include the following:

• Schedule major maintenance tasks during off-peak or closed hours so as to minimize conflicts with participants.
• Routine maintenance tasks conducted during operating hours should be performed by staff who have had public relations training.
• Preventive maintenance should be the number one priority, especially for equipment that participants come in contact with, such as amusement park rides, ski lifts, and elevators.
• Maintenance supervisors should not necessarily be the best skilled employees. Rather, they should have an adequate general background in most maintenance areas and be skilled supervisors of employees, including numerous seasonal employees.
• Special care must be taken when closing a facility for the off season. The objective is to protect the facility and make it easy to open again next season. Interiors should be put in order and cleaned, inventory taken, water pipes bled dry, windows and doors secured, etc.

Operating Procedures

Every commercial recreation facility needs a complete set of operating procedures. These procedures could be organized according to physical area (front desk area, retail area, food stands, rides and attractions, etc.), by functional responsibility (cash register operations, food handling, opening and closing, etc.) or a combination of the two. Figure 6-1 illustrates the opening procedures for the guest relations division of an amusement park.

Operating procedures should be written and in some cases illustrated by diagrams or photos. During training sessions, employees should be

Figure 6-1
Guest Relations Opening Checklist

1. Sign in at operations office
2. Turn on lights in guest relations office and ticket booths
3. Take out and raise flags
4. Sweep carpet corners
5. Vacuum floors and stairs
6. Set up toll turnstiles
7. Check daily sales projection to see how many tickets will be needed
8. Check out change drawers and tickets from controllers
9. Set up I.D. camera and laminating machine
10. Record items from previous day's lost and found
11. Log ticket numbers
12. Clean ticket booth windows inside and out
13. Clean tape player heads
14. Turn on background music to proper level
15. Check cashiers into ticket booths
16. Open front gate

provided with copies of all procedures that are relevent for their particular job. The employees may be tested on their knowledge of the procedures and/or be required to acknowledge by signature their understanding of the procedures.

It is advisable to have regular and periodic reviews of all procedures. The input of seasoned employees should be solicited for these reviews, and the employees should also have input on any changes that are made.

Security

The commercial recreation manager must recognize the importance of security. Substantial losses and lawsuits can occur if there are problems with guest safety, guest security, and/or security of financial operations. General areas of concern include crowd control and safety, emergency procedures, and facility security. Each topic may warrant extensive written procedures and training of employees. Professional consultants are available to help develop security procedures and to provide security service on a contractual basis.

Crowd control procedures are essential at amusement parks, sports events, concerts, or any other event that draws a large number of people. Some specific suggestions for crowd control include the following (*Managing The Leisure Facility*, 1979):

- Know your facilty—it's capacity, traffic bottlenecks, emergency exits, etc.
- Have special entrances for groups.
- Be ready for special group problems such as preschoolers, handi-capped, aged, foreign visitors, etc.
- Monitor sales to avoid overselling the facility.
- If sold out, station people out front to tell patrons.

- Have special parking areas for buses.
- Channel vehicle traffic in one direction.
- Have attendants in the parking lots at all times.
- Be prepared for emergencies and disasters.
- Use "peer group" security staff to monitor crowds.
- Have security staff trained in nonconfrontational public relations.
- Resort to police intervention only when a situation is beyond the control of the security staff.
- Check all areas after closing, including every corner and every restroom stall.

Emergency Procedures should be developed for all possible problem scenarios and rehearsed on a periodic basis. In some cases, proper preparation may require a large expense. A major stadium concert, for example, may require a staff of 100 EMT's, nurses, and doctors plus a couple of ambulances on duty. Some cities have volunteer organizations to assist in these functions. Specific emergency procedures should be developed for fire, serious illness or injury to a guest, disappearance of a guest, power failure, severe weather, natural disaster, vandalism, bomb threats, and terrorist activities. Procedures for all of these should be coordinated with appropriate authorities such as police, hospitals, fire departments, and civil defense.

Facility Security has benefited from a number of technical innovations in the last 10 to 15 years. Communication between staff has been greatly improved by the use of walkie talkies and pagers. Closed-circuit TVs can be used to monitor entrances, hallways, vaults, ticket booths, or any other important area. Microwave and infrared intrusion sensing systems provide "night eyes" to guard against trespassers. Photo I.D. cards help identify staff and can be used for season pass holders. In many situations, however, facility security is best accomplished by employees stationed in key areas. It is also a good idea to keep facilities attractive and well maintained. Such facilities are more likely to be appreciated and are less likely to be abused. Night lighting also may reduce trespassing and vandalism. If facilities or equipment are vandalized, they should be repaired immediately.

MARKETING AND PROMOTION

Marketing is the collective process that moves goods and services from the producer to the consumer. If a company has a market orientation, everything in the organization is oriented to the market place. Products and services will be developed based upon a knowledge of what the customer wants, how much they are willing to pay, and how they want it provided. By following a market orientation, the company should be able to keep current with customer desires and therefore be a valued provider of products/services.

The opposite side of the coin is product orientation. Here, the company decides what it can do best and most effectively, develops its products/services on that criteria, and then strives to sell it to the public.

The danger with this approach is that the company could develop an efficient product/service that is completely unwanted by the public.

A company that has a market orientation must have a marketing strategy. Bank of America (1986) has suggested the following marketing strategy for small businesses:

1. Expand Your Market Knowledge—through library research, customer surveys, business community information, and data from industry associations.
2. Carve Out Your Niche—by identifying the market segments and defining your target market.
3. Set Promotional Objectives—by developing your message, communicating the message, create awareness of products/services, and motivating customers to buy.

Many aspects of this marketing strategy have been previously discussed in Chapter 4. Market research, demand projections, competition analysis, market segmentation, market concept, and market positioning were among those topics. This section will concentrate on the promotional aspects of marketing.

Promotion of Products and Services

Most traditional marketing literature addresses the marketing of products. There are differences however, when it comes to marketing services or intangible products (Renaghan, 1981; Levitt, 1981).

- Services are intangible.—They cannot be tried out, tested, experienced, or held. Customers can swing a tennis racquet, test drive an R.V., or check the stitching in a baseball glove. We can only look at pictures of surrogates engaged in a service or listen to their comments about the activity.
- Services are produced and consumed simultaneously.—This makes location paramount and limits the choice of alternatives.
- Services are highly perishable.—An unsold airline seat, hotel room, or tennis court hour represents revenue lost forever. Unsold running shoes can be marked down and still sold for profit.
- Service quality can be highly variable.—Room service staff, aerobics instructors and tour guides have good days and bad days. Quality of a service is much more difficult to control than the quality of a mass produced product.
- Services are easily duplicated.—This allows competitors to copy a service faster, and there are fewer barriers to entering a service market.
- There is greater consumer risk with services.—Due to the aforementioned problems with services it may be more difficult to convince a customer to commit to a large expenditure for a service.

Making Intangible Products/Services Seem Tangible. If an intangible product or service can be made to seem more tangible, it can improve sales. There are a number of ways to make this occur (Levitt, 1981). Customers can be offered trial memberships or special prices for first-time visitors. Advertising can feature the endorsement of a respected celebrity. There can be tangible evidence provided to prove a service was completed, such as a sanitized paper band across hotel room toilet seats. Also, the customer can be guaranteed satisfaction with a money-back promise. Finally, there can be post-purchase reinforcements such as newsletters and free services.

Constructing The Message

A good product/service and accurate market research will be wasted if the promotional message is not communicated to the target audience. Ask yourself the following questions about your promotions. Are they visually unattractive or confusing to listen to? Are they the same advertisements or promotions you have had for years? Do they fail to inform customers about the benefits the product/service can provide? Do they fail to motivate the customer? If so, then it might be beneficial to try some of the promotional guidelines and visual communication tips listed below (Samuals, 1983; Harrison, 1983; Kelly, 1985; Bullaro and Edgington, 1986).

- Know your media—their target market, deadlines, etc.
- Use first class promotions to demonstrate quality.
- Do not clutter a promotion with too many ideas.
- Create a unique image and spotlight unique differences.
- Have attention-getting slogans with vivid action verbs.
- Stress "value," "benefit," "quality," and "investment," not "cost," or "price."
- Avoid long sentences and long paragraphs in written materials.
- Sell the benefits that are important to the target market.
- Illustrations should be able to stand on their own merits.
- Have a distinctive logo that communicates your market concept.
- Have consistency in all communications that use the company name, logo or slogan—letterheads, envelopes, advertisements, brochures, signs, direct mail, etc.
- Remember that color contrasts get attention, earth tones invite involvement.
- Use facts instead of generalizations.
- Alleviate anxiety about new products or strange places.
- Try provocative new ideas.
- Try more direct contact—displays in malls, presentations, etc.
- Try stunts and gimmicks—specialty advertising (t-shirts, pens), special events, celebrities, contests, price promotions.
- Don't waste words, keep it simple and direct.
- Mention the product/service as often as is feasible.
- Remember that bargains and "free" still get attention.
- Call for action at the end—tell where to buy it.

Promotional Strategies

There are four basic types of promotional strategy: advertising, promotional events, publicity, and personal selling.

Advertising—the nonpersonal presentation of ideas, product, or services using paid mass communication methods. Advertising objectives are to gain exposure, create need awareness, and stress brand superiority.

Promotional Events—special activities that stimulate consumer awareness and purchasing. Examples are race sponsorships, contests, open houses, entertainment programs, etc.

Publicity—the nonpaid significant news about a company, its products, or its services. Newspaper feature stories often highlight a new resort, a product innovation, or a unique service or individual.

Personal Selling—personal assistance and persuasion of a prospect to buy a product or service. It is important to "fine tune" the presentation of the product/service to customers needs.

Figure 6-2 illustrates the use of numerous specific types of promotion by different recreation industries. Note that no singular type of promotion is the prominent choice in every industry. This is because each type of promotion has its own advantages and disadvantages. The best choice depends upon the industry, the community, the market, available resources, and other factors. The remainder of this section examines a variety of specific promotional tools, primarily types of advertising (Bank of America, 1986).

Figure 6-2
Types of Promotion in Commercial Recreation

Type of Promotion	Percent Use By Type Industry							
	Golf & Country Clubs	Resort Hotels & Motels	Racquet-ball & Tennis Clubs	Multi-Purpose Athletic Club	Camp-grounds	Sport & Recreation Camps	Theme & Amuse-ment Parks	Stadiums Arenas,& Tracks
Telemarketing	0%	3%	10%	9%	2%	9%	14%	5%
Direct Mail	24	73	60	70	45	72	46	44
Radio Ads	24	27	23	46	18	26	57	44
TV Ads	7	0	15	12	3	19	35	39
Yellow Page Ads	59	67	55	73	51	40	46	18
Family Discounts	20	27	25	52	21	32	60	33
Group Discounts	13	42	38	70	8	15	46	26
Introductory Rate	15	9	40	49	5	11	0	3
Free Intro Use	13	9	40	49	7	8	11	3
Tours	2	30	15	70	9	32	22	10
Newsletter	17	36	65	85	23	74	3	39
Sales Force	7	27	27	49	6	13	27	18

Source: Anderson (1985).

Newspapers are one of the most widely used advertising media, reaching 90 percent of homes in some communities. Ads can present as much information as you want and can be targeted for sections of the paper read by certain target markets. There can be editions for specific geographic zones and inserts for special interest. Other advantages of newspapers include broad consumer acceptance, no limits on the amount of information presented, and short deadlines for submission of ads. Disadvantages include short life of advertisements, a small "pass-along" audience (additional people who read one copy), and the risk that your message can get lost in the clutter of numerous ads.

Television is the glamour advertising media, and most Americans watch several hours of TV a day. Television offers an effective combination of sight and sound that can show motion and close-ups. There is also favorable consumer reaction to good TV ads, which can be targeted by the type of program. However, TV provides only a fleeting impression, amid much commercial clutter and at a very high cost.

Radio is a very popular choice for local businesses. Each local station has a particular format and attracts a specific audience. Almost everyone has at least one radio, and ads can be targeted on the basis of a station's format. Ads can reach people in vehicles, and there is relatively low cost for local coverage. In addition, radio ads can be produced quickly. The disadvantage of radio is that it provides a fleeting message of one dimensional nature. Another disadvantage is that radio ads allow only a limited time to get the message across.

Magazines have diversified in recent years to include a wide variety of special interest publications, which allow ads to be targeted to very special audiences. Numerous national publications have demographic and geographic editions that allow further specialized targeting of ads. Also, magazines have high pass-along rates and can include features such as tear-out pages and coupons. Unfortunately, there is a long lead time to produce magazine ads, and high cost is involved in most cases. As with many mass media ads, the message may be lost in the clutter of other ads.

Outdoor Advertising includes roadside billboards and advertisements on busses. There is great flexibility to put colorful and eye catching ads where and when you want. Outdoor ads also provide repeat exposure, especially for commuters. A disadvantage is the creative limitation. There is time for only one picture, one idea. Another problem is the recent environmental attack on billboards, restricting their use in some areas.

Direct Mail is specific correspondence with individuals, usually persons on a targeted mailing list. Bulk or junk mail to "occupant" is not considered here. Direct mail can be very selectively targeted, depending upon the mailing list. There are no limits to space and format, and no distractions when the reader opens it. In spite of the poor reputation of direct mail, the fact is that most direct mail is read if it is personally addressed and properly targeted. There is however, difficulty in obtaining and maintaining a good mailing list. In addition, high creative skill is needed to create readership of the entire mailing, and there is a high cost to reach a large audience.

Point of Purchase Displays are displays positioned at check-in counters, cash register lines, and so on. Such displays can trigger impulse buying and may evoke the feeling that an item is on sale. However, only a limited number of these are practical to have at one time and they should be changed often.

Yellow Page Ads are almost essential for many types of retail businesses: sporting goods stores, high quality restaurants and hotels, and so on. The yellow pages are heavily used by people, especially newcomers and tourists. Obviously though, there is limited space to communicate the message, which is further limited by its one dimensional nature.

Telemarketing has become a popular way to reach consumers and other product/service suppliers. If a good prospect list can be obtained, telemarketing can be low cost and effective. There is, however, low receptivity to indiscriminant calls. In addition, a telemarketing campaign needs a good script and well trained callers.

Posters and Flyers are often used for local events, sales, concerts, and so on. They are low cost, can be distributed widely, and can be quickly produced. Disadvantages of posters and flyers include their short life and tendency to be regarded as litter.

Budgeting For Promotion

How do you determine how much money to spend for promotion? There are several approaches, but none is necessarily the best way. It is fairly common, however, to spend more money to promote a new business than to promote an established business that has a loyal clientele. Budgeting methods include the following (Bank of America, 1986):

All You Can Afford Approach is a simple method wherein you spend more money for advertising when business is good, and cut back when business is bad. The problem is that spending a lot more may not increase sales much. Even worse, in tough times can you afford to go without advertising?

Keep Up With The Competition Approach is a reactive strategy whereby you spend as much as your competition does. Unfortunately, you may not be able to afford to keep up.

Percentage of Sales Approach is a popular way to figure a budget and achieve parity with an industry norm. Most businesses spend about 5 to 10 percent of their projected revenue for marketing. This approach however, is like the proverbial chicken/egg question. Do you get more sales because you spend more on advertising or do you have more to spend on advertising because of increased sales?

Cost and Objective Approach is more complicated than other methods. The manager first sets specific objectives for *reach* and *frequency* of the promotion. *Reach* is the number of target consumers exposed to the promotion. *Frequency* is the number of times the average target consumer is reached. Next, the various promotional alternatives are analyzed and priced to determine which method will accomplish the objectives in the most cost effective manner. A problem with this approach is that many managers plan their objectives too optimistically and then cannot afford to achieve them.

A combination of the four approaches might be most practical: Keep an eye on the competition and set a budget that is within an affordable range of the percent of sales approach. Then utilize the cost and objective approach to determine which promotional tool (or combination of tools) will be most cost effective.

Cooperative Advertising has become a popular method in recent years to get more advertising for the dollar (Delano, 1983). In cooperative ads, two or more companies seeking to reach the same target market combine their efforts. For example, upscale ski resorts Vail and Beaver Creek combined with American Express to promote the 1987 American Ski Classic race series. Further, individual races within the series were sponsored by Rolex, Ford, and Subaru.

Marketing For Group Business

Groups represent a major source of revenue for many types of commercial recreation. Theme parks, resorts, airlines, cruise ships, bus tour lines, white water rafting companies, convention centers, and town wholesalers are among the businesses that count heavily on group sales. It is very common for such businesses to employ one or more group sales coordinators. These employees typically work on a commission basis or salary plus commission.

Some commercial recreation businesses such as theme and amusement parks seek group sales but prefer that it not exceed 25-30 percent of gate revenue. This is because too much group discounting can undermine the integrity of the basic price structure.

Some of the most common types of group discount methods are presented next (Opsata, 1979; *Managing The Leisure Facility*, 1982).

Regular Group Discounts are the foundation of group sales. Small groups of friends, family reunions, scout groups, singles clubs, day camps, and other groups prearrange to attend a recreation attraction on a specific day. In return, the groups are given discounts ranging from half a dollar to half price. There is always a minimum number of participants required to qualify for the discount. Minimums are typically 15, 20, or 25.

Industrial Group Discounts are provided to company employee groups. The minimum might be higher (50 to 100), but the discounts are usually deeper than for the regular groups.

Consignment Tickets are commonly issued to large companies, college student unions, military bases, or other major organizations. A set of prenumbered tickets are issued to the organization with the written agreement that they will be sold at a certain price or returned by a certain date. Some organizations take a small percentage of the sales price in order to cover their cost of staffing the ticket outlets. Figure 6-3 illustrates a typical consignment ticket agreement for a hypothetical tourist attraction.

Discount Cards are prenumbered cards issued to individuals in an organization. The individual receives a predetermined discount whenever they present the card at the ticket window of the given attraction.

Group Buyouts are also called group parties, group exclusives, or charters. In any case, a group contracts for the exclusive use of a recreation facility or transporation carrier (plane, bus, etc.). This of course has to be scheduled to avoid conflict with regular users. The minimum number of participants for a buyout may be quite substantial; for example, 1000 persons in the case of a water theme park. Sometimes two or more groups are allowed to combine their numbers to have enough participation to meet the minimum number.

Cooperative Packages can be developed between two or more noncompetitive businesses. Individuals or groups buying into one facility or service are given a discount for a second attraction. An example would be a tour operator who puts together an attractively priced group package that includes transportation, hotel accommodations, and admission to a sports event, worlds fair, expo or other special event.

Group Sales Management Tips. A variety of good ideas have been suggested (Opsata, 1979; *Managing the Leisure Facility*, 1982) that make group sales more effective.

- Try to get group business for off-peak periods when you need the volume most.
- Try to get up-front payment or at least a deposit. This may be relaxed for proven groups that have been reliable clients.
- Have a well organized mailing list of all prospect groups in your area with over 100 members.
- Promote group rates at least six weeks before the season opening.
- As soon as a group order comes in, assign them the best unsold seats (or rooms) available at that time (within the given rate structure).
- Check back with the group to confirm their attendance.
- Provide tickets to the group leader in advance by personal delivery, insured mail, or alone at the facility entrance/ticket window. Group members should wait in a designated area away from the entrance congestion.
- Groups should utilize a separate entrance if available.
- Make the group feel welcome by announcing their presence, providing a personal greeting, or even surprising them with special programs, refreshments, meal discount coupons, etc.
- Contact the group after their visit to make sure everything went well.

OTHER ASPECTS OF MANAGEMENT

Three additional aspects of management deserve attention before this chapter is concluded. Those topics are risk management, guest relations, and computer use.

140

Figure 6-3
CONSIGNMENT AGREEMENT

NO. 040

The Seminole Sports Hall of Fame (SSHF), subject to the terms and conditions hereof, agrees to consign to _____

(consignee, company name)

_____adult tickets to SSHF
_____child tickets to SSHF

from _____ to _____

1. The consignee agrees to remit on or prior to _____ (final settlement data) to SSHF $_____ per adult ticket, $_____ per children's ticket unreturned on or prior to final settlement date (less any payments made on interim dates).

2. On reorder (interim payment dates) consignee agrees to remit to SSHF $_____ per adult ticket, $_____ per children's ticket for each sold to date.

3. Should consignee fail to meet any of the interim payments, SSHF may, at its option, cancel this agreement by written notice to consignee and, in such event, consignee shall immediately deliver all tickets in its possession to SSHF and/or its authorized representative. All funds due for tickets unreturned shall be immediately payable in accordance with the above schedule upon demand.

4. Consignee assumes full responsibility for tickets received and agrees to pay SSHF (upon final settlement date, unless prior arrangements have been made) in accordance with the prices set forth herein for tickets unreturned regardless of reason for said nonreturn and agrees to reimburse SSHF for all legal fees and court costs relevant to the execution of this consignment agreement dated _____.

5. All payments due hereunder are to be paid by check payable to the Seminole Sports Hall of Fame to an authorized representative of the Seminole Sports Hall of Fame or forwarded to the attention of Accounting, 401 East Tait Drive, Tallahassee, Florida. All payments must refer to the document number at the top of this agreement or a copy of this agreement may be returned with the payment.

_____   _____
Representative of SSHF   Representative of Consignee (date)

_____   _____
Title   Title

_____   _____
Date   Company Name

                                     _____
                                     Address

                                     _____
                                     City   State   Zip

Risk Management

There is some evidence that the liability and insurance crisis that plagues the country has at last moderated a little. After receiving tens of thousands of formal complaints, numerous states have passed legislation affecting lawsuits. By 1987, about 20 states had adopted reform in varying degrees: by putting limits on awards, by creating stricter definitions of "pain and suffering," by limiting "joint and several liability" damages (wherein a wealthy "deep pockets" company pays the majority of a liability claim even though they were found to be less at fault than another defendent in the case), by imposing penalties for filing frivolous suits, and by setting limits on contingency fees. A number of states have also adopted a new legal ethics code, endorsed by the American Bar Association (Jensen, 1987; Shapiro, 1987).

There is still, however, a tremendous need for commercial recreation managers to develop a risk management plan. Such a plan has three major components.

1. Identify All Risks—This can be accomplished by analysis of past accident records, through facility and program inspection, and by staff input. Also, risk specialists from most insurance companies provide this service.
2. Analyze Every Risk—Analyze and classify every risk according to the Risk Management Strategy Grid presented in Figure 6-4. Each risk is classified according to its frequency of occurance and severity of injury when it does occur. It is important to note that some organizations will be very conservative at this step because of their service philosophy, their past history, and their insurance rates.
3. Implement Risk Strategies—According to frequency and severity, different action is suggested by the Risk Management Strategy Grid. Each quadrant is discussed below.

Lower Risk/Acceptance. Certain accidents happen infrequently and with minor injury. For example, a participant might cut a finger on a piece of paper in an arts and crafts class. Such injuries are very difficult to anticipate or prevent. Many organizations and their participants accept these minor risks as a natural part of engaging in the activity. Typically, the cost of any such accident falls below the deductible limits of the organization's insurance policy. Therefore, if there is any expense involved, it is picked up directly by the organization or by the participant.

Moderate Risk/Insurance. On rare occasions, there are accidents with major injury and/or property loss. Usually their occurances are also very difficult to anticipate or prevent. An example would be a hotel fire caused by an angered employee or guest. In such instances, adequate insurance coverage is the best remedy. Although rates are very high, insurance purchased through major carriers is the most common approach. Some organizations are joining together with peer organizations and contributing to cooperative insurance pools to collectively insure themselves.

Figure 6-4
Risk Management Strategy Grid

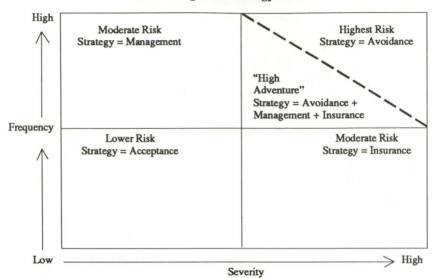

Adapted From Nilson and Edginton (1982).

Moderate Risk/Management. There are many recreation activities in which minor injuries are relatively common: slipping on the deck of a water theme park, sprained ankles and broken bones in sports competition, and so on. While insurance is advised to back up the organization in these instances, the best strategy is to manage the activity better. This means providing safety conscious supervisors for age group competition, and training lifeguards to prevent situations where injury may occure. A number of other management guidelines are present in Figure 6-5.

Highest Risk/Avoidance. There are some recreation activities that have relatively frequent accidents, with rather severe consequences. Examples include competitive boxing, ski-jumping, and hang gliding. Some conservative managers also put rugby, tackle football, sky diving, backcountry skiing, scuba diving and other popular activities into the high risk category. The best strategy for highest risk activities is to avoid offering them to the public. Some organizations, however, specialize in these activities: Helicopter Ski Tours, Wilderness Challenge Schools, Amazon Jungle Tours, and others. These providers of high risk/high adventure recreation must combine the strategies of management, insurance, and avoidance. For example, the skydiving service operator must be well insured, extremely professional in all aspects of the operation, and avoid going up during marginal weather conditions.

Guest Services/Relations

There is an area of management that may involve many of the specializations of facility maintenance, marketing, and financial man-

Figure 6-5
Risk Management Guidelines

General Guidelines

1. Have clear objectives
2. Corporate charter, by-laws, etc., must be up to date with all legal regulations.
3. Review the security of office files and safe.
4. Have all contracts in writing.
5. Do not advertise facilities, equipment, personnel, or programs you cannot provide.
6. Have a public information officer to be the spokesperson regarding any accidents.
7. Develop safety policies and procedures.
8. Practice emergency procedures.
9. Conduct analysis of all accidents.
10. Provide notice and/or post signs regarding any hazards or damages involving facilities, equipment, or programs.
11. Adhere to advertised time schedules for facilities and programs.
12. Provide transportation of participants only by insured qualified operators with chauffeurs licensing using appropriate, insured vehicles.

Personnel Guidelines—for employees and volunteers

1. Carefully screen all applicants.
2. Provide appropriate orientation and training.
3. Be sure staff have appropriate licenses, certificates, or other requirements for the work.
4. Monitor job performances.
5. Do not go beyond the scope of the job.
6. Provide emergency training to all staff.
7. Staff should not make reckless statements regarding accidents.
8. Never tell participants not to seek medical attention.
9. Keep supervisors informed of any problem.
10. Staff must stay active in the profession and up to date in competency areas.

Facility and Equipment Guidelines

1. Facilities should comply with all design standards.
2. Use only approved equipment that meets all appropriate industry standards.
3. Avoid using unsafe and/or damaged equipment.
4. Have proper security systems, especially smoke detectors, fire alarms, and sprinklers, etc.
5. Provide security and lighting for parking area.
6. Inspect facilities and equipment regularly.
7. Perform preventive maintenance in accordance with standards.
8. Repair damaged facilities/equipment immediately or remove them from service.
9. Train employees regarding proper use of all equipment.
10. Restrict the use of hazardous facilities and equipment (guns, horses, chainsaws, boats, etc.) to employees with proper training.
11. Know facility capacities and avoid overcrowding.
12. Have appropriate emergency equipment available.
13. Post emergency numbers by telephone.

Figure 6-5 (cont.)

Program Guidelines

1. Be sure that leaders have proper qualifications.
2. Design programs for safety—use buddy system, rest periods, etc.
3. Instruct participants in safety practices.
4. Keep activities within the ability of participants.
5. Adhere to proper ratios of staff to participants.
6. Comply with recognized program standards, procedures, rules, etc.
7. Instruct participants in program skills prior to their participation.
8. Know the health status of participants when appropriate to activity.
9. Have consent forms and release forms for participants.
10. Monitor activities including warm-ups.
11. Strive to match competitors and provide balanced team competition.
12. Participants should be placed in appropriate age group, ability level, or weight class in competitive activities.
13. Provide equipment and clothing lists for trip participants.

Special Guidelines for Release Forms

1. Realize that release forms do not absolve you from liability.
2. Explain all potential hazards and risks.
3. Explain participation procedures, rules, etc.
4. Participation in the activity should be voluntary.
5. Urge participants to purchase insurance.
6. Participants should be aware that they cannot collect damages if they sign consent. (Note: This may not hold up in court, however).
7. Information must be in conspicuous print so that the participant has fair notice of what they are signing.

---

agement. This middle ground is guest services and guest relations. Depending upon the type of commercial recreation business, guest services/relations may include any of the following functions:

Switchboard Operation	Reservations
Message Service	Room Service
Customer Complaint Department	Valet Service
Gift/Package Wrapping	Coat Check
Shuttle/Transportation	Greeters
Day Care Program	Information Service
Lost and Found	First Aid Station

Some commercial recreation businesses are large enough to have separate staff for each of these functions or a combination of two or three. Some organizations such as hotels may place several of these responsibilities under the auspices of the concierge service. The expanding rule of the concierge service is examined in greater detail in the next chapter. One particular task that guest relations staff (and all other employees to some degree) must be competent in is the fine art of handling guest/customer complaints. Figure 6-6 provides some general guidelines for handling complaints.

Figure 6-6
Checklist for Handling Guest/Customer Complaints

1. Identify yourself and your position.
2. Listen to the guests problem without interrupting.Allowing them to let off steam helps diffuse the situation.
3. Do not treat the problem as insignificant.Do not say "No Problem" when you mean to say "We can take care of that."
4. Be an understanding and pleasant recipient of their comments.You do not have to agree with everything.
5. Apologize for any inconveniences, dissatisfaction, or discomfort the guest has experienced.
6. Evaluate the problem and explain the proper policy or procedure to the guest.
7. Tell the guest what can be done, not what can't be done.
8. Invite the guest to choose between some logical and helpful alternatives.
9. Never talk down to a guest or make them feel stupid.
10. Try to use the customer's name in your conversation.
11. Let the guest see you record their complaints, especially if it needs to be referred to higher management.
12. If the guest is not satisfied, serve as their link to higher management, and present the guest (and their problem) with due dignity.
13. If you are the higher management, again present alternatives (room change, merchandise exchange, refund, etc.) and let the guest choose.
14. Invite the customer to call back regarding the resolution of the problem, or in some instances, initiate the follow-up contact yourself.
15. If the guest becomes abusive or physically belligerent, summon authorities who are trained and equipped to handle such problems.

Computer Use

There is little doubt that computers have been the most important innovation in management in recent years. Any aspect of management that is data based can probably be accomplished more efficiently through computer use. Specifically, the computer has three benefits: (1) it can store large amounts of information and access it quickly, (2) it can sort that information by any criteria defined, and (3) it can make logical decisions based on mathematic calculations and prescribed instructions (Bullaro and Edginton, 1986). Although the original investment in computers is very significant, the payback can be tremendous. It is not unusual for a commercial recreation business to save 30 percent of its labor cost for the business office because of computer efficiencies. Similar savings have been found when computers are used to control a facility's heating, cooling, and lighting (Patterson, 1981).

It is likely and recommended that every student and future manager take a course or two in the use of computers. Therefore, this section will not duplicate the standard material regarding computer technology and use. Instead, this section will concentrate on expanding the perspective of the many potential uses of a computer system.

It should be remembered that a computer system that is used for only a few functions is probably wasted. Every dollar saved through computer efficiencies may translate into an extra dollar of profit for the company. Presented below is a categorization of many of the potential computer uses (Cassell, 1986; Bullaro and Edginton, 1986; Patterson, 1981).

Accounting and Financial Functions—payroll, accounts payable, accounts receivable, general ledger, financial statements, ratio analysis, breakeven analysis, sales and cash flow forecasts, budgeting, material and labor forecasts, profit sharing tabulations.

Sales and Inventory Functions—register sales, inventory tracking and control, inventory valuation, status of ordered merchandise.

Marketing Functions—mailing lists, target market profiles, market analysis and demand forecasts, ticket printing, ticket/seating inventory, reservations, storage and access of press releases and advertising copy.

Program Management—team roster maintenance, program registration, league and tournament scheduling, membership list maintenance, tour scheduling, class and facility scheduling, progress reports for individual fitness programs.

Graphic Programs—headlines, clip art, original art, bar graphs, line graphs, pie charts, color features, shading.

Word Processing—upgraded office typewriter functions to add or delete material, spelling and grammar corrections, letter production from mailing lists.

Personnel Administration Functions—employee records, benefit calculation, absence and leave records, accidents, insurance claims, keys and property check-out records, employee orientation material, employee training programs.

Environmental Management—programs to control heating, cooling, lights, irrigation, pool chemicals, facility special effects.

Maintenance Management—inspection records, preventive maintenance records, preventive maintenance requirements, work-order tracking and tabulation, material and labor forecasts, project scheduling, project progress reports.

SUMMARY

Successful operations management relies heavily upon sound administrative practices in the areas of personnel, facilities, and marketing. Personnel management takes into account the hiring, training, and compensation of staff, the development of staff morale, the handling of part-time and seasonal labor, and interaction with unions. Facility management deals with maintenance, development of sound operating procedures, security, safety, and accident prevention.

Marketing and promotional efforts may utilize numerous means to get the product/service message to the consumer. Promotional strategies include advertising, promotional events, publicity, and personal selling. A myriad of means are available to create quality promotional efforts such as use of news and broadcast media, magazines, direct mail, point of purchase displays, and outdoor advertising.

Every commercial recreation enterprise can benefit from a comprehensive risk management program that includes insurance, preventive management, and if necessary, avoidance of certain activities. Another area of importance for any company is guest services/relations, which may take many forms depending upon the type of product/service involved. Finally, computer technology can help any company manage its operations more efficiently, especially in the area of accounting, inventory, marketing, word processing, and maintenance.

STUDY QUESTIONS

1. How does the use of a large number of part-time and seasonal labor affect the personnel management function of a commercial recreation business?
2. How can a company encourage repeat business on the part of the consumers.
3. What are four key objectives of a well-maintained facility?
4. Describe key aspects of ensuring that commercial recreation facilities are secure.
5. Describe how the marketing mix for products and services differ.
6. What are the strengths and weaknesses of five promotional strategies in commercial recreation.

PROJECT IDEAS

1. Visit a commercial recreation facility in your home town or campus. Assess the facility in terms of its maintenance standards, security, and apparent risk management procedures.
2. Collect several types of promotional literature from a commercial recreation business of your choice. How effective is the promotional literature in attracting you to the product or service described? Why or why not?

148

SPOTLIGHT ON: La Costa Resort Facility Renovation

Founded by owners who recognize top quality and want the best for their guests, La Costa Resort has always been considered a showpiece of exclusive resort spas. La Costa is a top choice among those wealthy enough to involve themselves in the most luxurious of vacations or health retreats. Maintaining this image was the purpose of a recent $100 million renovation of the La Costa facilities. The entire resort received a major facelift, transforming it from the brightly colored rooms popular in the 1960s to the more subtle pastels tones of contemporary times. While the layout did not change much, the number of rooms increased from 250 to 482, according to Kim Marshall, Public Relations Director for La Costa. The facility added a seventh restaurant offering the finest cuisine available and updated the menu at its six other restaurants. In addition, in order to attract the business convention market, a 50,000-square-foot meeting room facility was constructed.

Renovation of the facility was just part of the contemporary upgrading needed to continue to attract the $100,000-a-year-income client. A new program, Lifestyle Education, features a full-service wellness screening that includes analysis of nutrition, body fat composition, aerobic capacity and other factors. The program also includes a prescription for an improved lifestyle.

Marketing for the new facility has undergone major changes, also.

International markets such as Japan have been approached as have a younger segment of Americans. The young affluent market is being courted with recreation amenities that include two golf courses, a movie theater, swimming pools, a full-service spa program, 25 tennis courts, and excellent cuisine. Business clientele come to La Costa for the state-of-the-art technology in meeting rooms and amenities offered during conferences.

Marshall states that guests at La Costa appreciate the facility renovations, but are quick to note that the staff service is what makes La Costa successful. There is a ratio of three employees for each guest, and every employee is an expert at gracious service.

La Costa owners formerly managed the Desert Inn and Stardust Inn in Las Vegas and introduced the concept of the Lido stage to La Costa. The upbeat stage entertainment provides guests with a unique experience—top notch entertainment at a health spa resort. Another owner was the CEO of Lorimar Motion Pictures and brings current movies to La Costa for viewers. The commitment of the owners to the quality of the operation is what allows La Costa to enjoy a reputation untouched by other resorts.

Sources: Marshall (1987); *California Business* (1984).

REFERENCES

Anderson, B. (editor). *Managed Recreation Research Report.* Minneapolis; Lakewood Publications, 1985, 1986, and 1987.

Bank of America. *Marketing Small Business.* San Francisco: 1986.

Bullaro, J. and Edginton, C. *Commercial Leisure Services.* New York: Macmillan Publishing Company, 1986.

California Business. "$50 Million Renovation Updates La Costa's Image." October, 1984, pp. 177-181.

Cassell, D. "Retail: Profiting By The Numbers." *Fitness Management,* November/December, 1986, pp. 26;51.

Daschler, J., and Ninemeir, J. *Supervision in the Hospitality Industry.* East Lansing, Michigan: Educational Institute of the American Hotel and Motel Association, 1984.

Delano, S. "How To Get A Fix On Free Ad Dollars." *INC,* July 1983. pp. 94-96.

Drucker, P. *Innovation and Entrepreneurship.* New York: Harper & Row Publishers, 1985.

Epperson, A. *Private and Commercial Recreation: A Text and Reference.* New York: John Wiley & Sons, 1977.

Epperson, A. *Private and Commercial Recreation.* State College, Pennsylvania: Venture Publishing, Inc., 1986.

Feld, L. "Watch Out For The Minimum Wage Pitfalls." *Managing the Leisure Facility,* January, 1981, pp. 14-15.

Harrison, D. "Promotion Through Communication." Presentation at the Southwest Regional Conference of the National Employee Services and Recreation Association, Dallas, Texas, October, 1983.

Howard, D. and, Crompton, J. *Financing, Managing and Marketing Recreation and Park Resources.* Dubuque, Iowa: Wm. C. Brown Company, 1980.

Hurst, M. "Put A Wiggle In Your Walk." Presentation at the Annual Congress of the National Recreation and Park Association, Miami, Florida, October 1977.

Jensen, M. (editor). "Liability Insurance Crisis Scenario Similar to Oil Crisis?" *Recreation Executive Report,* February, 1987, p. 4.

Kelly, J. *Recreation Business.* New York: John Wiley and Sons, 1985.

Kohl, J., and Stephens, D. "On Strike: Legal Developments in Labor Management Relations." *The Cornell Hotel and Restaurant Administration Quarterly,* February, 1985, pp. 71-75.

Lee, E. "Back to Basics: A Primer on Security." *Managing the Leisure Facility,* May/June, 1979, pp. 32-36.

Levitt, T. "Marketing Intangible Products and Product Intangibles." *The Cornell Hotel and Restaurant Administration Quarterly,* August, 1981, pp. 37-44.

Managing the Leisure Facility. "Special Events Need Special Crowd Control." September/October, 1979, p. 6.

Managing The Leisure Facility. "Going After Group Business." February, 1982, pp. 22-23.

Marshal, K. Public Relations Director, La Costa Resort, California. Personal Interview, August, 1987.

McKenzie, B. "Repeat Business--New Dealing For Dollars." *Recreation, Sports, and Leisure,* July, 1983, pp. 10-14.

Mintzberg, H. "The Managers Job: Folklore and Fact," in *Perspectives on Management* (5th Edition), by J. Donnelly, J. Gibson, and J. Ivancevich. Plano, Texas: Business Publications, Inc., 1984.

Newman, R. "Is Your Maintenance Costing You Too Much?" *Managing the Leisure Facility,* January/February, 1980, pp. 5-8.

Nilson, R. and Edginton, C. "Risk Management" A Tool for Park and Recreation Administrators." *Parks and Recreation,* August, 1982, pp. 34-37.

Opsata, M. "Test Your Box Office Savvy; It May Need Sharpening." *Managing the Leisure Facility,* July/August, 1979, pp. 18-27.

Patterson, D. "Computers Cut Attrax Costs." *Managing the Leisure Facility,* February, 1981, pp. 22-23.

Renaghan, L. "A New Marketing Mix For The Hospitality Industry." *The Cornell Hotel and Restaurant Administration Quarterly,* August, 1981, pp. 31- 35.

Samuals, J. "Strategies For Improved Marketing: Cash In On Success In The 1980's." *Recreation Sports and Leisure,* July, 1983, pp. 7; 15-17.

Shapiro, R. "Tomorrow." *U.S. News and World Report,* March 2, 1987, p. 27.

Sternloff, R., and Warren, R. *Park and Recreation Maintenance Management* (2nd Edition). New York: John Wiley & Sons, 1984.

U.S. Department of Labor. *The Fair Labor Standards Act of 1938,* As Amended. Washington, D.C., 1984.

Veiders, T. "Park Clean-up Rated A Must By Top Park Management." *Managing The Leisure Facility,* January/February, 1979, pp. 12-16.

Chapter 7

COMMERCIAL RECREATION PROGRAMMING

Traditionally, university recreation curricula prepared students to become activity leaders, program supervisors, and administrators of governmental and nonprofit community recreation agencies. Students traditionally received an activity skill background in sports, arts, outdoor recreation, social recreation, and so on. There were usually several other courses in leadership techniques, program supervision, and program development. In short, as a popular textbook proclaimed, "The Program is King" (Tillman, 1973).

Today, many recreation curricula have become more management oriented, and others have dropped the heavy core of activity classes. Still, most curricula have a small core of program-related classes, and many recreation majors have a relatively rich personal background in recreation activities. Thus, programming remains as one of the key elements in the preparation of the recreation professional.

Many of the pioneers in commercial recreation did not gain this background in programming because they did not come from recreation curricula. They came from curricula in business, hotel management, communications, and so forth, or from the school of hard knocks. These people managed transportation systems, sold retail products, maintained lodging and dining facilities, and occasionally offered recreation via "amenity" facilities.

In recent years, however, many of these traditional recreation managers have come to learn what the recreation professionals have known all along: that programming can make a big difference in the success of a business. There are many ways that this can happen. When a sporting goods store sponsors a 10-kilometer run, the event can be a very cost effective marketing tool which puts the store's name in front of the public. When a bowling lanes conducts low cost instructional classes for children, it is building future clientele. When a campground offers square dance and live entertainment, it is probably building a base of repeat customers. When a hotel offers bicycle rentals it may discover a popular new "profit center." Recreation programming does not have to be a costly frill for a commercial business. Instead, recreation programming can be a very important part of the business concept, and it can often pay for itself.

Programming is probably the single most important skill that recreation professionals have to differentiate themselves from persons with other backgrounds. Theoretically, the recreation professional should be the person who is best equipped to understand the leisure interests of guests/customers, to visualize opportunities for programs, and to conduct successful programs without making structural or logistical errors.

There is no doubt that programming has become a viable part of the commercial recreation industry. Most of the major resorts in the southeastern states now have recreation program professionals on staff year round. Many hotels, retail stores, themed restaurants, tour operators and other enterprises are finding that recreation programs can improve business. This chapter will examine various types and purposes of recreation programs, review the programming process, and consider several special types of commercial programs.

TYPES AND PURPOSES OF RECREATION PROGRAMS

Not all recreation programs are the same, nor do all programs have the same purposes. In some cases, the recreation program serves as the primary way to provide benefits that customers seek. In other cases, recreation programs primarily embellish the overall experiences and benefits that customers gain at a resort, a restaurant, theme park, or other facility. Programs can be structured as the primary service, as a revenue-generating amenity, or as a supporting amenity. Further, commercial recreation businesses that do not directly conduct programs can benefit by facilitating programs.

Programming as the Primary Service

In many commercial recreation industries, the provision of a specific recreation activity or several activities is the primary focus of the business. Common examples include tennis clubs, bowling lanes, ballet schools, summer camps, party services, and guided tours. In every case, the facilities, equipment, and staff exist in order to facilitate the activity. As an example of programming in one industry, Figure 7-1 illustrates the variety of programs offered at three sport/fitness centers in California, Texas, and Utah.

Almost any activity may be offered in a *structured or nonstructured* format. Tournaments, leagues, instructional classes, and guided tours are examples of the structured format. The structure is provided by a combination of an established agenda, procedures or rules, and staff that take an active role in leading the participants. Individuals skating on their own at an ice rink, playing pool at a billiard hall, or working out on exercise equipment at a fitness club are involved in nonstructured activity. Some programmers call this "free play" or "open use." Staff supervision in nonstructured programs is present, but not actively and regularly engaging with the participants.

Entertainment activities have characteristics of structure and non-structure. The performers at a concert or in a movie are certainly leading an activity that has an established agenda, but the customer is basically a spectator. Any spectator can come or go, eat, drink, talk to friends, daydream or doze off while the activity is in progress. On the other hand, some persons would argue that their psychic involvement is extremely high while watching a play or a sports event.

Figure 7-1
Examples of Programs for Sports Clubs and Fitness Centers

Aerobic Dance	Racquetball Classes
Basketball League	Racquetball Leagues
Bike Race	Racquetball Tournament
Body Dynamics Class	Racquetball Video Clinic
Children's Ballet & Tap Classes	Scuba Diving Class
Children's Karate Tournament	Ski Trip
Dancercise	Swim Lessons
Fitness Assessment	Swimnastics
Fitness for Expectant Mothers	Swim Team
Group Trip to Jamaica	Tai Chi Demonstration
Infant Swim Classes	10 K Run
Jr. Tennis League	Tennis Camp
Karate Class	Tennis Clinic
Kids' Field Trips	T.G.I.F. Exercise/Social
Las Vegas Trip	3 on 3 Basketball Tournament
Member/Guest Tennis Tournament	Triathlon Club
New Member Social	Wallyball Tournament
Parent/Child Tennis Tournament	Weight Lifting Contest
Pizza Social	Western Barbecue
	Yoga Class

Generally speaking, it is easier for a commercial recreation business to provide a nonstructured activity than a structured activity. In a nonstructured activity, the customers must be provided with an attractive "opportunity setting" (facility, equipment, support personnel, etc.). The customers enter the opportunity setting and participate pretty much at their own discretion. They lift the weights, volley the tennis ball, or swim in the pool according to whatever agenda they wish. In a structured activity, the manager must provide the opportunity setting plus the additional staff to directly instruct, officiate, or lead people in the activity. In addition, there may be special rules, methods, or procedures that have to be followed during the activity.

Some commercial recreation managers do not have the basic understanding of leisure behavior to establish an attractive opportunity setting. Other managers may be able to establish the opportunity setting but do not have the programming background to provide a structured activity. It is not unusual to hear these managers rationalize their lack of programming background: "Our customers don't want any fancy programs" or "They just want to do their own thing." This view is indeed unfortunate because the managers may be missing certain customers who occasionally desire the benefits that a structured program can provide.

The key to good recreation programming is to realize that different people seek different benefits and to know how to provide these benefits. A successful programmer manipulates the choice of activity, the type of setting, and the type of activity structure to create the blend of benefits

154

which customers seek. More regarding this approach to programming will be covered later in this chapter.

Arts and crafts activities are common at many resorts that have started recreation programs for their guests. (Photo: Courtesy of Innisbrook Resort and M. Silver Associates)

Recreation Program As A Supporting Amenity

Whereas some commercial recreation businesses use recreation programming as a primary service, other businesses see recreation as an amenity to their main mission. That mission might be to sell rooms in a hotel, meals in a restaurant, supplies in a crafts store, spaces in a campground, or equipment in a sporting goods shop. Figure 7-2 illustrates some of the types of recreation programs that can complement a variety of businesses. These businesses are in the commercial recreation industry, but their primary revenue comes from selling a product and/or service that is not actually a planned recreation program.

Why then do such businesses occasionally offer recreation programs and amenities? The answer is that recreation is good for business. In general, recreation programs and amenities can help differentiate one business from another and be a key factor in generating repeat business. For example, recreation programs can be the difference in a family's selection of one hotel over another. The Las Vegas Hilton offers an extensive program that can accommodate up to 100 children per day. Several international travelers report that they stay at the Hilton because that's where their kids want to stay.

Some of the specific benefits that supporting amenity programs can provide are:

- People are introduced to new activities.
- Activity skills instruction may increase future participation.
- Social interaction increases contacts for future participation.
- Length of stay may be increased.

- Children can be meaningfully occupied, freeing parents to play.
- Programs improve relations between employees and customers.
- The overall experience is diversified and enriched.

These benefits translate into increased sales, diversification of sales, and repeat customers. This is the ultimate benefit of recreation programs to the commercial recreation business. Recreation programs can contribute to the overall success of the commercial recreation business even when they are not the primary product/service of the enterprise. Therefore, many resorts, retail stores, and other businesses find that recreation programs are a worthwhile amenity to offer their customers.

Figure 7-2
Examples of Recreation Programs As Supporting Amenities

Type of Business	Program Examples
Sporting Goods Store	Races, Sports Teams, Tournaments
Outdoor Specialty Shops	Climbing Clubs, Rafting Trips
Hunting & Fishing Sports Store	Hunter Safety Course, Fishing Contest
Arts & Crafts Store	Ceramics Classes, Arts & Crafts Shows
Hobby, Toy & Game Store	Hobby Show, Trivia Contest
Video Arcades	Video Games Contest
Nightclubs	Dance Classes, Lip Synch Contest, New Years Party
Casinos	Blackjack & Poker Tournaments
Boat Dealers	Boating Safety Course
Restaurants	Birthday Party Programs, Theme Parties
Hotels	Entertainment Events, Exercise Classes, Children's Programs
Music Stores	Instrument Classes, Sing Along Recording Booths
Campgrounds	Square Dances, Nightly Entertainment
Water Theme Parks	Concerts, Slide Contests, Tan Contests
Photography Store	Photography Classes and Contests

Recreation amenities may or may not bring in revenue of their own. The recreation facilities and programs may be relatively inexpensive to offer or they may represent a large financial commitment. The key to their justification is how strongly they contribute to the overall objective of the business. The commercial recreation business that believes in recreation programs evidently feels that there is a positive cost/benefit. An example of this attitude was demonstrated by the entire community of Steamboat Springs, Colorado. A summer-long festival called "The Way It Wuz Days" included over 50 special events and recreation programs. It is possible that some of the programs made enough money to pay for themselves, but the payoff was elsewhere. The festival brought people to town to stay in hotels, lodges, and condos; to eat in restaurants; and to make purchases in the many unique shops. Visitors found that Steamboat Springs was much more than a classic "ski town." The marketing value of the festival was tremendous, as many of these visitors make repeat trips and tell their friends about the good times they had. Figure 7-3 illustrates the programs held during the 1983 "The Way It Wuz Days."

Figure 7-3
"The Way It Wuz Days," 1983, Steamboat Springs, Colorado

Youth Art Show	Country Music Concert
Indian Dance Exhibition	Horsemanship Show
Crafts Demonstration	Horse Clinics & Lecture
Juried Art Show	Rocky Mtn. Oyster Fry
Square Dance Festival	Hot Air Balloon Rodeo
Enduro Motorcycle Race	Orienteering Race
Woodworkers Show	Old West Parade
Chili Cook-Off	Boots & Bare Legs Pageant
Rodeos	Golf Tournament
Horse Show	Bicycle Race
Soccer Camp	Kayak Competition
Old West Shootout	Fireworks Display
Liars Contest	Children's Musical
Dance Concert	Pottery Workshop
Mountain Folk Triathlon	Western Street Dance
Cowpie Ruby Classic	Health Hike
Bluegrass Festival	Airshow
Steamboat House Tour	Bi-Plane Exhibits
5 & 10-K Races	Barnstorming
Hobie Cat Clinic and Regatta	Hang Gliding
Old West Theatre Production	Sky Diving
Old West Character Look Alike Contest	Poker Championship & Saloon Party
Numerous Concerts	Yampa River Race
Mountain Man Rendezvous	Endurance Horse Race
Tomahawk Throws	Softball Invitational Tournament
Mountain Man Run	Hill Climb Contest
Shooting Events	Superteam Competition
Grandma's Feather Bed Race	County Fair
Cowboy & Donkey Obstacle Race	Chariot Races
Bicycle Hill Climb	Chuckwagon Barbecue

Programming As A Revenue Generating Amenity

Some commercial recreation facilities have taken the idea of the recreation amenity to a higher level. Not only is recreation used to draw new customers and repeat customers, the recreation program is expected to generate a profit.

To be a revenue generating amenity, the recreation program must be totally responsive to the interests of the customer. Otherwise, they will not participate and the program will yield a loss. The successful recreation manager must be up to date with recreation interests and fads, be alert to customers' comments and suggestions, understand the full program potential (and limitations) of the facility, know what support staff can be counted on, and be able to execute the details and logistics of a program. Ideas alone are not enough. A poorly planned or executed program can do more harm than good.

It is interesting to note that many of the most successful revenue-generating recreation amenity programs are at resorts in Florida and along the southern Atlantic coast. The recreation managers at these resorts happen to be the individuals who formed the nucleus for the development of the Resort and Commercial Recreation Association (RCRA). This association has been extremely instrumental in spreading the practice of recreation programming in resort and campground settings.

Two examples of revenue-generating programs have been Kiawah Island, South Carolina, and Marriott's Tan-Tar-A Resort in Missouri. Some of their most financially successful programs are listed below (Van Oordt and Lodwick, 1985). Note that these are 1985 figures, and some changes have occurred in the management of the resorts since then.

- Bicycle Rentals (Kiawah)—One thousand wide tire, single speed bicycles were available. During peak weeks, all of them were rented on a weekly basis. The program had $370,000 revenue in a year, with 70% profit.
- Poolside Retail Shops (Kiawah)—Swim aids were sold and rented with $150,000 revenue with 21 percent profit.
- Skate Rentals (Kiawah)--The skate purchase price was covered in one and one-half years. Revenue was $4,000.
- Youth Programs (Kiawah)—Half day and full day programs were provided for elementary children. Revenue was $50,000 with 30 percent profit.
- Video Taping (Kiawah)—Videotapes of a group's activity, a family's vacation, were sold. Revenue was $13,400 with 75 percent profit.
- Marine Livery (Tan-Tar-A)—Fifty boats including speedboats, excursion boats, and paddle boats were rented. Revenue was $500,000 with 42 percent profit.
- Sports Complex Activities (Tan-Tar-A)—Court use, tournaments, classes, fitness, etc., were available. Revenue was $300,000 with 47 percent profit.
- Recreation Buttons (Tan-Tar-A)—Guests purchase a button that entitles them to full use of 23 different activities each day. They participate as much or as little as they want. Revenues were $250,000.

Facilitating Recreation

Many commercial recreation businesses will not be in the business of directly providing recreation amenities or programs. They might not have the facilities, staff expertise, financial resources, or philosophical orientation to do so. This would not mean, however, that they only sell hotel rooms, meals, sports equipment, or crafts supplies. These businesses exist to satisfy customers, and one way to help do this is by "facilitating" recreation. This means to act as an information resource, an encourager, a catalyst, or an enabler. It really doesn't take much time, effort, or resources to do this. What facilitating does, however, is to improve the business image with its customers. The key idea is that the manager should help customers find the benefits they seek, even if it is not something that business has to offer. This makes a positive impression on the customer and a satisfied customer leads to repeat business.

The Children's Ski School at Snowbird provides a variety of activities for youngsters while their parents explore more challenging terrain. (Photo: Courtesy of Snowbird Ski & Summer Resort)

Some of the ways to facilitate recreation are listed below:

- Keep a Calendar of Community Events—Help your guest and customers know what is going on in the community. For example, a sporting goods store should keep listings of bicycle races, fun runs, tennis tournaments, etc.
- Serve as a Referral Service—Refer guests to community agencies and businesses that have the programs they desire. For example, a hotel should know where a guest can go for a fitness workout or cultural activity.
- Provide "How To" Information—Have game rules, skills information, equipment use guides, etc. A hotel might have maps of local jogging trails, and a sports shop might have books and videos for sports skills.
- Provide Loan or Rental Equipment—To make it easy to participate, a theme park might have baby strollers available. A condominium resort might have table games and books on loan.
- Publicize Other Programs—Include posters, flyers, and brochures of other community programs and attractions on counter tops. Similarly, your business promotional literature should be available at those other locations.

- Provide Day Care—To enable parents more time to shop or recreate, provide a day care service. This has been done successfully in hotels, health clubs, and shopping malls.
- Employees Should Be Interested and Informed—Employees should be trained to show interest and help facilitate a positive experience for their guests and customers. Therefore, employees need to be informed of the opportunities and resources available. Another subcategory of recreation programming, the concierge service, is an expansion of this concept.

Concierge Services

Long a hallmark of better European hotels, a concierge provides services limited only by human ability and resourcefulness. A hotel/resort guest is likely to ask for anything, and the concierge's job is to make it happen. In this way, a concierge is almost a personal recreation programmer for a guest.

There is a confusion of titles for concierge service in the United States, possibly because the concept is not yet well established here. Some hotels have concierge service, others have a guest service director, or a guest relations director. Bell captains at other hotels provide many of the same duties.

A concierge service can be a competitive advantage for a hotel and is viewed as a "necessary extra" for service oriented hotels. At one Hyatt hotel, three fourths of the guests surveyed reported that they return to the Hyatt because of its extra service (Withiam, 1983).

Most concierge duties can be considered as information or services. Information requests typically concern dining, shopping, hotel amenities, entertainment, recreation activities, transportation, or general information about the city. The range of services offered varies greatly from one hotel to another, but may include any of the following (Withiam, 1983; Hobbs, 1985): arrangement of local tours, tickets to concerts and sports events; express check in/check out; and flight, hotel, and restaurant reservations.

Under an expanded concept of "guest services" (which may be seen more in the future), services may include babysitting, youth recreation, exercise classes, and tour programs.

To be a good concierge or guest services director, a person must be friendly, polite, polished, and resourceful. The ability to speak foreign languages is highly valued in some hotels. There is a prestigious professional fraternity for concierges, "Les Clefs D'or," and its presence now in the United Stated marks the emergence of concierge service as a major trend in the hospitality industry.

THE PROGRAM PROCESS

Whether a recreation program is a primary service or an amenity, the program must be planned and carried out effectively. There are numerous textbooks devoted to this topic; the recreation programming process.

160

Figure 7-4 illustrates a composite of the programming process as described in several of these textbooks.

Recreation programming occurs within a framework that is created by a combination of the organization's philosophy, the organization's goals, the social environment, and the economic environment. Within the limits imposed by this framework, recreation programming is a process that completes a cycle of events and starts over again.

The programming cycle begins with an understanding and assessment of the needs and interests of the target market. Next, program objectives are established that are designed to fulfill those needs and interests. Different types of program alternatives are then considered, and a determination is made as to what type of program can best fulfill the objectives. Next is the program design phase where the logistics of the program are planned. The program is then implemented according to the design. Finally, the program is evaluated. This evaluation provides feedback that confirms or amends the organization's perception of the target market's interests. Thus, the cycle begins anew.

This traditional concept of program planning is taught in most recreation curricula. From a practical standpoint, however, one strong criticism of the traditional concept can be made. This criticism concerns the unrealistically low emphasis on the design and implementation phases of the program cycle. These phases represent one third of the

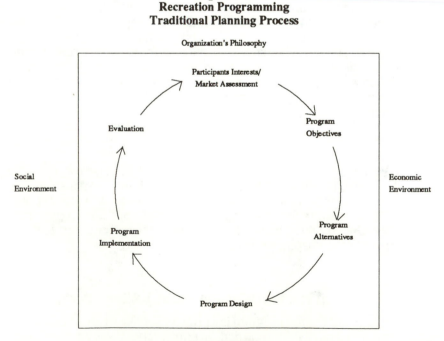

Figure 7-4
Recreation Programming
Traditional Planning Process

theoretical process but are often given about one tenth of the consideration in text literature. In reality, the recreation programmer often spends 80 percent of the time on "nuts and bolts" work of program design and implementation.

Therefore, a new recreation program process is proposed here. It is a process that emphasizes the many tasks that must be done to successfully conduct a program. It is also a process that is well suited for the commercial recreation manager who may not have much background in recreation programming, thus needing a more practical approach. This approach, for lack of a better description will be called the "nuts and bolts" programming approach (as opposed to an "ivory tower," theoretical approach).

The "Nuts and Bolts" Programming Process

Although the steps presented in this program process are listed in a numerical order, that order could change under certain circumstances. For example, if it typically takes an organization more time to recruit and train staff than to order equipment, then the time sequencing of the two steps could be reversed. Some commercial recreation businesses need to generate advertising for an event as much as a year in advance. Therefore, step #7, promotion, could have certain aspects occur anytime after step #1, initial planning. The promotional effort could continue right up to the start of the program. With these timing considerations in mind, the steps in the "nuts and bolts" approach to programming are presented below:

1. *Initial Planning*—Several tasks are essential from the outset:
   A. Assess the interests and needs of the target market.
   B. Determine objectives, both from the participant and organization's standpoint.
   C. Analyze the program alternatives that could accomplish the objectives and select the best alternative.
   D. Establish a budget for the program, considering both the direct costs and the overhead costs. Be conservative in estimating revenues.
   E. Coordinate the initial plan with other divisions within the organization, particularly maintenance, security, finance, and legal departments.

2. *Arrange For The Facility*—If the organization manages the facility that is needed for the program, then scheduling arrangements may be simple. Otherwise, it is necessary to lease or contract the facility from another organization.

3. *Obtain Equipment and Supplies*—This may involve writing specifications for equipment and going through a lengthy purchasing process. Equipment might also be borrowed, leased, solicited for donation, or repaired or reconditioned.

4. *Staff Recruitment and Training*—New employees may have to be hired or existing employees may have to be reassigned. In either case, training to some degree may be needed. Volunteers may also need to be recruited and trained.

5. *Make Special Arrangements*—Depending upon the program, there may be a variety of special arrangements required:

Bus use	Sponsors
Lodging and meals	Prizes and awards
Special maintenance	Medical assistance
Permits	Traffic control
Portable toilets	Concessions
Entertainment	Insurance

6. *Develop Specific Procedures/Operating Manuals*—Depending upon the complexity of the program, it may be necessary to develop specific time schedules, rules, activity procedures, program information, emergency procedures, etc.

7. *Program Promotion*—A variety of promotional methods may be utilized: advertising, publicity, special promotions, etc.

8. *Program Registration*—If registration is necessary will it be in advance or on site, by phone, mail, or in person? What form of payment will be accepted? Is a deposit required? When the participants register it may be appropriate to provide them with information sheets, schedules, and waivers as previously developed in step #6.

9. *Program Set-Up*—This step involves the physical set-up of the facility for the program: seating, trash cans, sports field preparation, equipment distribution, etc.

10. *Final Safety Check*—Prior to starting the program, make a final check of the area and equipment to be sure safety standards are met.

11. *Conduct The Program*—Finally! Most people only see this phase and don't realize all the preparation that went into it.

12. *Program Wrap-Up*—Schedule staff for this or they will disappear when the program ends. Tasks include:

Clean-up	Various report forms
Equipment return	Expense and revenue reconciliation
Post-event publicity	Sponsor thank you letters
Payrolls	Volunteer recognition

13. *Evaluate Results*—Consider if the program results, attendance, revenue, expenses, etc., met the objectives originally established. This step leads back to initial planning for the next program.

An Approach to Programming

One mistake that many recreation programmers make is to fall into the "stereotype trap." That means to program a certain type of activity in the same way, repeatedly. For example, basketball is usually offered at a sports club as free play or as a league activity. As such, it provides certain benefits to the participant, primarily physical activity, competition, and some social interaction. However, a good programmer would see how a variety of other program structures would provide different benefits to additional sports club members. Alternative approaches could include:

"Slam Dunk" league with lower baskets	3 on 3 leagues & tournaments
"Slow Break" league for age 30+	1 on 1 contest
Father and son, 2 on 2 tournament	"Hot Shot" contest
Demonstration/exhibit by pro/college players	Half court league
Booster club for local college/pro team	Co-rec league or tournament
Group outings to local college/pro games	Instructional classes
Trips/excursions to national tournaments	Basketball films
Exhibit of basketball memorabilia	Basketball trivia contest
Basketball photography exhibit/contest	Basketball officiating class
Bobby Knight chair throwing contest	League awards party

As stated previously, the key to good recreation programming is to provide the benefits people seek. This is done by manipulating and blending the choice of activity, the program format, and the program structure that best brings out the particular benefits sought. Program formats include leagues, tournaments, instructional classes, clinics, exhibits, demonstrations, clubs, trips, special events, and free play. Program structure variations include frequency of program, duration of program, skill level, and number of participants. For any given activity, there may be some participants who want the program offered in one way, while other participants desire it differently. As long as the participation volume allows it, why not offer activities in two or three different ways so that participants can choose the program they like best.

SPECIAL TYPES OF COMMERCIAL PROGRAMS

Most conventional textbooks about recreation programming give attention to the planning of games, tournaments, leagues, and instructional classes. Since many commercial recreation programs utilize these program formats, the traditional text content is generally of value. However, certain other types of recreation programs are typically overlooked in program textbooks. Examples are special/promotional events, food and beverage events, entertainment events, resort summer programs, and trips and tours. Since these types of programs are important in commercial recreation, some extra attention should be devoted to them. This section will focus on these special types of commercial recreation programs and examine some practical operational strategies for each.

Special/Promotional Events

Special/promotion events are a great way to announce the start of a new season, kick off a new product/service, spice up the old program, provide a change of pace, and attract new customers. Staff as well as participants can get charged up because of a special event. Many special/promotional events can be based around a holiday theme. Examples include a Valentine's Day Dance at a resort, Fourth of July fireworks party at an amusement park, or a Turkey Trot race sponsored by a sporting goods store.

In order to generate the most promotional value, it is very common to co-sponsor an event with a radio or TV station or a newspaper. An example would be a "Beach Party" at a water theme park. A radio station could sponsor the event and broadcast live from the park throughout the day. Activities could include tan contests, water slide relays, volleyball games, record giveaways, and bands playing Beach Boys tunes.

Ideas and operational strategies for special/promotional events can come from many sources including customers, staff, media people, and product representatives. One excellent source is the International Events Group (213 West Institute Place, Suite 303, Chicago, Illinois 60610), which publishes the *Special Events Report*, and the *International Directory of Special Events and Festivals*, and conducts event marketing seminars. Some specific strategies for special/promotion events include the following (Pogge, 1985; Brown, Jones, and Jensen, 1987):

- Have a Fun Idea and Good Program—No amount of publicity can offset a dull concept, and it must be a good program to get repeat visitors.
- Keep It Simple—Make it easy to promote with a central theme.
- Target Large Crowds—Sporting events and concerts lend themselves to visibility and crowds.
- Tie-In to the Market—Plan events that capture the target audience of the business and be the sponsors.
- Seek Community Involvement—Take every opportunity to involve community groups in the event in order to expand the base of support.
- Recognize Co-Sponsors and Contributors—Provide recognition in all brochures, during the event, and with follow up after the event.
- Involve the Media in Planning Meetings—For major events, invite the media to planning meetings in order to build interest and anticipation for the event.
- Maintain Events—Keep the ball rolling to the next year or next time so the event can build on past success.
- Develop Programs That Can Change—Although the main theme or concept may remain the same, have some variety from one year to the next in specific activities. Avoid staleness.
- Have Different Activities Each Day—For a multi-day event, have a variety of activities so people will want to come back each day.
- Utilize Personalities—Media personalities, sports and music stars, politicians, beauty pageant winners, etc., all draw more visitors.

- Control Spending—Limit the individuals who have authority to spend funds and stick as closely as possible to budget plans. Otherwise, special events can get out of hand.
- Have a Broad Base of Funding—Don't rely too heavily on a single financial source. Seek resources and revenues from ticket sales, concessions, donations, advertising, co-sponsors, etc.

One additional idea is to develop a special event checklist that serves as a reminder during the planning process. Rather than neglect a certain topic, review the list every time an event is planned. Figure 7-5 illustrates the special event checklist. It should also be noted that many of these ideas including the checklist can be adapted to the other programs in this section.

Food and Beverage Events

Throughout history, some of mankind's merriest moments have occurred around a full table of food and drink. Consider the feasts that are associated with the Greeks, Romans, Medieval Kings, and even some of the pioneers and settlers in the United States. Today, food and beverage events are a major service of hotels, restaurants, and resorts. Typically, the leadership in this area of recreation has been assumed by convention and meeting managers and banquet or catering departments of hotels. Occasionally, however, recreation staff generate an idea that can become a successful event with the help of a food service professional.

There are many types of food and beverage events and they range from the relatively simple to the very complex: wine and cheese parties, open house socials, receptions, western style barbecues, beach party clambakes, dinner theater, buffets, and complete themed parties.

The Amfac Hotel at the Dallas-Fort Worth Airport has a complete set of stage props, background sets, costumes for all personnel, and entertainment programs for a variety of food and beverage theme parties including Wild West, Hawaiian Luau, and Mexican Fiesta. Tourists to the Aviya-Sonesta Hotel in Israel can experience a "Beduin Party on the Red Sea" for only $30 per person. Guests are encouraged to wear robes and are provided with Keffiyehs (arab headdresses) to get them in the spirit. The event takes place in a large Beduin tent with low tables, comfortable sitting cushions, Beduin music, costumed waiters, and belly dancers for entertainment. Dinner consists of Oriental lamb on a bed of rice garnished with salads, followed by sweet meats, strong Beduin coffee, pita breads and cinnamon tea. Guest VIP's are brought into the tent on camel back (Robinson, 1985).

To manage a successful food and beverage event, Robinson (1985), Hosansky (1985), and Tannehaus (1985) have suggested a number of strategies and planning tips.

- Realize that theme parties require some risk.
- Do not let the theme replace quality service.
- Anticipate problems posed by colorful themes and locations.

Figure 7-5
Special Event Checklist

Site Suitability and Impact on:
   Neighborhood and Community
   Facility
   Turf and Vegetation

Facility:
   Accessibility
   Parking
   Traffic Flow
   Road Signs
   Information/Direction Signs
   Information Booth

Maintenance:
   Water Availability
   Trash Cans
   Electric Demands
   Electric Outlets
   Reserve Generator
   On-Site Maintenance
   Set-Up Crew
   Clean-Up Crew

Extra Equipment:
   Projector Bulbs
   Tools, Batteries
   Magic Markers, Pens
   Tape, String
   Trash Bags

Safety/Security:
   First Aid Station
   Ambulance (large crowds)
   Fire Extinguisher
   Walkie Talkies Telephone
   Security Personnel

Notice of Event to:
   Fire Department
   Hospital
   Police/Highway Patrol

Amenities:
   Restroom or Portable Toilets
   Shade and Rest Area
   Tents/Umbrella
   On-site Transportation
   Concessions
   Food and Beverage Service
   Drinking Water
   Entertainment
   Background Music
   Special Effects Displays

Other:
   Theme
   Schedule
   Press Package
   Announcer
   P.A. System
   Back-Up P.A.
   Change Fund
   Revenue Security
   Lost and Found Department
   Alternate/Extra Activities
   Site Supervision
   Publicity
   Registration Forms
   Staff Area
   VIP Area
   List of Contributors
   Insurance

- For outdoor events anticipate changes in weather. Have alternatives.
- Be familiar with local customs and cuisine. Avoid local holidays if staff will be off duty.
- Work closely with the caterer; be sure to have accurate estimates of attendance.

- Be up front about your budget capabilities.
- Know your customers. Some groups today are very health food conscious.
- Avoid "pasta shock," high starch meals that make people drowsy.
- The last night banquet should be the most extravagant, except on a cruise or a tour or other occasion requiring early morning departure.
- Service and ambiance can count as much as food quality.
- Create variety with different foods, decorations, table cloths, center pieces, costumes, and entertainment.
- Use buffet service with discrimination—it takes longer and people eat more.
- Keep close control over cocktail parties; do not schedule them for more than one hour.
- Use foreign and exotic dishes sparingly, especially at a U.S. location.
- Structure themed events around history, literature, show biz, sports, or countries.

Lastly, a separate planning checklist can be devised for food and beverage events. Figure 7-6 illustrates a list devised by Hosansky (1985).

Entertainment Events

Entertainment events can take many forms such as night club acts, dances, concerts, entertainment at receptions, or shows at fairs and carnivals. Proper planning and management can make these events an enjoyable experience for all persons involved. On the other hand, a poorly managed event can be a nightmare. Some of the important planning and management considerations for an entertainment event are as follows:

- Allow adequate time in planning the event—Local entertainers usually require at least a month notice, while regionally or nationally known entertainers may need to be booked three months to a year in advance.
- Match the entertainment to the clientele—If the theme is "Western Days," don't schedule a punk rock band.
- Consider the clientele when arranging security—Some entertainers have a following that requires tight security.
- Utilize booking agents—Agents have access to numerous entertainers at various prices.
- Determine the method of payment—Kelly (1985) reports that the most common contract involves a minimum guarantee to the performer, a fixed or cost-based amount to the presentor, and a percentage split after both these costs are covered. Be aware that cancellations may cost half of the guarantee.
- Reach agreement on expenses—Travel, lodging, food, etc., for entertainers and support crew.
- For major national entertainers contact record companies—Tours are usually booked a year in advance to coincide with the release of a new record.

Figure 7-6
CHECK LIST FOR FOOD AND BEVERAGE FUNCTIONS

☐ **Breakfast/Lunch/Brunch/**
Dinner/Buffets/Coffee Break:

___ Location
___ Number of each
___ Number to be served
___ Menu/cuisine
___ Wine/liquor/champagne
___ Cost
___ Gratuities
___ Guaranteed minimum
___ Serving time

☐ **Room:**

___ Size
___ Seating capacity
___ Air conditioning
___ Lighting
___ Acoustics
___ Decor/Decoration
___ Diagram of set-up

☐ **Tables:**

___ Shape (oval, round,
      rectangular, etc.)
___ Number
___ Number seated at each
___ Table covering:
      Cloth
      Place mats
      Other covering
      Color
___ Chairs:
      Number
      Type
___ Reserved seating
      Alphabetical seating list
___ Table numbers/reserved
      signs
___ Place cards
___ Floral arrangements
___ Other table decorations

☐ **Dance Floors**

      ___ Permanent or portable

☐ **Check Rooms**

☐ **Restrooms**

☐ **Telephones**

☐ **Music**

☐ **Speakers**

☐ **Entertainment**

      ___ Program timetable

☐ **Photographers**

☐ **Gifts & Souvenirs**

☐ **Printed Menu & Program**

☐ **Deadline for Confirmation**
   And Attendance

☐ **Cocktail Receptions &**
   Happy Hours:
   ___ Location
   ___ Location of bars:
      Public
      Private
      Full bar
      Limited bar
      Hosted bar
      Cash bar
   ___ Brands:
      Liquor
      Wine
      Champagne
      Mixers
   ___ Hors d'oeuvres:
      Hot
      Cold

☐ **Cocktail Receptions**
   & Happy Hours (cont)
   ___ Service:
   ___ Bartenders
   ___ Waiters
   ___ Attendants
      (door, check-
      room, other)
   ___ Decoration
   ___ Guaranteed minimum
   ___ Corkage charges
   ___ Gratuities
      included/at will
   ___ Attendance expected
   ___ Estimated cost
      per event

☐ **Head Table:**

   ___ Location
   ___ Configuration
   ___ Level
      Floor level
      raised
   ___ Floor covering
   ___ Dias covering
   ___ Number to be seated
      Seating arrangements
      Place cards
   ___ Lectern
   ___ Microphones
   ___ PA system
   ___ AV facilities
   ___ Floral & other
      decoration

☐ **Buffet Table**

   ___ Size
   ___ Number
   ___ Table cover
   ___ Decoration
   ___ Service/self-
      service

Source: Hosansky (1985)

Resort Summer Programs

Increasingly, resorts are offering special programs for parents who want to take children on vacation but not have them constantly underfoot. The idea is to provide recreation for the kids, not just babysit them. Meanwhile the parents have time to spend with each other without worrying about their children's activity and supervision.

Club Med is among the resort chains that have taken a leadership role in providing youth programs, by designating certain clubs as "Mini Club" locations. These mini clubs have full programs, much like a day camp. There are sports, games, aquatic activities, music, crafts, meals, and snacks. At the Eleuthra Island Club Med, there is a circus school where kids can learn to be clowns and trapeze artists. The Paradise Island Club Med features a "Baby Club" for infants who are between four months and one year old (Maynard, 1986).

In the United States, some of the best summer programs for kids are offered at major resorts in Florida, Georgia, and South Carolina. Figure 7-7 illustrates programs that are available at three of these resorts: South Seas Plantation near Fort Meyers, Florida; Amelia Island Plantation, north of Jacksonville, Florida; and Innisbrook Resort and Golf Club at Tarpon Springs, Florida.

In developing a resort summer program, many of the activities are similar to those offered at day camps and playgrounds under the auspices of YMCAs and city recreation departments. There are some major differences, however. Parents and children often expect a better program at a resort and are quite sophisticated in those expectations. They are willing to pay for a good program, and the program should be priced accordingly. Finally, the children may only attend for several days to a week, so the staff cannot really get to know the kids as well as they would at a community day camp. Some other important planning considerations are as follows (Nagel, 1987):

- Check to see if the resort program comes under state regulations for day care programs. If it does, be sure that all standards are complied with.
- Consider carefully the ages to be served. Some resorts have found it difficult to work with children under five. Other resorts develop programs for five and over and provide day care for children three and under. Four year olds may be too mature for day care but not mature enough for a recreation program. Therefore some resort programs find it best not to accept four year olds.
- Be sure there is an adequate ratio of staff to children; at least one staff to 10 to 25 children depending upon age.
- Be sure that meals and snacks meet all applicable health codes.
- It may be wise to restrict access of the program to certain areas such as the ocean beach.
- Programs should be flexible enough to accommodate variable numbers of children from day to day.

Trips and Tours

More than 5,000 outfitters, tour guide companies, and specialty travel agencies offer or arrange adventure tours. Samples include an 18-day bicycle tour of China, a two-week safari through Africa, an Alaskan glacier skiing trip, or a fishing trip on the Amazon River (Bauer, 1987).

Although these adventure trips seem quite glamorous, such trips are in the minority. For most Americans, a group tour is a 5 to 15 day motor coach trip with overnight stops at hotels. Typical destinations are to festivals, historic sites, cultural events, major cities, or scenic attractions. These tours are not only conducted by commercial operators, but by many municipal park and recreation departments and nonprofit recrea-

Figure 7-7
Examples of Summer Program Activities
South Seas Plantation, Amelia Island Plantation, and
Innisbrook Resort and Golf Club

Children 3-6

Shell Collecting	Mini Golf	Puppet Creations
Nature Craft	Fishing Trip	Animal Charades
Group Games	Treasure Hunt	Exercise
Swim Pool Fun	Ice Cream Making	Storytelling
Sandcastle Creations	Senses Hike	Cartoons
Arts and Crafts	Mini Bowling	Tots Tumbling
Name Bingo	Creative Movement	Face Painting
Scavenger Hunt	Parachute Game	

Kids 7-12

Weekly themes:	Tug-O-War	Swimming
Great Outdoor Adventure	Jewelry Making	Parachute Games
Pirates of the Carribean	Mini Golf	Crafts
Clown Carnival	Treasure Hunt	Sports Activities
Magic Week	Sportsfest	Games Tournaments
Rods, Reels & Red Fish	Action Skits	Table Games
Space Adventures	Ethnic Dancing	Tennis Clinic
Olympic Games	Frisbee Golf	Ice Cream Making
Beach Walks	Earthball Games	Plaster Craft
Mexican Fiesta	Bike Hike	Beach Party
Candy Making	Superstars Contest	Scavenger Hunt
Memories Mural	Kite Making	Oyster Diving
Water Battle	Cookie Making	Cartoon Party
Children's Dinner Theater	Pajama Party	Birthday Parties
Character and Improvization	Story Hour	Beach Party
Moonlight Swimming Party	Show Biz Pizza Party	

Teen Activities

Surf Boards/Boogie Boards	Western Night	Wallyball
Video Games Tournament	Horseback Riding	Golf Clinic
Moonlight Volleyball	MTV Night	Nature Hike
Ping Pong Tournament	Bike Hike	Miniature Golf
Teen's Dinner Theater	Pool Party	Scavenger Hunt
Basketball Game	Bonfires	Racquetball Clinic
Anything Goes Contest	Beach Party	Water Volleyball
Special Field Trips	Tennis Clinic	Pizza and Movie
Co-ed Flag Football	Windsurfing	Movie Night
Woodworking Crafts		

tion agencies. All of these tours should be directed and lead in a professional manner.

In conducting a tour, all the responsibilities may be handled by one organization or by several organizations working together through contracts. The possible parties involved include the following (Kelly, 1985).

1. Tour Operator/Wholesaler—develops the overall tour itinerary, (hotels, transportation, etc.) prices it, and markets it.
2. Retail Agents—sell the tour to the public.
3. Tour Manager—operates the day to day aspects of the tour and hires the tour director, escorts, and/or guides.

    a. Tour Director—goes with the group, represents the company, directs day to day events and provides narration to the group.
    b. Tour Escorts—similar to tour director, but do not provide tour narration.
    c. Tour Guides—Join the group at a specific location and provide expert narration for the specific area or site. Also called "step-on guides."

d. Local Providers—rent their resources to the tour (hotels, restaurants, attractions, events, etc.).
e. Transportation Carriers—rent transportation (charter buses, planes, cruise ships, etc.) to the tour operator.

The tour manager and director have the most contact with the group and generally coordinate everything once the tour is in progress. They are consumer advocates, trouble shooters, quality control persons, social directors, public relation specialists, and ambassadors of good will. They must enjoy working with people and have common sense.

Tour Itinerary. The basic idea in planning a tour is to provide an interesting itinerary without wearing the participants out. One way to do this is to build in several optional tours or events. Participants can choose to go along or have free time on their own. Figure 7-8 illustrates a typical itinerary for an eight-day tour with a single primary destination and side tours eminating from that hub location.

The remainder of this section will examine some specific suggestions for working with hotels and motor coach operations, for leading the group, and for handling emergencies. (Calhoun, 1986.)

Tips for Working With Hotels

- Know the published rates (rack rate) and competitor's rates.
- Talk to the highest decision maker and ask for better rates.
- Expect better rates with higher volume at the same hotel or same chain.
- Get the best rate for volume business (net-net rate) from the Hotel's national sales representative.

Figure 7-8
8-Day Tour Itinerary Format

Day	AM	Afternoon	Evening
Sunday	Travel	Travel and Check In	Rest/on own
Monday	Half day tour	Optional tour	Group Meal
Tuesday	All day tour	All day tour	On own
Wednesday	Optional tour	Half day tour	Group meal and entertainment
Thursday	All day tour	All day tour	On own
Friday	Half day tour	Optional tour	Major evening event
Saturday	Half day tour	Open for shopping, packing, etc.	Short meeting re: return, then free time
Sunday	Check out/ travel	Travel home	

Note: All day and half day tours may be sightseeing tours, shopping tours, or scheduled activities (round of golf, chartered fishing trips, sporting event, theme park visit, etc.)

- Strive for savings in related areas such as hotel restaurants.
- Know the peak seasons of the hotel.
- Know exchange rates if foreign hotels are involved.
- Make realistic room blocks (reservations).
- Compare what you are getting for the price.
- Be prepared to make a deposit unless you are a proven customer.
- Payment in full upon arrival will give you leverage in negotiations with the hotel.
- Be aware that the hotel's cancellation policy is usually nonnegotiable. Most require 10 days written notice but prefer 30 days notice.
- Major hotels and chains offer consistency of product but have difficulty making quick decisions.
- Independent hotels may have more character and can make quicker decisions but quality may not be known until arrival.
- Provide the hotel with a rooming list 14 days in advance.
- Call the hotel the day before arrival to verify room lists, special requests (handicapped, adjoining rooms, medication storage, number of beds in each room, etc.) arrival time, number of luggage, food and beverage arrangements, drivers room, activities and events planned.

- Upon Arrival:

  Keep people on the bus,
  Check the group in and bring the keys back for distribution as the group steps off the bus,
  Find out about bag pull time and location for the departure,
  Get special luggage tags for the group,
  Get to know the bell captain,
  Be in the lobby for half an hour to give information and answer questions.

- Upon Departure:

  Confirm the bag pull,
  Check with accounting office to be sure guests paid their incidental charges (phone, room service, etc.),
  Tell the hotel where you are going next,
  Count the luggage and check the tags,
  Thank the bell captain,
  Collect room keys on the bus and count the passengers.

Figure 7-9 illustrates the paperwork flow when booking a hotel. Figure 7-10 illustrates the confirmation agreement that is sent to the tour company for signature.

Figure 7-9
Paperwork Flow In Booking Hotels

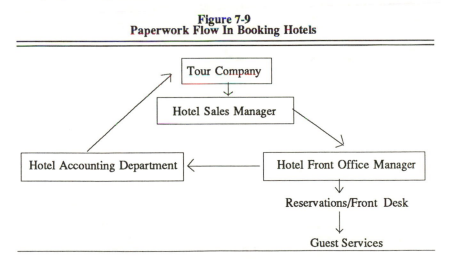

Motor Coach Procedures

- Check out the PA system upon boarding.
- Introduce the driver at the start.
- If there are four points of interest within 100 yards, stop the bus.
- If you are running late, do not cut out a stop that is advertised, cut out an unscheduled site stop.

Figure 7-10

ᙯarriott Hotel

75 South West Temple • Salt Lake City, Utah 84101 • 801/531-0800

GROUP TOUR CONFIRMATION AGREEMENT

Definite ☐   Revised ☐   From _____   File Number_____

Arrival Date_____   Number of Guests _____

Departure Date _____   Number of Rooms _____

Date Confirmed _____   Todays Date _____

Group Tour Name _____

Contact _____   Title _____

Company_____   Phone (___)

Address _____
CITY   STATE   ZIP

Rates Are: _____

Rates: Singles_____   Doubles_____   Twins_____   Triples_____   Quads_____   Suites_____

E.P. _____   M.A.P. _____   F.A.P. _____   Other _____

Rollaway(s) _____   (HOTEL TAX OF _____   NOT INCLUDED)

Day	Su	M	T	W	Th	F	S	Su	M	T	W	Th	F	S
Date														
Rooms														

CHECK-IN TIME: 4:00 p.m.

CHECK-OUT TIME: 12:00 Noon
Luggage storage is available through the Bell Captain for later departure.

BAGGAGE HANDLING:
$ _____ per person (round trip) covers check-in and check-out.

DEPOSIT:
In order to confirm reservations a deposit will be due by _____, along with your rooming list and name of tour guide. Total deposit amount _____

CANCELLATION POLICY:
If your deposit or rooming list is not received by the respective deadline dates, your group reservations will be subject to automatic cancellation.

LOSS OF DEPOSIT:
A loss of deposit will result if cancellation is less than 2 weeks before arrival.

COMPLEMENTARY ROOM POLICY:
One complimentary room for tour escort with _____ rooms occupied.

CREDIT ARRANGEMENTS:
Direct billing or voucher billing must be approved in advance with our Credit Department.

INCIDENTAL CHARGES:
It is the obligation of the tour escort, to insist that all incidental charges for each individual are paid prior to check-out or such charges will be billed directly to the agency and will be due and payable upon receipt.

GROUP MEALS:
For group functions, Catering Manager _____ will be in contact with you soon to discuss menus, special requirements, etc. according to attached agenda.

_____

_____

_____

_____

SALT LAKE CITY MARRIOTT HOTEL

NAME _____

TITLE _____

DATE _____

ACCEPTED AND AGREED TO:

NAME _____

TITLE _____

DATE _____   COMPANY _____
(WHO IS AN AUTHORIZED AND RESPONSIBLE AGENT FOR THE ABOVE ORGANIZATION)

WHITE COPY PLEASE SIGN AND RETURN TO SALT LAKE CITY MARRIOTT HOTEL SALES DEPT CANARY COPY: CUSTOMER COPY

- Have frequent rest stops—don't encourage use of the bus rest room.
- Encourage passengers to use the trash can.
- Don't block the drivers mirror or lean against the door.
- Designate a loading/unloading procedure such as first on/first off.
- Plan seat rotation twice a day—more often is a problem with personal items in the overhead racks.
- Plan rest stops before and after lunch.
- When stopping for the day tell the group: when the restaurant opens; departure time and location; baggage pick-up time and location; restaurant location and hours; how to dress the next day; information about shopping, entertainment, and safes for valuables.
- Count people everytime they load and unload.
- Ask group members if they have special requests or desire picture stops.

Tips for Tour Directors and Guides

- Talk loud enough.
- Stand where you can make visual contact.
- Don't dispense drugs or medication.
- Help people get on and off a bus (or boat).
- Point out hazards when the group is walking.
- Be sincere no matter how difficult it is.
- Avoid political, religious, and personal views.
- Don't bring up negative things.
- Make explanations understandable.
- Use first hand experiences.
- Relate to the participant's generation.
- Relate everything (including questions) to the group.
- Use humor when appropriate.
- Be topical to the area.
- Let the group know the rules at the start.
- Ask participants to write down all key information about arrivals, departures, or other procedures.
- Try to discover the tour members' expectations.
- Tell people about local customs, laws, etc.
- Show people what they expect to see.
- Strive to provide accurate information.
- Remember that the job itself is entertainment.

Handling Emergencies

There is no set way to handle emergencies. Each situation requires calmness, visibility, assertiveness, and common sense. Some general suggestions are:

- For illness, do not diagnose it or dispense drugs—seek medical attention if possible.
- For detours or bus problems, notify the hotel and the home office of the problem and delay.

- If bumped ("walked") from a hotel due to overbooking get the hotel to provide alternate accomodations and a refund—if the group is split up make sure everyone knows where you are.
- If there is a death, report it to authorities and inform tour members of the situation—phone the tour company, take care of the spouse/friend/family, and continue the tour.

SUMMARY

Recreation programming is becoming an important part of the Commercial Recreation Industry. Even the industries that are retail or hospitality oriented have found that recreation programs can help them differentiate their product/service from competitors and in the process gain repeat customers. Programs may be offered as a primary service, as a supporting amenity, or as a revenue-generating amenity. Recreation may also be provided through a "facilitating" approach and through concierge service in the hotel industry.

The programming process consists of an assessment of market segment interests, the establishment of program objectives, consideration of program alternatives, the design of the program, implementation of the program, and finally, evaluation. Much of the actual time that is spent in programming occurs at the design and implementation stage. Tasks to be accomplished at this time include arrangement for facilities, equipment and staff, training of staff, development of a procedure manual, program promotion, activity registration, safety check, program "showtime," and various wrap-up tasks.

Certain types of programs are more common to commercial recreation settings than to public or nonprofit agencies. These programs include special/promotional events, food and beverage events, resort summer programs, entertainment events, and trips and tours. Each type requires strict attention to details, many of which are suggested in this chapter.

STUDY QUESTIONS

1. Define how recreation programming may be a primary service, a supporting amenity, or a revenue-generating amenity.
2. How does recreation support a total amenity package? Give examples.
3. What are some examples of ways that programming can be revenue generating?
4. Describe the basic aspects of the recreation programming process.
5. Review key planning considerations for trips and tours, summer resort programs, promotional events, food and beverage events, and entertainment events.

PROJECT IDEAS

1. Find an example of a primary recreation service business, one where recreation is a supportive function, and one where recreation is a self-supporting amenity.
2. Select a favorite recreational activity. Develop a complete plan for the provision of that activity in a commercial recreation setting.

SPOTLIGHT ON: RENAISSANCE PLEASURE FAIRE

In 1963, the first Renaissance Pleasure Faire was held in Agoura, California. The founder, Phyllis Patterson, had been using the faire concept to combine history and drama in a summer project for her elementary school pupils. She expanded the concept by re-creating a Renaissance village in a participatory theater concept. Thus, the first festival was inaugurated with over 6000 people attending.

This event, almost 25 years later, has some 50 imitations across the country, and through the Living History Center, a nonprofit corporation founded by Patterson, a major northern and southern California faire is held each year in Agoura and Novato. In addition, a Dickens Christmas Fair is held in San Francisco and other harvest celebrations are programmed across the state.

The event evolves around a philosophy that it is good for people to interact with a period of history that is as culturally enriched as the Renaissance. The theme of the fair is carried out to authentic details with over 30 full-time staff, 13 guild masters, over 700 performers and history hobbyists re-creating the Renaissance period for thousands of participants on approximately 8,000 square feet of a re-created London town. The event is held over several weekends, attracting residents, tourists, and players alike.

The logistics of developing a faire of this magnitude involves 150 contractors who provide food service, games, arts and crafts of the period, and other merchandise services. In addition, all the complexities of an outdoor faire must be planned for. One rainy season can virtually wipe out a year of planning. Permits must be secured through the various zoning and planning requirements of over 50 government agencies. Then, the recruitment and training of numerous volunteers must create as authentic a theme as possible.

According to Phyllis Patterson, those who volunteer for the faires become involved in an exciting sociological structure that extends to a social group for the remainder of the year. Education is the key goal in re-creating the historical significance of the past through the medium of games, music, drama, and food. Through this activity base, the public can learn to do things that were common during that period, such as spinning, playing a flute, and singing a folk song.

In addition to the faire, the Centre sponsors the College of Renaissance Delights to train the staff and volunteers for the various Renaissance events. These workshops are also open to the public in the true spirit of service to the customer.

New projects of this very active operation include a destination resort built around an early California history theme. The creativity of a single entrepreneur with a goal to "popularize the arts" has mushroomed into a major programming event today.

Source: Patterson (1987).

REFERENCES

Bauer, B. "Buying Adventure—With or Without Frills." *U.S. News and World Report,* January 12, 1987, pp. 52-53.

Brown, T., Jones, R., and Jensen, M. "Development and Promotion of Tourist Events." Governors Conference on Tourism, Salt Lake City, Utah, February, 1987.

Calhoun, L. "Tour Directors Training Program." University of Utah course, Department of Recreation and Leisure, Spring, 1986.

Hobbs, N. "A Concierge Can Provide Those Extra Amenities." *Salt Lake Tribune,* January 13, 1985, p. A1

Hosansky, M. "The Way To A Meeting Planner's Heart." *Meetings and Conventions,* August, 1985, pp. 37-40.

Kelly, J. *Recreation Business.* New York: John Wiley & Sons, 1985.

Maynard, M. "Places That Pamper Your Kids." *U.S. News and World Report,* July 28, 1986, p. 43.

Nagel, A. "One of My Favorite Programs." *RCRA Newsletter,* February, 1987. p. 3.

Patterson, P. President of the Living History Center, Personal Interview, September, 1987.

Pogge, J. "Updating Audience Promotion Strategies." *Radio Only,* August, 1985, p. 36.

Robinson, D. "Food For Pleasure and Health." *Meetings and Conventions,* August, 1985, pp. 43-50.

Tannehaus, N. "Eating Outside or on the Water." *Meetings and Conventions,* November, 1985, pp. 174-175.

Tillman, A. *The Program Book For Recreation Professionals.* Palo Alto, California: Mayfield Publishing Company, 1973.

Van Oordt, L., and Lodwick, M. "Profit Centers and Revenue Generating Programs." The Resort and Commercial Recreation Association, Annual Convention, Phoenix, Arizona, January, 1985.

Witham, G. "Keepers of the Keys: Concierges In American Hotels." *The Cornell Hotel and Restaurant Administration Quarterly,* November, 1983, pp. 40-43.

PART III

INDUSTRY PROFILES

Part I (Chapters 1-3) of this text established an introduction to the basic nature of commercial recreation. Part II (Chapters 4-7) examined the initiation and management of the commercial recreation enterprise. The content in all of these chapters was oriented to the overall commercial recreation industry. Therefore, the content was rather generic in order to cover a wide range of concepts having some degree of universal application to the commercial recreation field. Part III (Chapters 8-10) reverses this approach and examines specific commercial recreation industries.

As explained in Chapter 1, commercial recreation may be thought of as three major industry groups: travel, hospitality, and local commercial recreation. These groups overlap in many instances. For example, cruise ships may be considered as part of the travel industry and as part of the hospitality industry. Rather than present the many overlapping "hybrid" industries in a separate chapter, they will be presented within just one of the major industry groups to which they belong.

There are hundreds of commercial recreation industries that could be examined in this text; some very large industries and some very small. The industries that will be presented in Chapters 8-10 each meet one or more of the following criteria:

1. An industry that presents significant career opportunities for students in recreation, tourism, or hospitality curricula.
2. An industry that is a major component of the overall commercial recreation industry. It is important to have a basic knowledge of the "big picture" of commercial recreation in order to be a successful entrepreneur, manager, and/or investor in any specific segment of the leisure industry.
3. An industry that has an important supporting relationship to any of the industries covered in #1 or #2 above. For example, campground managers need to understand the recreation vehicle industry even though they probably will not be involved in RV retailing.

It is therefore the objective of Chapters 8-10 to inform readers about the overall commercial recreation industry and several specific industries. Content will be presented that covers the basic status of each industry, its operational nature, and career opportunities.

It must be noted that there are numerous professional and trade associations and publications affiliated with each industry. Rather than use many pages listing these resources, it is suggested that readers utilize the *Encyclopedia of Business Information Sources, The National Trade and Professional Associations of the U.S.*, or the *Standard Periodical Directory*, available at most libraries, to gain current addresses for the association or publication of your choice.

Chapter 8

THE TRAVEL INDUSTRY

Consider the following data regarding the travel industry (Wynegar, 1987A; Hunt, 1986):

- It is a $286 billion industry in the United States.
- It involves over 1.1 billion trips away from home by Americans.
- It employs about 5.4 million persons in the United States.
- It accounts for 6 percent to 7 percent of the Gross National Product.
- It is one of the top three industries in almost every state.
- It is forecast to be the largest business activity in the world by the year 2000.

Obviously travel, transportation, and tourism are major factors in the overall commercial recreation industry. If you recall the data from Chapter 1 regarding expenditures for leisure, it might be observed that $286 billion represents almost the entire amount estimated to be spent for leisure in the United States. How can it be that one industry is so large? The answer is that definitions overlap. The U.S. Travel Data Center's definition of travel services includes expenditures for transportation, lodging, food and beverage, entertainment, and some types of recreation. It is recognized that much of the money spent for these services is spent by a traveler/tourist. However, we must also recognize that much of the money spent for entertainment, food and beverage, and recreation is spent by Americans within their own community.

This chapter will present an overview of the travel industry including definitions, distribution system, trends and expenditures, travel psychology and behavior, and important issues related to travel. Reviews of several specific travel industries will also be presented.

BACKGROUND OF THE INDUSTRY

This section will present definitions and distribution characteristics of the travel industry.

Definitions

McIntosh and Goeldner (1984), Jafari (1983), VanDoren (1983), Gunn (1979) and others have presented a variety of definitions relative to the travel industry. An assimilation of these definitions is used for this text.

Travel—all overnight trips away from home, and day trips to places 100 miles or more away from a travelers origin. This includes trips for business or pleasure.

Tour—a combination of services including transportation and one or more of the following: accommodations, meals, recreation activities, entertainment, or sightseeing, which are provided to individual or group pleasure travelers.

Tourist—a temporary visitor staying overnight at a location away from home. The purpose may be for business or for pleasure. In recent years, the word tourist has assumed a somewhat negative connotation. Therefore it is becoming more popular to use the word *traveler*, which includes the subclassifications of "business traveler" and "pleasure traveler."

Excursionist—a temporary visitor 100 miles or more away from the travelers origin, but not staying overnight. Again, the purpose may be business or pleasure.

Tourism or Travel Industry—a broad industry comprised of a loose network of businesses that serve tourists/travelers. According to this definition, the industry would include transportation carriers, travel agencies, tour companies, plus most of the hospitality industry and part of the local commercial recreation industry.

For practical purposes, it must be realized that the terms "tourism" and "travel industry" are often used interchangeably. It is also important to realize that the industry does not function in isolation; it intermingles with the natural, physical, social, and political environments (Hunt, 1986). More specifically, the components of the travel industry include (McIntosh and Goeldner, 1984; Gunn, 1979):

- *The traveler* who seeks psychic and physical experiences and satisfaction.
- *The businesses* providing transportation, lodging, products, and other services to the traveler.
- *The government* of the host country, region, or community.
- *The host community* including the resident's cultural background.
- *The natural resource base* and physical environment.

This is indeed an industry of complex interactions. The complexity should be apparent throughout the rest of this chapter.

Travel Industry Sales and Distribution System

Today, travel and transportation is a huge industry with thousands of businesses competing for the travel dollar, yet working together in many instances. Because the industry is so large, complex, and interrelated, there is no single process by which sales are made to the consumer. Instead, there is a distribution system in which sales occur through a variety of methods. Figure 8-1 illustrates the travel industry sales distribution system as adapted from Gee (1984).

In a one-stage sale, the supplier sells directly to the consumer. The consumer may make several purchases separately in order to arrange a vacation involving air transportation, rental car, lodging, and activities. In a two-stage system, the transaction goes through a travel agent, tour operator, or specialty channeler who makes all the arrangements. A specialty channeler could be a travel coordinator for an organization such as a park and recreation department, corporate recreation program, or large club. In a three-step sales system, a travel wholesaler may also be used. Wholesalers purchase large blocks of space with airlines, cruise ships, and resorts at a substantial discount. Then they market the space through travel agents or directly to the consumer. A four-stage system can bring all these middlemen into play. It would seem logical that the more complex transactions would wind up costing the consumer more, but such is seldom the case. Whenever middlemen exist, you can be assured that they are purchasing the product at a low enough cost to make a profit and to pass a reasonable value on to the consumer. In addition, the various wholesalers, tour operators, and travel agents also provide services such as travel counseling and itinerary coordination.

Figure 8-1
Travel Sales Distribution System

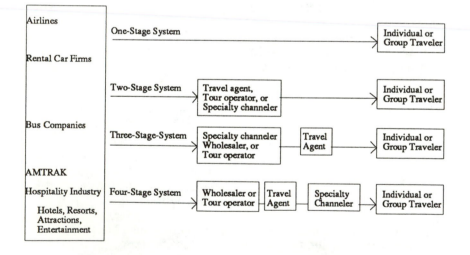

TRAVEL TRENDS AND EXPENDITURES

As mentioned previously, the travel business is a huge industry in the United States, serving over 1.1 billion persons on trips, staying 5.8 billion nights, and spending $286 billion. This industry has grown at least 6 percent every year since 1976. During this period, travel-related sales have grown 22 percent faster than the Gross National Product (GNP) of the United States, while travel prices have lagged behind the rise of the Consumer Price Index (Frechtling, 1987A). Such was not true in the 1970s when travel prices grew faster than the CPI due to outrageous oil price increases from the OPEC countries.

The recent travel boom has been influenced by several factors (Frechtling, 1987B):

1. Disunity among OPEC producers has led to an oil glut, that has kept prices down. Gasoline prices dropped 25 percent from 1982 to 1986.
2. Deregulation of airlines and competition within the industry has kept prices down (except in areas with little competition).
3. Hotel and motel construction has lead to overcapacity in the lodging industry resulting in competition and stable prices.
4. Tax reforms in the United States have given Americans more discretionary income. The tendency has been to spend the extra money first for a home mortgage or auto, then for travel.

Presently, about two thirds of all United States residents take at least one trip per year of 100 miles or more (Borcover, 1987). Most of this travel (75 percent) occurs by auto, followed by air travel (20 percent) and other types such as bus and train (5 percent). This travel can be analyzed from several perspectives: domestic travel, international travel, pleasure versus business travel, and weekend travel.

Domestic Travel

Within the United States, domestic travel accounts for 92 percent of the overall American travel industry. Some of the characteristics of domestic travel are reviewed below.

- The most popular destinations are Florida and California, followed by Texas, Michigan, Hawaii, Colorado, and New York (Zigli, 1986A).
- Overall, the Mountain Region (Colorado, Utah, Wyoming, Montana, Idaho, and New Mexico) is the largest "magnet region" with 40 million more visitors to it than residents traveling from it (U.S. Travel Data Center, 1986).
- Most visitors to a given destination are from within 500 miles (Mason, 1987).
- The National Parks, Monuments, and Recreation Areas are also major destinations, with about 290 million visitors in 1986 (Borcover, 1986A).
- The average family vacation trip involves 3.0 people for 5.6 nights, and covers 910 miles round trip (Mason, 1987).
- The average spending per vacation is $1503, but most vacationers (57 percent) spend $1000 or less. Only 12 percent of vacationers spend $2500 or more (Zigli, 1986A).
- The average spending on a trip is 39.8 percent for transportation, 28.9 percent for food, 14.6 percent for lodging, 8.3 percent for entertainment, and 8.3 percent for incidentals (Gee, 1984).

- About 5-7 percent of all trips are on package tours (U.S. Travel Data Center, 1986).

International Travel

International travel has seen major changes in recent years. From 1981 to 1984, the American dollar appreciated by at least 25 percent and as much as 115 percent compared to most foreign currencies. During this time, American travel to Europe doubled and travel to other countries also increased significantly. Overall, United States travel spending overseas increased from $16 billion in 1981 to $24.6 billion in 1986. This travel satisfied an excess demand that had built up in the United States during a previous period of an undervalued dollar. Conversely, travel became expensive for foreign visitors to the United States. International tourists declined each year from 23.6 million visitors ($15.5 billion expended) in 1981 to 21 million visitors ($14.1 billion expended) in 1985 (*U.S. News and World Report*, 1987; Beekhuis, 1986). In 1985 however, the dollar peaked. This event coincided with a rash of terrorism in Europe and the Mediterranean. Suddenly, the tide turned, and it became less appealing and more expensive for Americans to travel overseas. Travel to Europe decreased by 25 percent in 1986. As the dollar dropped in value, the United States became an attractive bargain for international travelers. Visitors from Europe and Asia have increased greatly, but this was offset by decreases in visitors from Mexico and Canada (Wynegar, 1987B). It is expected that international visitors will exceed the 1981 peak if the U.S. dollar remains weak.

In order to understand the overall international travel industry, the following data and trends are presented.

- International travel arrivals to the United States come from the following locations: Canada, 50 percent; Europe, 17 percent; Mexico, 10 percent; Asia, 10 percent; South American, 4 percent; other countries, 9 percent (Wynegar, 1987B). Europeans, Asians, and South Americans spend proportionately more than do Canadians, who come for frequent short visits.
- U.S. departures to foreign countries are to: Canada, 48 percent; Europe, 17 percent; Mexico, 13 percent; Asia, 6 percent; the Carribean, 11 percent; other countries, 5 percent (Wynegar, 1987B). Americans spend proportionally less per visit to Canada than overseas.
- International travelers to the United States use proportionally more domestic airlines, rental cars, bus tours, and hotel/motel rooms than Americans traveling domestically (Wynegar, 1987B).
- The leading destinations for worldwide travel, as measured by travel revenues, are in this order: the United States, Italy, Spain, France, and England (Beekhuis, 1986).
- The leading destinations for worldwide travel as measured by number of tourists are, in this order: Italy, Spain, France, United States, and Czechoslovakia (Beekhuis, 1986).

- Overseas visitors to the United States average 22 to 27 nights and spend $877 while here (Beekhuis, 1986).
- United States visitors overseas stay an average of 11 nights and spend $825 while there (Beekhuis, 1986).
- 28 percent of overseas visitors to the United States come on a prepaid package tour (Beekhuis, 1986).
- Foreign visitors to the United States tend to be looking for an outdoor, wide-open experience, and have a huge interest in our national parks (Borcover, 1987).
- Only 35 percent of Canadians who visit the United States come in the summer while 66 percent of American visits to Canada occur in the summer (Beekhuis, 1986).
- For Americans with children, 70 percent take the children on domestic trips but only 49 percent take them on foreign trips (Zigli, 1986A).
- About 22 percent of American professional women take foreign trips each year, compared with 10 percent of working women and 1 percent of nonworking women (*Leisure Industry Digest, March 31, 1986*).

Business vs. Pleasure Travel

It is difficult to determine what portion of the overall travel industry should be attributed to pleasure travel, and what portion should be considered as business travel. Cook (1987) reports that about 25 percent of all trips are for business and that 75 percent are for pleasure. It should be noted that "pleasure travel" includes visits to friends and relatives, which for some Americans is more of an obligation than a form of recreation. It is also important to note that a 75 percent pleasure travel rate is a major increase from the 50 percent rate that was commonly reported 10-15 years ago.

There is also an important trend in combining business with pleasure. Frechtling (1987A), reported that 4.7 percent of travel in 1980 was for business and pleasure. By 1986, this rate had increased to 18 percent of all trips.

Figure 8-2 illustrates some of the important differences between business and pleasure travelers (Cook, 1987). These differences can be extremely important in management and marketing decisions. For example, the data shows that pleasure travel is more seasonal than business travel. When vacations are considered, the seasonal influence is even greater, with about half of all vacation trips occurring in the summer. This has pricing and marketing implications for a resort that intends to be open year round.

Weekend Travel

One of the major social trends of the last 20 years is the increase in the number of women who enter the work force. This has lead to a dramatic increase in the number of "two career families." Many of these families find it difficult to coordinate their work schedules to allow time for long vacations. As a result, mini-vacations have become one of the significant travel trends of recent years. Weekend and long weekend

Figure 8-2
Comparison of Business and Pleasure Travel

	Business Travel	Pleasure Travel
Men	61%	50%
Women	39%	50%
College Educated	45%	34%
Income $40,000 or higher	39%	26%
2 wage earners in family	53%	44%
Mode of Transportation:		
Own Car	50%	73%
Air	42%	21%
Rental Car	15%	6%
Average Distance (Round Trip)	1180 miles	1010 miles
Average Duration	4.2 days	5.5 days
Average Party Size	1.4 persons	2.0 persons
Stayed in Hotel/Motel	71%	39%
Stayed in Home of Friend Relative	18%	48%
Other (includes R.V.s, condos, etc.)	11%	13%
Summer Trips	24.1%	33.4%
Fall Trips	31.2%	25.2%
Winter Trips	20.6%	18.9%
Spring Trips	24.1%	22.5%

Source: Cook (1987).

trips now account for 50 percent of American vacation trips (Frechtling, 1987A). Among two career families, this rate is even higher. Zigli (1986B) reports that 60 percent of Americans actually prefer to take several short trips rather than one long vacation. It is interesting to note, however, that there is a counter-trend among the extended vacation market. Trips which average 15 nights and 2000 miles or more round trip, have increased by 10 percent per year recently (Borcover, 1987). This segment, however, is overshadowed by the much larger mini-vacation market.

The mini-vacation market differs somewhat from the overall travel market. Obviously, the duration of stay is shorter, averaging 2.6 nights. Use of the auto or recreational vehicle is also higher, accounting for 86 percent of trips compared to only 10 percent by airplane. This market is also more likely to visit friends and relatives than other travel segments do (U.S. Travel Data Center, 1986).

TRAVEL PSYCHOLOGY AND BEHAVIOR

Some of the most interesting aspects of any study of the travel industry are the underlying psychological and behavioral aspects. These include motives and attractions for travel, barriers to travel, allocentric/psychocentric travelers, and market segmentation. Each of these aspects is considered in this section. The importance of these topics lies in the implications they have for marketing and managing a travel-related enterprise.

Motives and Attractions for Travel

Various motives and attractions for travel have been identified by Hudman (1980), Epperson (1983), McIntosh and Goeldner (1984), Siegel (1986), and others. Often the reasons for travel are identified as either "push" factors or "pull" attractions. Push factors are those forces within us that motivate us to travel. Typical push motivators include:

- Health Pursuits
- Curiosity
- Escape
- Rest and Relaxation
- Prestige/Ego
- Cultural Interest
- Pleasure Seeking
  (entertainment, gambling
  honeymoon, shopping, etc.)
- Physical Activity
- Friends and Relatives
- Novelty/Change
- Adventure
- Challenge
- Spiritual/Religious
- Search for Roots/Family Heritage
- Professional Development
- Business
- Learn New Skills
- Social Interaction

Pull factors are those attractions that strive to draw a person once they have the urge to travel. Typical pull/attractions include:

- Natural Scenic Areas
- Historic Areas
- Cultural Events and
  Attractions
- Entertainment Events &
  Facilities
- Sports Participation Facilities
- Educational Events & Meetings
- Wildlife
- Religious Shrines
- Comfortable Climates
- Sports Events

Periodically, studies are conducted to assess these motives for travel. Figure 8-3 illustrates the findings of five such studies. Note that four of the studies assessed vacation or pleasure trips, while another study is a broader measure of reasons for all trips. Also note that there is not uniformity in the categories of reasons; some are push/motivators and some are pull/attractions. This is not really a fault, it just reflects the different research orientations that may be taken. There are some similarities in the results, however. Notice that "visits to friends and relatives" is consistently ranked high.

It must be realized that the studies in Figure 8-3 represent the travel motives of a very broad market segment, the general public. In realistic

Figure 8-3
Motives for Travel: Five Studies

Rubenstein (1980) Reasons for Vacations:		U.S. Travel Data Center (1986) Purpose of all trips:	
Rest and Relaxation	63%	Friends and Relatives	40%
Escape Routine	52%	Other Pleasure	35%
Friends and Relatives	45%	Business/Conventions	17%
Recharge/Renewal	45%	Other Purposes	8%
Explore New Places	35%		

Cook (1987) Motives for Pleasure Trips:		Zigli (1986A) Motives for Vacations:	
Friends and Relatives	50%	Sightseeing	41%
Sightseeing and Entertainment	30%	Rest and Relaxation	28%
Outdoor Recreation	20%	Swim and Water Sports	14%
		Fish and Hunt	10%
		Sports Participation	10%
		Camping	6%
		Shopping	6%

Beekhuis (1986) Primary Reasons for Pleasure Travel:	
Friends and Relatives	44%
Touring	14%
Visits Close to Home	13%
Outdoor Trips	10%
Visit Resorts	8%
Visit Cities	7%
Visit Theme Parks	3%
Go on Cruise	1%

application, each particular travel-related company and destination resort needs to analyze the travel motives of their own particular market segments.

Barriers to Travel

Just as there are motives for travel, there are also reasons why people do not travel or travel less frequently. McIntosh and Goeldner (1984), Frechtling (1987A), and Hudman (1980) have enumerated what the major barriers are.

- Expense—Travel can be expensive compared to other forms of recreation. In one study, 63 percent of the people reported that expense is a barrier.
- Lack of Time—This may actually reflect a lack of priority.

- Health—Poor health is a major problem particularly among senior citizens.
- Lack of Skills—Children and many adults lack skills to engage in many outdoor activities at travel destinations.
- Lack of Interest—Some people would simply rather stay home.
- Family Stage--Families with young children are often limited in their travel.
- Lack of Information—It may be surprising, but many people are not aware of the range of travel opportunities and values.
- Lack of Travel Companion—About 20 percent of all Americans travel alone on vacation, and the percentage is increasing due to delayed marriages and divorce.
- Security—More than ever, Americans are concerned with crime and terrorism.

Each travel industry business must determine what barriers are relevant to their particular market segments. Next, strategies must be developed to combat the relevant barriers. Examples are reduced fares for infants on airlines, clubs for single travelers, and marketing programs that emphasize the ease and convenience of AMTRAK.

Allocentric and Psychocentric Travelers
Motives for travel are a key aspect of a psychographic model developed by Dr. Stanley Plog (McIntosh and Goeldner, 1984). This model classified travelers according to two psychographic types: allocentrics and psychocentrics. Plog found that the United States population was normally distributed along a continuum between these two types. Figure 8-4 illustrates the allocentric/psychocentric curve. Note that the majority of the population is "mid-centric" sharing some characteristics of both types.

Figure 8-4
Psychocentric/Allocentric Travel

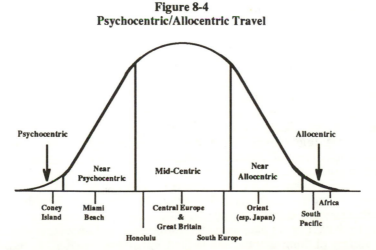

Adapted from Plog in McIntosh and Goeldner (1984).

An allocentric traveler is a person who seeks new experiences and adventure in a variety of activities. This person is outgoing and self-confident in behavior, with higher income and more educational/cultural interests. An allocentric person prefers to fly and to explore nontouristy areas before others have visited the area. Allocentrics enjoy meeting people from foreign or different cultures. While they prefer good hotels and food, modern chain-type hotels are not necessarily sought. For a tour package, an allocentric would like to have the basics (transporation and lodging) but not be committed to a structured agenda. They would rather have the freedom to explore an area, making their own arrangements and choosing a variety of activities.

Psychocentrics on the other hand are more conservatively oriented. They prefer to return to familiar travel destinations where they can relax and know what types of food and activity to expect. Psychocentrics prefer to drive to destinations, stay in typical tourist accommodations, and eat at family type restaurants. Not surprisingly, psychocentrics are a lower income group than allocentrics or even mid-centrics. When arranging a package tour, a psychocentric would prefer a heavily struc-tured agenda so that they know what to expect. Safety and security are very important to this group.

Some groups of people, such as college students and young profes-sional couples with infants may be allocentric by nature, but not able to afford an allocentric-type vacation. Therefore they demonstrate mid-centric or near- psychocentric travel patterns or save up for a less frequent allocentric-type trip.

Plog's model has many implications for travel marketing. For example, a tour company might promote to allocentrics the adventure of flying to Brazil for an Amazon river trip "before the jungle is tamed forever." On the other hand, a destination that appeals to the psychocen-tric market should promote the comforts, reliability, and security found in a familiar resort. A scenario such as "an easy drive to your own timeshare cabin by the lake, where you can fish with old friends," might catch the eye of the psychocentric traveler.

Travel Market Segmentation and Lifestyles

Many businesses in the travel industry are interested in market segmentation. Travel businesses typically want to know demographic characteristics such as area of residence, age, income, family stage, and transporation mode. It is also helpful to know behavioral characteristics such as those related to Plog's allocentric/psychocentric model. If travel businesses understand their market segments, they will do a better job in providing the product/service that the market seeks and will do a better job in communicating the message to the target market.

Travel businesses often develop market segment profiles to help characterize and understand their clientele. One example is the vacation market segmentation developed by Crask (1981). In this study, vacation-ers from the Great Lakes area and southeastern states were segmented by a variety of demographic and behavioral characteristics. Crask identi-fied five different market segments:

R and R Vacationers (32 percent of the market)—These were typically middle aged couples whose children no longer lived at home. The husband was college educated, and the couple had higher income than the norm. They wanted to rest and relax and "get away from it all."

Cost Conscious/Attraction Oriented (25 percent of the market)— These were lower and middle income young couples with children. They averaged less education than the R & R segment. Cost and travel distance was very important, and they had fewer days vacation. They favored visits to man-made attractions such as theme parks and they were more likely to drive to their vacations.

Campers (21 percent of the market)—These were also young adults with children. They had less education and vacation time than the R & R group. Cost and travel distance were important, but the primary vacation considerations were camping facilities and opportunities for sightseeing.

Sightseers (13 percent of the market)—These were older couples with high education and income. Children were no longer at home. Their primary vacation interest was to sightsee, while cost and travel distance were not too important.

Sports Enthusiasts (9 percent of the market)—This segment was the least likely group to be married. If they were married, they were young adults or older couples without children. Education was above average, but income was not necessarily above average, possibly because they were just starting careers. Nevertheless, this group would go on relatively expensive vacations because they would save for their trips. They were less concerned with sightseeing, cost, or travel distance. What they wanted were resorts with amenities and sports opportunities.

Brown (1986) conducted a very interesting study that compared travel motivators with other demographic data such as sex and income level. For this study, an income of $50,000 or more was considered to be the "high market," while lower incomes were in the "mass market." Some of the key findings were as follows:

- Thirty-seven percent desire low cost travel packages, but this is much less important with the high market.
- Nineteen percent sought health and sports facilities. In the mass market this was more important among males than females, but in the high market, females had more interest in sports.
- Only 12 percent sought cultural pursuits. It was the lowest overall travel motivation, but among the highest market ($100,000 income) it had a 31 percent rating as the prime motive.
- Information from friends and relatives was the most important travel influence, followed by travel advertising, travel agency advice, magazine articles, and newspaper feature articles.
- Females were more likely to collect travel brochures, advertisements, articles, and other information than males were.
- The high market planned their travel more in advance.
- Although both the mass and high markets had an interest in travel, and

sought information from travel agents, only 12 percent of the mass market actually took a foreign trip in the past year, compared to 36 percent of the high market.

Brown concluded that travel for the mass market is mostly a fantasy. They will read information and visit travel agents, but they won't buy. The prime market, especially for advertising, is the upscale market.

Finally, Kelly (1985) has made a number of sound observations about the general market for travel.

- Singles travel to destinations to meet peers.
- Two career couples with discretionary income are limited by the necessity of coordinating two work schedules. Time is scarce (and thus the increase in weekend travel).
- Parents of preschoolers must travel in ways that utilize space and services for small children. This often means trips by auto.
- Families with school-age children must coordinate schedules carefully, often resulting in late summer vacation trips. Destinations are closer to home to facilitate common interest activity and interaction.
- "Postlaunching adults" (adults with children no longer at home) have great freedom and resources to travel. Air travel, group tours, and trips for cultural and historical reasons are common.
- Whenever there is a break in the family cycle (death, divorce, etc.), travel becomes important for those in the transition stage, because of its escape and social interaction aspects.

IMPORTANT ISSUES IN THE TRAVEL INDUSTRY

Before examining specific types of travel businesses, it is appropriate to consider several important issues in the travel industry. These topics include the role of government, deregulation, and terrorism.

The Role of Government in Travel and Tourism

In many foreign countries, the national government takes a very active role in the travel and tourism industry. Airlines, railroads, and even some resorts are owned and operated by many foreign governments. They also coordinate travel and tourism planning and directly stimulate development of tourism destinations. Almost every major country spends more to promote inbound tourism than the United States does. It should be noted, however, that many U.S. cities and states spend considerable sums to promote tourism although most of the money is to promote domestic tourism.

While United States federal, state, and local governments are not as directly active as many foreign countries are in travel and tourism, there are nevertheless, many important roles for government such as provision of system structure, protection of natural resources, stimulation of the free enterprise system, and regulation of development and business operations in the public interest.

In addition to the above, the United States government in 1981 passed the National Tourism Policy Act. This act has three elements (Gunn, 1983; Guadagnolo, Kerstetter, and Corazza, 1983):

- Title I—recognizes the need to coordinate and respond to national, state, and local interests in tourism, such as global relationships, balance of trade, tourism opportunities, historic preservation, natural resources conservation, and travel research and planning.
- Title II—established the United States Travel and Tourism Administration, which is to prepare an annual tourism marketing plan.
- Title III—established a Tourism Policy Council to coordinate the policies and programs of federal agencies as they relate to tourism. It also established a Travel and Tourism Advisory Board to provide creative ideas in the development of tourism programs and in the implementation of national tourism policy.

Deregulation of the Travel Industry

The Airlines Deregulation Act of 1978 eliminated government control of the airlines industry. Since then, there have been other deregulation measures affecting travel agencies and bus companies. Although most of us associate deregulation with the idea of free enterprise and competitive pricing, there have been numerous problems (Borcover, 1986B). A plethora of everchanging airfares has led to confusion in airline reservations and ticketing. Airline consolidations, route changes, and company failures have left some cities without major service, and expansion of some routes has led to overcrowding of airports. Airline and bus company failures have left passengers stranded and/or holding worthless tickets, while route cancellations have left many cities without service. Reduced airfares mean reduced sales margins for travel agencies, and 852 agencies defaulted in 1986. Meanwhile, the rise of computerized travel ticket outlets through convenience stores and shopping mall booths have eliminated the counseling and service aspect of ticketing.

All of these problems alert us to the fact that sudden changes in the regulation of an industry are accompanied by a difficult period of transition. During this period, problems occur that may not have been anticipated. Managers of businesses that do not have a strong financial balance sheet or are not flexible, may find it difficult to survive the "shake out" period that follows a major industry change.

Terrorism in the Travel Industry

Terrorism is an age old political weapon and in recent years it has become an all too common occurrence. In 1972 there were 206 major incidents of terrorism worldwide, but this grew to 3010 incidents in 1985. Many of these attacks have involved the travel industry.

Authorities report that Americans are targeted in 14 percent of the terrorist incidents. This has profoundly affected American travel overseas in recent years. After a flurry of terrorist activities in late 1985 and early 1986, 1.4 million of these potential travelers cancelled their trips

(*Leisure Industry Digest*, May 30, 1986). Europe lost $1.1 billion of American travel and tourism business, with Mediterranean countries suffering most (Tuttle, 1987). This represented an overall reduction in travel to Europe of about 30 percent, and Canadian travel to Europe also declined by about 20 percent.

In order to counter this disastrous decline, many countries initiated aggressive new marketing campaigns. For example, Greece lost $100 million in tourist revenue after a TWA hijacking in 1985. The Greek National Tourism Organization soon put $3 million into an advertising campaign to bring tourists back. Familiarization tours were also given to 2000 American travel agents (Blumenthal, 1986). British Airways started a $6 million promotion called "Go For It America," Pan American Airlines offered "two for one" tickets to Europe, and European hotels reduced room rates by 25-50 percent (D'Amore, 1986).

INDUSTRY PROFILE: AIRLINES

How many commercial recreation graduates are going to own or manage an airlines? The answer is probably none, but this does not mean that there are not opportunities. Most airlines require that all employees start at the bottom and work their way up. Flight attendants can become senior attendants, supervisors, and trainers. Reservationists may have to work as baggage handlers at first, but may move up through ticket counter work to marketing positions. Both career paths can build upon the leadership skills, public relations skills, business skills, and knowledge of the travel industry that is gained by a commercial recreation major.

It is also important for students who are interested in the hotel industry and in other travel services to understand the airlines industry. Much of the travel business is interrelated, and career-minded students must understand airlines in order to understand the overall travel environment.

Airlines Industry Overview

Although only about 15 percent of American trips are by plane, air travel accounts for about 25 percent of the trip mileage (Frechtling, 1987B). Perhaps more importantly, air travel is the preferred transportation mode of the upscale tourist. The typical air traveler covers three times the distance of an auto trip, stays longer, and spends more money (U.S. Travel Data Center, 1986).

A milestone in the history of the airline industry occurred with Deregulation in 1978. This change allowed airlines to set their own routes, schedules, and fares. In a Darwinian struggle of the fittest, route systems expanded to meet new opportunities, and unprofitable routes were eliminated. Within six years, the number of certified airlines quadrupled, but there were also 161 companies that went broke or merged with other airlines (Work, 1986B).

By 1987, there were about 250 commercial air carriers in the United States, with 4500 aircraft and 355,000 employees, but only 57 of these carriers have scheduled passenger service. It should be noted that 38 of those 57 airlines did not exist before deregulation. While these new companies carry only 13 percent of the air passenger volume, they are growing much faster than the older airlines (Elliot, 1987).

The remainder of this section will examine the types of airlines and major trends that affect their operation: hub and spoke concept, operating costs, discount fares, and other trends.

Types of Airlines

There are two major classifications of airline flights: international and domestic. Airlines operating internationally must have their routes, schedules, and fares approved by the governments of the countries involved. There are particular problems inherent with international flights: time zone differences, baggage handling difficulties, passports and visas, custom regulations, and foreign currencies. International airlines may also operate domestically (Manjone, 1986).

Domestic air carrier flights originate and terminate within the United States. There are four types of domestic carriers, each presented below (Capousis, 1986; Work, 1986A; Elliot, 1987; Beekhuis, 1986; Standard and Poors, 1986; Manjone, 1986.).

Major Carriers have at least $1 billion in annual revenue. Twelve major airlines qualify for this honor and account for 84 percent of all passenger miles in the United States. The top five, Texas Air, United, American, Delta, and Northwest, account for about 70 percent of the volume. These five dominant carriers share a similar success format:

- A national route system based on hubs in four or five key cities.
- Controlled labor costs.
- Sophisticated reservation systems.
- Seat occupancy without discounting most seats.
- Smart, aggressive management.
- Strong cash position; liquidity.

National Carriers have revenues between $75 million and $1 billion. Most of these carriers, such as Southwest, PSA, and Alaska Airlines, serve regional routes. National carriers have had higher growth rates than the major carriers and serve as a source of competition in some markets.

Regional and Commuter Airlines have revenues under $75 million and provide service between small cities and major hubs. For this reason, many of the regional/commuter airlines form alliances with major airlines, and some are being taken over by the majors. Most of the regional/commuter lines are low fare, no frill, and have nonunion labor. These aggressively managed airlines exemplify the deregulated free market, but failure rate is high.

Charter Flights have declined in volume recently and now account for only about 3 percent of air travel. Usually, a plane, its crew and service are rented from a major or national airline by a company that specializes in charter flights. This arrangement is popular for large group tours and athletic team travel. The demise of charter flights, particularly for tours, can be attributed to the low fares on regularly scheduled flights.

The Hub and Spoke Concept

The Hub and Spoke Concept (see Figure 8-5 for travel definitions) has become the most popular routing system in the airline industry. The concept has numerous advantages (Work, 1986A; Standard and Poors, 1986).

- A large number of destinations are connected with fewer total flights.
- Aircraft and personnel are used more efficiently.
- Load factors (percent seat occupancy) are higher.
- Passengers stay with the same airline to make connecting flights.
- Average revenue per passenger is higher.

There are now about 50 hubs at 31 airports, and some of these airports operate above their design capacity. The increased congestion of the hubs has caused chaos at some locations. It is not unusual for one airline company to schedule 40 or more flights to arrive at a hub within a 50-minute period. While the planes refuel and baggage is transferred, passengers scramble to make their connecting flights. About 35 minutes later, the "bank" of 40 plus planes are scheduled to take off again (Powell, 1986).

The lack of airport congestion has become so unusual that it has become part of the marketing campaign for some destination areas. For example, the Utah ski resorts emphasize their accessibility through Salt Lake International Airport in contrast to the congestion that Colorado skiers face when they fly into Denver's Stapleton Airport.

Airline Operating Costs

In 1978, the price of jet fuel began a tremendous escalation, reaching $1.05 per gallon in 1981, a 153 percent increase. Fuel prices began to drop in 1983 and reached 52 cents per gallon in 1986. It is not just coincidence that the airline industry experienced huge losses from 1980 to 1982, but has been profitable since 1983. Today, fuel represents about 20-25 percent of the operating costs of airlines (Elliot, 1987). At this rate, each one cent per gallon drop in price translates into an additional $100 million profit for the airline industry (Standard and Poors, 1986).

Wages now represent about 37 percent of the operating costs for airlines, but at one time this was much higher. In 1983 American Airlines pioneered "B- tier" wages in which new employees were hired at 30-50 percent lower rates. Many other airlines followed suit, but not without protest from the unions (Standard and Poors, 1986).

Continental was one of the airlines that achieved low labor costs in a particularly aggressive manner. In 1983, Continental declared bankruptcy and discarded its union contract. The airline recruited new, nonunion workers and was back in the air 56 hours after it had closed

Figure 8-5
Travel Dictionary

Hub and Spoke—A concept wherein an airline uses a central point for connecting flights to numerous destinations. This reduces the overall number of direct flights that would have been necessary to connect all the perimeter destinations.

Connecting Flight—One that requires passengers to get off one flight and change to another flight.

Direct Flight—Not necessarily a nonstop flight, but passengers stay on the same plane to their final destinations.

Bank—A group of flights of one airline that converge on a hub, trade connecting passengers, and depart from the hub within a short period of time. One late plane bringing numerous connecting passengers can delay the departure of the entire bank of flights.

Transfer—The ground transportation, usually by van or bus, that takes passengers from the airport to their resort or hotel.

Joint Fare—A discount fare wherein a traveler flys one airline to a gateway city and takes another airline to the final destination.

Class F—First class airfare; the wide seats and extra service in the front of the plane.

Class Y—Coach air fare in the middle and rear of the plane.

Supersaver—A discounted fare, usually for domestic round trip flights that must be booked and paid for a specific number of days before flight time. There may be requirements for staying a specific number of days and/or a Saturday night (so business travelers do not take advantage of a bargain designed to lure discretionary travelers.)

Q, V, or M Fares—Computer names for various promotional air fares that may carry marketing names such as "Paradise Holiday."

Advance Purchase Excursion Fare (Apex)—A "supersaver" for international flights.

Group Inclusive Tour (GIT)—A discounted fare, usually for international flights, available for a group of people (minimum may be five, ten, or more), who travel on the same flight.

Travel Package or Tour Package—A combination of whatever a tour operator decides to offer. It may include airfare, lodging, ground transfers, meals, entertainment, and/or activities.

All-Inclusive Tour—A tour that includes round trip transportation plus a package tour of hotel, transfers, local tours, and possibly meals for one price.

Net Rate—A wholesale rate to be marked up for resale to the consumer.

Rack Rate—The list price for a lodging unit, the highest rate listed. This is usually charged to drop-ins or persons contacting the establishment directly. Package deals are usually cheaper.

Private Bath—A bath inside your room.

Semi-Private Bath—A bath outside your room shared by occupants of one other room.

Shared Bath—A bath between two rooms and available to occupants of each.

American Plan (AP)—Breakfast, lunch, and dinner included in the lodging package.

Modified American Plan (MAP)—Breakfast and dinner included in the lodging package.

European Plan—A hotel rate that includes bed only; meals are extra.

Half Board—Breakfast and either lunch or dinner included in a lodging package.

Land Price—The cost for the land arrangements only: hotel, local tours, activities, and possibly meals.

Escorted Tour—Tour in which an escort or tour manager accompanies the participants.

Independent Tour—Package tour for individuals who wish to travel on their own, without an escort.

Fly/Drive Tour—An independent tour featuring use of a rental car.

Single Supplement—Additional fee for single persons not sharing a room.

Guaranteed Share—Tour company pairs single travelers of the same sex, or company will not charge a single supplement.

Add-on Fare—Air fare to the city where a tour originates.

Single Room—Room with one bed for one person.

Twin Room—Room with two beds for two people.

Double Room—Room with one double bed for two persons.

Dorm—A room shared by four or more persons who might be strangers. Accommodations may be beds, cots, or bunk beds.

Double Occupancy Rate—Price per person if two people share a room.

Double Room Rate—Total price of a room that is shared by two persons.

Vouchers—Documents issued by tour operations to be exchanged for lodging, meals, sightseeing, etc.

Passport—Official government document certifying identity and citizenship, permitting a person to travel abroad.

Visa—Official authorization, added to a passport permitting travel to and within a particular country.

Ocean Front Room—Hotel room directly facing the ocean.

Gateway—City, airport or area from which a tour departs.

Ocean View Room—A room from which you can see the ocean; usually on the side of the hotel.

High Season Supplement—Additional charge imposed during the busiest time of the year.

Service Charges, Gratuities, and Taxes—A fixed percentage automatically added to room and meal charges. Taxes may be set by city, state, and federal government.

Pension—A European guesthouse or small inn.

Drop-Off Charge—A fee charged by a car rental company to defray the cost of returning the auto to its original location.

First Class Hotel—An average comfortable hotel.

Tourist Class Hotel—A budget hotel with few private baths and limited services.

Deluxe Hotel—A top grade hotel. All rooms have private bath, standards are high.

Incentive Travel—A trip offered as a prize, often used to reward employees in sales positions.

Land Operator—A company that provides local travel services, sightseeing, guides, etc.

Override—An extra commission paid by a travel carrier or hotel as bonuses for volume business.

Tour Shells—Brochures (of resorts and carriers) containing artwork and graphics but without written copy, which are then overprinted by tour operators or wholesalers.

Sources: Rand (1986); U.S. Tour Operators Association (No Date); Price (1986).

operations (Shrzychi, 1984). These lower labor costs, combined with lower fuel costs have made a big difference in airline profitability.

Discount Fares

One of the major outgrowths of deregulation is the competition that has led to a variety of airfare discounts. From 1981 to 1985, the average air fare per mile dropped 30 percent. Over an 8-year period, customers saved a total of $6 billion (Scocozza, 1987). Discounts now apply to 85 percent of all domestic flights, and the average savings per discount fare is about 56 percent. Some fares however are cut by more than 70 percent (Elliot, 1987), but the cheaper the fare, the more restrictions exist. These cheap fares are used to lure the leisure travelers who might not otherwise fly. Complex computer programs keep track of demand history and parcel out just enough discount fares to avoid damaging their full fare business (Work, 1986A; Carroll, 1986; Work and Shrzychi, 1987).

Other Important Trends

There are several other trends in the airline industry that deserve mention here.

Historically, airline load factors have been about 60 percent and this may even have dropped a little recently. Since some of the airlines have lower labor costs, and some have more fuel-efficient planes, the load factor that is required to break even varies from one airline to the next. Presently, the range is about 43 percent to 66 percent (Standard and Poors, 1986).

- Senior citizens, age 60 and over, represent the fastest growing market in the country. They have more discretionary time and money, possibly because 80 percent have paid off their homes. Some airlines are targeting this market with offers for unlimited flight for a year at a cost of about $1,200 (Dallos, 1986).
- Air travelers on package tours represent about 17% of the market (U.S. Travel Data Center, 1986). This is expected to continue to increase.
- Some airlines are making good revenue by leasing out their computer reservation systems to travel agencies. American Airlines Sabre system and United's Appolo system command 70 percent of this business. The Sabre system leases bring American Airlines about $338 million revenue a year.
- Several problems lurk on the horizon for the airline industry (Derchin, 1987). First, it is a cyclical business that can change rapidly with economic conditions, especially recessions or increases of oil prices. Next, terrorism could reduce travel demand to certain destinations, thus hurting the airlines that fly those routes. Finally, the consolidation and mergers of airlines could ruin the competition that has kept prices low enough to stimulate travel.

INDUSTRY PROFILE: CRUISE LINES

In 1970 only about 500,000 Americans went on cruises, but during the mid 1970s a successful television show "The Loveboat" introduced the concept of cruising to millions of viewers. This TV show has been given credit for broadening the cruise market and lowering the average passenger age (Beekhuis, 1984). By 1987, the U.S. cruise industry served about 3 million passengers and earned revenues around $5 billion. Growth rates in recent years have doubled the increase in the overall travel industry. To serve this booming industry, there are about 120 cruise vessels in North America, and most of these are new or refurbished. Some of the ships carry as many as 2600 passengers, while others, capable of sailing to smaller and more exotic ports, carry only 120 (Godsman, 1987; Davis, 1987).

The new cruise ships have taken advantage of modern technologies including stabilizers, lighter materials, modular construction, fuel-efficient design, and satellite assisted navigation. Newer ships have larger pools, theme restaurants, stereo/light show discos, health spas, TVs, VCRs, and youth centers (Reichel, 1986). These facilities complement the usual sun decks, casinos, libraries, shops, lounges, and showrooms.

Modern Cruise Ships are floating luxury hotels with sundecks, pools, recreation programs, entertainment, and fine dining for as many as 2,500 guests. (Photo: Courtesy of Carnival Cruise Lines.)

Major Trends

The United States is the largest cruise market in the world, accounting for 75 percent of the world's passenger volume. Even so, only 5 percent of the United States population has ever cruised (Reichel, 1986). Interest in cruising is much higher however. A study of 2000 vacationers revealed that 56 percent of the population is interested in taking a cruise. Indeed, great changes in the market have occurred. Once, cruise passengers were primarily wealthy senior citizens. This has changed; 37

percent are under 35 years of age, 25 percent are 35-54, and 38 percent are over 55 (Beekhuis, 1984). Most of these passengers are first timers, but once they go, 76 percent want to repeat.

Another major market change is the length of cruises. The industry average is 7 days, but the 3 to 4 day cruise is the fastest growing area of business, accounting for 24 percent of cruise volume in 1986. This represents a 35 percent growth over the previous year (Godsman, 1987).

A second major trend is the use of discounts and incentives to attract new markets. Many of today's prices are close to those charged in the early 1970s (Levin, 1986). There are also changes in pricing for single passengers. Instead of charging single passengers at double rate, most cruise lines are building more single cabins into the ships or creating room share programs for single travelers. Other incentives include free air fare and package deals linked to land-based attractions such as Disneyworld.

The third trend is the increased diversity in the cruises and destinations. Most cruises in North America depart from Florida ports and visit destinations in the Carribean. West coast cruises typically go to Alaska or to the Mexican beaches of Mazatlan, Puerto Vallerta, and Acapulco. More adventure cruises, however, are gaining great popularity. Destinations include the Nile, Amazon, and Yangtze rivers, plus numerous exotic islands.

Many cruises have a variety of programs available such as golf, skeet shooting, exercise classes, shore excursions, and talent shows. Theme cruises take the programming one step further with a variety of themed entertainment, classes, or other activities. Norwegian Cruise Lines has presented such themes as Country-Western Days, Viking Festival, Jazz Festivals, and the Fabulous 50s.

Overall, the cruise industry is now positioning itself as "New, Affordable, and Fun" to counter its traditional stigma of "Old, Rich, and Boring." It needs broader markets to fill the many new ships. The future may include new technology such as speedy jetfoil ships or even hovercrafts. Another view of the future sees numerous small excursion boats attached to one huge "mothership." The smaller boats will be able to take mini-cruises to exotic beaches and remote native towns where the larger vessels cannot find adequate ports (Reichel, 1986).

Opportunities In The Cruise Industry

While there are opportunities for employment in the cruise industry, students should not be deceived by staff profiles from "Love Boat" episodes. Ships officers are almost always non-Americans from the cruise line's home country: often Italy, Holland or Norway. Crew members are also non-Americans (Indonesia, Philippines, Portugal, etc.) who fill low paying, nonprofessional positions. The primary opportunities therefore are for positions with the social staff or with the on-shore offices.

A ships social staff is headed by the Cruise Director, who as a professional entertainer, must host shows, sing, dance, and be a comic. The assistant cruise director also entertains and helps the cruise director supervise the ship's recreation programs. Sports Directors and Youth Activity Coordinators are hired by some cruise lines to supervise these programs. Such positions pay about $300-$400 per week and have some potential for tip income. Students who wish to compete for these positions are advised to serve as "workaways," without pay, in order to gain experience. Some cruise lines also contract specialists for golf, tennis, snorkeling/diving, adult arts and crafts, bridge, and other activities.

All these social staff members get private rooms, meals, and airfare to the port cities. Employment may be contracted for eight months or as little as two weeks.

Cruiseline offices also hire reservationists, personnel specialists, marketing staff, and office managers. Students wishing to apply with cruise lines should first get the correct addresses from *The Steamship Directory*, which is available at many travel agencies and libraries (Powers, 1987; Henry, 1986).

Another possibility for cruise-related employment is to work as a tour group escort. Alumni groups, singles travel clubs, travel agencies, and tour operators may all occasionally employ tour escorts. See the spotlight at the end of this chapter for a profile of this position.

INDUSTRY PROFILE: TRAVEL AGENCIES

Travel agencies are a high tech, high growth industry where young people with management skills can begin a career in the travel industry. Every major city has several travel schools where students can learn the computer reservation skills needed to become a travel agent. Entry level positions are low paying, about $12,000 to $20,000 a year, and the work is stressful. Agents must try to please customers, some of whom can be obnoxious. Benefits are good however, since agents get free or discount air fares and hotel accommodations. Agents also go on occasional "familiarization tours," which are mini-vacations to inspect hotels and resorts (Walsh, 1986).

The mark of a professional agent is the achievement of "Certified Travel Counselor" status. This certification requires five years experience and additional training (Panos, 1986). The next step is to become an agency manager. At this level, skills gained in a college degree program become more important and the pay is more on a professional level. Some agents and managers go on to become travel agency owners. This can be a very risky proposition, even though it doesn't take much capital to open an agency.

Another career track for an experienced agent is to become travel coordinator for a major corporation or manager with a tour company, travel council, or convention/visitor bureau. In all these positions, it is important to have good interpersonal and communication skills plus knowledge of geography, travel interests, computers, and business.

Travel agencies were not a major industry until air travel began to flourish. In 1978 the airline deregulation act led to many changes in routes, schedules, and fares, causing people to begin to seek help in finding the best air fares. The number of travel agencies doubled to 28,933 by 1986. Most air travel, cruises, and international hotel rooms are currently booked through travel agencies (Treber, 1987). It has become an industry with revenues of about $70 billion a year.

Services of a Travel Agency

The primary duty of a travel agency is to arrange transportation and lodging for its clients. An agency should first become knowledgeable about the suppliers of transportation and lodging. A good agent will then help match the travelers expectations and financial ability with the appropriate travel options. The agent also has a duty to provide necessary information about the trip (visas, currency, civil unrest, etc.). Reservations for the transportation, accommodations, and other services must be made, and at a later date, confirmed if necessary. Ticketing and the processing of payments must also be completed.

A second major service is the retailing of tour packages. In some cases, the agency may develop the tour package and even provide escorts. It is more common however, to purchase the tour package through a tour operator or wholesaler, and then retail the package to the client.

The provision of auxiliary services is the third major responsibility of the travel agency. Such services include passports, travelers checks, maps, guidebooks, and tourist convenience items.

In exhange for its services, the travel agency receives commissions from the various travel suppliers, usually about 10 percent. However, some package tours, if sold in quantity, may pay as much as 18 percent. Occasionally an extra commission or "override" is paid by a supplier when the agency books a high volume of business (Hartzman, 1986).

Travel Agency Markets

An agency's total sales volume comes from two different markets: business travel and leisure travel. Even though leisure travel represents the majority of overall trips, the business market accounts for more than half of travel agency business. This difference exists because business travelers are more likely to utilize travel agencies, are more likely to fly full fare, and stay in more expensive hotels.

Air travel is by far the biggest revenue area, accounting for 62 percent of agency revenues. This is followed by cruise bookings, hotels, rail travel and, finally, motorcoach travel (Beekhuis, 1986).

Most travel agencies serve both the business and leisure markets. Beyond that, agencies may focus on a variety of target clientele. The best markets appear to be the following: business executives, high income groups, married couples (old or young) without children at home, upscale singles, families with teenage children, and higher educated individuals. People seeking cruises, package tours or international travel are very likely to use an agency's services. As with many commercial recreation industries, repeat business is critical for success; about 70 percent of travel agency bookings are made by repeat customers (Harris, 1984).

Travel Agency Operations

There are very few federal, state, or city requirements specifically oriented to travel agencies, and it is relatively inexpensive to open a business. This helps explain why 3000 new agencies opened in 1986. Unfortunately, 852 agencies defaulted.

One of the first expenses in starting an agency is to post a $20,000 performance bond to guarantee that all accounts between the agency and suppliers will be settled. The Airlines Reporting Corporation requires this bond, plus proof of adequate cash reserves (Borcover, 1986B). Another key initial expense is a minimum of $1000 a month to lease a couple of computer reservation terminals. Altogether, it should take $30,000 to $60,000 to start an agency, but another $60,000 per year will probably be lost for two years until a solid customer base is developed. Banks and other conventional lending sources are reluctant to loan this amount, so personal resources or partnerships are typically the financial sources for agency start-ups (Witcomb, 1986).

Areas such as shopping malls are good locations to attract leisure travelers, while city business centers are better for the corporate travel market. Both locations need to be on the ground floor with easy access for walk-in business. Professionally operated travel agencies are usually members of ASTA, the American Society of Travel Agents (Freemont, 1983).

In recent years, the tremendous discounting of airline fares have posed major problems for travel agencies. Counting all overhead, it costs an agency about $20 to counsel the traveler and write an airline ticket. Since they make about 10 percent commission, any fare below $200 loses money. It is not surprising, therefore, that the typical agency operates on a profit margin of under 2 percent, so volume is crucial for success. Recently, many small agencies have been caught in the squeeze between low margin and low volume and have been driven out of business. Another new development is to charge a $10-$15 service fee for writing low fare tickets (Work, 1986B).

Travel Agency Alternatives

Three types of alternative travel services have emerged in recent years: discount agencies, travel clubs, and ticket brokers. Each is designed to serve a special niche in an effective manner and draw customers by offering discount tickets.

A discount travel agency writes airlines or cruise tickets at full price in order to claim its commission, but then rebates part of the commission to the customer. In effect, it charges a flat fee, $10-$20, to write tickets, and customers usually save 5 percent to 8 percent of the fare. The catch is that there is no travel consulting and no changing of itineraries.

Travel clubs offer "distress merchandise"—unsold space on charter flights, cruises, and tours. Each travel club charges a fee of $25-$60 per year for a family who can call a toll free hot-line to hear a tape of available trips. This approach works best for travelers who can decide on a trip just days before its departure. Discounts range from 20-70 percent, yet the club still makes a good profit because they buy the unsold space at deep discounts.

Ticket brokers purchase frequent flyer coupons from individuals and sell the coupons at a profit. It is not unusual to find business travelers with so much frequent flyer credit that they can't use it all. Instead, they sell it to a broker for about two cents a mile. The broker may triple that price and still provide a discount for the new buyer. This semi-scam works best with first class or full fare travel where discounts are attractive and profitable (McGrath, 1986).

INDUSTRY PROFILE: TOUR COMPANIES

Tour and group travel today is a $10 billion industry, serving about 200 million passengers a year. The industry is growing at a rate of about 10-15 percent annually, which is faster than the overall travel industry. About 500 specialty travel and tour operators belong to the National Tour Association, but there are about 2500 operators who are not members.

Most of the NTA affiliated companies operate "intermodel" tours that incorporate motorcoach travel with planes, cruises, river runners, or rail carriers. Only 30 percent of NTA tour operators own their own motor coaches. The majority contract space with various carriers or charter the transportation necessary for the tour.

Tour patrons come from all across the United States and markets vary from company to company. Most NTA tour operators list senior citizens as the prime target market, followed by mixed adult groups, school groups, young adults, and families. These patrons have many types of tours to choose from. Direct mail is the favored promotional method used by 75 percent of NTA tour operators. This is followed by newspapers, group presentations, newsletters, trade shows, and radio (Lippencott, 1987; Bauer, 1987; National Tour Association, 1986).

Advantages and Disadvantages of Group Travel

Why do people go on group tours? There are numerous advantages and disadvantages (Calhoun, 1986; Manjone, 1986; Lippencott, 1987). For some travelers the advantages are:

- Financial savings of group rates.
- Economic simplification—travelers know what they'll spend.
- Solves the problem of what to see—inexperienced travelers appreciate this most. The best sights and activities are usually included.
- A shared experience—group interaction increases the trip value.
- A carefree experience—the traveler is released from the work of planning and executing the trip.
- Greater security with group travel and a tour guide to act as a buffer to the foreign environment.

There are of course, disadvantages of group travel for some people:

- It may be too regimented or too slow for some adventurous travelers.
- It may move too fast for the person who seeks depth and quality of experience.
- Passive sightseeing, the heart of most tours, is still important, but more travelers are now seeking activity and adventure.
- A sick, hurt, or lost group member can ruin the experience for many people on the tour.

Types of Tour Companies

There are several different types of tour companies: tour wholesalers, motorcoach companies, recipient operators, and outdoor adventure services. Each type may provide all the elements of a tour (make arrangements, market tour, lead tour) or they may specialize in one or two elements while contracting out the other aspects. Travel agencies may also perform any of the functions.

Tour Wholesalers specialize in putting tours together and selling the package to travel agencies, who retail the tour to the public. Some tour wholesalers also market the package directly to the public. Because wholesalers "block out" or reserve thousands of hotel rooms, cruise berths, motorcoach tour seats, and so on, they can command great discounts from the suppliers. These discounts can be built into an attractively priced tour package and still leave room for a healthy profit.

Some wholesalers work with a variety of destinations, markets, tour lengths, prices, and activities. They continually evaluate the tours, adding, dropping, or changing the tour to meet market interests. This approach has strength in its diversity and is less seasonal.

There are also a number of specialty tour wholesalers who concentrate on a particular market or destination. One example is "Singleworld" operated by Gramercy Travel Agency. Singleworld offers about 500 different trips a year that enable single travelers of all ages to meet and travel with other singles (Kerstetter, 1986).

Motorcoach Companies provide regularly scheduled intercity (between cities) transportation and/or chartered bus service. Overall, it is a $2.5 billion industry, with about 3000 authorized companies. In recent years, however, there has been a decline in the intercity route business, and many cities no longer have bus terminals. Low airfares are blamed for most of this decline. On the other hand, the charter and tour segment of the industry has seen a 44 percent increase from 1976 to 1985. About 19 million Americans per year go on tours that utilize motorcoach transportation. Today, a modern motorcoach costs about $170,000. It is air conditioned with plush reclining seats and extra large windows for sightseeing. Some motorcoaches even show movies and have concessions for food and drinks. Due to the decline in fuel prices, the operating cost for a motorcoach has declined since 1984. This has been offset, however, by huge increases for insurance, which averaged $2500 per vehicle in 1982, but $10,000 in 1987 (Beekhuis, 1986; Knapper, 1987; *Leisure Industry Digest*, October 31, 1986).

Receptive Operators are businesses that offer tour services to incoming groups of travelers. These businesses specialize in knowing a particular local area and provide many types of services:

- Planning and arrangements for tours coming into their area, including arrangements for lodging, meals, sports events, theme parks, etc.
- "Step on Guides" for incoming motorcoach tour groups.
- Motorcoaches for tour groups who fly into the area. The motorcoach may be owned by the receptive operator or leased from a separate company.
- Guided tours for local residents or for tourists who are traveling on their own. Horse drawn carriages, tour vans, tour boats, or motorcoaches may be used.

Because they know an area so well, receptive operators are often contracted by tour wholesalers to provide all the local arrangements for a particular geographic segment of a wholesaler's package. This saves the wholesaler valuable time. One 15-minute phone call can set up arrangements that would otherwise take hours to complete. It can also save money because receptive operators may get better rates by dealing frequently with their local market. Perhaps more importantly, the receptive operator should improve the quality of any tour, since they know the best places to go and the best way to present their local area. It is not surprising therefore that business for receptive operators has mushroomed in recent years (Rumpke, 1986).

Outdoor Adventure Tours are a booming segment of the travel industry. For example, in 1968 there were only two whitewater river tour companies in the Eastern United States, but by 1986, there were 200 companies. About 35 million people have now tried whitewater rafting (Crandall, 1987). The boom has coincided with two other growth areas: the fitness industry and air travel. Active, physically oriented "YUPPIES" can easily afford the air fare to numerous origination points for adventure tours. Many people choose the group tour approach because the necessary equipment, guides, instructors, and permits are supplied in one complete package. Popular types of tours include white water river rafting, ski touring, hiking/backpacking trips, bicycle tours, scuba dive excursions, helicopter ski weeks, guided fishing/hunting trips, mountain climbing, archaeological digs, and wilderness challenge outings. Adventure tours can also vary by length, from 1-30 days, and by price. For example, backpacking trips where participants supply their own equipment can be relatively inexpensive. On the other hand, heli-ski weeks are high priced due to the use of helicopters, expensive ski lodges, and fine restaurants. Although some adventure tours serve special segments of youth, women, seniors, or handicapped persons, the most frequent participants are college educated males age 25-45 with higher than average income.

Many outdoor adventure companies start on a limited basis with only a small investment. Banks, however, are reluctant to loan money for such start ups, so personal resources or partners are the typical funding sources. While the company's office location may be in a city for marketing purposes, a base location is needed close to rivers, mountains, deserts, or other appropriate natural resources.

One of the major barriers to starting an outdoor adventure company is the acquisition of permits for use of those natural resources. The Bureau of Land Management, the National Park Service, and the Forest Service limit the number of commercial users. Once the permit ceiling is reached, no new permits are issued. Some aggressive new companies try to buy out the older or marginal companies in order to secure their permits.

For an outdoor adventure tour company to be successful it must offer exciting activities in a picturesque environment. Tours should have some variety: some short, some long, some easy, some challenging. Food, equipment, and tour guides must be of the highest caliber, and safety must not be compromised.

Opportunities With Tour Companies

There are numerous opportunities for employment with different types of tour companies. Operators of local, overland, international, and adventure tour companies all prefer clean-cut, outgoing persons with good communication skills to work as tour guides. In some cases, specific skills in river rafting, horsemanship, bicycle touring, and so on may also be needed, but these are skills some companies are willing to teach a prospective employee. Wages for tour guides are not high, but tips income can substantially supplement the salary. Since many tour guide positions are seasonal, an off season strategy is important. Options include guide work in other seasonal tours, return to school, or seasonal work in other occupations.

It is not unusual for experienced tour guides to move up to management positions where they develop tour itineraries, negotiate with transportation carriers and hotels, train and supervise guides, market the tours, and so on. These opportunities seem to be more abundant with the larger tour companies. At this level of employment, the skills and knowledge gained from a university program in recreation or tourism become very important.

There are also numerous instances where tour guides and managers have learned the business well and started their own companies. By starting small and contracting for transportation, a tour operator can get off the ground without a huge capital investment (Calhoun, 1986).

OTHER TRAVEL INDUSTRIES

Auto rental companies, railroads, and the RV industry do not have a proven record of opportunity for students of commercial recreation and tourism. They, however, have important supporting roles in the overall travel industry. Therefore, this section will provide a brief inspection of these three industries.

Auto Rental Companies

The auto rental industry is tied closely to the airline industry. Of the $4 billion revenue from auto rentals, 88 percent of the business comes from airport locations. This is because airline travelers are the most frequent rental car users. Traditionally, most of the rental car users were business travelers who rented the cars Tuesdays through Thursdays. This changed with airline deregulation and lower air fares, as more people became "discretionary flyers." Now about 40 percent of the auto renters are pleasure travelers. This market is more weekend oriented, which helps pick up the slack in rentals and helps make the industry more cost efficient. With the increase in discretionary travelers, there has been intense price competition among auto rental companies.

An industry problem has been the decline of the used car market. Each year, many of the 500,000 rental cars in service are sold as used vehicles. The years 1984-1986 were disastrous for the sale of used cars because new car sales did so well. Another problem has been the change of tax laws, which no longer allow auto rental companies to take tax credits (reductions) for the purchase of new vehicles. These problems have impacted the profitability of the industry in spite of its growth in recent years (Beekhuis, 1986; Herbert, 1987, Vervaeke, 1987; Sullivan, 1987).

Railroads

Through the first half of this century, railroads were a prime carrier of American travelers. Then, improvements in air transportation and the development of the interstate highway system eroded the railroad's clientele base. Railroads and bus lines were left as the low cost transportation alternative.

In 1970, most of the nation's rail system merged into one organization, the National Railroad Corporation, also called Amtrak. The system has struggled with a huge investment in track, equipment, and facilities while facing a declining share of the travel industry. Recently, even the low price niche has been eroded due to decreases in air fares and gasoline prices. Nevertheless, the railroad travel industry has survived (Beekhuis, 1986; Gardner, 1987; and Scocazza, 1987).

An interesting survival strategy is the marketing of railroad travel as a distinctive experience. Railroads are touted as the scenic way to see America while enjoying comfortable accommodations, good food, lounge car entertainment, and planned activities such as bingo, movies, and happy hour.

In Europe, railroads remain a popular travel option, particularly among young tourists. The Eurail Pass, valid for unlimited travel for 21-90 days, is a good value. Rail travel is also important as a major connecting link between international airports and remote tourist towns and ski resorts in Europe.

Recreation Vehicles

A recreation vehicle is considered to be a wheeled vehicle with temporary living quarters. This includes travel trailers, folding campers, truck campers, and converted vans, while motorbikes and snowmobiles are not considered true RVs. There are about 8 million privately owned RVs in the United States and about 25 million people who use them. Sales volume is inversely related to gasoline prices and interest rates, although only half of all RV sales are financed.

Historically, RV owners are in the 35-54 year age group, which is a major growth market. RV vacation costs are about 50 percent less than comparable trips by auto or air, and savings occur mostly in the area of accommodations and food. RV families however, enjoy the experience as well as the cost savings. Almost 64 percent of RV owners think that their version of camping is the best vacation a family could have.

There are several important trends in the RV industry. First, new models with front wheel drive are getting 20-30 miles per gallon. This is significant in that it might help buffer the industry when the next oil crisis occurs. Another trend is the continuing growth of RV destination resorts (including timesharing) having recreation amenities and programs. Finally, there are a number of RV dealers who are doing a thriving rental business. This trend is expected to continue (Humphreys, 1987). Overall, the recreation vehicle industry appears to have a good future, particularly if oil prices remain stable.

SUMMARY

The travel industry is a huge and complex network of transportation carriers, travel agencies, tour companies, hotels, attractions, and many other services. Historically people traveled mostly for war, religion, or business, but pleasure travel has finally become a major component. There are significant differences between business and pleasure travel, as well as differences between domestic and international travel. Many of the trends in these areas can be attributed to changes in economic conditions, fuel availability, and political stability.

People travel for many reasons. Successful travel services must understand the motives of their particular markets, and strive to overcome any barriers to travel. Destinations and services for conservative psychocentric travelers would be quite different than for the outgoing allocentric travelers. A major travel trend is the increasing popularity of weekend travel, particularly for families with two working adults who have too much difficulty in coordinating careers to allow for extended vacations.

Opportunities exist in numerous travel industries: airlines, travel agencies, cruise lines, and several types of tour companies. In each, however, entry positions are low paying, but the benefits of free or discounted travel make the careers appealing. Advancement can occur if the employee has good interpersonal and communication skills, sound business sense, a knowledge of geography and the travel industry, and desire to help others enjoy their travel and recreation.

The individual travel industries are all enjoying a period of relative prosperity. Deregulation and fuel availability have helped keep prices down, and Americans are traveling more than ever.

STUDY QUESTIONS

1. What definitions are used to identify the travel and transportation area?
2. What is considered the most dramatic development in travel?
3. What factors have affected the recent travel boom?
4. Distinguish between business and pleasure travel.
5. Cite ten motivations and five barriers to travel.
6. How does an allocentric traveler differ from a psychocentric traveler?
7. Describe the hub and spoke concept.
8. Explain three trends in each of the following industries: airlines, travel agencies, tour companies, and cruise lines.

PROJECT IDEAS

1. Visit a local airport and determine the types of travelers arriving to the area.
2. Using Plog's psychographic model for travel, classify the travel tendencies of five of your friends.
3. Interview the manager or other professional in a travel business of your choice and ask what are the keys to operating a successful business and having a successful career.

SPOTLIGHT ON: TOUR ESCORT RICK HENRY

Cruise tour escorts are employed by travel wholesalers, travel agencies, or other tour organizers to accompany groups on cruises. The escort serves as the on-site service link between the tour organizer and the tour group. The escort coordinates group activities such as get acquainted parties, cocktail parties, information sessions, and shore excursions. Problem solving and social facilitating are other typical duties. On any given cruise ship there may be several escorted tour groups, while the majority of passengers cruise independently or in nonescorted groups.

Rick Henry has worked for two tour wholesalers and has escorted groups on several different cruise lines. He reports that being a tour guide is a classic "good news/bad news" type of job. The good news includes travel to exotic ports, great food, satisfaction in helping people enjoy their vacation, and the potential to make as much as three thousand dollars in tips on a one-week cruise. The bad news is that some groups and individuals can be very difficult to work with, and that tips may be only $300 a week for a job that pays no salary. It is not surprising therefore that most cruise escorts are young single people age 21-35 who are flexible enough to "roll with the punches" and surprises of the job.

According to Henry, older and more upscale people go on the higher priced cruises, and these vacationers give higher tips. It is a greater challenge, however, to work with a younger crowd because they want more activities. Unfortunately, the younger tour groups typically book on lower priced cruises and tip less. In working with either type of group it is essential to be friendly and personable while at the same time being a master of detail in making activity arrangements. A common problem in working with shore excursions is the unreliability and inconsistency of some of the local service providers in foreign countries.

There is little upward mobility for most tour escorts. Few move up into scheduling, marketing, or management positions in the tour company offices. The job is, however, an interesting way to travel, meet people, and bank some money before moving on to a more regular career (Henry, 1986).

REFERENCES

Bauer, B. "Buying Adventure--With or Without Frills." *U.S. News and World Report*, January 12, 1987, pp. 52-53.

Beekhuis, J. "The Cruise Industry." *World Tourism Overview*. New York: American Express Publishing Corporation, 1984.

Beekhuis, J. *World Travel Overview 1986/87*. New York: American Express Publishing Corporation, 1986.

Blumenthal, R. "On Terrorism and Tourism, Americans Alter Travel Plans." *The New York Times*, April 2, 1986, pp. 1; 13.

Borcover, A. "Where Have U.S. Summer Vacationers Gone This Year." *Salt Lake Tribune*, August 31, 1986A, p. T6.

Borcover, A. "Since Deregulation Some Degree of Chaos Has Reigned." *Salt Lake Tribune*, December 14, 1986B, p. 4T.

Borcover, A. "Vacations Will Cost More in 1987." *Salt Lake Tribune*. January 11, 1987, p. 71.

Brown, R. "1985 Travel Cross-Tab Study." *The Battle For Market Share: Strategies in Research and Marketing*. Salt Lake City: Travel and Tourism Resort Association, 1986, pp. 95-100.

Calhoun, L. "Tour Directors Training Program." University of Utah course, Department of Recreation and Leisure, Spring, 1986.

Capousis, H. "Texas Air Soars to No. 1." *USA Today*, December 31, 1986. p. B1.

Carroll, D. "Airlines Dogfighting In Denver." *USA Today*, March 15, 1986, p. 1B.

Cook, S. "1986 Domestic Travel in Review." *First Annual Travel Review Conference: Proceedings*. Washington, D.C.: U.S. Travel and Tourism Administration, 1987, pp. 15-24.

Crandall, D. "Recreation Trends." *First Annual Travel Review Conference: Proceedings*. Washington, D.C.: U.S. Travel and Tourism Administration, 1987, pp. 75-79.

Crask, M. "Segmenting the Vacationer Market: Identifying the Vacation Preferences, Demographics, and Magazine Readership of Each Group." *Journal of Travel Research*, Fall, 1981, pp. 29-34.

Dallos, R. "Airlines Look to Capture Lucrative Seniors Markets." *Salt Lake Tribune*, February 23, 1986, p. 2F.

D'Amore, L. "International Terrorism: Implication and Challenges for Global Tourism." Reprint of *Business Quarterly*, Fall, 1986.

Davis, W. "Largest Ship Specifically For Cruising Tests The Waters." *Salt Lake Tribune*, October 11, 1987, p. T9.

Derchin, M. "1987 Outlook For Airlines." *1987 Outlook for Travel and Tourism*. Washington, D.C.: U.S. Travel Data Center, 1987, pp. 89-95.

Elliot, F. "Transportation Services." *U.S. Industrial Outlook 1987*. Washington, D.C.: U.S. Department of Commerce, 1987, pp. 55-1 to 55-3.

Epperson, A. "Why People Travel." *Leisure Today*, April, 1983, pp. 31-32.

Frechtling, D. "1986 U.S. Travel Activity and Industry Trends." *First Annual Travel Review Conference: Proceedings*. Washington, D.C.: U.S. Travel and Tourism Administration, 1987A, pp. 1-13.

Frechtling, D. "Travel Trends in 1986." *1987 Outlook for Travel and Tourism*. Washington, D.C.: U.S. Travel Data Center, 1987B. pp. 5-8.

Freemont, P. *How to Open and Run a Money-Making Travel Agency*. New York: John Wiley & Sons, 1983.

Gardner, T. "1987 Outlook for Rail Travel." *1987 Outlook for Travel and Tourism*. Washington, D.C.: U.S. Travel Data Center, 1987, pp. 115-119.

Gee, C.M. *The Travel Industry*. Westport, Connecticut: AVI Publishing Co., 1984.

Godsman, J. "The Years Transportation in Review: Water Travel in 1986." *First Annual Travel Review Conference: Proceedings*. Washington, D.C.: U.S. Travel and Tourism Administration, 1987, pp. 67-70.

Guadagnolo, F., Kerstetter, D., and Corazza. "The National Tourism Policy Act." *Leisure Today*, April, 1983, pp. 30-31.

Gunn, C. "U.S. Tourism Policy Development." *Leisure Today*, April, 1983. pp. 10-12.

Gunn, C. *Tourism Planning*. New York: Crane Russak, 1979.

Harris, L. "Agency Growth: The Dimension of the Travel Agency Market." *Travel Weekly*, June 30, 1984, p. 57.

Hartzman, R. "Using Travel Agents." *Meetings and Conventions*, May, 1986. p. 263; January 1986, p. 91.

Henry, R. Tour Escort, Grammarcy Travel. Personal Interview, Matzalan, Mexico, September 1986.

Herbert, R. "1987 Outlook for Auto Travel." *1987 Outlook for Travel and Tourism*. Washington, D.C.: U.S. Travel Data Center, 1987, pp. 105-110.

Hudman, L. *Tourism, A Shrinking World*. Columbus, Ohio: Grid Inc., 1980.

Humphreys, D. "1987 Outlook for Outdoor Recreation." *1987 Outlook for Travel and Tourism*. Washington, D.C.: U.S. Travel Data Center, 1987, pp. 123-130.

Hunt, John D. "Tourism Comes of Age in the 1980's." *Parks and Recreation*, October, 1986, pp. 30-36; 66-67.

Jafari, J. "Tourism Today." *Leisure Today*, April, 1983, pp. 3-4.

Kelly, J. *Recreation Business*. New York: John Wiley & Sons, 1985.

Kerstetter, D. "Cruise Ships" and "Travel Clubs." In *Private and Commercial Recreation* (Arlin Epperson, editor). State College, Pennsylvania: Venture Publishing, Inc. 1986, pp. 97-123.

Knapper, T. "1987 Outlook for Bus Travel." *1987 Outlook for Travel and Tourism*. Washington, D.C.: U.S. Travel Data Center, 1987, pp. 111-114.

Leisure Industry Digest, Content from issues March 31, 1986, July 30, 1986, May 30, 1986, June 15, 1986, October 31, 1986, March 87.

Levin, M. "All The Ships At Sea." *Endless Vacation*, December, 1986, pp. 50-53.

Lippincott, D. "Tour Operations and Travel in 1986." *First Annual Travel Review Conference: Proceedings*. Washington, D.C.: U.S. Travel and Tourism Administration, 1987, pp. 43-46.

Manjone, J. "Travel." In *Private and Commercial Recreation* (Arlin Epperson, editor). State College, Pennsylvania: Venture Publishing, Inc, 1986, pp. 80-81.

Mason, P. "1987 Outlook for Regional Trends in the Family Vacation Market." *1987 Outlook for Travel and Tourism.* Washington, D.C.: U.S. Travel Data Center, 1987, pp. 151-161.

McGrath, A. "The Frequent-Flier Coupon Market." *U.S. News and World Report,* May 19, 1986, p. T3.

McGrath, A. and Tooley, J. "Shipping Out With A Winter Cruise." *U.S. News and World Report,* December 1, 1986. pp. 56-57.

McIntosh, R.W., and Goeldner, C.R. *Tourism: Principles, Practices, Philosophy* (4th Edition). New York: John Wiley & Sons, 1984.

Mullins, M. "Tallying The Tab." *USA Today,* May 5, 1986, p. 1B.

NTA Today. Lexington, Kentucky: National Tour Association, Inc., 1986.

Panos, J. "See Your Travel Agent." *Endless Vacation,* Fall, 1986, pp. 62-65.

Powell, S. "The Late, Late Show." *U.S. News and World Report,* December 22, 1986, pp. 14-19.

Powers, P. "Love Boat: Fantasy vs. Reality." 1987 Congress of The National Recreation and Park Association, New Orleans, Louisiana, September 1987.

Price, J. "ABC's of Travel Planning." *Employee Services Management,* March, 1986, pp. 14-21.

Quinn, J. "American Airlines is Trying to Ground Travel Agent Discounts." *Salt Lake Tribune,* November 7, 1985, p. B7.

Rand, A. "A Tightfisted Traveler's Dictionary." *SKI,* October, 1986, pp. 63-68.

Reichel, G. "Pleasure Cruises in the 1990's." *Proceedings of the TTRS 19th Annual Conference.* Salt Lake City, Utah: University of Utah Bureau of Economic and Business Research, 1986, pp. 239-243.

Rubenstein, C. "Vacations." *Psychology Today.* May, 1980, pp. 62-67.

Rumpke, R. "Receptive Operators Offer Destination Management." *Courier.* October, 1986, pp. 85-89.

Scocozza, M. "The Year's Transporation in Review." *First Annual Travel Review Conference: Proceedings.* Washington, D.C.: U.S Travel and Tourism Administration, 1987, pp. 57-61.

Shrzycki, C. "Continental Air Soars Above Union Turbulence." *U.S. News and World Report,* July 23, 1984, pp. 69-70.

Siegel, B. "The U.S. Pleasure Travel Market." In *World Travel Overview, 1986/87.* New York: American Express Publisihing Corporation, 1986, pp. 116-119.

Standard and Poors Industry Surveys. "Air Transport Outlook." January 9, 1986. pp. A28--A35.

Sullivan, J. "The Trends in the Car Rental Industry." *First Annual Travel Review Conference: Proceedings.* Washington, D.C.: U.S. Travel and Tourism Administration, 1987, pp. 63-65.

Treber, J. "The Travel Agency Industry and International Travel in 1986." *First Annual Travel Review Conference: Proceedings.* Washington, D.C.: U.S. Travel and Tourism Administration, 1987, pp. 47-49.

Tuttle, D. "Discerning the Shadows Cast by Coming Events: A Dozen Developments Which Will Shape The Travel Industry's Future." *First Annual Travel Review Conference: Proceedings.* Washington, D.C.: U.S. Travel and Tourism Administration, 1987, pp. 51-56.

U.S. Travel Data Center. *1985 Full Year Report: National Travel Service.* Washington, D.C., 1986.

U.S. Tour Operators Associations. *How to Read a Tour Brochure.* New York, No Date.

U.S. News and World Report . "The Travel Deficit." October 12, 1987, p. 84.

VanDoren, C. "The Future of Tourism." *Leisure Today,* April 1983, pp. 27-29; 42.

Vervaeke, W. "1987 Outlook for Auto Rental." *1987 Outlook for Travel and Tourism.* Washington, D.C.: U.S. Travel Data Center, 1987, pp. 97-101.

Walsh, C. "Travel Your Way to Success." *Business Week's Guide To Careers*, 1986, pp. 83-85.

Witcomb, P. "Travel Agents and Survival Strategies." *Colorado Business*, May 1986, pp. 34-37.

Work, C. "Fewer Airlines Are Flying High." *U.S. News and World Report*, September 22, 1986A, pp. 60-61.

Work, C. "Survival of the Biggest." *U.S. News and World Report*, August 25, 1986B, p. 37.

Work, C. and Shrzychi, C. "Cheap Fares: Come Fly With Me." *U.S. News and World Report,* February 23, 1987, pp. 43-44.

Wynegar, D. "Travel Services." *U.S. Industrial Outlook, 1987*. Washington, D.C.: Department of Commerce, 1987A, pp. 60-1 to 60-4.

Wynegar, D. "The Year's International Travel in Review." *First Annual Travel Review Conference: Proceedings.* Washington, D.C.: U.S. Travel and Tourism Administration, 1987B, pp. 31-41.

Zigli, B. "We're Going on Vacation In, Near U.S.A." *USA Today*, May 5, 1986A, pp. 1E--2E.

Zigli, B. "Searching For The Right Travel Package." *USA Today,* March 17, 1986B, p. 3E.

Chapter 9

THE HOSPITALITY INDUSTRY

The hospitality industry is sometimes considered to be an extremely broad range of businesses that meet the needs of the traveler or recreation seeker. This perspective could include any of the following: hotels, resorts, restaurants, travel agencies, tour operators, theme parks, health clubs, and night clubs. Obviously this represents overlap with the travel industry and the local commercial recreation industry. Therefore the definition of the hospitality industry needs to be narrowed.

For this text, the hospitality industry will be considered to be those businesses that provide overnight accommodations, food and beverage service, and supporting amenities (such as hotel pools, shops, concierge, etc.) that contribute to the customer's leisure experience. In its pure form, the industry has only a few categories: hotels, motels, restaurants, and taverns. There are also many ways in which the hospitality industry combines with travel and local recreation. For example, campgrounds, meeting and convention services, and timeshare exchange services are each part of the hospitality industry and the travel industry. Leisure theme restaurants, night clubs, and residential recreation communities are also in the hospitality industry, but they primarily serve local commercial recreation purposes.

Resorts are part of the hospitality industry, but they have a unique role because they link all the major categories of commercial recreation together. Resorts provide accommodations, food and beverage, recreation programs, retail services, and entertainment. This chapter will examine several aspects of resort development and then consider several specific industries within the hospitality field.

RESORT DEVELOPMENT

According to Kelly (1985) resorts can be classified as theme resorts or variety resorts. A second approach is to consider them as comprehensive resorts or complementary resorts. A theme resort, therefore, could be either comprehensive or complementary.

Theme Resorts are based on a particular type of natural resource or manmade attraction. Examples include resorts located at the ocean, ski areas, hot springs, historical attractions, and gambling towns. A problem of the theme resort is that it may be highly seasonal in nature and/or dependent upon a single interest that could change over time. Therefore, many theme resorts are striving to diversify in order to stabilize their revenue base.

Variety Resorts offer a range of resources, attractions, and activities. Due to the diversity, they may be more capital and labor intensive. Some variety resorts have a ratio of more than one staff per guest. Kiawah Island, South Carolina, is an example of a variety resort that offers numerous beach and aquatic activities plus golf, tennis, live entertainment, social activities, childrens programs, shopping, and gourmet dining.

Comprehensive Resorts have control of their basic recreation resources. It is in their best interest to protect the overall ecology of the area. This can be costly and may involve development of an extensive infrastructure. Disneyworld is an example of a comprehensive resort.

Complementary Resorts have hospitality services, but the major natural resource or attraction of the area is located off site. The resort has access to the resource or attraction, but not control of it. Obviously, this can be an uneasy situation even though there is a complementary relationship between the resort and the resource. The town of West Yellowstone is a complementary resort for the major attraction, Yellowstone Park.

Why Develop Resorts?

Profits from the operation of a resort (sale of rooms, food, services, merchandise, etc.) are not the only reasons for developing a resort. Other reasons for resort development include the following:

- Profit from land development—Resort property may be sold or leased for the development of condominiums, hotels, retail areas, etc.
- Land appreciation—Property held by the resort or by local residents may appreciate with the development of a quality resort.
- Boost adjacent business—Tourists stimulate business for local merchants.
- Increased economic development—Government authorities often encourage resort development because it creates jobs and boosts tax revenues.
- Political reasons and national/regional pride—Resorts showcase an area and add to its image and prestige.
- Tax write-offs—Prior to tax changes in 1986, there were numerous tax advantages such as investment credits and accelerated depreciation. Tax write-offs are less attractive now.

Characteristics of Successful Resorts

Resorts must have several ingredients in order to be successful. They must be based on an attractive natural resource or have significant manmade physical attractions. In addition, the resort must be close to, or have good access to, a large population base. Lastly, it helps immensely to have a unique feature or gimmick that differentiates the resort from others.

Las Vegas is an example of a resort city that meets these criteria. Although there are natural resource attractions nearby (Lake Mead), the city features over a dozen resort hotels with impressive amenities. The

Food and Beverage events are popular opportunities for socializing as well as fine dining. (Photo: Courtesy of Marriott's Tan-Tar-Resort)

city is tied to major populations via excellent airline connections and an interstate highway to Southern California. Legal gambling is of course, the unique gimmick, but several resort hotels have added other features: championship boxing and racing at Caesar's Palace, circus entertainment at Circus Circus, and childrens programs at the Las Vegas Hilton.

There are several other characteristics that are common in many successful resorts (Hudman, 1980; Schnidman, 1983; Masterson, 1986):

- Development that is compatible with the environment.
- A political climate that advocates growth.
- Capacity of the water and sewer systems to handle the development.
- Plenty of reserve capital to overcome unforseen problems and delays in the development.
- Lack of manufacturing in the community.
- Comfortable and clean accommodations of a wide price range.
- A good internal transporation system.
- Plenty of long- and short-term parking.
- Nearby medical services.
- A large commuter population for a labor source.
- An attractive aesthetic atmosphere including scenic vistas, gardens, promenades, open spaces, parks, etc.
- A wide range of recreation amenities including sports facilities, shops, restaurants, lounges and night spots, swimming pools, tennis courts, golf courses, food and beverage events, fairs and festivals, fitness activities, youth recreation programs, trips and tours, social events, and recreation equipment rental.
- A variety of meeting and convention facilities.

INDUSTRY PROFILE: HOTELS AND MOTELS

Throughout ancient times and the middle ages, hotels or "inns" were just rooms within private dwellings. By the time of the industrial revolution in England, more people began to travel and competition for the lodging business led to improvements. English Inns soon gained a reputation for being the finest in the world because they were clean and had friendly service. Eventually, English standards began to be emulated. In 1794, the City Hotel in New York became the first building in the United States to be erected specifically as a hotel.

A revolution of sorts occurred in 1908 in Buffalo, where Ellsworth Statler started the first of the modern commercial hotels. It had electric lights, private baths, fire doors, circulating water, full length dressing mirrors, free morning newspapers, and courteous service. This led to a boom in hotel construction and to books on hotel management.

The Great Depression brought on the worst period in United States lodging history, and 85 percent of the nation's hotels went through some form of bankruptcy or other failure. World War II, however, revived the demand for hotel space as millions of Americans traveled to defense plants or military camps. After the war, Americans took to the highways in autos, and there was a tremendous boom in the construction of motels along the roads.

In the 1960s, major hotel companies started to go after specific market segments. Hotels and motels were built for airport locations, along the new interstate highways, and at resort areas. Several budget chains were started as well. By the 1970s there was further specialization, with condominium and timeshare developments at resorts, all-suite hotels, and more budget chains (Lattin, 1985).

Overall Status of the Industry

Today there are about 54,000 hotels and motels in the United States, with a total of 2.8 million rooms. This is a $44 billion industry with about 1.36 million employees (Sousane, 1987; Maynard, 1986; Lattin, 1985).

Revenues average $24,792 per room per year with 62 percent of it coming from room rents. Food sales account for 23 percent of revenue, followed by beverage sales, telephone charges, facility rentals, and other revenue including recreation amenities (Pannell Kerr Forster, 1986).

These revenues come from an average room rate of $62.60. Rates are highest in the Northeast, at resorts, and at center city hotels. Many hotels and motels offer substantial discounts to business travelers and tour groups. Figure 9-1 illustrates the average room rates and discount percentages at different types of hotels.

Average occupancy rate in the U.S. is about 64 percent, but due to business travel, occupancy is higher on weekdays. It drops to about 50 percent nationwide on weekends. The highest occupancy rates (70 percent) are in the northeast and at airport hotels, while the lowest occupancy rates (57 percent) are in the overbuilt south central states and at center city hotels. Some hotels such as large chains and good resort

220

Figure 9-1
Advertised Room Rates and Average Discount Percent

Type	Hotel/MotelNumber of Rooms			
	Under 150	150-249	250-449	450+
Center City	$37.00 (16.5%)	$53.00 (20.1%)	$74.00 (26.5%)	$101.00 (28.1%)
Suburban	$35.00 (11.1%)	$52.00 (15.3%)	$71.00 (21.0%)	--
Airport	--	$53.00 (24.4%)	$73.00 (29.1%)	$91.00 (33.1%)
Highway	$32.00 (10.7%)	$45.00 (17.7%)	$59.00 (22.7%)	--
Resorts	$52.00 (15.2%)	$66.00 (21.2%)	$80.00 (29.9%)	$99.50 (31.7%)

Source: Carroll (1986)

hotels, tend to have higher occupancy rates. Hotels in the Disneyworld area of central Florida average about 72 percent for the year. Factors related to high occupancy include a strong ratio of demand to supply, good climate, and popular recreation attractions (Sousane, 1987; Beekhuis, 1986).

Hotel and Motel Marketing

Business travelers account for 40 percent of the total room nights at hotels and motels. Pleasure travel and conferences/conventions account for about 25 percent each, followed by government business, and other personal travel (Sousane, 1987). Research shows that people select hotels primarily due to location, followed by rate, cleanliness, food, and courteous service. It is interesting to note, however, that people choose to return to hotels primarily because of the courteous service. Cleanliness and the hotel's amenities are the next highest ranked reasons for returns.

Each year the Mobile Travel Guide announces its Five Star Award winners. Only about 30 hotels, resorts, and restaurants earn this prestigious award, which is proudly highlighted in the winner's marketing literature. To earn the award, a resort hotel must have a gracious lobby with tasteful furnishings and decor, elegant guest rooms, fine art, superior restaurants, meticulous landscaping, twice daily maid service, extensive recreation facilities, and the services of a social/recreation director.

To market its properties, 73 percent of resort hotels utilize direct mailings to travel agencies, previous clientele, targeted organizations and individuals. Yellow page advertising is used by 67 percent of resort hotels. Other marketing methods include corporate group discounts, newsletters, facility tours, radio ads, family discounts, and outside sales force, (Anderson, 1985).

Types of Hotel Operations

There are two major types of hotel/motel operations. Independents account for 46 percent of all hotels/motels, while the rest are types of chain operations including franchises (31 percent), chain owned (12 percent), and chain managed (9 percent), (McCoy, 1986).

Independents are single location operations. These used to be the bulk of the industry, but have lost ground to the chains. Independent operator/owners often have greater pride in their properties and have total management flexibility, but they typically lack marketing clout and financial reserves. If a small independent hotel or motel can fill a specialty niche within an area market, it can be very successful.

Chain hotels and motels offer consistency of product and name recognition. They are efficient due to volume purchasing, personnel training programs, standardized operating methods and procedures, national marketing programs, major financial availability, and nation-wide computer reservation systems. Chain hotels may or may not be franchised. Holiday Corporation for example, owns only 211 of its 1696 Holiday Inns; the rest are franchised.

Many hotel chain properties are built, owned, and operated by the parent company. This gives the company the most control. On the other hand, some chains have contracted operators. Marriott, for example, designs, builds, finances, and manages but does not own its hotels. Most new Marriotts are sold to limited partnerships who then contract the management back to Marriott. In other cases, the parent chain owns the

Hotels such as the Hotel Jerome in Aspen may draw guests with their character and ambience. (Photo: Courtesy of Aspen Skiing Company)

222

hotel, but contracts out for the management (Standard and Poors, 1986; Lattin, 1985).

Figure 9-2 illustrates the organizational chart of a large hotel. Small hotels and motels perform most of the same functions, but people may have to fill several roles.

Figure 9-2
Organization Chart For A Large Hotel

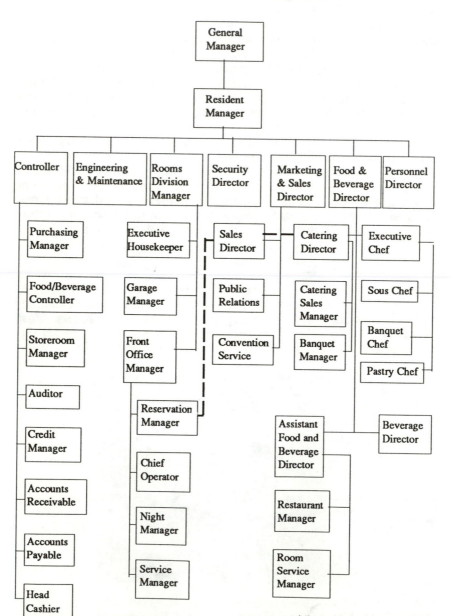

Adapted from Lattin (1985)

Hotel/Motel Classifications

In addition to being an independent or a chain property, hotels can be classified according to their primary function. Types include commercial hotels, airport hotels, economy properties, bed and breakfast inns, suite hotels, residential hotels, casino hotels, and resorts (Lattin, 1985).

Commercial Hotels cater to business clients and small conventions. Center city locations are best for commercial hotels. Typically, they have excellent food and beverage facilities plus a variety of convenient services such as valet laundry, concierge, and health clubs.

Airport Hotels are primarily a convenience to travelers, but some airport hotels are reaching out to other markets. The largest, the AMFAC Hotel and Resort at the Dallas-Fort Worth Airport, markets heavily to convention groups. It can serve 5000 at a banquet and create 50 different special events. The hotel also arranges golf tournaments and theme park outings.

Economy Properties provide for the basic needs of vacationing families and budget-minded business travelers. Most guests stay only one or two nights and seek only clean accommodations with a TV and small pool. Economy hotels and motels increased by 82 percent from 1980 to 1984 and continue to expand today. Rates are typically 20-50 percent less than full service hotels in their area (Kelly, 1985).

Bed and Breakfast Inns are usually Victorian homes or renovated small hotels, lodges or farmhouses. They offer sleeping accommodations and a breakfast in a charming and unique atmosphere. Rates are typically $50-$150 a night. Target markets include business travelers who desire a change of pace plus honeymoon and anniversary couples.

Highway/Roadside Motels usually provide overnight accommodations to travelers on their way to a final destination. In small towns, such properties provide the primary lodging facilities for business or recreation travelers staying several days or more. Few roadside motels have recreation amenities other than a small pool or play area. Since many roadside motels do not have the instant image that a chain operated property enjoys, a favorable rating by the AAA (American Automobile Association) can help attract customers.

Suite Hotels offer accommodations with separate bedroom and living room/kitchens. They are typically located in city centers and cater to business travelers, vacationers, and persons who are relocating.

Residential Hotels are also usually in city centers and function as primary homes or as secondary homes for frequent travelers. The best residential hotels have suite accommodations plus housekeeping service and dining facilities.

Casino Hotels are often quite luxurious while being moderately priced. The idea of course is to make the profits through gambling revenues. Casinos are highlighted in a later industry profile.

Resort Hotels differ from other types of hotels in several ways. Most importantly, the target clientele is much different. About 57 percent of resort hotel guests are there on vacations. This is about double the typical hotel percentage. Groups and conventions account for 29 percent of volume, while only 14 percent are there on business (Cornell HRA, 1986). Length of stay is also longer at resort hotels, and guests are more interested in recreation amenities. Most resort hotels have a bar/lounge, game room, meeting/conference rooms, restaurants, swimming pool, and sports/recreation facilities (combinations of tennis courts, dance floor, boating/fishing area, playground, fitness center, shops, sauna/ steam room/whirlpool, etc. (Anderson, 1987).

Recreation programs are also more important at resort hotels although only 30-50 percent of resorts have professional recreation staff. Typical programs include social activities, food and beverage events, trips and tours, entertainment, teen and youth programs, fitness activities, sports, and equipment rental (Masterson, 1986). Because of the recreation programs and amenities, the increased length of stay, and the service orientation of resorts, there are stronger personal relationships between guests and staff. This helps contribute to the return rate (Lattin, 1985).

Some resort hotels have relatively short seasons, having good occupancy only from late May through Labor Day. Winter oriented resort hotels face the opposite seasonality. Another problem is that fewer Americans return to the same vacation resort year after year. The solution to both problems is diversification, as previously mentioned. Those resorts that solve this problem and serve an upscale market can be very profitable. Resorts such as Caneel Bay Plantation in the Virgin Islands and the Cloisters at Sea Island, Georgia, generate over $125,000 per room per year. This is four times more than the industry average (Beekhuis, 1986).

Hotel Operation Trends and Problems

Examined here are several operational trends and problems that have occurred in recent years.

Computerized Reservation Systems have proved to be extremely beneficial to hotel chains. The systems allow sales to be made directly through travel agents, corporate travel departments, and airlines. Commissions to the travel agent can be tracked easily and paid centrally once a month. Guest check-in time is reduced by 60-70 percent, and customers are billed more efficiently. The computer systems also provide a self adjusting perpetual inventory of rooms by type and rate (Geoglein, 1986).

New Markets are being sought by hotels. Everyone is seeking the business of the 25,000 professional, trade, and fraternal organizations that hold conventions and conferences. Hotels give big discounts for this convention business if it occurs in the off season or shoulder season. Research has shown that one third of conference attendees return someday to the same hotel and that many convention travelers stay over an extra few days for vacation purposes (Lattin, 1985; Hotel and Motel Management, 1983). Over 2000 hotels have added fitness facilities or programs in order to draw the health conscious, and other hotels have designated entire "no smoking" floors. Increased security is advertised in order to draw women executives, and practically every hotel chain now has a "frequent guest" incentive plan. Many hotels are adding amenities aimed at enticing the business traveler: built-in hair dryers, private label toiletries, secretarial service, disposable swimsuits, personal computers, stock market quote service, morning newspapers and so on.

New Construction has slowed somewhat due to the loss of certain tax advantages. Nevertheless, some hotel chains are still diversifying in order to reach different markets. For example, Marriott has developed the economy level "Courtyard" chain, which is getting 80-90 percent occupancy (Copley News Service, 1986).

Labor Shortages are beginning to occur in some areas of the country as the population ages. It is expected that the demand for hotel industry jobs will increase tremendously in the next ten years, but there may not be enough young semi-skilled labor to fill the positions. Solutions could include a combination of the following: labor saving design and mechanization, senior citizen staff, increased wage scales, and increased use of foreign nationals in entry level jobs.

Opportunities In The Hotel/Motel Industry

Hotels and motels are one of the largest employers in the nation. Many of the positions of course, are nonprofessional, such as room attendants, bell boys, and porters. Even so, students who take these jobs while in school learn many of the practical, grass roots aspects of the business. Before they graduate, students can often move up to positions such as bell captains, concierge, front desk clerk, reservations clerk, assistant housekeeper, sales representative or night auditor. After graduation the student may be ready to move up to mid-level management positions such as front office manager, executive housekeeper, or guest service manager. With further experience the young professional may move up to be personnel director, sales manager, convention manager, marketing manager, and eventually general manager.

It must be noted that many people currently in managerial positions have come up through the ranks without academic training. The trend now, however, is to advance those employees who have combined academic training with practical experience. Most of the larger hotel/motel chains have training programs that prepare young professionals for managerial positions.

Some hotels and many major resorts employ recreation activity staff. In large programs there may be specialists for sports, fitness, golf, tennis, crafts, youth programs, or other activities. The recreation director for a major resort is usually a trained professional and is compensated accordingly. However, recreation directors seldom get into the career track that leads to being a general manager. According to hospitality authority Jim Burke, the commercial recreation/tourism major has better long term career opportunity pursuing the human resource management positions in hotels. These include positions in front desk and personnel management, guest services, and convention services management. Experience has shown that commercial recreation graduates have also done well in sales and marketing positions (Lattin, 1985; Burke, 1987; Bullaro and Edginton, 1986).

The entrepreneurs with interest in owning their own hotel should first gain experience in the industry and start with buying a small property. Bed and breakfast inns are popular with entrepreneurs, but even these take $250,000 or more to start.

INDUSTRY PROFILE: SKI RESORTS

Although skiing is usually considered a recreation activity (activity businesses are profiled in the next chapter), most of the revenues associated with a ski vacation actually come through the hospitality industry. On a typical ski vacation, the average American spends about $27-$29 per day on lodging, $19-$27 for food, and $22-$28 on lifts and lessons (Berry, 1986).

The ski area industry was born in 1934 when a crude rope tow was installed on a hill outside Woodstock, Vermont. In 1936, Sun Valley, Idaho became the first real ski resort when a mechanized chair lift was introduced. Sun Valley lured movie stars and helped give skiing a glamorous label. By 1955 there were 78 lift-served ski areas in North America (Ski Industries America, 1984). It soon became apparent that ski areas were excellent locations for hotels, lodges, condominiums, restaurants, and retail shops. Growth averaged 15-20 percent a year as skiing became the fastest rising sport in the United States from 1973-1982. At one time there were about 1000 ski areas in North America, but about one third of them (mostly smaller areas) have since failed (Haddow, 1986).

Today there are about 680 ski areas with 54 million skier/days participation annually. The industry takes in about $1.6 billion annually, but this does not include all of the restaurant, hotel, and real estate revenue associated with ski resorts. As everyone knows, skiing is an expensive sport. The average ski vacationer spends about $101 per day. In eastern states, however, the overall cost is less because most people drive less distance to reach a ski resort. Prices for lift tickets have increased about 40 percent faster than the consumer price index over the last 10 years due largely to rising insurance costs. Insurance rates at some ski areas have increased 400 percent and a few areas each pay $2.5 million in premiums for a year's coverage. Debt service for the tremendous facility development is also very high, averaging $5-$10 out of every lift ticket. In spite of these high costs, ski areas average a pretax profit of about 7 percent. The top 45 areas do even better, averaging 20 percent profit before taxes (Berry, 1986; Donnelly, 1986; Recreation Executive Report, 1987; Berry, 1986; Heitsmith, 1987; Janofsky, 1986).

The Ski Market

The National Ski Areas Association (1986) classified skiers as Dilettantes, Stalwarts, and Aficionados. Dilettantes make up 38 percent of the market and ski less than nine times a year. They have lower than average income (due to a large percentage of students), and cost is important to this segment. Stalwarts ski up to 20 days a year and comprise 38 percent of the market. There are many persons age 25-44 in this segment, the majority of whom are married, however only 45 percent have children. Aficionados ski 20 or more days a year and comprise 22 percent of the market. This group is 66 percent male, includes more singles and expert skiers who tend to live closer to ski areas than do the other segments. Commercial lodging and airlines travel are more likely to be used by the dilettantes and stalwarts than the aficionados. Overall, the stalwarts are considered to be the prime market segment for ski resorts, so most promotional campaigns are targeted at this group.

Another market is the cross-country skier, who represents about 29 percent of the 21 million skiers in the United States. Cross-country skiers tend to be older, more family oriented, and more educated.

Ski Area Development and Operation

The traditional wisdom for ski area location and design suggests the following:

- A minimum of 60-100 days of weather with 28 degrees or less and 70-100 inches annual snowfall.
- North facing trails with beginner terrain at 10-15 percent slope, intermediate trails at 20-25 percent slope, and advanced trails at 30-50 percent slope.
- Minimum of 80-foot-wide trails with key runs 150-200 feet wide.
- Adequate natural drainage.
- Adequate water supply and electricity nearby to install snowmaking equipment.
- Enough parking space for one car for every two skiers on peak days.
- A signage system to mark trails and provide skier safety information.
- Ski shops, food and beverage facilities, retail shops, and lodging that is contracted out or self-operated. All should have good access to the ski slopes and/or be linked by ground transportation.

Ski area development is costly. New chairlifts cost $100-$200 per linear foot, snow grooming vehicles cost about $200,000 including attachments, and snowmaking costs about $10,000 per acre covered (Berry, 1986).

Figure 9-3 illustrates the organization chart for a ski area that operates its own ski school but contracts out for the operation of rental shops, food and beverage facilities, retail shops, and lodging.

Cross-country ski areas require less capital development; about $200,000 for a small area. A minimum of four to five kilometers of multiple tracked trails should be available. Such an area could serve about 600 skiers a day. Base facilities for a small cross-country area should include a lodge with 3000 square feet, snackbar, retail counter, and rental shop with 200 pairs of equipment (Ski Industries America, 1985).

Figure 9-3
Ski Area Organization Chart

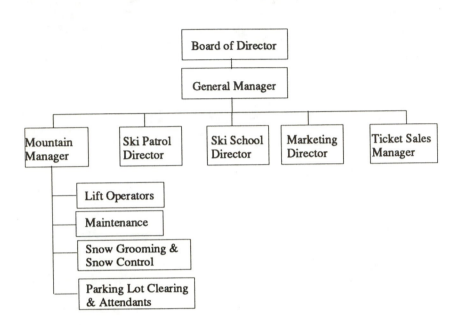

Trends and Problems in the Industry

There is some suspicion that demographic changes in the United States will soon cause demand for skiing to flatten out. To counter this problem, the National Ski Areas Association (1986) has suggested several strategies:

- Improve services—variable time lift tickets, more flexible hours for ski schools, "ski guides" to assist intermediate and advanced skiers.
- Place more emphasis on women's interests and programs for children—the future lifeblood of the industry.
- Provide promotion and encouragement to skiers over age 45, a time when too many people quit the sport. Well groomed runs are most attractive to this group.
- Provide reinforcement for return clientele—welcome parties, beer discounts, social activities, etc.
- Provide incentives for first timers—discount packages, free lessons, etc.

Another problem is the off season. Many ski areas are making major efforts to bring participants back during the summer. Common strategies include discount lodging, tram rides, hot air balloon rides, alpine slides, water slides, music concerts, art shows, festivals, backpacking, horseback rides, boating, windsurfing, fly fishing, and white water river trips

(Winslow, 1986). It is also difficult to find and keep quality seasonal employees. A ski resort with year round activity can attract more permanent and career-minded employees.

Opportunities At Ski Resorts

Ski resorts have numerous positions in hotels, restaurants, and retail shops, but these opportunities are dealt with in other sections of this text. Most of the positions at the actual ski area are seasonal: ski instructors, lift attendents, ski patrollers, ticket sales persons, reservation clerks, snow grooming crew, ski area hosts/hostesses, and so on. A few students who gain experience in these areas may advance to the very few positions that are year round at major resorts: mountain manager (and a core of assistants), ski school director, and office manager. Commercial recreation graduates have also gained positions as communications director and assistant marketing manager, but both positions require additional background in communications and marketing. Some large ski areas have also employed a sports coordinator and an arts and entertainment coordinator to develop year round programs.

For persons who aspire to be the general manager of a ski resort, the most common career path seems to be promotion from the positions of mountain manager or marketing manager. According to a national survey several years ago, the general manager must have expertise in many areas including general administration, labor cost control, personnel management, business correspondence, lift operations, reserve management, liability and risk management, snow making and hill maintenance, accounting, and public relations (Seid and Christie-Mill, 1980).

INDUSTRY PROFILE: CASINO RESORTS

Another very different type of resort is the Casino Hotel Resort. What makes it different, of course, is the legalized gambling, or "gaming" as the industry prefers to call it. Casino gaming was only a $1 billion industry in 1975, but it has grown at least 10 percent a year to yield about $6 billion in "wins" (wagers less payout) by 1987. Las Vegas area casinos account for about 40 percent of the gaming wins, while Atlantic City brings in about 36 percent. The remaining 24 percent is split between Reno, Lake Tahoe, and several smaller locations (Leonard, 1987; Standard and Poors, February 8, 1986; Las Vegas Convention and Visitors Authority, 1986).

Slot machines are the most popular gaming attraction, and account for about 53 percent of the typical casino's gaming revenue. Blackjack yields 24 percent of the win revenue, followed by craps at 14 percent. To put revenue in another perspective, the win per square foot of casino space is about $4,000 per year. (Las Vegas Convention and Visitors Authority, 1986; Scherschel, 1987). Casinos do not have to be dishonest because there is a house advantage built into every game.

A study of gamblers in Las Vegas (Dandurand, 1986), revealed that slot machine and keno players tend to be lower educated, have lower income, and are older than players of other casino games. Blackjack players were younger and had higher income and higher education.

Atlantic City and Las Vegas: Market Contrasts

There are tremendous differences in the markets of Atlantic City and Las Vegas casinos. Atlantic City draws more visitors, but they are a poor tourist market. Their average stay is less than one day and they spend $2.4 million. In Las Vegas, visitors stay an average of 4.3 days and spend a collective $7 million. Whereas Atlantic City was once a classic seaside resort, it now markets itself as a gambling city. On the other hand, Las Vegas gained fame for its gambling, but is now marketing itself as a complete destination resort. Las Vegas has several golf courses, numerous parks, shopping malls, sports facilities, and a water theme park. Several hotels such as the Circus Circus, Bally Grand, and especially the Las Vegas Hilton have children's activities and supervised programs. There is also boating, sailing, skiing, and water skiing opportunities within a short drive (Manfredi, 1985; Leonard, 1987; Standard and Poors, 1986; Scherschel, 1987).

Las Vegas has also become very successful in attracting the convention trade. It hosts about 500 conventions a year that average over 2000 delegates each. These combination business/pleasure travelers spend about $810 per person and account for 42 percent of Las Vegas hotel occupancy (Las Vegas Convention and Visitors Authority, 1986).

Casino Resort Operations

There are several considerations in the planning and management of casino hotels/resorts that are somewhat different than for other types of hospitality businesses (Lord-Wood, 1982).

- Legislative controls, especially in New Jersey, are more complex. There is licensing and extensive investigation of personnel, conflict of interest regulations, and complex accounting requirements.
- Casino Resort Hotels are more labor intensive than other hotels because of the 24-hour activity. This drives operating costs up.
- Managers must be trained in handling a variety of problems that are unique to the industry: more transient labor, 24-hour operations, increased security, entertainment management, gaming management, and control of undesirables—drunk conventioners, prostitutes, etc.
- Lodging and/or food and beverage operations may be priced cheaply to be a marketing tool to draw customers, rather than being priced to make profits.

Due to the above problems, casino resorts have very high operating costs. In order to be successful, the casino must have a very high occupancy rate and entice its guests to gamble on premises rather than at another casino. Casino hotels in Las Vegas accomplish this fairly well, having average occupancy rates of 84.7 percent compared to 70.1 percent in local non-casino motels. In Lake Tahoe, occupancy is even higher—93 percent (Las Vegas Convention and Visitors Authority, 1986). Successful casino operators see that their business is part of the overall leisure time and travel industry. This is reflected in their pricing, marketing, and diversification to a wider range of recreation interests.

Opportunities At Casino Resorts

Casino resorts have many of the same opportunities available in the hotel industry, but there are also some differences. One recreation student gained additional training at a blackjack dealers school then got an internship with a casino. After a few years the student had advanced to a position supervising the gaming area of the casino. Another student took a job as parking valet at a top casino resort and made over $3000 a month in tips. After three months he dropped out of school. Some casino resorts employ recreation staff to manage their youth programs, special promotional events, and recreation facilities. In summary, there is no defined career path for recreation/tourism graduates in the casino resort industry. Opportunities may be there, but they must be pursued on a case by case basis.

INDUSTRY REPORT: TIMESHARING

Timesharing is the sale of luxury accommodations to numerous people, wherein the occupancy of the units is divided into increments of one or more weeks. Resort timesharing was first developed and marketed in the French Alps in 1964 (Masterson, 1986). By the mid-1970s three things combined to bring this vacation concept to the United States:

1. Hotel and resort room rates escalated with inflation.
2. Condominiums and houses became so expensive that most Americans could not purchase vacation homes.
3. Americans began to realize that they did not have to own an entire vacation home in order to have dependable lodging available.

By 1986 there were over 1000 timesharing resorts in the United States, mostly in Florida, Colorado, California, Hawaii, South Carolina, and Texas. Prices for fully outfitted units including furniture, dishes, and silverware range between $2,000 and $20,000 for an annual week of use. The average price is about $7,000 to $8,000. It varies according to a resort's location, its amenities, and whether the week is in the peak, shoulder, or off season. Developers typically provide customer financing with a down payment of 10 percent to 20 percent. Most timeshare resorts charge an annual maintenance fee of about $200-$300 (*U.S. News and World Report*, 1986).

Timeshares may be purchased in fee simple, wherein owners gain title to a specific unit for a specific period of weeks. Another approach is to purchase a "right to use" license, lease, or membership. The buyer does not gain title, but does have the right to use a particular unit for a specific period of weeks, for a fixed number of years. Variations of this method allow club members to use other units at other resorts in the same chain, or to have "floating time" right to use privileges within a particular season (Paananen, 1984).

Timeshare Marketing

It is the marketing of timeshare resorts that has clouded the industry's reputation. A typical timeshare project including land and amenities may be built for $50,000 to $100,000 per unit. Therefore, a 100-unit project may cost $6 million. If each unit is sold for an average of $6,000 per week for 50 weeks, the total yield is $30 million, for a margin of $20 to $24 million. It is however, often difficult to sell the nonprime weeks, so they may be heavily discounted to $3,000 while prime weeks sell for $8,000.

In order to attract potential buyers to see the resort, invitations promising free gifts are mailed to the target market: married couples who own their home and earn average or higher income. Typically 1 percent to 3 percent of the people solicited by mail accept the offer to visit the property. The gifts usually turn out to be worth $50-$100 total, but some timeshare resorts use much cheaper prizes. High pressure sales tactics are often used, and an average of 10-20 percent of those who visit the resort end up signing a contract to buy. The total marketing cost per unit/ week sold is about $1000-$2000, or as much as 40 percent of the price. This may seem high, but since timeshares are basically an "unsought good," they must be marketed aggressively (Huntley, 1984; Changing Times, 1983; American Land Development Association, 1981). In order to protect buyers from unscrupulous sales tactics, about 30 states permit a "cooling off" period of several days where a person can change their mind.

Most timeshare buyers are well satisfied, even though their unit seldom can resell for its original price. Reasons for satisfaction include: (a) affordable ownership--you pay for only the weeks you use, (b) ownership is a hedge against inflation, (c) hassle-free reservations— space is guaranteed, and (d) exchange privileges with other resorts (Paananen, 1984).

Timeshare Exchange Services

There are several timeshare exchange services, the largest being Resort Condominiums International, founded in 1974. By 1986, RCI had exchange service contracts with 1280 different resorts, and 665,000 timeshare owner/members. Each year about one third of the members trade their week and vacation at a different resort (DeHaan, 1987). In recent years, some hotels in resort areas have designated certain units or wings for timeshare sales and exchange. This has helped improve the legitimacy of the timeshare and exchange concept.

Timeshare Resort Operations

The operation of a timeshare resort is like other resorts and hotels in many ways. There are, however, some differences. Almost all the guests arrive and depart on the same day of the week, the "turnaround day", usually Friday, Saturday, or Sunday. Between check-out time at 10:00 AM and check-in time of 4:00 PM, all the units must be cleaned and prepared for the next wave of vacation weekers. This is a hectic time when all staff are very busy.

The regularity of the timeshare week allows the resort recreation director to structure a very attractive program. The first evening, a get acquainted dinner or social is very common. Recreation classes, trips, and special events can be promoted at this time to a rather captive audience. By keeping records of programs and attendance, interest patterns become clear over a period of several years. For example, owners of week #20 may enjoy golf outings while week #5 owners enjoy bridge tournaments. The repeat nature of owner's visits also helps build social interactions that in turn, helps facilitate programs. Most large timeshare resorts offer a wide range of recreation amenities and programs (Masterson, 1986).

Ultimately, the success of a timeshare resort depends on several factors: the ability to keep high standards of quality, the satisfaction of timeshare owners and guests, and the ability to sell the off season and shoulder season weeks. This last hurdle is much easier to do if standards are high and owners happy.

Opportunities In Timeshare Resorts

Timeshare resorts often have many of the opportunities found in the hotel industry plus a few more. All timeshare resorts employ a team of sales people until the property is sold out. While many timeshare sales staff are overly aggressive, it is possible to have sincere belief in the resort and communicate tastefully and ethically to prospective buyers. A successful timeshare sales person can earn excellent income through commissions, and some advance to management positions.

Large timeshare resorts frequently employ recreation managers and activity directors. While some of these positions do not pay well, advancement is possible to the position of property manager.

INDUSTRY PROFILE: RECREATION COMMUNITIES

According to the National Association of Home Builders (Schiffres, 1986), there are about 4.2 million second home owners in the United States. Many of these homes are in real estate developments that exist primarily because of a recreation orientation. These may include ski condo projects, beach front villas, hunting cabins, golf resort condos, and some retirement communities. The average value of all types of second homes nationwide is $70,500. By comparison, primary residential homes average $97,000. There was a period during the recession years of the early 1980s when second homes did not sell very well, but this changed when interest rates came down.

People buy property in a recreation community because they want to take advantage of the recreation opportunities, to entertain business clients, to purchase a home in advance for retirement, and/or because they are looking for an investment. Therefore, developers stress the following market considerations: (1) easy access to the area, (2) access to the primary recreation attraction, (3) rental potential, and (4) resale value.

Resale value of second homes is not very stable in bad economic times. For example, prices in many resort areas fell 10-20 percent after the federal government in 1984 proposed a limit on the deduction of mortgage interest paid on second homes (Schiffres, 1986). This did not occur, however, and sales rebounded, particularly when aided by the lure of lower interest rates in 1985 and 1986. Tax considerations also determine how long some people live in their recreation residence. A person can rent out their vacation home for 14 days a year without having to pay tax on the money received. If their property is used primarily for rental purposes, they can personally use it 14 days a year, or ten percent of the time it is rented out, and still claim all depreciation, maintenance or other expenses for tax write-offs. Owners who split their occupancy more evenly can only charge off proportionate depreciation and maintenance for tax purposes.

There are several approaches to selling vacation homes in a recreation community. The most obvious is to sell the units to individual owners in fee simple title. A new approach is to sell an "undivided resort interest" in which investors buy a share in the entire resort. This is somewhat like timesharing, but more flexible. For example, 10 individuals per unit pay $10,000 each for a share of the resort and each gets five weeks use per year.

Kelly (1985) has classified recreation communities into three different types: retirement developments, mixed communities, and resource focused communities. These plus a fourth type, local recreation communities, are examined further below. One common feature is that most of these communities charge their residents a monthly fee to cover maintenance of the recreation facilities.

Retirement Developments are common in the sunbelt area from Florida to California. Homes and condominiums are typically well integrated into a comprehensive land-use plan and adapted to the local climate, terrain, and aesthetics. Recreation amenities are prevalent, but mostly of a social nature: swimming pools, golf, social hall, and so on. Recreation programming may be provided by paid staff and/or through resident committees.

Mixed Communities have a combination of temporary and full-time residents, and offer a range of recreation opportunities. Hilton Head, South Carolina, is a good example of a "mixed recreation community." Such an area has year round residents, retirees, seasonal vacation home owners, timeshare properties, rental condominiums, and hotels for convention and tourist trade.

Resource-Focused Communities are developments based on a specific activity such as skiing or beach vacationing. There is less emphasis on full-time residents, and the development is designed for short-term visitors. This might mean proportionately more restaurants, night clubs, retail shops, and recreation activities. Second homes and condominium projects in these settings are often affiliated with a property rental company. The property rental company markets the unit and handles reservations, check-ins and maintenance. In return, they keep 40-50 percent of the rental revenue. Owners may stay in their properties a few weeks of the year but rent out the majority of the time. Owners may get only 50 percent of the income but often have higher rental occupancy rates due to the marketing of the Property Rental Company.

Local Recreation Communities include apartment, condominium, and single residence communities that are based on a recreation concept. Often, the concept is a golf course, marina, or sports facility. It is much more common now than 20 years ago to see residential areas sold because of their recreation opportunities.

Opportunities In Recreation Communities

Many recreation communities employ full-time recreation coordinators and offer extensive programs. Some smaller properties with only 100 to 200 units may combine their resources with other such properties and jointly employ a recreation coordinator. This is not uncommon with companies that manage several apartment complexes in one community.

Duties in managing the recreation programs and facilities for a residential community are somewhat similar to those in managing a municipal program. There are some differences, however, particularly in recreation communities that have major seasonal variations in residents. Special events rather than on-going programs can be more popular in such settings.

INDUSTRY PROFILE: CAMPGROUNDS

Camping is one of the most popular recreation activities in North America. It is not surprising therefore that the provision of campgrounds is a large industry. There are about 5,500 campgrounds in the United States, which is a slightly lower number than reported in previous years (Anderson, 1986). Most of these campgrounds provide space, amenities and services for the recreation vehicle camper or the family that is "car camping" (tents, etc., based out of their vehicle). Most campgrounds are very small and are privately owned single establishments with few recreation amenities. In many cases these are sole proprietorships established to supplement primary sources of income already being generated from the land. Owners of gas stations, restaurants, small motels, and farms often provide small campgrounds to transient overnighters in an attempt to generate extra income. These "mom and pop" operations open and close down continuously. It is, however, the large chain-operated campgrounds that represent the greatest area of growth as a commercial recreation business. The majority of this industry profile will concentrate on several types of these large campgrounds.

Types of Campgrounds

Campgrounds can be classified as destination, overnight (or enroute), and urban campgrounds. Each type is examined here.

Destination Campgrounds first emerged in the 1970s on the west coast. Several hundred acres are utilized with about half being used for campsites and half for recreation areas. Facilities are often very elaborate including pool, clubhouse, tennis courts, sports fields, and even golf courses. Supervised recreation programs are recognized now as a great way to stimulate the social contact and satisfaction that leads to repeat business.

A popular variation of the destination campground is the membership campground. Space is sold just as with the timeshare resort concept: fee simple title or right to use methods. Typically there are no more than 15 owners per site. Members can also reserve or trade space at other camp resorts of the same chain. Some of the better known destination campground chains are Outdoor World, Thousand Trails, and Camp Coast to Coast (with over 500 member facilities).

The market for destination membership campgrounds is predominantly middle age and retired couples. Only about one third of them have incomes over $25,000. The marketing schemes and sales pitches are similar to the timeshare industry: mailed invitations and prizes to see the facilities. Sales costs are often 40-50 percent of the price to buy, which may be as high as $8,000 (Masterson, 1986). Persons who buy memberships but do not own RVs can be provided with a fully equiped RV at many of the destination campgrounds.

Overnight or En-Route Campgrounds serve the needs of people traveling between destinations. Since most guests stay only one or two nights, recreation amenities are usually less extensive than at a destination campground. Nevertheless, there is usually a pool, a store, and a game room. Kampgrounds of America (KOA) is the largest private campground system in North America, and most would be considered as enroute facilities. In 1986, KOA hosted 25 million campers at their 650 franchised locations (Crandall, 1987). The initial fee to purchase a KOA franchise is not very high, but operators must also pay 8 percent of camping fees to the parent company. One trend in overnight campgrounds is to add more recreation amenities and programs in order to keep guests there for longer stays (Kelly, 1985).

Urban Campgrounds serve RV travelers who need a place to hook up their vehicles (to electricity, water, and sewer service) while they are in a city. Spaces are very close together, and the majority of the facility may be asphalt. Nevertheless, some people stay at such locations for a week or more because of the attractions in the urban area. For example, the Circusland RV Park at the Circus Circus Hotel in Las Vegas offers 421 spaces, a variety of recreation attractions, and of course, casino gambling.

Campground Operations

Revenues come primarily from space rental and related user fees, while most of the expenditures are for payroll. The peak season, as to be expected, is May through September, which accounts for about 75 percent of many campgrounds' revenue.

Many campgrounds are situated on land that was originally acquired for other purposes. The value of the land itself may be the ultimate key to success if the property value appreciates significantly while the campground just breaks even. To earn operating profits, a campground should be located on a major throughfare that is close to or enroute to a popular natural resource or vacation attraction. An attractive environment with plenty of shade, vegetation, and a water source helps add to the ambience. Recreation amenities and friendly service help gain repeat visitors. The facility should be marketed to out-of-state travelers, RV groups, and with flyers at destination attractions. Yellow page ads, direct mail, and billboards are also used to attract visitors. In the off season, it may be necesssary to close down or offer alternative activities to draw business.

Opportunities In Campgrounds

The majority of campgrounds, being small privately owned establishments, have little need for year round employees other than the owner. Large campground chains, however, do present opportunities for the commercial recreation student. Many of the membership campgrounds such as Outdoor World employ recreation coordinators to develop extensive programs. Salaries have not proven to be very high; some are listed as low as $12,000 a year. Since the industry is growing, however, there is reported to be opportunity to move up to positions managing the overall property or in coordinating recreation programs for several campgrounds in a region.

INDUSTRY PROFILE: RESTAURANTS

Public restaurants as we know them were in evidence in London as early as 1400 A.D., and within 200 years the French had gained a reputation for serving fine food. In colonial America, restaurants were really just coffee houses and taverns. Most persons, however, still ate their three meals a day at home. The Volstead Act in 1919 changed this pattern, since it made the sale of liquor illegal. Taverns therefore were forced to increase their food service or close down. As Americans became more mobile through automobile travel, they began to dine out more often. After World War II, the population increased dramatically, and there was a boom in restaurant construction (Harael, 1977; Lattin, 1985).

Today, more than 40 percent of the American food dollar is spent on eating out, compared with only 25 percent in 1955. It is a $140 billion industry with a growth rate over 8 percent a year since 1975 (*U.S. Industrial Outlook*, 1987; Gottschalk, 1986).

The average American eats out 3.7 times a week, but business people, higher incomes, young adults, and singles exceed that rate. Quality of food, convenience, price, and service are the traditional criteria for selecting a restaurant, but more people now also seek atmosphere, amenities, and entertainment. Midscale restaurants with table service account for 27 percent of the nations dining out occasions, while 64 percent occurs in a fast food restaurant and only 9 percent at upscale full service restaurants (Robey and Russell, 1983; Gottschalk, 1986).

Type of Restaurants

There are four types of restaurants that fulfill different roles in the leisure service industry: full service, casual theme, fast food, and leisure theme restaurants. Each type is examined briefly in this section.

Full Service Restaurants have table service and typically middle income to upscale customers. About half offer a varied menu, while the others are a variety of specialty restaurants for steak, seafood, Italian, Oriental, and so on. The orientation may be that of a family restaurant, emphasizing variety of food and moderate price or that of an upscale restaurant emphasizing quality food and atmosphere. In the latter case, dining is likely to be a form of social or business entertaining. Indeed, about $30 billion is spent in the United States each year on meals for business entertainment (*Leisure Industry Digest*, July 15, 1986).

Casual Theme Restaurants include outlets such as Chi Chi's, Bennigan's, and TGI Fridays, who cater to young professionals and upscale students. Food selections are typically salads, nacho plates, sandwiches, Mexican dishes, and the like. Bar business is very important and the marketing, therefore, emphasizes socialization. Many casual theme restaurants have "happy hours," special events, birthday parties, sports viewing, New Years Eve parties, and other promotions to draw crowds.

Fast Food Restaurants are not all "burger joints." In fact, only about 40 percent of fast food restaurants have burger/beef orientations. The remainder are oriented toward pizza, chicken, ice cream, sandwiches, donuts, Mexican food, or other specialties. McDonald's is the leading fast food chain, with 9400 outlets worldwide, followed by Pizza Hut, Burger King, Dominos Pizza, and Wendy's. Some chains have expanded too rapidly, and in recent years several chains have suffered financial setbacks (Shriver, 1987).

Increasingly, fast food restaurants are using leisure amenities and activities to attract customers. Playground equipment, contests, discount toys, theme park coupons, birthday parties, and other promotions are common. McDonald's has an enviable record of community involvement through sponsorship of special olympics meets, scout jamborees, youth sports leagues, fun runs, and countless other events. Another trend is that many fast food chains have become more health conscious, offering low calorie salad bars and chicken dishes.

Leisure Theme Restaurants probably evolved in the early 1960s when Shakey's Pizza began to draw more people with its player piano, singing waiters, old movies, and cartoons than it did with its food. In the early 1980s there was a tremendous boom in the construction of Chuck E Cheese Pizza Time Theater and Show Biz Pizza establishments. These are basically fast food establishments, featuring computer synchronized robotic characters who sing and dance.

There are numerous video and arcade games and play attractions, plus dining rooms, TV viewing rooms, and party rooms. Some establishments serve 30 or more birthday party groups each Saturday. Special programs include sports team video parties, teen dances, and slumber parties. By 1984 there were 450 Pizza Time and Show Biz outlets, but overexpansion and a reputation for mediocre food forced the closing of many locations (*Business Week*, 1984).

Adult oriented leisure theme restaurants are also common in many cities. Dave and Busters promotes itself as the largest dining and entertainment establishment in Dallas. It features four bars, a large video game area, pool tables, dart game areas, and other attractions. As many as 2700 people flock to Dave and Busters at peak periods, but only about one third of its revenue comes from food sales. The rest is beverage and games revenues (Herold, 1983).

Operations and Keys to Success

The operations of any type of restaurant involve a variety of tasks, which are illustrated in Figure 9-4. In smaller restaurants, staff have to perform several of the tasks. There is no sure-fire formula for success, but the following factors probably contribute significantly (Lattin, 1985):

- A good location—near the population, accessible and visable.
- Good environment—a coordinated, clean, and tasteful theme.
- Good service—friendly, competent service that makes customers feel welcome.
- Good food and beverage products—that taste, smell, and look good.
- Value of the dollar—fair value for the total dining experience.
- Management controls—food costs held to about 35 percent of sales (lower with some fast foods) and liquor to 20 percent of sales, proper portion sizes, and inventory control.

Two recent trends present potential problems for the future. First, the trend toward healthier foods (salads, vegies, pasta) has been reflected in lower cost for the average meal. This has caused some restaurants to lose revenue even though customer volume has remained constant. Secondly, demographic trends indicate that labor will be a critical problem for restaurants in the future, particularly fast food establishments. In some areas it is already difficult to find enough eager young people to work part time jobs at low wages while in school (*U.S. Industrial Outlook* 1987).

Opportunities in the Restaurant Industry

Restaurants employ more people than any other single retail business in the country. The vast majority of positions however are of part-time or nonprofessional nature. Nevertheless, positions such as cooks, waiters/ waitresses, buspersons, and bartenders do provide essential background experience for persons interested in this field. Advancement to positions such as food controller, executive chef, dining room super-

Figure 9-4
Sample Organization Chart for a Large Restaurant

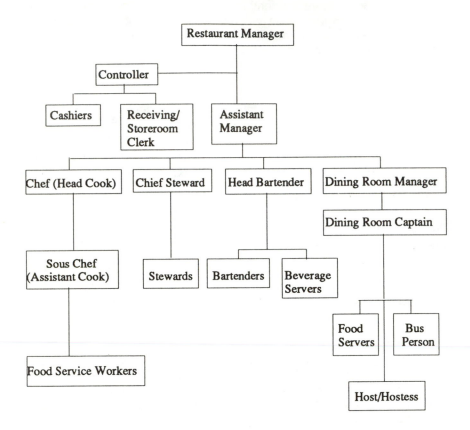

Source: Ninemeier (1984) p. 53.

vision, purchasing director, beverage manager, and restaurant manager require experience and in some cases academic or specialized training. Few commercial recreation and tourism curricula offer sufficient course-work in this area, but restaurant management programs, hospitality programs, and cooking schools do.

Contrary to popular opinion, fast food operations are usually more advanced in technology, methods, and operating procedures than are traditional full service restaurants. Salaries for managers in fast food operations are also very competitive, but the hours are very long. Fast food managers can also move up through the corporate structure to become training directors, area supervisors, and even franchise owners if they can get the capital (Lattin, 1985).

Another area of opportunity is to work with a major hotel or resort as the banquet manager or catering manager. Both positions require the programming flair of a good recreation professional and the food service background of a restaurant management graduate.

Finally, some leisure theme restaurants have employed persons as special promotion coordinators. Recreation graduates have filled these positions successfully.

INDUSTRY PROFILE: CITY CLUBS, NIGHTCLUBS, AND TAVERNS

About 80 percent of American adults drink alcoholic beverages to some degree (Beeman, 1985). Although much of the consumption occurs at home and at restaurants, much of it also occurs at some type of club or tavern. Such facilities have been common in the United States since colonial days and in fact, were the forerunners of the restaurant industry.

Today, city clubs, night clubs, and taverns have similar functions: entertainment and social interaction at establishments serving alcoholic beverages and some food. According to United States census data, there are about 60,000 drinking establishments in the United States, generating about $10 billion in revenue. Most are public night clubs and taverns, but about 2000 are city clubs (Lattin, 1985). Each type is briefly profiled in this section.

City clubs provide an upscale environment for business people to socialize and conduct business. Most have an initiation fee between $500 and $1000. Food and beverage sales account for 50 percent of revenues, and 33 percent comes from member dues, which average about $41 per month. The remaining 17 percent of club revenue comes from other sources such as overnight lodging or sports facility charges. Only one fifth of city clubs have athletic facilities, and fewer have swimming pools. Libraries, reading rooms, and meeting rooms are more common facilities (Pannell Kerr Forster, 1984; Holmberg, 1983).

Nightclubs feature entertainment in addition to alcoholic beverage service. The entertainment may be live music of many types, live comedy, or recorded music. Dance floors are a common amenity. Depending upon the state, clubs may be open to the public or may require memberships typically costing $25 to $50.

An example of a successful nightclub chain is Confetti's, which operates in 11 cities including Dallas, Atlanta, Denver, Tampa, and Memphis. The Confetti concept is to be a never-ending, ever-changing party. Facilities cover about 7500 square feet with a variety of levels, platforms, and connecting walkways. Dance floors are small and scattered about in order to minimize the feeling of empty space. When more people arrive, more levels are opened and soon the dancing spills into the aisles. Alcohol sales represent 86 percent of the revenue, and the Dallas location does about $500,000 in business each month, which is very profitable (Weiss, 1984).

Taverns are typically smaller than nightclubs and have less emphasis on entertainment. As with nightclubs, profits at a successful tavern can be quite high, due in part to the excellent margin on alcohol sales. Beverage costs typically are only 15-25 percent of sales. Another reason for profitability, similar with nightclubs, is that labor costs are low. Cocktail waitresses, bartenders, and bar-backs are paid low hourly wages. They expect to earn their living mostly on tips.

An important problem that has been recognized recently is the drunk driver. With the passage of Dramshop Acts in many states, the responsibility for drunk drivers has shifted from the drinker to the server. Therefore, nightclubs and taverns now instruct bartenders and waitresses to stop serving patrons who are becoming intoxicated. They also serve more food and snacks (to help neutralize the alcohol effects)(*Restaurants and Institutions*, 1985).

Opportunities In The Club Industry

There is no clear career path for commercial recreation/tourism graduates to become managers or owners of clubs, nightclubs, and taverns. Numerous opportunities exist however for the student who learns the basics of bartending, food and beverage control, and hospitality management. Depending upon the setting, experience in managing entertainment and coordinating promotions is also essential. These are all skill areas that complement the social and business skills acquired in a commercial recreation curricula. Experience and maturity is essential, however, and prospective club managers must regard the field as a business rather than as a personal playground. Otherwise, owners, managers, and staff have been known to give away and "drink away" the profits.

SUMMARY

The hospitality industry is comprised of businesses that provide overnight accommodations, food and beverage services, and supporting amenities. Specific types profiled in this chapter included hotels and motels, ski resorts, casinos, timeshare resorts, recreation communities, campgrounds, restaurants, and clubs. There are many variations of businesses within each type of industry. Although each type of industry is different, there are several commonalites shared by successful businesses. The manager must know who the consumer is and what he expects. Services provided must meet those expectations. There must be a good location and a reliable labor source. Management must control costs and have a diversity of revenue sources. Finally, some types of resorts, hotels, timeshares, campgrounds, and recreation communities are very dependent upon having natural resource attractions that must be protected.

STUDY QUESTIONS

1. Differentiate between the travel industry and the hospitality industry.

2. Name and describe the four types of resorts.
3. Explain the characteristics of successful resorts.
4. Differentiate the market and services of each variation of the following industries: hotels, campgrounds, recreation communities, restaurants, and clubs.
5. Explain four trends and problems in hotel operation.
6. What is a timeshare and what are its advantages and disadvantages?
7. What are the keys to success in the restaurant business?
8. Which type of resort has better opportunity for the recreation major: casino, timeshare or ski resort? Justify your answer.

PROJECT IDEAS

1. Visit two hospitality industry establishments in or near your community.
2. Interview three persons working in different hospitality industries and find out what skills and knowledge are essential to their work.

SPOTLIGHT ON: Club Med

Club Med, short for Club Mediterranean, has over 100 self-contained vacation villages in 28 countries spread through the Mediterranean, the Caribbean, Middle East, Africa, Mexico, the Bahamas, South Pacific, South America, Asia, and the United States. In fact, this destination resort is considered the world's largest vacation village organization and the ninth largest hotel chain, having 93,000 beds and 20,000 employees. Over 9 million guests have come to Club Med since its start in 1950.

Club Med was conceived by a Belgian diamond cutter and water polo champion whose goal was to offer a unique getaway from post World War II Europe. He envisioned a resort where people of diverse backgrounds could find a new and different environment, built around the camaraderie of sports and shared experiences. The original purpose has survived almost four decades due to its uniqueness and the way in which the communal spirit is developed during a Club Med vacation.

Two key strengths exist in preserving this image of international understanding and fun. The first, personnel, exists in the form of the G.O.s (gentle organizers) who provide G.M.s (gracious members—vacationers) with constant activity during the vacation. In addition, friendly service personnel handle the duties of food preparation, maintenance, and so on. A typical village contains one Chef du Village (Chief of the Village) who manages 90 to 110 G.O.s and a multitude of service personnel. All G.O.s and the chief are rotated from village to village every six months to keep ideas and personnel fresh. G.O.s come from all around the world, with approximately 18 percent from the United States. G.O.s must have some foreign language proficiency, skills in sport or entertainment, and enthusiasm to allow for a full day of work, seven days a week. There are typically two types of G.O.s: those who are short-term for the international experience and those who become serious and stay for a career. The career path of a G.O. may start with several years of six-month rotations to many clubs, then advance to being in charge of an activity department, then chief, then zone manager, and finally a main office administrator. All personnel are on fixed salary and are subject to being "on call" with respect to assignment.

The spirit of the village rests with the creative ideas and contact generated by the staff. It continues through the vacationers who are, in fact, club members year around. A quarterly newsletter *L'esprit des Villages* is sent to vacationers to keep contact and maintain rapport once the vacation is over.

The second strength is the diverse program of activities available at each village. The program includes instruction in sailing, snorkeling, scuba diving, wind surfing, water-skiing, tennis, archery, arts and crafts, and aerobic exercise. In addition, there is nightly entertainment, dancing, volleyball, basketball, ping pong, bicycling, horseback riding, exercise, group games, and numerous excursions.

A Club Med vacation is all-inclusive with one rate paying for flight and transfers, meals, lodging, and all activities during the stay. Additional services such as deep sea fishing and excursions are arranged for an additional fee. These additional services utilize local contractors and add an important international and cooperative dimension to the vacation.

Market research and promotion is conducted by the main office in France and also by each zone office. Through extensive market research, Club Med has identified its key market segments and their interests. Recently, Club Med initiated mini clubs and baby clubs to accommodate couples with children that wish to vacation together, thus shedding its "singles only" image. Club Med is also expanding its American locations and considering ways to attract older vacationers. Its commitment to changing with the times should help Club Med retain its position as the superstar of destination resort organizations. (Sources: Club Med Sales Inc. (1986); Herin (1987).

REFERENCES

American Land Development Association. *Resort Timesharing: A Consumers Guide.* Washington, D.C., 1981, p. 140.

Anderson, B. (editor). *Managed Recreation Research Report.* Minneapolis; Lakewood Publications, 1985, 1986, and 1987.

Beekhuis, J. *World Travel Overview 1986/87.* New York: American Express Publishing Corporation, 1986.

Beeman, D. "Is The Social Drinker Killing Your Company." *Business Horizons,* January/February 1985, p. 54.

Berry, I.W. "What Price Skiing." *SKI,* November, 1986, pp. 159-167.

Bullaro, J., and Edginton, C. *Commercial Leisure Services.* New York: Macmillan Publishing Company, 1986.

Burke, J. "Resort Management." Presentation at the 1987 Congress of The National Recreation and Parks Association, New Orleans, Louisiana, September, 1987.

Business Week. "The Pitfalls In Mixing Pizza and Video Games." March 12, 1984, p. 33.

Carroll, J. "Focus on Discounting Hotel Rack Rates." *The Cornell Hotel and Restaurant Administration Quarterly,* August, 1986, p. 13.

Changing Times. "Timeshare Sweepstakes." Volume 37, 1983, pp. 46-47.

Club Med Sales, Inc. *Club Med Expert: Travel Agent School Training Manual.* New York, 1986.

Copley News Service. "Major Hotel Chains Splitting Images to Gain New Markets." *Las Vegas Sun,* June 23, 1986, p. C1.

Cornell Hotel and Restaurant Administration Quarterly. "Hotel Industry Trends." May, 1986, p. 101.

Crandall, D. "Recreation Trends" in *First Annual Travel Review Conference.* Washington, D.C.: U.S. Travel and Tourism Administration, 1987.

Dandurand, L. *Las Vegas Visitor Profile Study.* Las Vegas, Nevada: Las Vegas Convention and Visitors Authority, First, Second, and Third   Quarter, 1986.

DeHaan, J. "RCI: A Tradition of Firsts." *Endless Vacation,* April/May 1987, p. 66.

Donnelly, J. "Changing Atmosphere of Today's Ski Resorts Mean Bigger Costs." *Salt Lake Tribune,* April 16, 1986, p. SV9.

Geoglein, R. "Technology and Tourism: A Growing Partnership." *Proceedings of the TTRA 19th Annual Conference.* Salt Lake City: University of Utah Bureau of Economic and Business Research, 1986, pp. 1-4.

Gottschalk, E. "Dining Chic to Chic." *Wall Street Journal,* April 21, 1986. Section 4, p. 130W.

Haddow, E. "Colorado's Ski Industry at a Watershed in 80's." *Salt Lake Tribune,* April 6, 1986, p. F15.

Harael, A. "Food Service: How It All Began." In *Readings on Managing Hotels, Restaurants and Institutions* (Sapienza, Abby, and Vallen, editors). New Jersey: Hayden Book Company, Inc., 1977.

Heitsmith, G. "Comparison of Ski Price Increases." *Ski Business,* March, 1987, p. 12.

Helyer, J. "A New Way To Reserve A Holiday Spot. Purchase Equity In A Developing Resort." *Wall Street Journal,* June 10, 1986.

Herin, R. Chef du Village, Club Med Ixtapa, Ixtapa, Mexico. Personal Interview, June 1987.

Herold, L. "A Place For Grown Ups To Play." *Dallas Morning News,* December 2, 1983, p. C1.

Holmberg, S. *Operational Profile of Private Clubs.* Bethesda, Maryland: Club Managers Association of America, 1983.

Hotel and Motel Management. "Resort Biz Rebounds With Traffic Up 53%." March, 1983, p.1.

Hudman, L. *Tourism A Shrinking World.* Columbus, Ohio: Grid Publishing, Inc. 1980.

Huntley, S. "If You Answer Those Pitches For Resorts." *U.S. News and World Report,* July 30, 1984, pp. 63-64.

Janofsky, M. "Insurance Rates May Snow Ski Industry." *Salt Lake Tribune,* February 17, 1986, p. B6.

Kelly, E. "Cheap Hotel Is Not Necessarily A Derogatory Term." *USA Today,* August 5, 1985, p. 6B.

Kelly, J. *Recreation Business.* New York: John Wiley & Sons, 1985.

Las Vegas Convention and Visitors Authority. *Marketing Bulletin: 1985 Summary.* Las Vegas, 1986.

Lattin, G. *The Lodging and Food Service Industry.* East Lansing, Michigan: The Educational Institute of the American Hotel and Motel Association, 1985.

Leisure Industry Digest. April 30, 1986, June 30, 1986, August 15, 1986, September 15, 1986.

Leonard, S. "1987 Outlook For Gaming." *1987 Outlook For Travel and Tourism.* Washington, D.C.: U.S. Travel Data Center, 1987, pp. 134.

Lord-Wood, F. "The Casino Resort Hotel." *The Cornell Hotel and Restaurant Administration Quarterly,* February, 1982, pp. 54-60.

Manfredi, V., Marketing Director, Paddlewheel Casino and Hotel, Las Vegas. Personal Interview, December, 1985.

Masterson, L. "Camp Resorts," "Time-Share Resorts," and "Resorts." *In Private and Commercial Recreation* (Arlin Epperson, editor). State College, Pennsylvania: Venture Publishing, Inc, 1986.

Maynard, M. "Hotel Weekends on the Cheap." *U.S. News and World Report,* May 26, 1986, p. 47.

McCoy, M. "Lodging's 400 Top Performers." *Hospitality,* August, 1986, p. 68.

National Ski Areas Association. *National Ski Opinion Survey,* 1986.

Ninemeir, J. *Principles of Food and Beverage Operations.* East Lansing, Michigan: American Hotel and Motel Association, 1984.

Paananen, C. *Condominiums and Timesharing in the Lodging Industry.* East Lansing, Michigan: American Hotel and Motel Association, 1984.

Pannell Kerr Forster. *Clubs In Town and Country.* Houston, Texas, 1984.

Pannell Kerr Forster. *Trends in the Hotel Industry.* Houston, Texas 1986.

Recreation Executive Report. "Ski Areas Anticipate Another Record Season, Invest $192 Million In Expansion, Improvements." October, 1987, p. 4.

Restaurants and Institutions, May 1, 1985, p. 208-A.

Robey, B. and Russell, C. "How Consumers Spend." *American Demographics,* October, 1983, pp. 17-25.

Scherschel, P. "Battle Royal On Old Boardwalk." *U.S. News and World Report,* April 27, 1986, pp. 60-61.

Schiffres, M. "Buying A Vacation Home." *U.S. News and World Report,* May 12, 1986, pp. 53-55.

Schnidman, F. (editor). *The Approval Process: Recreation and Resort Development Experience.* Washington, D.C.: Urban Land Institute, 1983.

Seid, B., and Christie-Mill, R. *Job Specification and Skills Necessary For Area Managers.* East Lansing, Michigan: Michigan State University, Agricultural Experiment Station, 1980.

Shiver, J. "Burger Wars Resulting in Layoffs and Losses." *Salt Lake Tribune.* May 17, 1987, p. F1.

Sing, B. "Sales of Vacation Homes Have Revived." *Deseret News,* December 8, 1985.

Ski Industries America. *White Paper on Skiing.* McLean, Virginia, 1984.

Ski Industries America. *Cross-Country USA.* McLean, Virginia, 1985.

Sousane, J. "Hotels and Motels." *U.S. Industrial Outlook 1987,* Washington, D.C.: U.S. Department of Commerce, 1987.

Standard and Poors Industry Surveys. "Gaming." February 8, 1986, pp. 26-30.

Standard and Poors Industry Surveys. "Lodging." February 6, 1986, pp. 31-33.

U.S. Industrial Outlook 1987. "Eating and Drinking Places." Washington, D.C.: U.S. Department of Commerce, 1987, pp. 56-7.

U.S. News and World Report. "News You Can Use: Resort Time Shares." May 26, 1986, p. 63.

Weiss, M. "Confetti Owner Goes Public to Fuel Growth." *Dallas Morning News,* April 8, 1984, p. 1H.

Winslow, J. "Ski Resort Prices Slide Into Summer." *USA Today,* May 5, 1986, p. 17E.

Chapter 10

LOCAL COMMERCIAL RECREATION

This chapter deals with recreation products and services that are purchased by people in their home communities. For lack of a better title, "Local Commercial Recreation" is used. In some cases, tourists may account for much of the participation, but overall, it is the local residents who are the primary consumers. For example, Disney World, the largest theme park in the world, draws most of its revenue from tourists. Most other theme and amusement parks, however, draw primarily from their local communities or metropolitan regions.

Local commercial recreation can be divided into three major groupings: recreation activity providers, recreation product retailers, and entertainment providers. Each category contains numerous recreation industries, some of which overlap into other categories.

Recreation Activity Providers include health clubs, racquet clubs, bowling centers, dance studios, golf courses, and summer camps. These businesses make their revenue primarily through the provision of recreation programs and facilities. Activity may occur as unstructured use of facilities (ie., round of golf) or it may be a highly structured program such as an instructional class, tournament, or league.

Recreation Product Retailers include general sporting goods stores, arts and crafts shops, and stores selling scuba gear, toys and games, bicycles, cameras, motorbikes, and music. Some provide a wide range of merchandise, and others are highly specialized. In many cases recreation retailers also offer instructional classes and sponsor special events in order to draw and/or keep customers.

Entertainment Providers include movie theaters, amusement parks, fairs and festivals, auditoriums and arenas, and pro sports. These businesses provide facilities where customers view entertainment (movies, concerts, sports events, etc.) or engage in nonactive participation such as riding a roller coaster.

The operation of a local commercial recreation business typically involves many of the task areas that have been discussed in previous sections of this text: marketing, recreation programming, retailing, facility management, and so on. Therefore, in order to avoid duplication, these areas will not be covered again. As with previous industry profile chapters, the purpose of this chapter is to overview the operation of several important commercial recreation industries. Some of the smaller industries will be profiled in a collective section at the end of the chapter.

INDUSTRY PROFILE: SPORT, FITNESS, AND HEALTH CLUBS

Sport, fitness, and health clubs have existed in various forms since ancient times. The Baths of Trajan in Rome included a swimming bath, running track, gymnasium, exercise area, courts for ball games, and refreshment rooms (Kraus, 1984). Later, many European "health spa" resorts were based on the presence of a mineral hot springs.

By the early 1900s the YMCAs began to exert an influence by offering sports facilities and programs. The Ys, though nonprofit, were pioneers in basketball, swimming, and weight training. Commercial health clubs also began to evolve, offering men's and women's exercise on alternating days.

As the sports and fitness movement grew, clubs tended to become oriented toward special interests. Now, clubs can be classified as follows: figure salons, health clubs, body-building gyms, tennis clubs, racquetball centers, or multipurpose clubs.

According to a 1984 Gallup poll, 59 percent of Americans exercise regularly, which is double the participation rate for 1981 (Huntley, 1984). Americans spend over $5 billion a year for fitness and much of that is spent at the various types of clubs. Overall, there are about 7545 racquetball, tennis, and multipurpose health clubs (Anderson, 1986).

Clientele at the various clubs differ somewhat, but most clubs strive to attract young professionals age 21-35. Secondary markets, particularly for off-peak daytime hours are students, housewives, and night shift workers. A recent study reports that 80 percent of members join the clubs to get in shape or to stay in shape (McCarthy, 1986), but clubs can also be a great setting for socialization and informal business contacts. Members tend to be more loyal at tennis clubs, where the average membership is over three years, compared to nine months at fitness centers.

Overall, the most popular activities at sport, fitness, and health clubs are the use of weight machines, racquetball, steamroom, and sauna, and aerobic exercise (Richards, 1986). According to the International Dance Exercise Association, 89 percent of the aerobic exercisers are women, with the largest segment aged 25-34 (Dominguez, 1987).

Unfortunately, some members do not get what they expect when they join a club. Complaints against health clubs typically concern dirty facilities, high-pressure sales tactics, and false advertising. Numerous clubs have sold "lifetime memberships," reaped thousands of dollars, and then closed abruptly. Many other people purchase memberships and attend only a few times after which they quit due to several reasons: they lose interest, facilities are too crowded, or they don't get the service they expected. These problems are generally more common in the various types of health clubs than with the racquet clubs and multipurpose sports clubs.

Figure Salons, Bodybuilder Gyms, and Other Health Clubs

Figure salons are the most elementary type of fitness facility. They typically are low overhead storefront facilities with a small exercise floor and limited equipment. A "bare bones" figure salon can be opened for under $10,000 but it is more likely to cost several times more. Locations in strip- mall shopping centers offer good visibility and access, which is critical since membership turnover is very high. In recent years, figure salons have fallen on hard times because larger clubs offer much more at competitive prices. Many figure salons have gone out of business in recent years.

Body-builder gyms, devoted to serious weight trainers, existed prior to the fitness boom. These gyms still exist in some areas but have very little market share today. Most people seek a co-ed environment and a broader range of activities than is offered in the male-dominated gyms.

Health and fitness clubs offer a greater variety of facilities and services than do the salons and gyms. Facilities typically include an open exercise floor with sound system, sophisticated weight training equipment, free weights, steam room, sauna, jacuzzi, and possibly a small pool for lap swim. Health clubs need 50,000 to 70,000 population within a several mile radius in order to draw a sufficient membership of at least 500 to 1000. Some clubs believe that it is impossible to sell too many memberships. For example, one club had 4000 members yet had a capacity for only 100 people at a time. Fortunately, some managers do emphasize quality and are successful in keeping repeat customers.

Promotional efforts for health clubs begin two or three months prior to opening with direct mail and phone campaigns. A month prior to opening there are big newspaper ads, radio spots, and finally an open house. Some pre-opening campaigns raise as much as $150,000, which covers equipment purchase for the facility and much of the advertising costs (Kilberg and Strischeck, 1985; Huntley, 1983; Entrepreneur Magazine, 1979).

Health club instructors are usually enthusiastic young men and women in good condition. They are employed at a ratio of one staff member for approximately 100 participants. Many instructors learn what they know about fitness through crash training programs or reading equipment instruction manuals. For management positions, sales background is often considered more important than knowledge of fitness. Recognizing the dangers of this improper training, the American College of Sports Medicine has begun offering a certification program for health club professionals. Other associations have begun to offer certification programs for aerobic instructors, weight training instructors, and managers.

Racquetball, Tennis, and MultiPurpose Sport Clubs

Racquetball and tennis clubs feature indoor and outdoor court facilities, plus a pro shop and possibly some fitness facilities. Multipurpose sports clubs serve the widest range of fitness and sport interests, usually combining many of the features of the racquet clubs and health clubs.

Obviously, multipurpose clubs are usually larger than racquet clubs or health clubs. The average operating budget is about $820,000 for multipurpose clubs compared to $434,000 for racquet clubs. Since they occupy considerable land, both types of clubs are usually located outside the center city area. Clubs should be within a 15 minute drive of the target market's workplace or residence. Many clubs are planned to have only 50 to 100 members per racquetball court and 25 to 50 members per tennis court in order to assure availability of playing time (Goss, 1984). However, by combining racquetball, tennis, fitness and other facilities, higher ratios can be served by the multipurpose club.

Racquetball and tennis clubs average about 1000 members while multipurpose clubs average over 2400 members. Families constitute the largest membership category for racquet clubs, but single memberships are the largest group in multipurpose clubs. About three fourths of the clubs charge an initiation fee averaging $210 for individuals at multipurpose clubs, but $592 at racquet clubs. Most clubs also charge monthly fees in the range of $30-$70 (Anderson, 1987). These fees account for about half of the revenue at most clubs. Other revenue comes from user fees, lesson fees, pro shop sales, and food and beverage sales, as illustrated in Figure 10-1.

Personnel accounts for about two thirds of the expenses of most clubs. It is interesting to note that multipurpose clubs pay out much more for marketing expenses than do the racquet clubs. This reflects the higher turnover of members at the multipurpose clubs, and therefore, the need to advertise. After all the expenses are deducted, profits average about 23 percent of revenues at multipurpose clubs and 14 percent at racquet clubs (Anderson, 1986, 1987).The return on investment, however, is generally lower.

Figure 10-1
Revenue Sources

	Type of Commercial Recreation				
Revenue Source	Multi-Purpose Sports Club	Racquet & Tennis Club	Theme & Amuse-ment Park	Public Golf Course	Golf & Country Club
Membership Fees	55 %	32 %	1 %	17 %	44 %
User Fees	11	29	39	38	10
Lesson Fees	10	9	4	3	1
Guest Fees	3	6	21	11	5
Equipment Rental	1	0	1	8	4
Nonfood Sales	2	1	11	2	1
Food & Beverage Sales	5	6	13	8	21
Pro Shop Sales	4	11	1	7	6
Facility Rental	2	4	1	1	2
Special Events	2	2	2	1	3
Other	7	1	7	5	3

Source: Anderson (1987).

Recreation programs at racquet clubs and multipurpose clubs are much more extensive than at the health clubs. Leagues, tournaments, and classes are common for the racquet sports, and most clubs offer several types of fitness classes. Some clubs offer volleyball, basketball, gymnastics, swimming, fitness assessments, wellness programs, theme parties, trips, and children's day camps. A few clubs have become so innovative as to offer automatic bank tellers, stock market quote service, computer matching for tennis competition, auto detailing, laundry and dry cleaning service, and wine cellar storage (Feld, 1987). Promotion of these activities is usually achieved through direct mail, club newsletters, yellow page ads, and special promotions.

Multipurpose clubs average about 11 full-time employees and 17 part-timers, compared to seven full-time staff and ten part-time at racquet clubs. Figure 10-2 illustrates the typical organization chart at a generic multipurpose club.

Figure 10-2
Organization Chart for a Multipurpose Sports Club

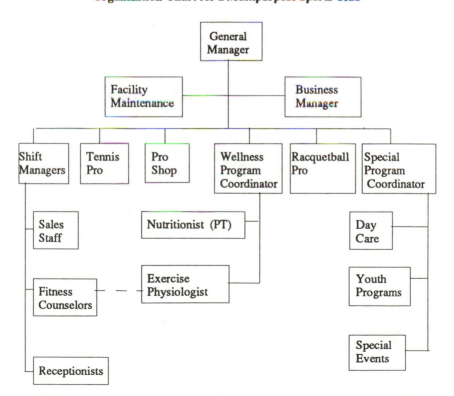

Operational Trends

While interest in fitness is high and possibly still growing, demand for racquetball and tennis has leveled off. A popular solution to this problem is to redefine and diversify the business. Aerobics and weight training are now the core of the industry, but a broader orientation to "wellness" is the emerging concept. This approach includes fitness and lifestyle assessment, health and nutrition programs, stress reduction, smoking cessation, and a wide range of sport and social activities. Without this diversification, single purpose health or racquet clubs are losing their market share (McCarthy, 1986). Larger multipurpose clubs keep their members longer and generate revenue from a variety of sources.

A major problem in the industry is increased competition from nonprofit facilities such as YMCAs. John McCarthy (1986), Executive Director of the International Racquet Sports Association, feels that many Ys are no longer oriented to the traditional markets and services that justify the Ys tax exempt status. According to McCarthy, "these yuppie clubs, in my judgment are simply a form of tax evasion." In fact, congressional hearings have been held regarding this topic, but little has been done.

Opportunities In Sports and Fitness Clubs

To gain an entry level position, career oriented students should have a high level proficiency in tennis, racquetball, fitness, and/or aquatics. There are many part-time and some full-time positions as instructor in these areas. Beyond this level, programming and business skills are needed. Positions include tennis or racquetball director/pro, aquatics director, fitness program manager, and club program director. People in these positions develop new programs, supervise instructional staff, and manage facilities in their area. They also continue to teach group classes and private lessons and supervise other programs. They may also work as a shift manager, opening and closing the facilities, overseeing the front desk, and providing general supervision to all areas.

Many clubs also employ sales representatives on a full-time basis. Depending upon the club, this position may or may not require program background. Some clubs also employ youth program coordinators, food and beverage staff, retail shop staff, health and nutrition counselors, and exercise physiologists.

Prospective managers should have skills in at least one program area and a working knowledge of the other areas. Experience in sales, retailing, public relations, facility management, and personnel management are also critical. It appears that most manager positions are filled through promotions within the organization (NRPA January 1986; Graydon, 1987; Anderson, 1987).

INDUSTRY PROFILE: GOLF COURSES AND COUNTRY CLUBS

Games similar to golf have existed since the middle ages, but the first golf course was started at St. Andrews, Scotland, in 1754. The first course in the United States was the St. Andrews Club in New York, which had six holes in 1888 (Cornish and Whitter, 1982). In just 100 years, the game has grown to involve about 18 million golfers in the United States. This represents about 12 percent of the adult population. Most of the rounds, however, are played by a loyal core of one-fourth of those golfers (*Leisure Industry Digest*, March 31, 1986). Although there is a growing number of women players, most golfers are males with higher than average income. The biggest growth market, however, is senior citizens, who represent about 40 percent of all golfers.

Types of Golf Courses

There are two major approaches to the classification of golf courses; (a) type of course, and (b) type of operation. The types of courses are regulation, executive, par three, and miniature. Types of operation include public course, private country club, and municipal course.

Regulation golf courses require about 90 acres and have a predominance of par four holes. Land and construction is very expensive; a championship course can cost $80,000 to $250,000 per hole (Kerstetter, 1986).

Executive courses require less land and less capital. There are more par three holes than par fours, and the course can be played (by the busy executive!) in less time.

Par three courses have much shorter holes but they can still be constructed in a way that is a challenge to play. As little as ten acres may be needed, and the cost per hole for construction is about half that of a regulation course. These courses can also be lighted for night play.

Miniature golf courses are often developed as part of an outdoor entertainment complex at resorts, amusement parks, or along suburban highways. A good location can be very profitable, making nine times the return on investment over the facility's ten year life span (*Wall Street Journal*, Nov. 2, 1985).

Considering the other approach to classification, there are about 5573 public golf course in the United States, 4861 private country clubs, and 1912 municipal courses (Anderson, 1986). Most of the public courses and country clubs are privately operated whereas municipal courses tend to be operated by local government. Public courses and country clubs are contrasted in the next section.

Operations

Country clubs have substantially more facilities than do public courses. The public courses often have bars and lounges, pro shops, and restaurants. Country Clubs usually have these facilities, plus tennis courts, swimming pools, dance floors, better restaurants, meeting rooms, game rooms, and sauna/steam rooms.

Country clubs depend more upon memberships than do public golf courses. The typical country club has 900 to 1200 regular members, over half of which are family memberships. Most clubs charge an initiation fee under $5000, but 16 percent of clubs charge over $10,000 for initiations. In addition, there are monthly dues, usually in the $100 to $150 range (Anderson, 1987; Pannell Kerr Forster, 1986).

Country clubs count on membership fees for about 44 percent of their overall revenue. This figure is much lower for public golf courses who, lacking a membership orientation, earn about half of their revenue through daily greens fees. Food and beverage sales are also much higher at country clubs. Figure 10-1 illustrates the revenues for both types of golf operations. Payroll is the majority expense and is slightly higher with country clubs, reflecting their service orientation. It costs about $13,000 per hole to maintain a golf course. Maintenance is a high priority and must be accomplished by knowledgeable professionals in horticulture or landscaping. About three fourths of all clubs have automated watering systems, which reduces labor substantially (Pannell Kerr Forster, 1986; Holmberg, 1983).

Neither country clubs nor public golf courses spend a high percentage of their revenues for promotion; the figures are one percent and four percent respectively. This is understandable since country clubs are oriented toward rather stable memberships.

Interesting and challenging course design can draw golfers to test their skills. (Photo: Courtesy of Amelia Island Plantation.)

Keys to Success

There are several keys to success in operating golf courses and country clubs. These include location, design, retail operations, programming, and real estate development.

Location. The simple natural beauty associated with the location of a golf course is one of the game's most important drawing cards. Courses should capitalize on a beautiful landscape rather than alter the terrain artificially.

Efficient Design and Maintenance. Slow play reduces revenue by limiting the number of rounds played. A successful course presents challenge to the golfer without slowing play. This can be accomplished through proper design of the links, hole length, hazzard placement, and greens design. In addition, good maintenance will help reduce the amount of time that golfers spend looking for errant balls (Rasmussen, 1985). A competent starter also keeps play moving by getting foursomes started quickly.

Retail Sales. Food, beverage, and merchandise sales can contribute substantially to a golf course's success. High mark-ups can be justified for many items purchased on impulse, such as balls, tees, caps, and drinks. Part of attracting these sales is to make club members feel personally welcome when they come to the course.

Effective Programming. A successful golf course finds ways to attract players on weekday mornings and early afternoons. One approach is to develop special programs and attractive prices for women and senior citizens. These programs can include lessons, mini-tournaments, and ladies day. Another approach is to develop package deals for tourists and convention goers. There has also been an increase recently in week-long golf instruction schools. Such programs feature video tape feedback and highly personalized instruction by teaching pros. Some courses handle 100 golfers per week in these schools and make additional revenue on food and beverage sales (Ryan, 1987).

Real Estate Development. For some areas, golf course development and the sale of real estate go hand in hand. Without the sale of adjoining land for homes and condominiums, the money would not be available to build a tournament quality course. By the same token, the presence of a quality golf course helps sell the real estate.

Opportunities In Golf and Country Clubs

There are three different career tracks in the golf course and country club industry: club pros, clubhouse managers, and greenskeeper/course managers.

Golf pros have demonstrated a high level of playing proficiency and should have the ability to teach golf to groups and individuals. Many golf pros also manage the potentially lucrative retail pro shop and cart rentals. There is a Professional Golf Association (PGA) Apprentice program that provides training in all areas of golf club operation. Numerous college level players with recreation degrees have done well in the PGA program.

Clubhouse managers usually have backgrounds in the food and beverage industry and manage these services in the golf/country club. Sometimes they also manage the retail shops.

Golf course greenskeepers manage the staff which keep the course in great playing condition. Although some old pros have no academic background, many now have degrees in agronomy or landscaping. Top golf clubs pay good salaries to people who can make a course attractive and playable.

General managers of golf courses and country clubs usually come from backgrounds as club pro or clubhouse manager. They must be a master at public relations to deal with the many diverse interests of members and they must also have solid business skills.

INDUSTRY PROFILE: ENTERTAINMENT/ACTIVITY CENTERS

The term "Entertainment/Activity Centers" has been created here to describe a commercial recreation industry that really doesn't have a common title. Nevertheless, most people have probably visited one of these centers, which are indoor or outdoor complexes that feature a variety of recreation attractions.

Most outdoor centers are based around a combination of activities such as miniature golf, batting cages, bumper boats, mini-racers, video game rooms, and snack bars. Some outdoor centers are part of regional or national chain operations. For example, there are over 30 Malibu Fun Centers in 13 states. Some of these facilities cost over $2.5 million to build, but they can bring in over $2 million a year at a good location. Since operating expenses average about $1 million a year, a very healthy cash flow can be realized. One area of concern, however, is the declining revenue from video games, which at one time represented 30-40 percent of revenues (Seay, 1983; Thornton, Skelton, and Tuomisto, No Date).

Indoor Entertainment/Activity centers can include any of the same amenities that outdoor centers have. In addition, indoor centers may include bowling lanes, bumper cars, ice rinks, roller rinks, theaters, indoor soccer, and arcade games. Two very innovative centers have been built in Denver and Salt Lake City.

The Celebrity Sports Center in Denver began in 1959 as a Walt Disney idea and was financed by Disney, Jack Benny, George Burns, Bing Crosby, and several other Hollywood personalities. The center features 80 bowling lanes, bumper cars, arcade games, billiard parlor, shops, restaurants, and an olympic size pool. It's unique feature, however, is the indoor water slides which drop six stories (Francis, 1987). The facility is heavily visited by groups from churches, recreation centers, schools, and day camps.

The 49th Street Galleria in Salt Lake City opened in 1984 as the first of eight projected facilities. Billed as "Americas Premier Indoor Entertainment Mall", it has two dozen recreation attractions including 30 bowling lanes, miniature golf, bumper cars, roller rink, batting cages, Laser Tag range, video arcade, recording studio, costume photo shop, childrens rides, live entertainment, and seven eating places (Green, 1987).

The key concept with entertainment/activity centers is to provide a variety of recreation choices so that customers stay longer. When people stay longer, they try several activities and spend more money. Also, they tend to spend more for food, beverages, and souvenirs. Another advantage is that maintenance, operations, marketing, and administration are usually more cost effective with a centralized complex than with numerous separate and specialized facilities.

Some of the typical attractions of an entertainment/activity center are examined here in greater detail. It must be remembered, however, that each type often exists as a separate recreation enterprise.

Bowling

Early bowling alleys were often smoke filled hangouts of blue collar types, and the game's image was not associated with high status or good family recreation. In the 1950s however, the invention of automatic pin setters and ball returns sparked a growth in the game. Many clean, bright, multi-lane bowling centers were constructed and marketed as family recreation centers. Bowling participation grew dramatically, but dropped off again in the 1960s as families were drawn to an increasing number of theme parks, shopping malls, and other attractions.

Today, bowling has been rejuvenated again through good marketing, and facelifts for the facilities. There is automatic scoring, video playbacks, upholstered furniture, carpeting, color-coded balls, themed restaurants, video games, and day care facilities. Bowling is now a $4 billion industry with 70 million participants at about 8000 facilities. It has a surprisingly upscale demographic profile compared to earlier years. Today the typical bowler is between 18 and 49 years of age and has higher than average education and income.

There appear to be several keys to operating a successful bowling center (beyond the standard good location, sound management, good public relations, etc.). First, a bowling center needs a solid core of league bowlers. Leagues usually fill the early evening hours, but about half of the lanes should be left available in the later evenings for nonleague open play. The best bowling centers also have successful day time leagues for shift workers, housewives, and senior citizens, plus Saturday and summer leagues for youth. Secondly, there needs to be a rising group of young bowlers at each center in order to assure future participation. The final key is that bowling centers need revenue producing amenities such as restaurants, video games, day care, and billiard room. At some locations, a night club with dance music has been a popular draw for young adults (Skrzychi, 1987; Kerstetter 1986; *Leisure Industry Digest*, September 30, 1986).

Miniature Golf

Fully packaged miniature golf courses cost only about $30,000, but this figure can be misleading. When the costs for land purchase or lease, land preparation, parking lot, utility installation, fencing, landscaping, lighting, rental/office building, restrooms, game room, snack bar, and pre- opening expenses are added in, the cost for an 18-hole course can reach $400,000. Annual income for such a complete complex in a warm climate location can reach $400,000 when video game and snack bar revenue are included. Operating expenses are about half that amount, so the entire facility can be paid off in two or three good years. Many of the operators of large miniature golf complexes are part of major national chains or franchises. The largest, Putt-Putt Golf, has over 600 courses in 40 states.

Overall, miniature golf probably has a good future because it can be incorporated into larger recreation complexes or operated as a single enterprise. It has broad appeal because everyone can play miniature golf and it is cheaper than a ticket to the movies. It is also one of the few active things a family can do together. A final advantage is that course layout can easily be changed for variety, and if unsuccessful, most of the course fixtures and structures can be sold or relocated (Thornton, Shelton, Tuomisto, No Date; *Dallas Morning News*, 1984).

Ice Skating Rinks

About five percent of the adult population of the United States participates in ice skating (Gallup, 1986). There are, however, many different types of participants, and some ice rinks cater more to one type than another. The largest segment includes the many youth and young adults who desire open skating sessions and occasional instructional classes. There is also heavy demand in some locations for hockey games and team practices. Another segment is the figure skaters who need practice time on ice and individualized instruction.

Building an indoor ice rink is very expensive. Initial costs include the building shell; mechanical, electrical, and plumbing expenses; ice rink equipment; a zamboni; and bleachers. A 40,000-square-foot ice arena plus office, shops, and lockers could cost over $2.5 million (Armstrong, 1985).

The major operating expenses for an ice rink are salaries, utilities, maintenance, and insurance. Utilities are higher at ice rinks than at most other recreation facilities due to the cost of maintaining the ice. In order to cover the huge expenses, many ice rinks stay open 20-24 hours a day. Hockey teams and figure skaters often use the less popular hours for practice times. Revenue comes from public skate-time fees, concession stands, pro shops, vending machines, hockey, private ice time, skate repair and sharpening, ice shows, and special events.

Skating demand falls off during the summer and some ice rinks close down or reduce their hours. Another quite profitable strategy is to conduct figure skating and ice hockey camps.

A key aspect for efficient management is to design the facility so that it can be supervised during slow periods by only one or two staff. Design that is centrally located and connects the cashier's booth, control room, and rental facilities can accomplish this objective.

Roller Rinks

Roller skating became very popular in the United States in the 1950s, and in some towns the local roller rink was the popular place for teens to meet on Saturday nights. As with bowling, there was a major decline in the 1960s and early 1970s when theme parks and shopping malls became popular. Many roller rinks closed down during this period. Several events in the mid-1970s turned the sport around. Most importantly, the use of polyurethane wheels gave skaters much more manuverability and control. This technology was also combined with the disco dance craze to create roller disco. Skating rinks installed high-tech sound systems and special effect lighting to create an attractive atmosphere for teens and young adults. About this time, cable TV started to carry "Roller Derby," but it is uncertain how much this stimulated skating, since few people admit to being roller derby fans.

Today about 9 percent of American adults participate in roller skating each year. Most are under age 35 and have higher than average income. Participation rates are probably higher among teens and pre-teens.

Skating is being positioned both as part of the fitness movement and as "pop culture." This is most evident at Venice Beach, California, where sidewalk skaters abound, entertaining people with disco freestyling and slalom course acrobatics.

Roller rinks often have about 9000 square feet of skating surface, plus concession stands, video games, and a skate rental counter. In many ways, operation is much like that of an ice rink, minus the ice. Revenues come from public skating periods, instruction, rentals, concessions, video games, parties, special events, and a few hockey leagues. It can be a profitable business if expense can be kept down. A big problem is that there is little demand for skating during morning and afternoon hours. Therefore many rinks are closed much of the day except for brief flurrys of business in prime time hours. Few roller rinks have found a good way to diversify their operations (Gallup, 1986; Kerstetter, 1986).

Opportunities in Entertainment/Activity Centers

With the diversity of businesses under this heading, there is no clear career path overall. Managers for each type of facility need to have experience in that activity area as well as general business skills, public relations ability, and personnel management skills. For example, bowling lanes managers need to know about lane and pinsetter maintenance, league scheduling, retail operations (including ball drilling), facility maintenance, and possibly food and beverage management, day care center operations, and video game management. In other words, the manager must be a jack of all trades. While a commercial recreation degree provides important knowledge of programming, business, and management, practical experience is absolutely essential. Job announcements for managerial positions in these entertainment/activity centers seldom mention specific academic requirements, but do require practical experience. Such experience can be gained through part-time positions, for example: activity instructors, league coordinators, retail sales, front desk operations, maintenance staff, and so on.

INDUSTRY PROFILE: SPORTING GOODS

One of the nation's first sporting goods stores, Abercrombie and Fitch, was founded in 1892. It gained a reputation for catering to affluent sports enthusiasts, and it outfitted personalities such as Teddy Roosevelt, Admiral Robert Perry, and Amelia Earhart. The store expanded to locations in numerous states where it competed primarily with independent sports retailers. By the 1970s however, Abercrombie and Fitch, plus other small chains and independents, were facing stiff competition from large chain stores. Often located at shopping malls, these new chains could purchase in large quantity, sell at lower price, and afford more advertising. In 1977 Abercrombie and Fitch went bankrupt and was acquired by Oshmans Sporting Goods, the largest sports chain at the time (Hansard, 1983). Since then, many other independent sporting goods stores have suffered a similar fate as Abercrombie and Fitch.

While the chain concepts are successful, they do not necessarily spell doom for all sports specialty stores. There is still a good market for well managed specialty stores in product lines where service is most important. Actually there are numerous ways in which sporting goods reach the American public.

Department Stores—usually carry at least a limited selection for the major sports in season. While product depth and service may be lacking, price is usually competitive.

Full Line Sporting Goods Stores—try to cover all the sports interests (with the exception of boats, snowmobiles, motorcycles, and other major items), while offering good product variety and service. Since there are many full line chain stores, this approach dominates sales volumes in the sports industry.

Specialty Sports Stores—count on expertise, service, and depth of product lines to draw customers. Specialty stores often exist for boating, scuba diving, mountaineering/climbing, motorcycles, snowmobiles, bicycles, and skis. Often an independent operator, it is usually necessary to diversify product lines for the off seasons.

Pro Shops and Concessions—are typically found at recreation facilities such as golf courses, tennis clubs, ski resorts, etc. Rental equipment and convenience items are important products, as are specialty items with the facility logo. Occasionally, wealthy tourists will buy an entire set of equipment and/or clothing in order to participate on short notice.

Sports Wholesalers—sell primarily in quantity to small stores and to institutions such as schools, local recreation departments, camps, and YMCA's. Competitive, written bids are often part of the sales process.

Mail Order Houses—often have specialty orientations. Some, like L.L. Bean (outdoor equipment and clothing), offer high quality products, while others offer cheap imitations.

Overall, sporting goods is an industry in which sales are about $30 billion a year. Product lines that have sold well in recent years include equipment for exercise, skiing, and golf. The biggest sales increase however has occurred with sports clothing and footwear (Urciuoli 1986).

The largest buying segment for sporting goods is males age 25-44, with above average income. There is, however, strong growth in the number of women who buy sporting goods (Stiltner, 1987). In order to gain market share, the full-line stores and specialty shops must not only sell products, they must sell expertise, experience, and service. This helps create repeat business that is essential for success. Some stores also issue newsletters, teach clinics, lead trips, start activity clubs, and sponsor special events such as races, tournaments, or fun runs. Denver-based Gart Brothers is a good example of such innovation. They have a ski machine hill, a golf driving cage with video camera, an adventure travel agency, basketball court, tennis court, boating pool, and meeting rooms for slide shows and classes. Sports stores spend about three percent to eight percent of sales revenue on conventional advertising. The vast majority is spent on newspaper ads and direct mail.

Keys To Success

While there is no sure-fire formula for success, there are several characteristics which are often shared by successful sporting goods stores.

Product Line Buying can yield great savings for stores if the correct merchandise is purchased in quantity. Major chain stores have an advantage in this area and often employ professional buyers. These specialists study consumer interests and they monitor the manufacturers in order to find the best deals. Trade shows are a good time to negotiate with the manufacturers because factory managers usually attend and have considerable discretion on making deals. A good payment history helps the sporting goods store to get better prices and service from suppliers (Greenidge, 1987).

Store Location should match the needs of the particular market. For example, full line sports stores need locations in regional or suburban shopping centers. These prime locations are justified by the high volume of walk-by traffic. On the other hand, many specialty shops do not need such expensive locations because their repeat customers know where to find them.

Off-Season Strategy is important to carry the store through the year. Full line sporting goods stores rotate their stock to carry whatever is "in" for the current season. Specialty shops may carry different but complementary product lines. For example, motorcycle shops may carry snowmobiles in the winter.

Sales Staff and Service must be knowledgeable and experienced. It is also important to have the optimum level of staff; just enough to be cost efficient yet not overextended. Motivation of sales staff may be enhanced through commissions, bonuses, and recognition in addition to an adequate base salary.

The following sections review several of the major components of the sporting goods industry.

Sports and Athletic Wearing Apparel

In recent years, the most consistent growth area of sporting goods sales has been wearing apparel. About one third of the $30 billion sporting goods industry is sales of wearing apparel. Much of the growth has been associated with the fitness boom. There has also been significant growth in the number of stores that specialize in wearing apparel. Almost every shopping mall has an "Athlete's Foot," "Fleet Foot," or similar specialty store.

Another successful approach has been in the sales of wearing apparel that is officially licensed by pro sports. Official team jerseys, jackets, and caps are usually big sellers. (Richards, 1986; Urciuoli, 1986; *Sport Style*, 1985).

Recreational Boating and Sailing

Boating retail is now a $15 billion industry whose success seems to be related to steady fuel prices and low interest rates (since many boats are financed). There are two major consumer markets: males age 25-34 with above average income, and males age 35-54 who are often repeat purchasers buying a more expensive boat.

The typical boat dealer has gross revenues of about $900,000 from boat sales, repairs, and accessory sales. Dealers report that store location is not a major key to success, but that low interest rates are a key. Aluminum boats have been the best sellers because they are cheaper and have long hull life.

During the years of the energy crisis, sailboats and windsurfers came on strong. Sales dropped when gasoline prices came down in 1984, but since then the nonpower boat industry has stabilized (Urciuoli, 1986; Shuman, 1987; Crandal, 1987).

Skiing

The sale of ski equipment and apparel reached about $1.5 billion in 1986. Less than half of the total is for equipment, with the rest being apparel. Historically, women purchase more ski apparel; but this is starting to balance out as men become more fashion conscious.

The ski season traditionally begins with Labor Day Sales, then moves into the Christmas season (including January) when 63 percent of all ski gear is sold. Business is best when it is a good snow year. Good snow also correlates with good preseason sales the following fall.

Many ski shops and full line sports stores in ski country have equipment rental services. While most rentals are for beginners, there is a market for renting high performance equipment to advanced skiers on a "demo" basis. This can help stimulate sales, as the rental price is usually credited against the sales price if the customer buys (Urciuoli, 1986; Kahl, 1985; *Leisure Industry Digest*, September 30, 1986).

Bicycles

About 41 percent of Americans participate in bicycling, making it the second most popular recreation sport, surpassed only by swimming. However, only about 17 percent of the adult population rides on a regular basis (Market Opinion Research Corporation, 1986). It is now a $2 billion industry with about 11 million bikes sold a year (Urciuoli, 1986).

There are basically five types of bicycles sold:

(1) Touring bikes—for long distance riding.
(2) Racing bikes—lightweight and with a shorter wheelbase.

(3) Recreational bikes—lower quality, purchased for children and neighborhood riding.

(4) Bicycle Motorcross Bikes (BMX)—smaller, rugged, with coaster brakes.

(5) All terrain or mountain bikes—have fat tires, larger seats, upright handlebars and gearing for vertical climbs.

The BMX bikes have had a tremendous boom in popularity and represented 42 percent of all bikes sold in 1985. Due to the demographic trend for fewer youth, this should decline in favor of the all terrain bike, which is gaining popularity among adults (Ellis, 1987).

Bicycle specialty shops account for only about one third of all the bikes sold in the United States. The rest are sold in department stores, discount stores, full line sports shops, or through national distributors. The typical specialty shop has revenues of $255,000 a year of which 47 percent comes from bike sales, 32 percent from parts, clothing, and accessories, and 21 percent from repairs. Shops try to get a 35 percent margin on sales, but few really achieve this because of discounting. An average shop has only three employees, and it sells 557 bikes a year. The best months are in the summer, so in the winter the shop may offer cross-country ski equipment, ski rentals or indoor bike training. Shops build customer awareness through sponsorship of bicycle safety checks, races, and racing teams (Crandal, 1987; *Bicycle Business Journal*, 1985).

Opportunities in Sporting Goods Retail

Commercial recreation majors with advanced skills in several activity areas can be very valuable in the sporting goods industry, particularly if they also have retail experience. Employees who are accomplished participants can relate better to customers, can speak more knowledgeably about the equipment, and can discuss local opportunities for participation. In addition, such employees may be called upon to lead demonstrations and coordinate special programs and promotional events. Specialty shops in particular need staff who are business and people oriented, with expertise in the activity. There are, of course, those entrepreneurs who open specialty shops of their own. Some of the niches that may be the focus of a specialty retail store are scuba diving, hang-gliding, windsurfing, trophies, climbing, cross-country skiing, hunting, fishing, soccer, hockey, golf, athletic shoes, outdoor adventure sports, and any combination of these.

Another approach is to work as a manufacturer's representative. This requires high knowledge of the activity and the product line and the personality to aggressively cover an assigned territory. Manufacturer's representatives conduct demonstrations, clinics, and training programs for retailers; coordinate special promotional events; and service their retail accounts by processing orders, handling product-related problems, and generally expediting business. Sometimes manufacturer's reps switch into retail management and vice versa.

INDUSTRY PROFILE: THEME, AMUSEMENT, AND WATER PARKS

In the early 1600s several Russians operated a sled ride with a 70-foot verticle drop. It might be the first evidence of a business where people paid money to be terrified (Ruben, 1987). Other amusements evolved over the years throughout Europe, but it was not until 1857 that a permanent amusement park, Jones Woods in New York City, appeared in the United States.

The industry really began to take off in 1884 when the first modern roller coaster was built at Coney Island, New York. For the next 40 years, amusement parks with roller coasters, rides, and carnival-type entertainment sprang up across the country. However, in the 1930s the Great Depression and the growth of movie houses caused the amusement park industry to decline. A near fatal blow came during World War II when the government restricted the manufacture of rides costing over $5,000. This changed the industry into a lot of "kiddie-ride"-type parks with carnival-type arcade games. Amusement parks in general entered a period of disrepute and many closed down (Price, 1986; Ruben, 1987).

Everything turned around in 1955 when Walt Disney opened Disneyland, the world's first theme park. Disneyland was different because it combined big thrilling rides with a wide range of family entertainment. The facilities cost much more than any previous park, but more people attended, stayed longer and paid more. Cleanliness and employee courtesy were cornerstones of the Disney concept; the American public loved it.

A second Disney park, Disneyworld opened in 1971. The 28,000-acre park near Orlando includes a theme park, EPCOT (Experimental Prototype Community of Tomorrow), a major camping area, resort hotels, and by 1988, a 50-acre Water Park. The overall investment will exceed $3 billion. Many other parks have attempted to emulate the Disney characteristics of cleanliness, friendly service, and a family orientation.

Overall, about 235 million people visit theme/amusement parks each year in the United States. Surveys indicate that about 45 percent of the population makes an average of two visits each year (Graff, 1987). There are 40 major theme parks that get half this attendance, while 640 smaller amusement parks and attractions get the other half. Total revenues are over $2.8 billion, and the industry employs over 100,000 people (Price, 1986). Most of the parks are members of the International Association of Amusement Parks and Attractions (IAAPA).

Types of Theme/Amusement Parks and Attractions

There are a variety of parks and attractions, each with a different approach to drawing crowds and showing them a good time. Each type is profiled below.

Cultural and Education Parks are a remnant of the old-fashioned type of European park. Such parks feature formal greens, gardens, and fountains, with historical and educational exhibits. Musical entertainment may feature bands, string quartets, and choral groups. There are few of this type of park left in the United States.

Outdoor Amusement Parks are generally small parks that serve a metropolitan or regional market. These parks feature traditional thrill rides, carnival midways, and some entertainment. Most amusement parks lack a themed orientation to architecture, rides, and entertainment.

Theme Parks differ from amusement parks in several ways. Primarily, a theme park is a family oriented entertainment complex that has a particular subject as its theme. There is a major architectural idea throughout the park or in specified sections of the park. Theme parks tend to be larger and have a great variety of rides and attractions. Typically, more specialists are hired, especially in entertainment. Also, there usually are many specialty shops.

There are two areas of the country where a number of theme parks have clustered to form entire destination areas. These are Central Florida with Disneyworld, Epcot, Sea World, Cyprus Gardens, Wet-n-Wild, Boardwalk and Baseball, and six other specialty attractions and Southern California with Disneyland, Knotts Berry Farm, Universal Studios, Raging Waters, Six Flags Magic Mountain, Sea World, and numerous smaller specialty attractions.

Water Theme Parks are a rather recent phenomena, which have captured 40 percent of all attendance growth in the industry (Price, 1986). Large water parks feature wave action pools, river rides, steep vertical drop slides, and a variety of twisting flume slides. The idea for wave action pools originated in Germany during World War II as a way to test submarine design. The first wave pool in the United States opened at Point Mallard park in 1970 in Decatur, Alabama, and was profitable almost immediately. Water parks in some climates are a very "time intense" business where money must be earned in a very short period of time.

Specialty Attractions exist in hundreds of cities and towns. They include wax museums, sports hall of fames, roadside attractions, small water slides, specialty museums, and sealife parks. A problem with many of these attractions is that they may hold visitors for only an hour. This is not long enough to justify a large admission fee, and it is not conducive to food and beverage sales. Therefore, marketing is extremely critical in order to draw pass-by traffic. Unfortunately, some of these attractions turn out to be disappointing tourist traps.

Operations

As illustrated in Figure 10-1, about 60 percent of theme/amusement park revenue comes from admission fees (user fees and guest fees), while the rest comes pimarily from food, beverage, and merchandise sales. Most (76 percent) of the expense for theme/ amusement parks is for personnel.

To handle the admissions revenue a centralized ticket system is preferred. An all-inclusive admission price entitles the customer to as many rides and shows as they desire. This approach has led to longer stays at parks, which in turn has boosted food and beverage sales.

The $12 million Oasis Water Resort in Palm Springs, California, is an example of a relatively new industry: Water Theme Parks. (Photo: Courtesy of Palm Springs Convention and Visitors Bureau)

Another centralized admission method is to sell ride/show tickets in sets or coupon books. Usually these are "value priced" (i.e., five coupons for $5, but 12 coupons for $10). Either approach to centralized ticket sales minimizes the number of people handling money throughout the park, thus giving better efficiency and control.

Layout. Theme/amusement parks need to be designed with good inside and outside visability. People inside the park should be able to see some of the other attractions in order to stay excited. People outside should be able to see some of the exciting action inside the park. Rides should be balanced: some wild, some mild, and some in between. In this way different ages and temperaments will find something of interest. Popular rides should be spread around the park so people will pass by the smaller attractions and concessions and give them a try.

Facilities. In addition to rides of various types, theme/amusement parks are likely to have video game rooms, arcade games, concessions, gift shops, children's play apparatus, miniature golf, waterslides, restaurants, and show stages. Due to the need to draw repeat customers many parks constantly add new attractions and renovate old ones. Since the major rides often cost more than a million dollars, changes tend to occur more with the smaller attractions and amenities.

Organization and Staffing. As much as 80 percent to 90 percent of the personnel at a theme/amusement park are seasonal employees, which can be a problem at the end of summer. Many parks have incentive programs that give bonuses for young employees who stay for the full season before returning to school. Figure 10-3 illustrates the organization structure of a typical theme, amusement, or water park. It should be noted that the Operations Manager carries a major responsibility for the success of the park. It is a rare individual who has the technical and personal skills to perform this difficult job well.

Figure 10-3
Generic Organization Chart
for Theme, Amusement, and Water Parks

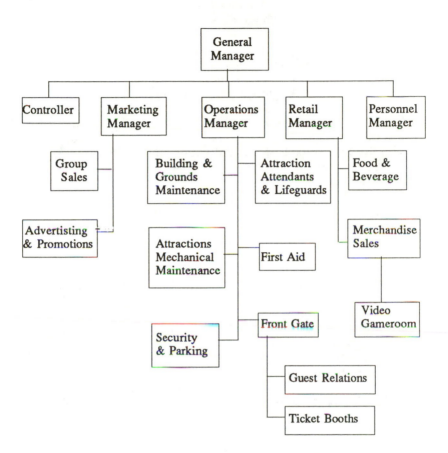

Marketing. The traditional appeal of theme/amusement parks is to preteens, teens, and young adults. Changing demographics are now causing most parks to think in terms of a broader market, particularly families, corporate groups, and even senior citizens. To reach these groups, parks are emphasizing increased beautification and diverse entertainment and food service. More parks are also working with tour operators to draw that trade (Graff, 1987).

There were a number of creative marketing strategies during the 1979 energy crisis. Parks advertised that they were "only five gallons away." Some operated their own gas stations or made arrangements to guarantee gas for people to get home. Others operated telephone "hotlines" to advise people outside the local area about gasoline availability (Kittle, 1980).

Theme/amusement parks spend about 10 percent of their expenditures for advertising. Radio, newspaper, and yellow page ads, family and group discounts, and direct mail are the most common promotional methods (Anderson, 1985, 1987). Among large theme parks television advertising is an excellent visual medium to capture the excitement. Therefore, a few parks use the majority of their advertising budget for television. There are five major market segments for theme/amusement parks:

1. Tourists—a substantial market for large theme parks in destination areas such as Florida and southern California.
2. Local Families—people within a day's drive who visit mostly on weekends.
3. Childrens Groups—schools, churches, recreation agencies, scouts, and other groups who come in busses on summer weekdays.
4. The Evening Market—teens and young adults who come for entertainment, concerts, and dancing at night.
5. Corporate Groups—include consignment sales and group parties.

Keys to Success
Following the Disney example, a number of keys to success may be suggested (Graff, 1986; Bullaro & Edginton, 1986; Kelly, 1985; Veiders, 1979).

- The attraction must be clean, safe, secure, and comfortable.
- Having maintenance people visable and active in the park helps the cleanliness image and is a psychological deterrent to littering.
- Exciting rides will help gain repeat local attendance particularly among teens.
- Employees must be personable and courteous, be trained well, and realize that they are "on stage" performers.
- If possible, the park should accumulate enough acreage to protect its adjoining buffer area from incompatible or unattractive developments.
- State of the art technology in rides and entertainment is more possible with computer technology to coordinate the timing of special effects.
- Preventive maintenance for rides is absolutely essential for safe operation.
- Luck—a solid week of rain or temperatures in the high 90's can ruin a season's profitability.

Industry Trends
There are a number of trends occurring in the industry which should be noted (Graff, 1986 and 1987; Price, 1986).

- There will probably be more attempts at linking small amusement parks with major shopping malls such as the West Edmonton Mall in Canada. Even if these parks just break even, they help draw people to the mall.
- With an aging population there is a saturation point being reached for

major theme parks. Growth will occur in middle-sized markets such as Denver, San Antonio, Seattle, and Indianapolis, and in foreign markets such as Australia and Asia.

- Although the industry safety record is very good, insurance rates continue to be a major concern. Many small attractions have been driven out of business.
- There is increased competition from major festivals and fairs. One strategy is to find a way to tie into these events.
- There may be a market for specialty parks in strong market areas. Sesame Place, an educational children's park near Philadelphia is an example.
- Indoor entertainment centers may be the answer to the seasonality problem, particularly in cold weather states.

Opportunities in Theme and Amusement Parks

Theme/Amusement parks employ thousands of college-age students on a seasonal basis, and in warm climates, the opportunities are year round. Most of the entry level positions pay near minimum wage, yet require positive, outgoing personalities, good communication skills, and the ability to work with all types of people. Many of the managers of theme/amusement parks started in entry level positions such as ride attendants, ticket salespersons, retail salespersons, maintenance staff, lifeguards, and guest relations staff. Each area of the park usually has several levels of positions, and good employees advance quickly through the levels.

Several large theme parks have college internship programs, but Disney's is the largest. The Walt Disneyworld college program accepts up to 500 college interns three times a year. In addition to the standard employee training program, interns attend ten business management seminars.

Experienced employees with good skills in personnel management, communications, and business can move up to mid-level management positions in personnel, marketing, group sales, promotional programs, merchandising, food service management, attractions operations, and guest relations. These department managers work extremely long hours for many days during the peak season, but may get extra long vacations during the off season. Many general managers and some department managers also receive bonus incentives if the park meets its goals for attendance, revenue and/or operations. Overall, the theme/amusement park industry offers excellent opportunity for students who can work their way up to become creative problem solvers and humanistically oriented managers (Samuals, 1983; NRPA April 1986).

INDUSTRY PROFILE: MOVIE THEATERS

The vast majority (87 percent) of movie theaters in the U.S. are indoor while only 13 percent are drive-ins and drive-ins have decreased in number each year since 1980. The rising value of land and cost of property taxes have squeezed profits and prompted owners to sell out in search of more profitable ventures. A major change with indoor theaters is the construction of multi-screen complexes and the conversion of single screen buildings to dual screens. Also, major theater chains have bought out many of the small chains and independent operations.

Box office revenues historically hit peaks every four years, with about $4 billion reported in 1984 and again in 1987. The reported revenues do not however include concession sales, which actually contribute to the majority of profits for a theater.

According to an advertising survey, the average American goes to see a motion picture about five times a year. Persons age 12-24 however, attend over eight times a year. About 85 percent of the moviegoers are between the ages 12 and 39. (Mulligan, 1987; *Leisure Industry Digest*, March 31, 1986; Market Opinion Research Corp. 1986).

Movie Theater Operations

One of the most important aspects of theater operations is the bidding for the films it shows. Typically, a potentially successful movie will be rented to the theater under a 90/10 split: 90 percent of ticket sales to the film distributor and 10 percent to the "house." This arrangement typically lasts seven to ten days, and then the split narrows to 80/20, 70/30, and so on, on a weekly basis. Theater operators may have to give the 90/10 split for three straight weeks to the distributor of a potential top hit such as a "Rocky" sequel (Urciuoli, 1986). On the other hand, a movie chain may successfully bid a 50/50 split for a little known "sleeper" that becomes a box office hit (Fairchild, 1983). The theater chain staff who screen films and bid on the splits need to have a good sense of what the public wants to see.

Overall, the average theater gets to keep little of the box office revenue (*Variety*, 1987). It is therefore very important to have good concession sales; which may contribute as much as 70 percent of a theater's profit. Typically, a theater earns an 85 percent margin on its concessions. Revenues can be increased through "value pricing" in which customers are encouraged to buy attractively priced larger sizes of drinks and popcorn. Some theaters with upscale audiences have expanded beyond the traditional concessions to offer imported beer, champagne, fresh croissants, and other specialty items (Cummings, 1986). A few theaters such as the Cinema N' Drafthouse International chain have table service for pizza, beer, and sandwiches within a renovated theater building.

Theaters can try to stimulate attendance by having discount nights, consignment tickets, Saturday children's matinees, family nights, midnight movies, and special promotional events. Drive-ins may use their asphalt areas during the day time for giant open air bazaars and "swap meets."

Even though revenues from the sale of video cassette movies have surpassed movie box office receipts, the motion picture theater business should continue to be a viable part of the entertainment industry. People enjoy the shared environment of seeing a first run movie in a high quality presentation environment. One theater segment that may fail, however, is the independently operated specialty theater showing classic films, cult movies, and discounted second run features. Video cassette rentals could take much of this market.

Opportunities With Movie Theaters
There are few full-time positions in a movie theater. Most of the work can be performed by high school and college students in part-time jobs. Typical positions include ticket sales, usher/ticket taker, and concession sales. Some theater chains prefer to hire college graduates for assistant manager positions. Much of this work involves supervision and training of the part-timers, but there are also financial responsibilities related to concession management and control of box office revenues. In addition, some assistant managers have responsibilities for arranging promotional events, screening films for future bookings, and working as the film projectionist. In many theaters, however, the projectionist is a full-time employee with union membership. Assistant managers with experience may move up to fill managerial positions and positions in the regional offices of major chains (Fairchild, 1983).

OTHER LOCAL RECREATION INDUSTRIES

There are several other components of the local commercial recreation industry that present occasional opportunities for the recreation/tourism student. These industries include sport and recreation camps, toy and game stores, craft and hobby shops, auditoriums and arenas, and fairs and festivals. This section will conclude with a brief review of several additional entrepreneurial possibilities in local commerical recreation.

Sport and Recreation Camps
There are thousands of sport and recreation camps in the U.S., but only about 16 percent are commercially operated. The vast majority are operated and often subsidized by government or nonprofit agencies (Anderson, 1987). Nevertheless, some camps are oriented to upscale markets of youth and adults. Examples include ski, tennis, and golf camps at resorts; dude ranch camps; youth sports camps; and adult baseball camps that resemble major league spring training.

Most revenues from camps come from registration fees, but food and beverage sales can be important secondary sources. Most expenses are for seasonal program staff and for facility upkeep. Promotion of camp programs is usually accomplished through direct mail, special interest magazines, and personal presentations to groups including camp "alumni" who are encouraged to bring along friends (Bounous, 1986).

There are many seasonal positions available in camps: activity specialists, group counselors, cooks, and so on. Pay is usually about $100-$200 per week plus room and board. Full-time positions are quite scarce because the typical camp employs only about six people year round (Anderson, 1987). Career oriented individuals must have a broad range of experience including maintenance and marketing to justify their retention year round.

Toys and Games

The toy and game industry has sales of about $12 billion a year, but retailers must keep in mind the fadish nature of the industry. Toys that are major hits usually have a life span of only two or three years. If a retailer gets stuck with too much inventory during the decline stage of a product, it may have to be sold at cost. On the other hand, it is difficult to anticipate success and have enough of a toy in stock to meet demand. For example, Cabbage Patch Kids were rejected by five companies before Coleco put them on the market. Another problem is the highly seasonal nature of the industry. About 60 percent of sales occur in November and December. This has management implications for stockroom size, floorspace utilization, part-time labor, and cash flow. Managers have to gear up and phase down for the peak season.

Looking ahead to the early 1990s, the toy and game industry should be healthy. Although there will be fewer teens, there will be more children age 5-9; the prime toy consumer years. Also, adults are becoming a more important market for interesting and challenging games (Hughes, 1987; Urciuoli, 1986; Tutelian, 1986).

Most toy and game stores are part of national chains that have management trainee programs and a career progression. It is, however, a career area few commercial recreation students pursue, even though courses in business and leisure behavior make a good background for this industry.

Crafts and Hobbies

The craft and hobby industry has annual sales around $4 billion and seems fairly resistant to economic downturns. This is because people enjoy crafts and hobbies (a) for creative reasons, (b) for personalized gifts, (c) as a revenue-producing hobby, (d) to save money on gifts, and (e) for therapeutic value. These factors make it a fairly stable industry.

There are three primary ways to sell crafts. The most obvious is through a full-line crafts store or a speciality shop featuring products such as ceramics or leather works. Another outlet is catalog sales, which is a good way to reach handicapped people, shut-ins, and rural residents. Finally, there is a large wholesale market for sales to schools, camps, recreation agencies, and seniors centers. Some craft stores utilize all three approaches. High quality and personalized service are extremely important because "word of mouth" is the primary way to reach new customers. Many shops offer instructional classes to help stimulate customer loyalty.

Craft and hobby shops may be chains operated such as Tandy Leather, but most are independently operated. It could therefore be an area for entrepreneurial pursuit, but the prospective operator should have a high level of crafts interest and experience before making such a commitment (Currie, 1983; Van Horn, 1985; *Profitable Craft Merchandising*, 1985).

Auditoriums and Arenas

Most cities and universities have some type of arena, civic center, or auditorium available for a wide range of events: basketball, hockey, concerts, tradeshows, rodeos, and so on. About half of these facilities are public tax-supported operations, and half are privately operated. Most of revenue comes from the rental of facilities to sports teams and concert promoters, followed by food and beverage concession revenue. Expenses are primarily for payroll, but liability insurance is taking a much bigger bite out of the budget than ever before. To meet these expenses, the key to success is to be highly scheduled. The Los Angeles Forum for example is in use two thirds of the time, which is a fairly full schedule.

Auditorium/civic center/arena managers are paid very well, but the work is demanding. They must manage a staff of employees who perform extremely diverse duties: facility management, ticket sales, concessions, entertainment management, security, marketing and promotions, and financial management. Commercial recreation students can occasionally find internships and entry level positions, then work their way up through this organization, where experience is essential (Anderson, 1987; *Leisure Industry Digest*, August 15, 1986, June 30, 1986).

Fairs and Festivals

Fairs and festivals are a fixture of community life in almost every city, county, and state. Most are operated as nonprofit but self-sustaining ventures. There are also numerous commercially operated fairs and festivals and occasional regional fairs and world expos. These events are big business; the top 50 fairs in the U.S. drew 47 million customers in 1986. The largest events, drawing about 4 million patrons each, are the state fairs of Texas and Ohio. Even larger, was Vancouver's World Expo in 1986, which drew 22 million. Such fairs and festivals have significant economic impact on a community, and provide numerous seasonal jobs.

Fair/festival revenues come from gate receipts, parking revenue, sale of exhibition space, and a percentage of revenue from contracted operators of rides, midway amusements, food and beverage stands, craft booths, and souvenir stands. The key to success however, is to earn significant revenue during the long off-season. This is accomplished through the profitable use of facilities for concerts, dances, wedding receptions, flea markets, private parties, trade shows, rodeos, and livestock exhibitions. Recently, another approach is to secure commercial sponsors. For example, American Express provided a $2.6 million grant to the New York International Festival of the Arts. A problem with large fairs/festivals is that they require huge amounts of capital investment in facilities. The 1992 Chicago Worlds Fair should cost over $800 million and cover 600 acres. Sometimes this outlay is not recovered by the operation of the event. For example, the New Orleans World's Fair left behind a $105 million debt.

Large fairs and festivals are managed by a combination of paid staff and volunteers. The Cheyenne Frontier Days has ten full-time staff who work with a budget of $2 million and 2500 volunteers. The fulltime staff work in a variety of responsibilities: managing facilities, booking entertainment, developing promotional events, contracting with concessionaires, personnel management, public relations, marketing, group sales, and so on. Many of these positions can be filled by persons with commercial recreation training and experience, but few students ever pursue this career area (Lee, 1981; Ries, 1984; Romero, 1987, *Leisure Industry Digest*, May 15, 1986, January, 1987).

Other Local Commercial Recreation Opportunities

There are numerous opportunities in every community for enterprising people to start successful businesses that fill specialized niches in recreation. Some of the successful examples, that might be repeated in other communities are illustrated below.

Commercial Softball Complex—A $2 million four field complex can serve as many as 200 teams in league play. With entry fees of $400 per team, it takes about 120 teams to break even. Other revenues come from tournament play, concessions, and advertising signs (Wackrow, 1984).

Dance Studios—A minimum of 1500 square feet is needed for a dance studio. Depending upon lease rates, a facilitiy of this size requires about 200 students to break even. Studios concentrate on youth ballet, tap and acrobatic classes, adult social dance, aerobic dance, or a combination of these. Additional revenue comes from the sale of wearing apparel, shoes, records, and tapes (Young, 1984).

Party and Message Services—Singing telegrams, comic messages, and party dancers can bring in $30 to $200 per booking for companies such as Eastern Onion. Some companies arrange 80 to 100 of these per day, indicating that public demand and acceptance certainly exists. Another service area, arranging and catering parties, is limited only by the imagination of the entrepreneur and the pocketbook of the customers (Shook, 1983).

Balloon Company—Starting with an investment of as little as $3000, a balloon company provides balloons for delivered bouquets, parties, dances, and special events. Some companies do volume of $120,000 a year with deliveries of as many as 140,000 balloons for a single event (Dishman, 1982).

Personal Fitness Trainer—Serving celebrities and executives, personal trainers charge $50-$150 for one and a half hour sessions at the customers home. A trainer must be highly personable as well as knowledgeable about fitness in order to be a success (Toufexis, 1985).

SUMMARY

Local commercial recreation businesses provide leisure products and services to people, primarily in their home communities. There are three major classifications of local commercial recreation, and each includes numerous distinct industries. Recreation activity providers include health clubs, racquet clubs, golf courses, bowling centers, and dance studios. Recreation product retailers include sporting goods stores, arts and crafts shops, toy and game stores, and sport specialty shops. Entertainment providers include theme parks, amusement parks, movie theaters, and fairs and festivals.

Many of the individual businesses within these industries function as national chains and/or franchises, but there are also opportunities for independent operators. Although the independents may be smaller, they can be successful by filling specialized niches within a given community.

Career opportunities exist in great numbers, but a recreation degree is not an automatic ticket to success. Students must have specific practical skills for entry level work in each industry. Some of the skills may be learned in an academic setting, but many are experience based. Advancement to managerial levels is usually based on experience even though the work tends to draw more heavily on the conceptual skills and knowledge gained in the academic program.

STUDY QUESTIONS

1. List and describe the major components of local commercial recreation.
2. Describe the different types of sport, fitness, and health clubs.
3. What are the keys to success in operating each of the businesses profiled in this chapter?
4. Explain which industries offer the best opportunity for commercial recreation and tourism majors and justify your answer.

PROJECT IDEAS

1. Looking through the yellow pages of a local phonebook, list names of local commercial recreation providers.
2. Visit five of the providers listed in the project above, and find out if their primary markets and operational trends are similar or different to those mentioned in this chapter.

SPOTLIGHT ON: Two Sports/Fitness Clubs

Sports and fitness clubs do not necessarily have to follow the same management concept in order to be successful. This spotlight will examine two sports/fitness clubs that have gained success while appealing to different market segments with different approaches to management and programming.

Holiday Spa Health Clubs

Step inside a Holiday Spa Health Club and the impression is immediate. It is clean, colorful, bright, and high tech. Activity is visable in almost every direction. Most of the participants are upscale young adults looking fairly fit and wearing attractive color coordinated workout apparel. They play racquetball, swim laps, jog on the overhead track, bounce to the beat in the aerobic dance room, relax in the steam room, sauna or jacuzzi, lounge at the nutrition center, or exercise on a wide variety of modern weight training machines. The atmosphere sparkles. If a music video were to be made about fitness clubs, this is the place to film it!

Holiday Spa Clubs are part of Bally Corporation's multi-million dollar leisure business. Gary Graydon manages the Holiday Club in Salt Lake City and will be responsible for developing four more clubs in Utah. The $3.7 million facility has 40,000 square feet and serves about 4000 members. The Holiday concept is fairly simple; sell the importance of fitness at a fair price to a wide middle class adult market, and package the product in a clean, attractive facility. All staff seem to fit the image; they are clean cut, young, attractive, and in good condition. Judging from the 70 percent membership renewal rate, the Holiday concept works.

Graydon is a good example of the Holiday chain's development of young employees. While a communications major in college, he became interested in fitness and worked as a part-time instructor. He moved up through a series of jobs that involved membership sales, weekend management, and then supervision for five clubs. Now, as Vice President and General Manager for the Utah clubs, he believes that promotion from within is a key to employee motivation. He says that staff will never see an advertisement in the paper for a manager position at one of his clubs. Graydon's straight-ahead approach to management carries through to programming. There are occasional classes and tournaments but not really an extensive variety of programs. The facility and the fitness movement basically sell themselves. The off-peak/off-season strategy is to "ride it out" rather than offer too many discounts or special programs. This allows basic membership rates to remain stable and a good dollar value. So far, this approach has worked very well (Graydon, 1986).

The Western Reserve Family Sports Center

The Western Reserve Family Sports Center in Tempe Arizona takes a very different approach when compared to the Holiday Clubs. Owner, Dave Brown has oriented his Western Reserve Club toward families because he feels that they are a more stable membership. In fact, families tend to be members six years or more, compared to only two or three years for single members. Brown's idea is to provide a place where the entire family can come and find something of interest. Indeed, 56 percent of the memberships are sold to families. The Western facility is similar to that of a Holiday club, but Western also has 31 outdoor tennis courts, an olympic size outdoor swimming pool, a physical therapy center, plus indoor basektball and volleyball courts.

A big difference with the Western Reserve Club is its approach to programming. Children as well as adults have many program opportunities, including leagues in basketball, soccer, and volleyball, as well as classes in swimming, martial arts, and gymnastics. There are also wellness seminars, children's sports camps, day care services (accommodating 100 children), and a children's activity club complete with its own newsletter. Brown believes that if children enjoy the programs, families will continue their membership, and the children will buy memberships when they get older.

Eventually, the Western Club will be the centerpiece of a planned unit development that will include an office park, specialty shops, and 100 luxury condominiums. The sports club will help draw tenants for all of these. Already, the first new amenity is in place: a high quality restaurant situated at the club's entrance (*Athletic Business*, 1987).

REFERENCES

Anderson, B. (editor). *Managed Recreation Research Report*. Minneapolis; Lakewood Publications, 1985, 1986, and 1987.

Anderson, K. "Summer's New Attractions." *Dallas Morning News*, June 17, 1983, p. 1c.

Armstrong, M., Assistant Manager of The Cottonwood Heights Ice Rink and Recreation Center, Salt Lake City, Utah, Interviewed by Shirly Wilson. November, 1985.

Athlete Business. "Arizona's One-Stop Family Sports Club." March 1987, pp. 76-80.

Bicycle Business Journal. "Independent Bicycle Dealer Survey." October, 1985.

Bounous, S., Director of Bounous International Ski Camps, Salt Lake City, Utah. Interviewed by John Carpenter, April, 1986.

Bullaro, J., and Edginton, C. *Commercial Leisure Services*. New York: Macmillan Publishing Company, 1986.

Cornish, G., and Whitter, R. *The Golf Course*. New York: Rutledge Press. 1982.

Crandal, D. "Recreation Trends." *First Annual Travel Review Conference Proceedings*. Washington, D.C.: U.S. Travel and Tourism Administration, 1987.

Cummings, J. "Movie Houses Offer Gourmet Foods For Upscale Audiences." *The Salt Lake Tribune*, November 28, 1986, p. 8M.

Currie, A., Owner and Manager of Audria's Crafts, Fort Worth, Texas. Personal Interview, May, 1983.

Dallas Morning News. "Stroke of Business Genius: Miniature Golf Finds Clear Path to Profitability." April 8, 1984, p. 24.

Dishman, P. "Entrepreneur." *Dallas/Fort Worth Business*, December 20, 1982, p. 11.

Dominguez, R. "Keep That Body Moving." *USA Today*, June 23, 1987, p. D1.

Ellis, K. "Bicycles," and "Motorcycles." *U.S. Industrial Outlook*, 1987. Washington, DC: U.S. Department of Commerce, 1987.

Entrepreneur Magazine, "Fitness Centers Muscle In On The Market." November, 1979, pp. 6-16.

Fairchild, B., Manager of Prestonwood AMC Theaters, Dallas, Texas. Personal Interview, April 1983.

Feld, J. "25 Great Service Ideas." *Club Industry*, September, 1987, pp. 22-28.

Francis, J. "Celebrity Sports Center: A Bit of History." A news release from *Celebrity Sports Center*, Denver, Colorado, 1987.

Gallup Organization Inc. in "The Business of Leisure." *The Wall Street Journal*, April 21, 1986, Section 4, p. 130.

Goss, G., Facilities Manager, AMFAC Bear Creek Golf and Racquet Center, Irving, Texas. Personal Interview, April, 1984.

Graydon, G., Vice President and General Manager, Holiday Spa Health Clubs of Utah, Salt Lake City, Utah. Personal Interview, April, 1987.

Graff, J. "Industry Viewpoint" in *Managed Recreation Research Report* (B. Anderson, editor). Minneapolis: Lakewood Publications, 1986.

Graff, J. "1987 Outlook For Theme Parks." *1987 Outlook For Travel and Tourism*, Washington, D.C.: U.S Travel Data Center, 1987, pp. 131-133.

Green, D., Manager of 49th Street Galleria, Salt Lake City, Utah. Personal Interview, March, 1987.

Greenidge, C. "Make Show Time Negotiating Time." *Skiing Trade News*, March, 1987, p. 14.

Hansard, D. "Bagging Wild Game." *Dallas Morning News*, October 16, 1983.

Holmberg, S. *Operational Profile of Private Clubs*. Bethesda, Maryland: Club Managers Association of America, 1983.

Hughes, P. "Dolls, Toys, Games, and Children's Vehicles." *U.S. Industrial Outlook*, Washington, D.C.: U.S. Department of Commerce, 1987.

Huntley, S. "Keeping In Shape, Everybody's Doing It." *U.S. News and World Report*, August 13, 1984, pp. 24-25.

Huntley, S. "The Not-So-Healthy Health SPA Industry." *U.S. News and World Report*, November 7, 1983, pp. 60-62.

Kahl, N. "Sale and Order Survey Shows Trends in Alpine Hard Goods." *Ski Business*, December, 1985, p. 14.

Kelly, J. *Recreation Business*. New York: John Wiley & Sons, 1985.

Kerstetter, D. "Golf," "Bowling," and "Roller Skating" in *Private and Commercial Recreation* (Arlin Epperson, editor). State College, Pennsylvania: Venture Publishing, Inc., 1986.

Kilberg, P., and Strischeck, D. "Lending to Health Clubs." *The Journal of Commercial Bank Lending*, August, 1985, pp. 8-20.

Kittle, K. "Attrax Need To Beat Fuel and Economy." *Managing The Leisure Facility*, March/April, 1980, p. 16.

Kraus, R. *Recreation and Leisure in Modern Society* (3rd Edition). Glenview, Illinois: Scott, Foresman and Company, 1984, p. 62.

Lee, D. "Variety In Format Key to A Healthy Fair." *Managing The Leisure Facility*, February, 1981, pp. 15-27.

Leisure Industry Digest. Selected content from the following issues. April 30, 1985, January 31, 1986, March 31, 1986, April 15, 1986, June 30, 1986, July 30, 1986, August 15, 1986, September 30, 1986, October 15, 1986, January, 1987, April, 1987.

Market Opinion Research Corporation. In "The Business of Leisure." *The Wall Street Journal*, April 21, 1986, Section 4, p. 130.

McCarthy, J. "The Club Business is Becoming a Major Industry" in *Managed Recreation Research Report* (B. Anderson, editor). Minneapolis: Lakewood Publications, 1986.

Mulligan, R. "Entertainment." *U.S. Industrial Outlook 1987*, Washington, D.C.: U.S. Department of Commerce, 1987.

National Recreation and Park Association. "Racquet and Fitness Club Industry." *Employ*, January, 1986.

National Recreation and Park Association. "The Amusement Park and Attraction Industry." *Employ*, April, 1986.

Pannell Kerr Forster. *Clubs in Town and Country.* Houston, Texas, 1986.

Price, H. "Outdoor Amusement Parks and Attractions" in *Private and Commercial Recreation* (Arlin Epperson, editor). State College, Pennslyvania: Venture Publishing, Inc., 1986.

Profitable Craft Merchandising. "The Industry's Growing Pains." November 15, 1985. p. 28.

Rasmussen, E. *Analyzing the Golf Course.* Michigan State University, 1985.

Rice, F. "Guess Who's the Sulton of Sweat?" *Fortune,* April 16, 1984.

Richards, B. "Misshapen Identities." *The Wall Street Journal,* April, 21, 1986, Section 4, p. 130.

Ries, W. "Worlds Fair Woes." *Dallas Morning News,* August 17, 1984.

Romero, D. "Tourism In Local Communities." *1987 Congress of the National Recreation and Parks Association,* New Orleans, September, 1987.

Ruben, P. "The Screem Machines." *USA Today,* May 4, 1987, p. 5E.

Ryan, H. "Golf Instruction Schools Booming Across The Country." *Salt Lake Tribune,* May 17, 1987, p. 75.

Samuals, J. "Theme Parks: Program Variety and Employment Options." *Parks and Recreation,* November, 1983, pp. 58-63; 75.

Seay, M., Manager of Malibu Grand Prix and Castle Golf, Dallas, Texas. Personal Interview, April, 1983.

Shook, R. "Salvaging Misfortune." *Dallas Morning News,* January 22, 1983, p. C-12.

Shuman, J. "Recreational Boats and Boating Equipment." *U.S. Industrial Outlook 1987,* Washington, D.C.: U.S. Department of Commerce, 1987.

Skrzychi, C. "Finding Big Bucks In The Alleys." *U.S. News and World Report,* February 16, 1987, pp. 48-49.

Soloman, J. "The Business of Leisure." *The Wall Street Journal,* April 21, 1986, Section 4, p. 130w.

Sports Style. "Eyeing the Future." *Sport Style,* November, 1985, p. 73.

Stiltner, K. "Sporting and Athletic Goods." *U.S. Industrial Outlook 1987,* Washington, D.C.: U.S. Department of Commerce, 1987.

Thornton, M., Skelton, S., and Tuomisto, R. *Construction and Budget Projection for Amusements Unlimited, Inc.* Tempe, Arizona. No Date.

Toufexis, A. "Body Styler of the Rich and Famous." *Time,* December 2, 1985, pp. 88-89.

Tutelian, L. "Barbie and Rambo Star At Toys Bash." *USA Today,* February 10, 1986, pp. 1B-2B.

Urciuoli, J. "Leisure Time Basic Analysis." *Standard and Poors Industry Surveys,* February 6, 1986, pp. L15-45.

Van Horn, J. "Hobby Industry Scores Points." *Business Journal of New Jersey,* January 3, 1985, p. 2.

Variety. "Where Our Movie Dollar Goes." March 7, 1987.

Veiders, T. "Park Clean Up Rated A Must." *Managing The Leisure Facility,* January/February, 1979, p. 12.

Wackrow, R. "Softball Fantasy." *Dallas Morning News,* May 28, 1984, pp. C-12.

Wall Street Journal. "Revivance of Miniature Golf." November 2, 1985.

Young, K., Owner, Kay Lynn's Dance Studio, Carrolton, Texas, Personal Interview. June, 1984.

Chapter 11

THE CAREER OF THE FUTURE

Dramatic changes in the economy, the work place, social structure, and lifestyles have occurred in the past decade. It is imperative to recognize these changes and forecast coming events with some degree of accuracy in order to plan for a preferred future. One's view of the future is affected not only by past events but also by attitude, intellectual orientation, and experience.

This chapter will examine an approach to the study of the future, and suggest a number of projected trends for the future in commercial recreation. This will help set the stage for a review of career strategies and opportunities in commercial recreation. The chapter will conclude with a section which considers curriculum implications for commercial recreation/tourism academic programs.

TREND ANALYSIS IN THE U.S.

The future may be analyzed in many ways, but one method has gained particular popularity. This method, content analysis, reviews trends through a study of print and broadcast media. The premise is that to look into the future one must know the past and see how trends have evolved to the present. Probably the most comprehensive content analysis was conducted by the Naisbitt corporation and published in John Naisbitt's (1982) best seller *Megatrends*. Several of the trends suggested in this publication have particular relevance for the leisure industry.

Move From Industrial-Based to Information-Based Society. The United States has moved from a manufacturing oriented society to a society that is based more on the communication and processing of information. Commercial recreation businesses can take advantage of this trend by providing information-based services. These include video tapes of vacation destinations and summer camps, skill instruction tapes, resource listing services, computerized home shopping, video dating services, hotel and campground reservations services, and timeshare and vacation time exchange services.

Move in Dual Directions of High Technology and High Touch. As technological advances become incorporated into society, various work efficiencies gained by that technology may yield increases in leisure time. Related change may be the increased stress of a fast-paced, impersonal, technological society. These changes will probably increase the demand for leisure products and services that can reduce stress and provide meaningful social interaction.

Move from National to Global Economy. The importance of world trade, worldwide communications, and the increased availability of information about foreign countries will cause an increase of travel for both business and leisure. It will also cause people to take more time to learn about foreign languages, lifestyles, and cultural norms. A tremendous global market will exist for leisure products and services.

Move From Centralization to Decentralization. Organizations with decentralized management and decision making will be able to respond more quickly to changes in the market place. Leisure service managers with broad generalist backgrounds will be better prepared to work in a decentralized organization than will a manager with a narrow specialized background.

Move From Industrial Cities of the North to the South and West. Due to demographic changes, commercial recreation industries may find greater opportunities in the growth states of the south and west. Businesses in the industrial heartland will have to be more flexible in their operations and marketing in order to cope with the possibility of reduced demand for their products and services.

Move From Hierarchical Structure to Networking. Changes in organizational structure of many institutions and businesses will affect the way in which leisure services are provided. The commercial recreation field will make use of networks and cooperative ventures in business approaches and marketing efforts.

Trend Away From Narrow Life Choices. Rather than few choices, there are now many choices regarding college education/vocational training, marriage, child bearing/rearing, home ownership, career employment, and so on. This trend will affect personal leisure consumption because market segments and purchases will be less predictable than in past years. New market strategies will need to reflect peoples' lifestyle variations by giving them choices in the products/services they desire.

In addition to these overall trends, there are several important issues that should, according to Weiner and Brown (1986), affect the future of commercial recreation. Some of these issues are:

- Rising health care costs could make preventive wellness and leisure activities more appealing and cost effective.
- Leisure environments could become the battlegrounds for conflicts between individual lifestyle excesses (ie., smoking, alcohol, drugs, loud noise, etc.) and the collective human rights of society to be free from such excesses.
- Limits upon development of the earth and use of its resources will have to be balanced with demands for development and consumption.
- The needs of the community and society in general must be balanced by the willingness of people to pay for government services. Any decline in government responsibilities will, by default, open the door for commercial opportunity.

Futuristic facility design and high tech equipment have helped fitness centers present an attractive image to health-conscious Americans.

(Photos: Courtesy of Holiday Spas, Inc.)

A LOOK AHEAD FOR COMMERCIAL RECREATION

Predictions about the future of commercial recreation are not a matter of anonymous agreement among industry authorities. Nevertheless, a review of the predictions and projections of Beekhuis (1986), Hunt (1986), Kelly (1985, 1987), Raymond (1986), Tuttle (1987), Wynegar (1987A, 1987B), and others does reveal some general consensus. Therefore, a variety of projections are presented here that should point general directions for the commercial recreation industry in the next five to ten years.

Economic Oriented Projections
1. Due to mergers, a few very large companies will dominate certain industries: airlines, travel agencies, hotels, movie theaters, theme parks, sporting goods stores, and health and fitness clubs. Entrepreneurial opportunities will come in small markets and with specialty niches.
2. If the U.S. National debt remains high, so will interest rates, making it difficult to finance new businesses and expansions.

3. Revenue oriented recreation facilities and programs operated by nonprofit and government agencies will increase and lead to more lawsuits wherein "unfair competition" is charged.

4. Oil prices should remain rather stable for several years due to competition among major producer countries. However, as oil reserves diminish over ten years, prices will creep upward, thereby increasing inflation, particularly travel costs.

5. American companies will seek more foreign business opportunities in an attempt to diversify their markets. Hotels, fast food restaurants, and theme parks have already begun this move.

6. Increases in the minimum wage will cause businesses to become less labor intensive wherever practical.

7. Senior citizens of the future will have even more discretionary income than today's seniors due to the prevalence of company and union retirement programs and tax sheltered IRAs.

8. There will be continued oversupply of hotel rooms, airline seats, cruise berths and bus seats, so competition in these industries will continue to be fierce. Discounts will continue for off-peak periods of demand.

Activity Projections

1. Leisure consumption and participation will increasingly occur in off-season and off-peak hours as the American work force shifts to less traditional scheduling of work hours.

2. Rising numbers of "confident minorities" will participate in activities traditionally associated with the white majority; skiing, golf, tennis, gymnastics, etc.

3. Commercial attractions will increasingly replace nonprofit service agencies such as Scouts as prime interests of youth.

5. Sales of RVs, motorboats, vacation homes and other big ticket items will fluctuate wildly with increases and decreases of interest rates.

6. Participation in golf, cruises, motorcoach tours, backpacking, and hiking are expected to increase while hunting, skiing, tennis, and racquetball are expected to level off and/or decline.

7. Females will be a more significant market for many recreation products and services.

8. By 2020, almost one third of the U.S. population will be at least 55 years of age, prime consumer age for expensive travel packages, vacation homes, recreation vehicles, and other big ticket items.

9. Health and fitness activities are expected to be more popular among tomorrow's senior citizens than among current seniors.

10. At home recreation activities such as gardening, reading, and video viewing should continue to increase.

11. Planners, architects, and real estate developers will design more of their products to feature recreation amenities.

Operational Projections
1. Multiple unit housing will continue to increase, and there will be more recreation provided through condominium associations, apartment management firms, etc.
2. More government services will be contracted out to private enterprise. This should include opportunities in golf courses, auditoriums and arenas, campgrounds, lodges, food and beverage service, marinas, etc.
3. A diminished youth labor pool will result in businesses utilizing more senior citizen and foreign labor sources.
4. There will be an increase in the number and variety of cooperative ventures between government and private enterprise. Contracted private management of golf courses, resort lodges, marinas, concession stands, auditoriums/arenas/stadiums, campgrounds, and other facilities and programs will be more common.
5. Computerized services will be common for securing travel reservations, concert tickets, sports event tickets, campground reservations, etc. Such ticketing will be available at convenient shopping mall locations and possibly through home computers with national networking tie-ins.
6. Recreation programming, particularly special events, will be used more frequently by resorts, restaurants, bars/social clubs, recreation equipment retailers, and other businesses to draw new customers and to keep repeat customers interested.

Travel Projections
1. Short vacations and weekend travel will continue to increase among two career couples who have difficulty in scheduling long vacations together.

Active Senior Citizens are a growing market for the travel industry .
(Photo: Courtesy of Busch Gardens, Tampa)

2. Tourism will continue to be one of the fastest growth industries, with most rapid growth in Asia.

3. Tourism and commercial recreation will be a primary focus in the economic redevelopment of urban cities.

4. Continuing weakness of theUnited States dollar will make travel to the United States a bargain for foreign tourists. Americans will continue to favor domestic travel over foreign travel.

5. The fastest growing element of the travel industry will be receptive services for foreigners who don't speak English.

6. Travelers will seek more "back to nature" experiences and personal enrichment to counter the depersonalization of the work place.

7. More travel will occur due to the older population, smaller families, and a better educated consumer base.

By understanding these future directions, prospective commercial recreation professionals may improve their search for entrepreneurial opportunities and career associations. The next section will present an overview of these career opportunities and suggest strategies for career development.

CAREERS IN COMMERCIAL RECREATION

There are abundant opportunities for job placement in commercial recreation settings, many of which draw upon a recreator's strong programming, leadership, and communication skills. Most settings additionally demand abundant business acumen whether it is learned as a part of formal education or acquired through experience. In fact, business educators are giving closer attention to the leisure industry as a place where business opportunities prevail. An article in *Forbes* noted: "Leisure management is one of the fastest growing, most lucrative fields for today's business majors" (Andresky, 1986). A well prepared commercial recreation major can be just as competitive as a business major for many positions and actually have an advantage in some positions. Masterson (1984) points out that "the marketing department is looking to the recreation professional to analyze consumer demands and interests and use the information to position the product more effectively."

There are many settings in which to find employment; so many, in fact, that a job search may appear to be confusing. It is this apparent fragmentation that not only causes difficulty when searching for a suitable site for employment, but also causes fragmentation in professional preparation programs.

The grouping of industries—travel, hospitality, and local commercial recreation—helps to focus the career search because there are some similarities within each major field. For the purpose of comparison, it might be interesting to first review the results of a survey by Jamieson (1985) that quantified the number of commercial recreation businesses within a geographic area. In a survey of 3600 recreation businesses in California, the product/service orientations were as follows:

Tourist Services	39%	Recreation Product Manufacturing	17%
Recreation Services	38%	Contractual Recreation Services	7%
Recreation Product Sales	29%	Employee Recreation Services	4%

The total percentage exceeds 100 percent because some businesses had more than one primary orientation. In addition, 17 percent of the businesses indicated that internships were available for students.

In the following sections, it must be realized that the categories overlap. For example, the skills needed for success in a resort may actually be a combination of the skills needed in travel, hospitality, and local programming. Similarly, opportunities suggested are composite summaries for the major industry categories. Specific aspects were covered in the industry profiles in Chapters 8 to 10.

Careers In The Travel Industry

The common thread in the travel industry is the transportation of people. Beyond that, the methods, amenities, and services differ according to the type of travel business. The primary employment areas are airlines, travel agencies, cruise ships, tour operations, bus companies, and travel promotion organizations.

As with all careers in commercial recreation, positions in the travel industry require a variety of personal qualities and skills: interpersonal communications, marketing, accounting, personal management, public speaking, initiative and motivation, knowledge of leisure behavior, attention to detail, and so on. These and other personal skills are discussed further in the career development section of this chapter. Some of the particular skills needed for most travel industry careers include knowledge and ability in the following areas:

- United States and world geography, history, and social customs.
- Computer reservation and ticketing systems.
- Transportation carriers and systems.
- United States and foreign regulations regarding travel.
- Foreign language.

Positions in the travel industry tend to be perceived as glamorous. Many employees get the opportunity to travel to world famous resorts as part of the job and/or get great savings on personal travel. The glamor however, is often tempered by long hours, low pay, repetitive work, and inconsiderate customers. Salaries are better after significant experience has qualified a person to advance into management positions. Experience is essential, because a degree alone seldom qualifies a person for a management position. For persons interested in starting their own travel agency, tour company, or other travel service, there is typically more chance of success by appealing to a specialized market niche.

Hospitality Industry Careers

The common thread in the hospitality industry is the provision of overnight accommodations, food, beverage, and related amenities. Within this industry, career paths in hotels, motels, resorts, restaurants, campgrounds, night clubs, timeshare condominiums, recreation communities, and meeting/convention services are diverse and interesting. Particular skills and knowledge needed for success in the hospitality industry include:

- Real estate principles, marketing, and sales.
- Food and beverage preparation, service, and management.
- Housekeeping management.
- Facility maintenance and safety.
- Front desk and reservation systems.
- Foreign languages—particularly with hotels having an international market.

Students interested in hospitality careers will probably be employed in a variety of positions before reaching their position of choice. Entry positions generally require less than a college education, and some persons have advanced to top management from this level without a formal education. Mid-management positions may be filled by persons who move up from entry level or who enter from specialized training programs. Top level management positions tend to favor college-trained individuals who have gained varied experience while moving up through the ranks. Management level salaries can be quite good in the hospitality industry and there are many benefits, particularly with large chains. For example, management level employees may be able to vacation at greatly reduced rates at the resort properties of other hotels in the chain.

Careers In Local Commercial Recreation

Local commercial recreation businesses provide activity programs, retail products, and entertainment to people primarily in their home communities. Since each of these types of businesses differ greatly from the others, each type will be reviewed separately.

Activity/Program Providers include health and fitness clubs, racquet clubs, multipurpose sports clubs, golf courses, skating rinks, bowling lanes, dance studios, and party services. In each case, the business provides facilities and staff for its customers to engage in a particular type of recreation activity. Some of the particular areas of expertise needed in this career area include:

- A high level of knowledge and proficiency in the program areas.
- Background knowledge for the particular skill area—this may include exercise physiology, sport psychology, coaching theory, etc.
- Maintenance and management skills for specialized facilities: pools, golf courses, ice rinks, tennis centers, etc.
- Membership sales technique.

- Recreation programming ability for a variety of program formats—
  classes, clinics, leagues, tournaments, trips and tours, demonstrations, clubs, special events, etc.

Entry level positions typically require the employee to work directly in the program area, teaching classes, supervising leagues, directing tournaments, and maintaining the facility. There may also be some retail sales work required as well as membership sales work. Managers are usually involved more in personnel management and training, facility scheduling and programming, marketing, and financial management.

Local Recreation Retailers include stores and specialty shops that sell sporting goods, boats, arts and crafts supplies, toys and games, and so on, primarily to local customers. Some of the particular skills necessary in this area include:

- In-depth knowledge of the product line.
- Direct sales and customer service ability.
- Inventory management, including purchasing, stock control, and merchandise display.
- Product service and repair.
- Sales force management and motivation.
- General programming skill for product oriented promotions and special events.

There are numerous entry level positions in recreation retailing that do not need to be filled by degreed staff. These positions typically receive a low hourly wage, but may also receive sales commissions and bonuses. Managers usually have sales experience and perform more work in the areas of marketing, purchasing, personnel, and financial management.

At the managerial level, the skills and knowledge gained in a college degree program become more applicable. In addition to a base salary, many managers participate in profit sharing or bonus programs. It is not unusual, particularly in small specialty shops, for the manager to be an owner or part owner in the business.

Entertainment Providers include movie theaters, amusement parks, water theme parks, arenas and auditoriums, and fairs and festivals. Although some of the customers are tourists, most are local residents. Some of the specialized areas of skill and knowledge needed for success in this industry include:

- Technical aspects of entertainment productions, including staging, lighting, sound systems, graphic projection, etc.
- Artistic aspects of entertainment production plus booking and management of entertainment acts.
- Maintenance and management of specialized facilities: theaters, auditoriums, amusement attractions, etc.
- Management of food and beverage concessions and souvenir stands.
- Event security, crowd control, and facility safety.

As with other types of local commercial recreation, there are numerous positions that do not require a degree. Entry level hourly wages are low and there are few opportunities for tips or commission. Therefore much of the work is performed by high school and college students. Experienced employees can move up to mid-level management positions. Some of these positions however, may also be seasonal or part time, particularly with water parks, amusement parks, and fairs and festivals that have seasonal periods of operation. Skills and knowledge gained through college programs are most applicable at upper management positions. Again, experience is a prerequisite for advancement.

CAREER DEVELOPMENT

Students who are interested in a career in commercial recreation will encounter several barriers. Each must be overcome to gain a good entry level position on a career track. The barriers are fragmentation of the field, uncertainty of the business, and position variety.

It should be very clear from reading the past several chapters that the commercial recreation industry is extremely diverse and fragmented. There is no professional association that bridges the spectrum of industries and provides career guidance, contacts, and job placement service. Rather, there are separate professional associations for hotels, restaurants, travel agencies, theme parks, campgrounds, sporting goods stores, golf courses and country clubs, fitness centers, racquet clubs, resorts, and probably many others. Some offer career guidance and job placement service, but all offer the opportunity for professional contacts. The student would be well advised to investigate membership in two or three associations and strive to attend state, regional, or national conventions whenever possible. The conventions provide an excellent opportunity to interact with the professionals, attend workshops, and apply for internships and full-time positions at scheduled job marts.

The second barrier is the uncertainty of the business. Since commercial recreation is dependent upon economic and market conditions, a major decline can result in reduced profits, personnel layoffs, and business closings. Even when business is booming and an employee has an excellent evaluation, there is no guarantee for sustained employment. A thriving company may be purchased by another company, who decides to bring in a new management team. There are three major strategies to cope with the uncertainty barrier. First, have a variety of skill and experience areas in order to pursue jobs in several different industries. This increases your chances to enter an industry that happens to be in a growth stage at the time. Second, make solid contacts with professionals in the industry because inside information from peers is the best way to find out about good opportunities. Third, live a notch below your income in order to save enough money to withstand a temporary setback. Rather than take the first new job that comes along, it may be more prudent to hold out a little longer for the job that is right for you.

The third barrier involves the variety of positions within many of the industries. Some positions may offer the best entry level opportunity, but others may offer the best career track. For example, a commercial recreation graduate might have the opportunity to work as a front desk clerk or as the assistant recreation director at a resort hotel. The recreation position might initially pay better and offer the better professional challenge. However, the front desk position might lead to a management training program and eventually to a higher position such as assistant manager or general manager.

Part of career development is to position oneself for future employment. Five strategies help accomplish this goal:

1. Utilize the time in school to develop career skills such as foreign language, communications, computer literacy, and sales technique, whether or not they are required in your program.
2. Gain a variety of practical experience through part-time employment while in school. Emphasize the quality of the work experience over the money received.
3. In both of the above, concentrate on improving personal skills such as attention to detail, patience, writing, interpersonal relations, dependability, public speaking, etc.
4. Consider fieldwork and internship opportunities that are well structured to provide you with exposure to all aspects of the business.
5. Concentrate on academic courses that provide a balance of quantitative skills and qualitative skills. The program should not be overloaded on the end of activity skills or on the other end—accounting and finance.

The remainder of this section will examine the topics of career skills and personal skills mentioned in strategies #1-3 above. The final section of this chapter will address curriculum implications of items #4 and #5 above.

Career Skills in Commercial Recreation

The commercial recreation specialist needs a variety of skills that usually differ from public sector training. According to Kelly (1985) a distinction may be made between commercial recreation business and public programs in that there are different aims and different clientele. Understanding those differences is important in developing career skills through postsecondary education and experience. It is important to have business competence with a grounding in leisure/recreation studies in order to deal with the "bottom line" profitability of a business and with leisure participation.

Generally, an aspiring commercial recreation professional should have an understanding of the motivations and feelings of participants as well as the social, political, and physical factors that affect their recreation environment. In addition, functional business skills should be attained to determine what the business must accomplish and how to accomplish it.

The following references to two separate studies present an overview of career skills needed by the commercial recreation professional. Surveys by Bonn (1984) of resort and commercial recreation managers in Michigan, North Carolina, and nationwide ranked a variety of tasks performed most.

As illustrated in Figure 11-1, there is general agreement regarding the tasks that are performed most often: general administration, labor cost control, personnel management, and business correspondence.

Figure 11-1
Tasks Most Frequently Performed by Resort and Commercial Recreation Managers

Item	1979 National Rank	1979 Michigan Rank	1983 N.C. Rank
General Administration & Management	1	3	1
Labor Cost Control	2	2	3
Personnel Management	3	1	4
Business Correspondence	4	—	2
Equipment Selection	5	—	8
Fees & Charges	6	5	5
Liability Insurance	7	14	9
Planning/Design	8	20	11
Maintenance	9	—	7
Application of Safety Regulations	10	14	6
Marketing	20	11	10

Source: Bonn (1984).

In another study, Ellard (1985) surveyed 930 managers and assistant managers of commercial sport businesses to assess competencies needed in the field. As illustrated in Figure 11-2 managers place higher priority on administrative tasks such as decision making, budget preparation, publicity promotion, hiring, pricing, and marketing than do assistant managers. On the other hand, assistant managers place higher priority on day-to-day operational tasks such as in-service training, staff communications, program planning, staff supervision, staff meetings, and first aid/safety than do managers.

Personal Skills and Attributes Needed in Commercial Recreation

An important feature of career development in commercial recreation is the need for certain personal skills and attributes. Such characteristics must be an integral part of an individual's personality or must be developed through awareness and experience. They are not directly teachable through an academic curriculum, although they should be reinforced in this setting. The following personal skills and attributes

Figure 11-2
Ranking of Competencies by Managers and Assistant Managers of Commercial Sport Businesses

	Ranking		
	Manager		Asst. Mgr
Decision Making	1		5
Communications with clientele	2		1
Complaint handling	3		2
Hiring	4		22
Program development	5		10
Leagues & tournaments	6		17 (Tie)
Facility management	7		6
Pricing fees and charges	8		17 (Tie)
Employee motivation	9		7
Area & facility Management	10		11
Staff & personnel supervision	11		3
Marketing	12		46
Publicity promotion	13		31
Employee evaluation	14		21
Staff communications	15		4
Organizational goals & objectives	16		15
Priority setting	17		32
Program planning	18		9
Personnel policies & procedures	19		25
Time management	20		17 (Tie)
Program goals & objectives	21		13
Facility scheduling	22		22
Problem solving techniques	23 (Tie)		14
Budget preparation	23 (Tie)		53
Equipment repair & replacement	25		33 (Tie)
Business procedures	26		17 (Tie)
Organization structure	27		24
Financial recordkeeping	28		47
Advertising	29		43
Security policies & procedures	30		44
Purchasing	31		30
Performance measures	32		26
Accounting & bookkeeping	33		48
Staff meetings	34		16
Budget review	35		54
Strategic planning	36		40
Clinics & special events	37		28
Program evaluation	38		29
Awards & recognition	39		42
In-service training	40		8
First aid & safety	41		23
Resource allocation	42		41
Instructional programming	43 (Tie)		33 (Tie)
Job analysis	43 (Tie)		39
Sports rules & regulations	45		37
Employee compensation	46		49
Job descriptions	47		36
Program policies	48		33 (Tie)
Employee recruitment	49		27
Program leadership techniques	50		38

Source: Ellard (1985)

have been mentioned often by commercial recreation managers as essential for entry level employment and success on the job.

Self-confidence. Part of the development of self-confidence comes in mastering a course of study successfully. Similarly, as one progresses in a job, managers advance people when they are ready for the increased responsibility. If one progresses too rapidly, mastery of a job and self-confidence may be lost (Lattin, 1985). One of the best avenues for self-confidence is mastering the tasks that are required for an entry level position.

Flexibility. Most commercial recreation positions demand long hours, working a variety of responsibilities. In catering to a passenger, hotel guest, or activity center member, many demands are on the employee's time. The ability to work with different people, work a variety of hours, work long hours, use a variety of skills, and respond to change is important for success.

People skills. People contact requires an extroverted individual or at least someone with assertive and friendly skills in dealing with people. Most commercial recreation businesses are client intensive, and the ability to work with people is imperative.

Motivation. Persons entering the field of commercial recreation often enter at the first rung of the career ladder and must demonstrate their motivation in order to advance. For example, a student with a B.S. degree took a job in the room service division of a luxury hotel. He was able to computerize the service operation and was soon promoted.

Attention to detail. This quality is related to organizational skill development, but is one step beyond simple task organization. The requirements of managing a successful people oriented leisure business necessitates an ability to see that all aspects of the operation are running smoothly. A missed detail can result in a very dissatisfied customer.

Initiative. People in the commercial recreation field are expected to take the leadership in developing new ideas, making decisions, and being innovative. While following job responsibilities is important, taking the initiative to solve problems, improve procedures, and find new opportunities are definite plusses in employment. The American Hotel and Motel Association (Lattin, 1985) puts it this way: "Don't worry about beginning your career in a different department or in a different type of hotel than someone else. Get on the job, give it the best you have, evaluate your present work, consider your past experiences, develop a new goal, and begin working to attain it."

Patience. Most commercial recreation managers started at entry level and moved up in the field. Students pursuing this field would benefit from being patient in career development. Too many students think they can start off as managers but in reality, lack maturity and understanding of the industry. Patience and hard work will help overcome this shortcoming.

Stability. Due to high turnover rates in the field, those with greater stability are able to progress more rapidly as openings occur. Most hotels promote from within as do fitness centers, sports clubs, theme parks, retail chains, and other local commercial recreation ventures.

Placement skills. Campus placement centers can help with the development of an application letter and a resume, plus improve a student's interviewing technique and job search skills. These skills require the student to understand their goals in order to best represent their education and experience to an employer.

The above personal skills are attainable by anyone who has the desire to achieve them. By practicing certain select qualities, a person's weaknesses may be overcome before actual employment.

CURRICULUM IMPLICATIONS

The field of commercial recreation requires certain essential skills as previously discussed. Some of these skills are developed best through practical experience, while others are developed better, or at least introducted better, through academic programs. Therefore, many universities have developed commercial recreation programs to respond to the academic needs of the industry. This section will examine the components of a well balanced academic curriculum in commercial recreation. These components include recreation courses, business courses, specialization courses, other supporting courses, and fieldwork or internship programs. Depending upon credit hours and semester length, some curricula may offer more than one course to address each topic area.

Recreation Courses. The student should gain a firm understanding of the overall recreation/leisure service field. This includes coursework in the following areas:

- Recreation Foundations—basic history, philosophy, social and economic impact, service providers, and interrelationships of the entire leisure industry.
- Leadership and Supervision—leadership theory, principles and practices as applied to participants, staff, and volunteers.
- Recreation Programming—needs/interests assessment, program areas and formats, program structure, operations, and evaluation.
- Leisure Behavior—background in the psychology, sociology, and economics of individual, family, and group leisure.
- Recreation Resources Planning and Management—principles of systems planning, site planning, facility design, maintenance, and operations management for outdoor and indoor recreation areas and facilities.
- Introduction to Commercial Recreation—an overview of the nature of commercial recreation and the major components of the industry; also, business concepts applied specifically to commercial recreation settings.
- Technical Aspects and Feasibility Studies in Commercial Recreation—advanced applications of business principles and economics to commercial recreation; also, the feasibility study process and steps to start a new business.

Business Courses. Each student should have coursework in the following areas:

- Accounting
- Economics
- Budgeting & Financial Management
- Marketing Principles
- Advertising
- Business Law
- Management Principles

- Personnel Administration
- Small Business Management
- Business Writing & Communications
- Entrepreneurial Development
- Optional Subjects (depending on interest)
  Retail Sales & Management
  Real Estate Development
  International Business

Specialization Courses. Each student should take a cluster of courses in one or more of the following specialization areas:

- Travel and Tourism
- Hotel/Motel Management
- Restaurant/Food Services Management
- Fitness and Sports Management
- Retail Sales & Management
- Arts/Entertainment Management
- Outdoor Recreation and Resources Management

Other Supporting Courses. To provide a well rounded background, the student should take as many of the following courses as possible:

- Public Speaking
- Mass Communications
- Computer Applications
- Foreign Languages
- First Aid & CPR

- Activity Courses (depending on career interest)
  Sports
  Fitness
  Outdoor Recreation
  Art, Theater, or Music

Fieldwork/Internships

The most effective way to secure quality initial experience in commercial recreation is through fieldwork or internship with an established business. This is because fieldwork or internship is (or should be) more than just a part-time or seasonal job. It is an opportunity to have an intensive, work-based exposure to a broad range of operations within a company. Certainly the student should expect to perform some regular and productive duties in one division of the company. The bonus, however, is that the intern usually has a unique opportunity to observe and/or work with many other divisions of the company, thereby enriching the experience. The student should seize this opportunity even if it requires 20 hours of volunteer work beyond the standard work week.

Fieldwork and internships vary in length, intensity, and requirements set by the business and the university. Perhaps the best system is to have a 3-5 credit fieldwork early in the academic program (sophomore year), followed by a 10-15 credit internship late in the program. The fieldwork serves as an exploratory experience where the student can test their interest in a practical setting, 15-20 hours a week. The internship should be more of a culminating experience, in which students receive a professional level work challenge. To get the most from the opportunity, it requires a full-time, 40-70 hour per week commitment.

Some students strive to gain an internship placement that will lead directly into a full-time professional level position or lead to industry contacts that will accomplish the same objective. It is also important to select an internship with a company that gives the student a high quality and varied experience. Unfortunately, students often accept higher paying internships with companies that return little benefit (except the money) to the student . Therefore, the student must be cautioned to consider the quality of the internship experience first and the pay second.

Another area of concern is the length of the fieldwork or internship commitment. Universities are often tied into 10-week quarters or 15-week semesters that do not coincide with the needs of the company, either for starting/ending dates or for duration of the program. It may be necessary for the student to sacrifice some personal vacation time or even forego a quarter/semester of school in order to be available when the company requires. For example, several resorts want interns for six-month commitments.

A final area of concern regards out-of-state internships. There are many out-of-state resorts, theme parks, tour operators, and other companies with excellent internship programs. Disneyworld for example, recruits students from 114 college campuses internship program that offers 500 positions. Sometimes these out-of-state positions pay less and/or have higher housing costs than convenient local placements. Again, the student must decide if their priorities are quality or expediency? The student who plans ahead and saves money while in school is in a better position to choose the quality experience, which in the long run usually pays higher dividends.

It should be mentioned that the Resort and Commercial Recreation Association (RCRA) publishes an internship directory detailing over 250 opportunities. RCRA and some other professional associations also have job marts at their annual conventions.

CONCLUDING NOTE

In developing a projections concerning the future of the commercial recreation field, it is necessary to predict the type of work place that may exist. According to the Los Angeles Chapter of the World Future Society (Murnane, 1984) the executive of the future will need to be able to:

- Re-examine existing values
- Anticipate changes
- Stimulate creativity
- Eliminate bureaucracy

- Communicate openly and clearly
- Develop a corporate vision
- Stimulate employee teamwork

- Eliminate fear of computers
- Be optimistic and welcome changes

By implication, the student of commercial recreation will need these same attributes to develop a successful career. Curriculum, too, will need to adapt to a constantly changing commercial recreation industry by developing responsiveness to the industry's needs.

STUDY QUESTIONS

1. Explain five of Naisbitts "megatrends" that will affect the recreation industry.
2. Explain five projections for the future of commercial recreation in each of the following areas: economics, operations, activities, and travel.
3. Describe career possibilities and skills needed in the hospitality, travel, and local commercial recreation industries.
4. What general competencies are needed in commercial recreation?
5. What problems are faced when seeking an internship?

PROJECT IDEAS

1. For a commercial recreation business of your choice, develop a scenario for the future 5-10 years and 20 years from now.
2. Design a career strategy based upon your entry level skills, personal skills, internship possibilities, and course development.

REFERENCES

Andresky, J. "Living Off Your Hobby." *Forbes*, November 17, 1986, pp. 248-254.

Beekhuis, J. *World Travel Overview 1986/87*. New York: American Express Publishing Corporation, 1986.

Bonn, M. "Job Specifications and Skills Necessary for Resort and Commercial Recreation Managers." Annual Conference of the Resort and Commercial Recreation Association, Wintergreen, Virginia, 1984.

Ellard, A. *A Competency Analysis of Managers of Commercial Recreational Sport Enterprises* (unpublished doctoral disseration). Indiana University, 1985.

Hunt, J. "Tourism Comes of Age in the 1980s." *Parks and Recreation*, October, 1986, pp. 30-36; 66-67.

Jamieson, L. "Private-Commercial Recreation: State of the Art in California." Research Section Proceedings from the 1985 Resort and Commercial Recreation Conference, Phoenix, Arizona.

Kelly, J. *Final Report: Job Analysis*. Alexandria, Virginia: National Recreation Conference, Phoenix, Arizona, 1985A.

Kelly, J. *Recreation Business*. New York: John Wiley & Sons, 1985.

Kelly, J. *Recreation Trends*. Champaign, IL: Management Learning Laboratories, Ltd., 1987.

Lattin, G. *The Lodging and Food Service Industry*. East Lansing, Michigan: American Hotel and Motel Association, 1985.

Masterson, L. "Making Money Out of Fun." *Parks and Recreation*, October, 1984, 19 (10), pp. 51-53, 70.

Murnane, T. "The Executive of Tomorrowland" *California Business*, July, 1984, pp. 65, 67-71.

Naisbitt, J. *Megatrends*. New York: Warner Books, 1982.

Negley, J. "Are You Considering Private Sector Employment?" *California Parks and Recreation*, August/September, 1980, pp. 13, 25-26.

Raymond, H. "Management in the Third Wave." *The Futurist*, September/October, 1986, pp. 15-18.

Tuttle, D. "Discerning the Shadows Cast by Coming Events: A Dozen Developments Which Will Shape the Travel Industry's Future." *First Annual Travel Review Conference: Proceedings*. Washington, D.C.: U.S. Travel and Tourism Administration, 1987.

Weiner, E., and Brown, A. "Should Robots Pay Taxes?" *The Futurist*, March/April, 1986, pp. 9-12.

Wynegar, D. "Travel Services." *U.S. Industrial Outlook 1987*. Washington, D.C.: Department of Commerce, 1987A, pp. 60-1 to 60-4.

Wynegar, D. "The Year's International Travel in Review." *First Annual Travel and Tourism Conference*. Washington, D.C.: U.S. Travel and Tourism Administration, 1987B.

INDEX

300